Lan

Language Diversity Endangered

edited by
Matthias Brenzinger

Mouton de Gruyter
Berlin · New York

Mouton de Gruyter (formerly Mouton, The Hague)
is a Division of Walter de Gruyter GmbH & Co. KG, Berlin.

♾ Printed on acid-free paper which falls within the guidelines
of the ANSI to ensure permanence and durability.

Library of Congress Cataloging-in-Publication Data

Language diversity endangered / edited by Matthias Brenzinger.
   p. cm. − (Trends in linguistics. Studies and monographs ; 181)
   Includes bibliographical references and indexes.
   ISBN 978-3-11-017049-8 (hc. : alk. paper)
   ISBN 978-3-11-017050-4 (pbk. : alk. paper)
   1. Language attrition.   I. Brenzinger, Matthias, 1957−
   P40.5.L28L36   2007
   306.44−dc22

                              2006035522

ISBN 978-3-11-017050-4

Bibliographic information published by the Deutsche Nationalbibliothek

The Deutsche Nationalbibliothek lists this publication in the Deutsche Nationalbibliografie;
detailed bibliographic data are available in the Internet at http://dnb.d-nb.de.

Preface

The present volume aims to familiarize interested readers with the extent and variation of the accelerating phenomena of language endangerment. They will find global overviews on endangered languages in chapters dealing with all major geographic regions of the world. These contributions provide insights into the specific areal dynamics of language endangerment, past and present. In addition, the authors discuss numerous key issues concerning the documentation of endangered languages. This book is aimed not only at scholars and students from the various sub-disciplines of linguistics, but also addresses issues that are relevant to educators, language planners, policy makers, language activists, historians and other researchers in human science.

The volume comprises updated versions of presentations from the Colloquium *Language Endangerment, Research and Documentation – Setting Priorities for the 21st Century* held in Bad Godesberg from February 12th–17th, 2000 and sponsored by the *Volkswagen Foundation*. Besides the present publication, the colloquium had a substantial impact on the genesis of the UNESCO report *Language Vitality and Endangerment*, as well as the *Recommendations for Action Plans*. Between 2001 and 2003, a UNESCO ad-hoc expert group on endangered languages (co-chaired by Akira Yamamoto and Matthias Brenzinger) collaborated with the UNESCO Intangible Cultural Heritage Section in Paris to draft a preliminary version.

I wish to thank the *Volkswagen Foundation* for their financial support in organizing the colloquium. Thanks also to Monika Feinen, cartographer at the Institut für Afrikanistik, University of Cologne, for her professional contribution. I would like to thank Anke Beck (Mouton de Gruyter) for her sustained support in this enduring publishing project. Thanks are also due, of course, to the authors of the volume and to all colleagues who contributed by sharing their experience in the study of endangered languages. I am particularly grateful to the *Research Institute for Languages and Cultures of Asia and Africa* at the *Tokyo University of Foreign Studies, Tokyo* for enabling me to finish the book manuscript during my stay there as a visiting professor in 2005–06.

Tokyo, April 2006   Matthias Brenzinger

Table of Contents

Language Endangerment Throughout the World

Matthias Brenzinger

1. Introduction

Questions concerning the origin of human language have recently re-gained significant scholarly attention and it is expected that ongoing studies may produce important new insights into basic issues of language evolution. One of the most fundamental questions in this context is: Was there ever a Homo sapiens proto-language which existed some 100,000 or 200,000 years ago and then gave rise to large number of very distinct languages about 12,000 years ago, which for their part have been reduced to the approximately 6,000 of today? No matter what possible scenario for language genesis may be conjectured, it seems most likely that the large number of languages spoken on earth in some distant past dramatically dropped when hunter-gatherers changed to a pastoral lifestyle and even more so, when humans become sedentary farmers. The few thousand languages currently spoken are remaining relics of a once much richer pool of languages, and the shrinking of language diversity has accelerated during the last few thousand years.

The currently disappearing and endangered languages of the world, featured in the present volume, are essential sources for studying not only diachronic and synchronic aspects of human language. They are of eminent importance in attaining knowledge on human prehistory in general. Languages are formed by and reflect the most basic human experiences. Without proper scientific documentation, the decline of these languages will result in the irrecoverable loss of unique knowledge that is based on specific cultural and historical experience. Furthermore, the speech communities themselves will often suffer from the loss of their heritage language as a crucial setback of ethnic and cultural identity.

2. Indicators for assessing language vitality

The evaluation of the state of vitality of any language is a challenging task, as one has to consider different, intertwining factors. Speech communities are complex and patterns of language use within these communities vary and, in addition, are difficult to explore. Even the number of speakers is not always a clear indicator of language vitality. Languages spoken by thousands of people might be endangered, while others with a few hundred speakers may be vital and stable for the time being.

General indicators for the assessment of language vitality and also indicators for selecting languages for documentation were proposed and circulated prior to the colloquium *Language Endangerment, Research and Documentation – Setting Priorities for the 21st Century* by the organizer (Brenzinger 2000). These indicators were discussed at the colloquium, and are employed (some in a modified form) in the tables in the following contributions to this volume.

The indicators of Set A aim at capturing various levels of endangerment by considering a) the percentage of speakers within a population, b) the extent of language transmission, c) loss of functions in language use, and d) attitudes towards one's own language. Language endangerment is an ongoing process, and all indicators therefore serve to capture changes within the speech community.

The indicators of Set B relate to the question of ranking endangered languages most urgently in need for documentation. The scientific (linguistic) value is mainly assigned by considering the genetic status of an endangered language, and the second indicator is the current status of its documentation. The third indicator, namely research conditions, has been removed from the list as they are too varied and complex to be reduced to mere numbers. Furthermore, conditions for fieldwork are subject to constant changes.

Discussions of these indicators at the colloquium served as a starting point for the work of an UNESCO Ad-hoc expert group on endangered languages that collaborated with the UNESCO Intangible Cultural Heritage Section in Paris. Between 2001 and 2003 the team drafted a report entitled *Language Vitality and Endangerment*, as well as, *Recommendations for Action Plans*. A final version of the report and the recommendations were prepared by linguists, language planners, representatives of NGO's, as well as members of endangered language speech communities at a meeting at the UNESCO headquarters in Paris in March 2003. The final document identifies nine core factors that may help to assess and understand the language situation of specific endangered languages.

Factor 1   Intergenerational language transmission
Factor 2   Absolute numbers of speakers
Factor 3   Proportion of speakers within the total population

Factor 4   Loss of existing language domains
Factor 5   Response to new domains and media
Factor 6   Material for language education and literacy
Factor 7   Governmental and institutional language attitudes and policies, in-
           cluding official language status and use
Factor 8   Community members' attitudes towards their own language
(Factor 9   Amount and quality of documentation)   *quantitative measures*

By applying these factors to individual languages, a 5 to 0 grading system
has been proposed in the UNESCO report. For instance, grade 5 with factor 1 shows that all members of the community are also speakers of the
heritage language. Grade 0 states that all speakers of the language have
passed away. All factors may be applied to a given language, and the table
of numbers, which is obtained in this way, can help to characterize the
kind and state of endangerment for a language. The tables may serve as
instruments not only for the assessment of the current situation of a community's language, but also for the formulation of appropriate support
measures for language documentation, maintenance, or revitalization.

Factors from (1) to (8) are applied to assess a language's vitality and its
state of endangerment by capturing the dynamics of the processes of a giv-
en language shift situation. The single most crucial factor among them is
intergenerational language transmission (1), which determines the extent of
language acquisition among the children within a community. Languages
without any young speakers are obviously seriously threatened by extinction. The *proportion of speakers within a community* (3) addresses among
others, a rather important aspect of language vitality: is the language still an
essential asset for being regarded a member of the community or not? If
membership of the community is possible without speaking the heritage
language, this language is highly endangered from within the community.

External threats may derive from the introduction of formal education
or new job opportunities for the members of a minority group. These
changes may result in the *loss of domains* (4) in which the heritage language has still been used. A shift in religious affiliation of a community
might also result in the shift to another mother tongue, a language that is
associated with the new religion (5). Not only *Arabic*, but also *Hausa* and
Dyula, for example, spread as first languages in West Africa along with Islam. Factor (6) relates to the stage of development of a given language
("Ausbau"). Does the community have an orthography? Have the community members agreed on a common standard form for writing the language? Are *teaching and learning materials* for the language available? Is

there literature, such as newsletters, stories, religious texts, etc. published in that language? Factor (7) deals with the *government's policies towards that language* and factor (8) assess the *speakers' attitudes* towards their ethnic language.

Finally, factor (9) aims at helping to determine the urgency for documentation by focusing on the quantity and quality of already existing and analyzed language data. This last factor is the remaining attempt to provide an indicator for the ranking of languages in urgent need for documentation, previously addressed in Set B above. Serious problems with the endeavor of prioritizing languages for documentation have been pointed out by Tryon (p. 438, this volume). He claims that the results gained from factors 1–8 might be overruled by criteria which arise in factor 9: The utmost importance of documenting language isolates, and the attempt to reach coherent language descriptions by choosing languages which are still spoken, not only remembered. While for the question of language documentation, factor 9 is the most crucial, it might be prove to be rather irrelevant for language revitalization efforts, as discussed by Grenoble and Whaley (2006: 4–5).

3. A global overview of endangered languages

Michael Krauss (University of Fairbanks, Alaska) opens the volume by proposing a refined terminology for categorizing degrees of language endangerment by considering the single factor language transmission. His scale comprises three basic categories, namely *safe, extinct,* and *endangered,* with the latter category being further refined by 5 subcategories.

The other chapters are assigned to regions and together capture the global extent of language endangerment. In addition, they analyze a wide range of different threats to individual languages and most importantly, draw attention to specific issues relevant for the research on and documentation of endangered languages.

Willem F. H. Adelaar (Leiden University, The Netherlands) reviews the complex history of language replacement in Hispanic South America from pre-colonial times to the present. *Quechua,* as the language of the Inca Empire, played a significant role in diminishing language diversity before *Spanish* and the European conquerors became a threat to South American languages and even to the people themselves.

Denny Moore (Museu Goeldi, Brasilia) presents a thorough overview of the enormous number of endangered languages of Lowland Tropical

South America. In discussing linguistic research and documentation carried out on these languages, he points out fundamental differences between non-missionary and missionary linguists in the important issues of training national and native linguists.

Colette Grinevald (University Lyon 2, France) shares her comprehension of the situation of endangered languages of Mexico and Central America with an activist approach. She approves achievements in language work on endangered languages that are reached by local, national and regional research institutions and calls for giving support to them. One concrete need in this respect is the training of Amerindian linguists.

Akira Yamamoto (University of Kansas, USA) presents an overview of endangered languages in the USA and Canada. He contrasts the language situation in three communities in some detail and discusses the language work going on in these communities. His main emphasis, however, is on issues that relate to the ethics and pragmatics of fieldwork.

Matthias Brenzinger (University of Cologne, Germany) focuses on endangered languages in Northern Africa. The spread of various "world" religions has had a major impact on the language map in this part of the world, the spread of *Arabic* along with Islam being the most significant.

In a second contribution, *Brenzinger* starts off with the endangered *Khoisan* languages of Southern Africa and moves on to deal with the Eastern African situation. The role of migration waves for language replacement is examined, followed by a typology of the various present settings of language replacement in this part of the world.

Roger Blench (Cambridge, UK) analyses the situation of endangered languages in West Africa by employing statistical methods. He captures national and regional differences, and stresses the importance of the still great number of languages for which no information exists at all.

Bruce Connell (York University, Canada) summarizes information on endangered languages of Central Africa. A brief account on the language history of the region is followed by an overview of endangered languages. This list is incomplete, as he states, due to the fact that even the most basic information for classifying languages does not exist for several countries in that region.

Tapani Salminen (University of Helsinki, Finland) provides on overview of the endangered language of Europe. The postscript added to his contribution just before the publication underlines a point he previously raises, that not all European languages are well studied and documented, and that even where they are, judgments on whether a language is endangered or not are not easily possible.

Olga Kazakevich (Lomonosov University of Moscow, CIS) and *Alexandr Kibrik* (Moscow State University, CIS) survey the endangered language in the CIS. In their contribution to this volume, they describe the importance of formal education in *Russian* as a major force in endangering all other languages that are and were spoken in the Russian Empire and the USSR.

Jonathan Owens (University of Bayreuth, Germany) centers his survey of endangered Middle East languages on Afghanistan, the country with the highest linguistic diversity in the region. He reviews linguistic research and provides diachronic information on languages and speech communities.

David Bradley (LaTrobe, Australia) examines the endangered languages of China and mainland Southeast Asia. For many languages, he adds details that are important for their endangerment to the basic statistical information.

George van Driem (Leiden University, The Netherlands) records the large number of endangered language in South Asia. Among other issues, he raises the question of whether it is in fact feasible to set up a universal code of conducting research is feasible.

Nicholas Evans (University of Melbourne, Australia) assesses the situation of Australian languages. He allows for an understanding not only of the linguistic characteristics of these languages, but also mentions aspects of the mythology and culture of the people.

Stephen Wurm † (Australian National University Canberra, Australia), one of the great scholars in the study of endangered languages, summarizes threatened languages in the Western Pacific area from Taiwan to, and including, Papua New Guinea.

Darrell Tryon (Australian National University Canberra, Australia) closes the volume by evaluating the endangerment of the Austronesian languages of the Pacific Region. Among other issues, he discusses practical questions concerning the setting up of local language archives.

4. The scope of the volume and further related topics

Linguists with regional expertise have contributed to the present volume, their investigations outlining the extent of language endangerment and analyzing threats to language and linguistic diversity. While the importance of language diversity in many other respects is acknowledged, the present studies choose to concentrate mainly on issues that relate to languages as resources for scientific research.

Yamamoto deals with fieldwork ethics, but for the actual linguistic fieldwork, we want to further refer to practical manuals, several of which explicitly consider the documentation of endangered languages (e.g. Newman and Ratcliff eds. 2001).

Language revitalization is an important related issue. Linguists such as, for example, Kenneth Hale and Thomas Kaufman, have been instrumental in setting up community programs that aim at countering language shift processes. For sustained success in language maintenance, however, language revitalization must be "a community-driven, a bottom-up kind of movement", as pointed out by Grenoble and Whaley (2006: 20). We refer the reader to their book, *Saving languages*, the key publication on academic and practical aspects of language revitalization.

Skutnabb-Kangas might be consulted on important questions concerning endangered languages and language (human) rights. She examines not only the language policy environment of her own marginalized Saami language, but also of many endangered languages from various countries and continents (Skutnabb-Kangas 2000, 2002).

Even though the volume outlines threats to language and linguistic diversity with a global framework, dimensions of other linguistic variability remain widely ignored. There is no doubt about the fact that the diversity of linguistic variability will continue to evolve as long as humans exist and communicate. Special vocabularies are generated, for example, with the progressing professional specialization and new terminologies develop with achievements reached in technologies. Also peer group-specific speech forms follow rapidly changing fashions and linguistic variability is employed to express affiliations to specific scenes. Even new languages may arise in the formation of young nations.

Regional varieties as well as secret codes and other special languages, i.e. linguistic variability that encapsulates linguistic heritage, seem to be disapearing throughout the world. The formation of nation states with one unifying language, as well as a global coverage – first by mass media and now by the WWW – has fostered the assimilation of regional "dialects" to national standard "languages".

In these processes, not only regional variants, but also distinct languages are often downgraded to mere "dialects" by national ideologies and as a result disappear, widely unnoticed. They may not be considered in the academic discourse on endangered languages and for that reason also not feature in the present volume. On the Okinawan Islands of Japan, for example, the entire language group of the *Ryukyuan* languages is about to disappear. The *Ryukyuan* languages are the only linguistic relatives of the otherwise isolated *Japanese* language; however, their distance to *Standard Japanese* is much greater than, for example, the one between *German* and *English* (Heinrich 2005). The *Okinawan* languages are being replaced by *Standard Japanese* as a result of the Japanization of Okinawa, which started with the annexation of the Ryukyu Kingdom in 1879. In public schools, Okinawan children were educated to become Japanese and they were no longer allowed to speak their own language. Mashide Ishihara describes the policy of "One nation, one people, and one language" (Ishihara 2004) by the government in Tokyo, which made strong efforts to turn the Okinawans into loyal Japanese-speaking citizens. The U.S. occupation of Okinawa after WWII, which – at least formally – ended in 1972, marks the final stage of the fade of the *Ryukyuan* languages. The Americans tried to separate Okinawa from Japan and for that reason emphasized the distinctiveness of the *Ryukyuan* language and culture. This US policy, however, fostered the Japanization movement and today, even the remaining – mainly elderly *Ryukyu*-speakers – themselves refer to their languages as *Japanese* "dialects".

Several contributions to the volume mention regions for which even the most fundamental information on minority languages does not exist, such as in Amazonia and parts of the African continent. During the past few years, financial support from various institutions and foundations allowed for quite a number of studies on endangered languages, for example, in *The Endangered Languages of the Pacific Rim* program of the Japanese government and the *DOBES (Dokumentation bedrohter Sprachen)* program of the *Volkswagen Foundation*, Germany. Other important programs for language documentation were set up by the *Rausing Foundation*, UK and the *Netherlands Organization for Scientific Research (NOW)*. Even though the *Endangered Language Fund*, USA and the *Foundation of Endangered Languages* provide relatively small grants, they have nevertheless had a significant impact on the discussions and the actual research of endangered languages. Research on language endangerment and the documentation of endangered languages will progress further, and we hope that the present volume will be a useful reference in these endeavours and encourage further discussions and studies on endangered languages.

References

Brenzinger, Matthias
   2000   Selection and ranking of endangered languages most urgently in need for documentation. Discussion paper prepared for the colloquium *Language Endangerment, Research and Documentation – Setting Priorities for the 21st Century,* February 12th–17th 2000.
Dwyer, Arienne; Brenzinger, Matthias and Akira Y. Yamamoto
   2003   Safeguarding of endangered languages, *The endangered language fund newsletter* 7,1: 1–4.
Grenoble, Lenore A. and Lindsay J. Whaley
   2006   *Saving languages.* An introduction to language revitalization. Cambridge: Cambridge University Press.
Heinrich, Patrick
   2005   Reversing language shift in Okinawa Island, in Crawhall, Nigel and Nicholas Ostler (eds.) *Creating outsiders: Endangered languages, migration and marginalization.* (Preceedings FEL IX, Stellenbosch, South Africa, 18–20 November 2005), Bath: FEL. 137–144.
Ishihara, Mashide
   2004   One nation, one people, and one language: Becoming Japanses in Okinawa, 平成 13, 14, 15 年度科学研究費補助金 (基盤 A)「日米における同化政策と 20 世紀沖縄」研究成果報告書 (琉球大学法学部 2004 年 3 月発行) 237–244. (Research report to the Grant-in-Aid for Scientific Research, "Nichibei ni okeru Doka-Seisaku to 20-seiki Okinawa", 2001–03: 237–244).
Newman, Paul and Martha Ratcliff (eds.)
   2001   *Linguistic fieldwork.* Cambridge: Cambridge University Press.
Skutnabb-Kangas, Tove
   2000   *Linguistic genocide in education – or worldwide diversity and human rights?* Mahwah, New Jersey, London: Lawrence Erlbaum Associates.
   2002   Irelands, Scotland, education and linguistic human rights: some international comparisons, in Kirk, John M. and Dónall P. Ó Baoill (eds.) 2002 *Language planning and education: Linguistic rights in Northern Ireland, the Republic of Ireland, and Scotland.* (*Belfast Studies in Language, Culture and Politics*, 6), Belfast: Cló Ollscoil na Banríona, 221–266.

Chapter 1
Classification and Terminology for Degrees of Language Endangerment

Michael Krauss

1. The following is a suggested framework or schema for classifying languages according to degree of viability, from *'safe'* to *extinct*, with terminology and designators.

		'safe'	*a+*	
e		*stable*	*a–*	all speak, children & up
n *d* *a*	*i* *n* *d*	*instable;* *eroded*	*a*	some children speak; all children speak in some places
n *g* *e*	*e* *c*	*definitively* *endangered*	*b*	spoken only by parental generation and up
r *e*	*l* *i* *n*	*severely* *endangered*	*c*	spoken only by grandparental generation and up
d	*e*	*critically* *endangered*	*d*	spoken only by very few, of great-grandparental generation
		extinct	*e*	no speakers

The schema and discussion do not address definition of "language" vs. "dialect" for example, or the type of rapid linguistic evolution or "decay" (such as loss of inflection, incorporation of loan words) which is considered by some also as "endangerment".

The three basic categories are *'safe'* and *extinct*, with everything in between *endangered*, by far the largest category, to be taken up last.

2. The term *'safe'*, designated *a+*, I have adopted as a technical term, so keep that in single quotes, to be used with caution, though perhaps that is inconsistent with the rest, also proposed as technical terms. *'Safe'* are those languages which are not only being learned as mother-tongue by children as the norm, but which we predict will still be being so learned

for the foreseeable future, i. e. throughout this new century, still having at least a viable community, critical mass, of children speakers in the year 2100. Such would be a very large proportion of languages which are now spoken by a million or more, including children, and/or are firmly supported by the power of a state or regional government, this including also, though the population may be well below a million, e. g. *Icelandic* or *Faroese*, 250,000 and 40,000 respectively. The total number of '*safe*' languages may thus currently be about 300 out of 6,000 or 5 %, the majority of those being both spoken by over a million and supported by state power, used in educational and media domains. Sometimes, however, state support does not suffice, as in the notorious case of *Irish*, already severely endangered before it gained that support, or, more often, a million does not suffice without that support, as in the case of *Breton*, or *Quechua*. Even so, other factors may prevail, as in the case of *Yiddish* in conservative or Hasidic communities, which might classify *Yiddish*, perhaps the most famously "dying" language, in the elite class of '*safe*' — to put the enormity of the *endangered* class in perspective — where *Yiddish* may well be at the 95th percentile for 'safety.' Probably no language with fewer than 10,000 speakers could anywhere be classified as '*safe*', and 10,000 is probably at least at the 65th percentile for language speakership size, the median size being closer to 5,000. (It remains a major study, not addressed here, to consider factors detracting from language '*safety*,' such as genocidal violence, industrial development, environmental degradation, demographic intrusion or upheaval, urbanization, indifference, television exclusively in the dominant language, along with the whole spectrum of attitudes, both of the minority and dominant language speakers).

3. *Extinct*, designated *e*, are languages no longer spoken or even potentially spoken (remembered) by anyone, so for which no new documentation can be obtained. Questionable cases of recent extinction of course are common, perhaps more common than cases where it is certain that not a single speaker anywhere survives. Borderline cases exist too, where a few words or phrases are remembered, which could be quite valuable in determining at least the genetic position of an otherwise undocumented language, though there is no one able to generate sentences in it. Such cases might be designated *e+*. Perhaps still more difficult to classify, but probably *e+*, are languages for which there are no fluent speakers or persons able to generate new sentences, but for which there are persons who may remember extensive rote ritual or epic text, such as *Ainu yukar*. (Similarly, however, there are or have been languages with extensive writ-

ten literature but with no native speakers, such as *Hebrew* until the late 19th century, *Coptic*, or clerical *Latin*, regularly used in ritual. Commonly these may have new text generated in writing may even be the only written language for the community, and may have persons potentially capable of conversation in them under special conditions. Along with other types, such as *Esperanto* or pidgins, these may perhaps be designated by the proposed scale, or something parallel to that, some perhaps even so high as '*safe*,' however restricted their domain may remain. These, or any language sufficiently documented, have also the potential to be revived and will be considered at the end of this discussion.).

4. Between '*safe*' and *extinct* is the entire spectrum of *endangered* languages, probably 95% of the 6,000. The term *endangered* is clearly adopted from its use in the field of biology, where "endangered species" are defined as "in danger of extinction throughout all or a significant portion of their range", as distinct from "threatened species", defined as "likely to become endangered within the foreseeable future throughout all or a significant portion of their range". For language we have agreed to use the term *endangered* much more broadly, to include a large category, perhaps already a third of "endangered" languages, which are no longer spoken by children; those would correspond in biology to species which have lost the capacity to reproduce. Rather than use terms like "dying", "doomed", "terminal", or even "moribund" or "non-viable", which might well have a discouraging or negative effect, we extend the term *endangered* to include those too, however euphemistic that use may seem, trusting that the term *endangered* may itself be sufficiently alarming. For our purposes, I do not see either that a distinction between *threatened* and *endangered* for language would be very useful; since we are using "endangered" already as a euphemism for a status much graver than what "endangered" means in biology, it seems wrong to compound the obfuscation by calling merely "threatened" (not yet endangered) what does in most cases correspond to "endangered" in biology. Perhaps in further elaboration of a separate study of factors endangering a language, "threatened" might be defined to designate an upper minority of the category of stable but unsafe languages, to double or triple the number of non-endangered languages ('*safe*' 5% + *threatened* 5–10% more).

4.1. At the top of the scale in the *endangered* category is the class designated *a, stable*. So long as a language is being learned as mother-tongue by the children, it remains classified as *stable*. This would generally require that virtually all children are so learning the language, in the family, and actually speaking it not only to their elders but to each other. Home is the essential domain, and so long as home use remains stable, though another language may be used increasingly in school, work, religion, etc., the language remains *stable*, however threatened it may be by factors external to the home. Failure of a language to expand into new technological domains may indeed increase the threat to it, but need not necessarily reclassify it as less than *stable*. A language might remain *stable* if it is merely the "norm" that children learn and speak it in the home, so long as cases where that is not so are truly exceptional, or are common only in a diaspora, e. g. permanently urbanized families, at some remove from the core area. The term *stable* seems detachedly realistic and not leading to complacency, so long as one remembers that that is merely the top category, still the majority worldwide, though probably for not much longer, of endangered languages. The use of the term *stable* is partly inspired by the phrase "Stabilizing Indigenous Languages" in the title for a series of North American conferences.

4.2. For the next subclass of *endangered* languages, incipiently in decline, I see no qualifier better than *instable* or *partly stable*, designated *a–*. (The designators, it is time to explain, are partly derived from the American public school grading system, where *a* is 'excellent', *b* 'good', *c* 'fair, average', *d* 'poor', and *f* 'failing', and *a–* is less than *a* but closer to *a* than to *b*, *b+* better than *b* but closer to *b* than to *a*, etc. They have the advantage of being more iconic than a numeral system, where it is not immediately clear whether the lower number 1 or I as opposed to the higher number 4 or IV is better.) There are clearly two different types of *a–* situations, both defined as where some of the children speak the language. The first type, *instable*, is where "some" of the children speak the language, e. g. some of the children in a single village, or scattered through a wider area, perhaps still a majority, but not constituting a stable or critical mass. *Instable* includes also a situation where the children speak the language some of the time, i. e. to elders, but amongst each other speak the replacing language, so seem destined to speak that to their spouses and children. The other subtype of *a–* might be *partly stable* or *eroding*, where for a more complex situation of several communities where the children all speak the language in one or more parts of it but there also is part or parts where only some children speak the language, especially where a clear geographical distinction is not easy to make. If it is easy to make such a distinction, then a further dimension of the designator system should be used, more than one designator separated by a comma, here namely *a, a–*, meaning that in a part of the language area all children are learning the language, but in another part only some children are learning it. The language in that case as a whole would be *a–, partly stable* or *eroding*, but could be further designated as *stable* plus *instable*. The term *instable* (c. f. instability) is used as a technical term instead of "unstable", in order to avoid the connotation of "mentally unstable".

4.3. The next subclass is *b, definitively endangered* (and definitively in decline) for lack of a better term, meaning that the language has passed the crucial basic threshold of viability, is no longer being learned as mother-tongue by children in the home, that the youngest speakers are of the parental generation, or more precisely that the youngest generation of which all are speakers is the parental generation. (That age could of course vary widely in different parts of the world, minimum probably from 15 to 20.). This might include also situations where the parents not only can but do speak the language to their children, yet permit the children regularly to respond in the replacing language, so that the children hardly become active speakers of the endangered language. Designated with variants of *b*, such as *b–*, might be cases where some of the parents speak the language, or where more uniformly the youngest speaker age is 25 or 30, again meaning in a different way that some parents speak the language. Another type of finer designation might be *b+*, for where the youngest speakers may be 5 or 15, but the intergenerational transmission is definitively interrupted. If the youngest speakers are already even five, the language has probably been definitively abandoned. Though numerically more children may still be able to speak it than cannot, the language should probably be designated *b+* rather than *a–*, because of the dynamic, which is always more important than sheer numbers. The system allows also for two more types of complexity. The first is as shown above, two designators divided by comma, e. g. here *a,b* for two communities or distinct geographical areas, in one of which all speak the language, in the other only parents and up. The second type, which I have very often used, is joining two designators with a hyphen, ambiguous in American notation as the same symbol as a minus sign, e. g. *a–b*, for a complex or continuum which ranges from all children speaking the language to only parents and older speaking it. Perhaps the joining symbol should not be used so ambiguously, so that a situation ranging from where some of the children speak the language in one part to where only parents and up speak it would be *a–b*, thus allowing very finely also, e. g. for *a–b+, a–b–*.

4.4. The next subclass is *severely endangered, c*, where the youngest speakers are of grandparental generation, middle aged (mutatis mutandis age span of 35–60 or even wider) where parents cannot teach the language to their children. I have picked "severely" over "seriously endangered", which implies that it is not "serious", or "gravely endangered", too funereal. This is by far the most common basic category for indigenous North American languages, for example, both because of historical timing and the breadth of the age-span. More complex distinctions such as *a–c*, *c–*, can of course be used. For example, the long *Inuit* continuum I have designated *a–c*, for *a* in Greenland and Eastern Canada, but not Labrador, *b* in Central Canada and a few parts of Alaska, *c* in Western Canada and most of Alaska. Another type of fine designation that I occasionally used in my circumpolar report was *–c*, for where the youngest speakers were in the range 35–40, i. e. youngish for grandparent but closer to *c* than to *b*; this should, according to the above, be better symbolized *c+*.

4.5. The last subclass before *extinct* is *critically endangered*, *d*, for languages of which the youngest speakers are in the great-grandparental generation, and are also very few, often fewer than 10 for most American languages, and constituting the second largest class, after *c*, for the U.S. Languages very close to extinction, with all speakers at the very end of life expectancy, and fewer than 10, could be designated *d–*. In this class too the numbers could be problematical. e. g. in the case of *Hawaiian* (not counting *Ni'ihau*, the one isolated island which is *a*), where the youngest speakers throughout are over 70, but with a large enough population that there may be still a thousand such elders, some of whom also could become centenarians; such a language might well resist extinction longer than small languages designated *c* where the number of speakers is 10, some aged only 55, but of whom none might reach 80. Sheer numbers should only secondarily be a factor in the classification however, the *Hawaiian* case being far less frequent than the smaller language populations. For languages in class *d* it should also be noted that the further toward extinction a language moves, the more the actual language ability of the last speakers may become an issue. Often neither academic linguistics nor community language interest can afford to discount speakers with less than eloquent or complete command of a language in this category; a designation of *d–* might well include or consist only of a very few speakers with less than complete competence, or very rusty speakers or semi-speakers. Some languages, e. g. *Sayan Samoyed*, resisted extinction for a generation or more on that basis, possibly also *Ubykh* now.

5. Finally, the designations so far have dealt only with unidirectional movement from *stable* downward to *extinct*. One type of exception would be languages traditionally learned in adulthood, e. g. as I have heard

about *Tarascan* in Mexico, where children learn only *Spanish*, but are expected to learn in young adulthood *Tarascan* and henceforth to speak that with other adults. It would be important to note other such cases. Possibly, *Esperanto* and pidgins could have similar special designations, or secret or ritual languages, such as *Demiin, Coptic* or clerical *Latin.* Before considering and designating those, however, we need to consider another type more frequent and important for our purposes, increasingly the result of community programs for reversal of language loss. One example is *Hawaiian*, which might be designated *a, d–a*; the *a* is for *Ni'ihau,* the small isolated island where the children all still speak the language, and *d–a* is for the rest of the islands, where until recently the only speakers were the generation of those now past 70 or 75, but where some younger adults began learning the language about 20 years ago, instituted the Punana Leo (Language Nest) movement now spanning kindergarten through high school (all basically taught through the medium of *Hawaiian*, graduates of which are now raising native *Hawaiian*-speaking children). *Maori* in New Zealand had probably reached a designation of *b–c* (maybe *a–c*), but the Kohanga Reo movement (parent to its Hawaiian counterpart) has now produced many child speakers; *Maori* thus might be designated *b–c–a* (or *a–c–a*). *Cornish* was indeed extinct for about a century, and insofar as revivalist claims are correct, that there are now some native-speaking *Cornish* children, could be designated *e–a*, or if not, then *b–a*. *Irish* is still *a* in some of the Gaeltachtaí (*Irish*-speaking districts), but has many more speakers who actually do speak it to each other as a second language and whose children are native speakers of it e. g. in Dublin, so *Irish* generally might be designated *a, b–a*. A pidgin in the process of becoming a creole might also be designated *b–a*.

Possibly, using *x+* instead of the *–y* device used occasionally in my circumpolar paper, the designation *–b* might be reserved for languages learned only in adulthood or school, such as *Tarascan, Esperanto*, pidgins, or clerical *Latin*, where the state of decline is not relevant. *Sanskrit* however, reportedly has children speakers, so should accordingly be designated *–a*. Also, until the late 19th century, *Hebrew,* which is now of course, *a+*, and still may have more second-language than native speakers, might be designated as *–a+*! Finally, cases like *Ainu* or successful results of the California-type master-apprentice program, insofar as one or very few adults have successfully learned the language from a last aged speaker, might be designated *d–b*, noting that the hyphen in those loss-reversal cases does not signify a range of speakers throughout the intermediate generations. Presumably terms could be assigned to various types of loss reversal, e. g. *revived* (from extinction) for *Cornish*, *e–a,* or even *e–b; revitalized* or *restabilized* or *restored*, variously, for cases like c–a, *d–a*, *d–b*; *renativized* for *Sanskrit* or *Hebrew, –b–a*, *nativized* or *creolized* for pidgins, also *–b–a*.

Chapter 2
Threatened Languages in Hispanic South America

Willem F. H. Adelaar

1. Introduction

In the western part of South America language endangerment is not a recent phenomenon. The process of linguistic reduction may have started during the 15th century with the conquest wars conducted by the Incas of Cuzco. At the height of their power the Incas dominated the Andean region from southern Colombia to the centre of Chile with the inclusion of all the coastal areas. The Incas introduced the habit of relocating entire populations from newly conquered areas to places in the centre of the empire, where they could be controlled more easily. Conversely, loyal populations from the centre were taken to the borders for reasons of defense. This practice, known as *mitma*, may have favored the use of the imperial language (*Quechua*) to the detriment of the original languages of some of the affected populations.

2. The linguistic consequences of conquest and colonization

The spread of epidemic diseases during the 16th century, as well as the actions of the Spanish conquerors, who had introduced them, had a devastating effect upon the ethnic and linguistic diversity existing in the area under discussion. Several coastal populations disappeared during the 16th and 17th centuries. If they had languages of their own, these fell into oblivion before they could be described or documented. An example is the *Quingnam* language, which was spoken along the Peruvian coast near Trujillo and further south. The survivors assimilated with the newcomers and turned to *Spanish*. Coastal cities such as Lima and Trujillo became predominantly European in culture and in language, as well as in the physiognomy of their inhabitants.

In the highlands of what are today Bolivia, Ecuador and Peru, the presence of the indigenous population remained strong. A language of communication and administration, known as 'the general language of the Inca', was widely used in the Inca Empire. If not as a mother tongue, it was used as a second language by most of the Inca's subjects, who often maintained local languages as well. This 'general language of the Inca' was a variety of the linguistic family later to become known as *Quechua*. In the former Inca Empire the Spanish authorities initially favored the use of three languages, in order of importance, *Quechua*, *Aymara* and *Puquina*. It shows the great interest of the Spanish rulers for the southern half of the former Inca Empire with its rich mineral resources. The languages spoken in the northern half of the former empire were seriously neglected and remained largely unstudied and undocumented (cf. Adelaar 1999). Standardized varieties of *Quechua* and *Aymara* were introduced in the aftermath of the 3rd Church Council of Lima (*Tercer Concilio Limense* 1582–83). They became instruments of Christianization and, in the case of *Quechua*, interregional contact. All other languages fell victim to neglect and were gradually replaced either by *Quechua*, or by *Spanish*. The relatively unimportant *Puquina* language also suffered that fate. *Aymara* survived in a much reduced part of its original territory, i. e. the area surrounding Lake Titicaca. The only language that benefited from the colonial policy was *Quechua*. It became more and more important. The introduction and stabilization of *Quechua* in the highlands of Bolivia and Ecuador, where it had hardly been present before, was remarkably successful.

In those parts of the Andes that did not originally belong to the Inca Empire (Colombia) or where its influence had been superficial (Chile) similar policies were followed. *Muysca* (*Chibcha*) and *Quechua* obtained an official status in the kingdom of Nueva Granada, present-day Colombia (Triana y Antorveza 1987: 163–70); *Araucanian* maintained a dominant position in Chile. The policy followed with regard to *Muysca* was not successful. The language died out during the 18th century. In Paraguay and adjacent areas, *Guaraní* became the leading language, its use being stimulated by the Jesuit missions. Today, *Paraguayan Guaraní* is the only native American language whose position can be considered unthreatened. The number of its speakers is growing constantly and comprises more than 90 % of the population of Paraguay. Large areas of what are today Argentina and Chile, as well as the Gran Chaco region, remained untouched by colonization until the 19th century. In those areas the native languages were not immediately threatened.

The influence of colonial rule in the Amazonian lowlands bordering on the Andes was of an intermittent character. In central Peru, an initially successful mission among the Asháninca and other Amazonian tribes was interrupted in 1742 by the rebellion of Juan Santos Atahuallpa. On the other hand, several numerous tribes, such as the Panatahua of the Huallaga river valley, disappeared as a result of epidemic disease introduced by the mission (Santos 1992). The plains of what is now eastern Bolivia were the scene of severe warfare during the first 150 years of colonization. In 1692 the Jesuits succeeded in establishing a successful mission among the Chiquito Indians (Marzal 1992, I: 421–55). They favored the use of the *Chiquitano* language at the cost of the languages of many other ethnic groups sharing the Chiquito culture and way of life, who were incorporated into the missionary domain. Another missionary experiment took place further west in the Moxos region, an old cultural area with an extraordinary linguistic diversity. In Moxos many of the local languages were preserved, although most of them are moribund today.

The policy of the Spanish colonial authorities with regard to the native languages changed radically in 1770. Three years before, the Jesuits, who were active protectors of the natives and their languages, had been expelled from the empire. Henceforth, forced 'Castilianization' (Hispanicization) became the rule, following the model of the Romans, who also had succeeded in imposing their language upon the populations they had conquered. The failed indigenous rebellion of 1780–81, headed by Tupac Amaru II, a descendant of the Inca elite, entailed a further repression of the use of the indigenous languages (cf. Triana y Antorveza 1987: 514–15).

Unfortunately, the independence of the Andean nations initially did not bring any improvement in the status of the native languages. All new states sustained the ideal of homogeneous European-style nations with a single national language, *Spanish*. The indigenous legacy was to be disposed of as soon as possible. It is in this period that we have to look for the roots of the profound feeling of inferiority that the Andean populations continue to nourish with respect to their native languages and which has been the cause of the major language shift that takes place in the Andes today. In the meantime previous shifts in language loyalty continued to be operational, as *Aymara* gained terrain on the *Uru* languages, and *Quechua* on *Aymara* and on the *Zaparoan* languages of the Ecuadorian Amazon. However, varieties of *Quechua* now became threatened throughout the Andes. The Chilean Araucanians conquered new territories in central and southern Argentina and imposed their language on the vanquished *Tehuelche*, *Teushen* and *Gününa Küne* (cf. Censabella 1999: 89–96).

3. Language loss through genocide

The new nation-states turned their attention towards areas to whose possession they considered themselves entitled and which had never been brought under Spanish control. The fierce resistance of the local Indians led to downright genocide in Argentina and in Uruguay. The last nomadic Indians of Uruguay were surrounded and slaughtered in 1831. The survivors were enslaved (Pi Hugarte 1993). The power of the free Indians of central and southern Argentina was broken in two successive campaigns, in 1833 under general Juan Manuel de Rosas, and above all in 1879, when general Julio Argentino Roca launched his infamous *Conquista del Desierto* 'Conquest of the Desert', preceded and accompanied by heated nationalist rhetoric. The campaign of 1879, which continued with a somewhat lower intensity until 1885, destroyed all hopes of a peaceful solution. Thousands of Indians were killed, native settlements destroyed, the survivors, including several famous chiefs, taken prisoner. Due to the harsh conditions of the campaign, many of them died in custody. The extermination war in the Pampas and Patagonia was followed by similar, but less effective actions in the Gran Chaco region (Martínez Sarasola 1992).

Tierra del Fuego became the scene of a particularly nasty case of genocide. The inhabitants of its main island, the nomadic *Ona* or *Selk'nam* Indians, were wiped out by headhunters hired by cattle-raising landowners, with the passive support of the Argentinian and Chilean authorities, mainly between 1890 and 1910 (Martínez Sarasola 1992: 311–15). At one time 500 died after eating whale meat that had been poisoned on purpose. Many *Onas* sought the protection of the Salesian mission, where starvation and disease caught up with them. In 1899 nine *Onas* were exhibited as 'cannibalistic Indians' in a cage at the World Fair in Paris. The *Onas* never gave up their language. Their language died in the 1970s with the death of the last full-blooded tribe members. Another tragic case is that of the *Yahgan* or *Yamana*, who inhabited the archipelago south of the main island of Tierra del Fuego. This once numerous southernmost nation on earth fell victim to diseases imported by missionaries. Most of them died between 1880 and 1910. Among the survivors only a few aged people remember the language. The *Alacaluf* or *Kawesqar*, who once inhabited the immense area of channels and fjords between Tierra del Fuego and the Chonos archipelago, are still present, but their number is now reduced to 28 (Viegas Barros, ms.). Their chances of survival are limited.

Another episode of postcolonial violence, which had consequences for the survival and distribution of peoples and languages, were the atrocities that accompanied the exploitation of wild rubber in the upper Amazon basin between 1880 and 1914. In 1894 the notorious rubber-baron Fitzcarraldo machine-gunned the *Toyeri*, a subgroup of the *Harakmbut* in the southern Peruvian jungle because of their refusal to work for him (Gray

1996). Survivors escaped to areas near the Andean slopes, where they had to fight an internecine war with their relatives over diminished resources. Rubber extraction companies, such as the Peruvian Casa Arana, persecuted and enslaved thousands of Amazonian Indians with utmost cruelty, causing tremendous mortality among them. Most severely hit was the area of the Putumayo river at the border between Colombia and Peru. *Huitoto* Indians were incited to hunt down members of other tribes, such as the *Andoque* and *Bora*. The atrocities are described in the Casement report (Casement 1988). The production of this report, presented to the British Parliament in 1911, was motivated by the fact that a British company held a considerable economic interest in Arana's activity in the area. As a consequence of deportations and forced labor, fragments of Indian tribes ended up a thousand miles away from their original habitat. The effects of the rubber-boom can still be felt today. Many until then thriving native groups were split up or fell down to critical numbers. The number of speakers of their languages was of course affected accordingly.

4. Language shift in the Andes

The second half of the 20th century brought a great deal of interest in the Andean languages and their situation. Several languages were documented and described. The distribution and the dialectal variety of *Aymara* and *Quechua* were thoroughly studied. The native languages became a political issue in 1975, when the military government in Peru issued a decree declaring *Quechua* to be the second national language along with *Spanish*. This measure had little immediate effect and was never seriously implemented, but the change in attitude of the dominant groups is significant. One issue that was raised was the question whether a unique standard variety had to be selected for *Quechua*, or several standards corresponding to the local dialectal variety, which is considerable in Peru. As a result six different dialects of *Quechua* were selected to be standard varieties. Grammars and dictionaries of these varieties were published by the Peruvian Ministry of Education and the Instituto de Estudios Peruanos (Escobar 1976).

At present, the multicultural and plurilingual character of Bolivia and Ecuador is duly recognized at different official levels. Ecuador furthermore has powerful Indian organizations, who give a high priority to the use of the native languages. The Colombian constitution of 1991 recognizes the cultural rights of all the native groups in the country. In Chile the

Mapuche Indians are also revindicating cultural and linguistic rights. The first experiments with bilingual education gradually developed into large-scale programs which now carry the epithet 'intercultural', thus showing the intention to preserve the native languages and cultures alongside knowledge of the national language and society. Best known are the experimental programs of bilingual education, run with German state development aid (GTZ – Deutsche Gesellschaft für technische Zusammenarbeit), that were operational in Puno (Peru) and in Quito (Ecuador) during the 1980s and 1990s, as well as the current intercultural bilingual education program PROEIB Andes in Cochabamba (Bolivia).

Although these developments give ground to optimism as to the preservation of the native languages, the reality is less cheerful. The Andean languages, *Quechua* in particular, are subject to a phenomenon that can be described as 'massive language shift'. The *Quechua* language is split up into a multitude of dialects, some of which differ considerably from each other. Therefore, some prefer to speak of '*Quechuan* languages', which is indeed more correct than the term 'dialects'. In particular, the varieties of Central Peru (*Quechua I*) are known for their great diversity and their historical interest. Precisely these Central Peruvian dialects are rapidly disappearing. Whereas in 1940 the percentage of *Quechua* speakers in the provinces of Junín, Pasco, Tarma and Yauli was still calculated at 75 % of the total population (Rowe 1947), it had fallen to less than 10 % in 1993 (Pozzi-Escot 1997: 258). In the countryside there are still children who learn the language but their number amounts to only a few percent. If *Quechua* will survive, its speakers will probably be users of four of five of the more successful dialects, most of which belong to the *Quechua IIB* and *IIC* subgroups (following Torero 1964). However, even the so far highly successful *Ayacucho dialect* (*Quechua IIC*) is under heavy pressure. During the period of violence of 1980–93 the population of the Peruvian department of *Ayacucho* dropped by 25 %, mainly through migration. The refugees filled the shanty towns of Lima and other coastal towns, where there is hardly any future for *Quechua* speakers. In the meantime *Quechua* is rapidly losing ground to *Spanish* in the Ayacuchan countryside (Chirinos 1999).

As we have seen, the great Andean language shift is probably due to historical causes which continue to have an effect, even though the social conditions are changing. As Cerrón-Palomino (1989: 27) puts it, "*Quechua* and *Aymara* speakers seem to have taken the project of assimilation begun by the dominating classes and made it their own." What the shift amounts to is an increase in the amount of bilingualism, coupled with a

sort of collective decision not to hand on the language to the next generation. Sometimes the shift appears to be quite abrupt. Whereas the parents' generation still has a poor command of *Spanish*, the children deny
active knowledge of their parents' language and address them in *Spanish*.
So, a traumatic communication gap appears to exist within the families.
Since the same phenomenon of language shift affects large unorganized
populations, spread out over hundreds of isolated villages and hamlets,
there is very little an outsider can do about it, even with the best of inten-
tions. In this respect, the situation of small language communities, such as
those found in the Amazon region, is more favorable, because there are
better possibilities to reach the community as a whole.

In the Andean countries the percentage of *Quechua* and *Aymara*
speakers has decreased in relation to the total population, probably
ever since the independence. At the same time, the absolute numbers of
speakers of these languages have increased, but much less drastically
than the national population in its totality. The Peruvian census of 1993
indicates a number of 3,199,474 of *Quechua* speakers and 420,215 *Aymara* speakers of five years and older (Godenzzi 1998) on a total population (all ages) of ± 23,000,000. In 1940 the total number of *Quechua*
speakers older than five was 2,444,523 and that of *Aymara* speakers
231,935 on a total population (all ages) of 6,673,111 (Rowe 1947). In
spite of the increase in absolute numbers, we have seen that the situation of *Quechua* at the local or regional level can be much more dramatic, than at the national level. In the near future we may begin to observe
a decrease in the absolute number of *Quechua* speakers, especially in
Peru, where the situation is particularly precarious. The situation in Bolivia, with 2,400,000 *Quechua* speakers and 1,600,000 *Aymara* speakers
(Albó 1995) on an estimated total population of ± 7,500,000, is less dramatic. There is a considerable overlap between the figures of *Aymara*
and *Quechua* speakers due to cases of bilingualism and trilingualism.
The Ecuadorian situation remains unclear as a result of considerable
fluctuations in the number of *Quechua* speakers (1,400,000 to 2,000,000)
provided by the statistics.

5. Tables of endangered languages in each country

The languages of Venezuela and those of the Amazonian parts of Bolivia,
Colombia, Ecuador and Peru are not included here. For these languages
I refer to Denny Moore's contribution chapter 3, this volume.

Table 1. Indigenous languages of Argentina. Data mainly based on Censabella
1999. For Tehuelche the source is Ana Fernández Garay (personal communication). Many languages have further speakers outside Argentina.
The Tupi-Guaraní languages are all very closely related.

Family, Languages	Speakers	Population	Trans-mission	Status
Araucanian				
Mapuche	less than 60,000	40,000 to 60,000 (preservation of pre-Araucanian substratum)	locally	a, b, c
Chon				
Gününa Yajich	extinct since the 1960s			e
Ona	extinct since the 1970s			e
Tehuelche, Aonek'enk	4	200	no	d
Guaicuruan				
Mocoví	most	3,000 ~ 5,000	yes	a—
Pilagá	most	2,000 ~ 5,000	yes	a—
Toba	most	36,000 ~ 60,000	yes	a, a—
Lule-Vilela				
Vilela	possibly a few speakers	11 (1974) (merged with Tobas)	no	d, e
Matacoan				
Chorote	most	1,200 ~ 2,100	yes	a
Chulupí, Ashluslay, Nivaclé	all	200 ~ 1,200 (more inParaguay)	yes	a
Mataco, Wichi	all	35,000 ~ 60,000	yes	a
Quechuan				
Collas	10,000 ~ 20,000 (more in Bolivia)	group not well defined	yes	a–, b
Santiago del Estero	60,000 ~ 120,000	no ethnic group	yes	a

Table 1. cont.

Family, Languages	Speakers	Population	Trans-mission	Status
Tupi-Guarani				
Chiriguano, Ava	most	15,000 ~ 21,000 (more in Bolivia)	yes	a, a–
Mbyá	all	2,500 ~ 3,500 (more in Brazil)	yes	a
Tapieté	no data	384 (more in Paraguay)		c
Guaraní correntino	100,000 or more	no ethnic group	yes	a–

Table 2. Indigenous languages of Chile. Data from various sources: Álvarez-Santullano Busch 1992; Gundermann 1994; Martinic 1989; Poblete and Salas 1997, 1999

Family, Languages	Speakers	Population	Trans-mission	Status
Alacalufan				
Kawesqar, Alacaluf	28	28	possibly	c
Araucanian				
Huilliche	a few 1,000		probably not	c
Mapuche	200,000 ~ 500,000	928,500 (census 1992)	yes	a–
Atacameño				
Atacameño, Kunza	only words and expressions are remembered	2,000		e
Aymaran				
Aymara	16,000	33,000 (more in Bolivia and Peru)	locally	b
Chon				
Ona, Selk'nam	extinct since the 1970s			e
Quechuan				
Quechua	no data	many outside Chile		
Yahgan				
Yahgan, Yamana	2 (1994)	100 (mixed)	no	d

Table 3. Indigenous languages of Paraguay. The figures for the Gran Chaco area
are based on the DGEEC census of 1992 and alternative counts discussed
in Melià (1997). Many groups of the Lengua-Mascoi family (all closely related) now live in mixed communities. The Tupi-Guaraní languages are all
very closely related. Lyle Campbell (personal communication) observes
that the number of Chorotí speakers must be substantially higher

Family, Languages	*Speakers*	*Population*	*Trans- mission*	*Status*
Guaicuruan				
Emok-Toba, Toba Qom	755	781 ~ 1,030	yes	b
Lengua-Mascoi				
Angaité	971	1,647	most	c
Guaná	24	84 (probably more)	mixed with other groups	d
Lengua, Enxet	9,387	9,501 ~ 13,050	most	a–
Sanapaná	789	1,063 ~ 1,358	most	b
Toba Mascoi	1,312	2,057	most	a–
Matacoan				
Chorotí, Manjui, Yofuajá	208	229 ~ 274 (more in Nivaclé communities)	yes	a
Chulupí, Nivaklé	7,780	7,934 ~ 12,504	yes	a
Mak'á	990	1,061	yes	a
Tupi-Guaraní				
Aché, Guayakí	538	639 ~ 883	yes	a
Guarayo, Guarani-eté	24	1,254 ~ 2,111	yes	c
Mbyá	2,435	4,744 ~ 10,990	yes	a
Chiripá, Nhandeva	1,930	6,918 ~ 8,602	assimilating to Paraguayan Guaraní	a–
Paí Taviterã, Kaiwá	500	8,026 ~ 8,750	assimilating to Paraguayan Guaraní	a
Tapieté	123	1,351 ~ 1,789	assimilating to Paraguayan Guaraní	d
Zamucoan				
Ayoreo	815	814 ~ 1,708	yes	a
Chamacoco	908	908 ~ 1,281	yes	a

Table 4. Indigenous languages of Bolivia: Highlands, Gran Chaco and Eastern plains. Data based on Albó 1995:19 and the Censo Rural Indígena de Tierras Bajas [Rural indigenous census of the Lowlands], cf. Rodríguez Bazán 2000; for Paunaca: de Haan personal communication; for Iru-Itu (Uru): Muysken personal communication

Family, Languages	Speakers	Population	Trans-mission	Status
Aymaran				
Aymara	1,600,000		yes	a, a–
mixed language				
Callahuaya	a few		probably not	c
Uru-Chipayan				
Chipaya	1,000	1,000	yes	a–
Iru-Itu, Uchumataco, Uru	1	142	no	d
Quechuan				
Quechua	2,400,000		yes	a
Arawakan				
Chané	possibly extinct (more in Argentina)			e?
Paunaca	a few		no	c
Chiquitoan				
Chiquitano, Besïro	5,855	47,086	locally	a–
Matacoan				
Mataco, Weenhayek	1,811	2,081	yes	a
Tupi-Guaraní				
Chiriguano, Guaraní boliviano	33,670	36,917	yes	a
Tapieté	70	74	yes?	c
Zamucoan				
Ayoreo	771	856	yes	a

Table 5. Indigenous languages of Peru: Highlands and coast. Data based on the 1993 census of INEI (Chirinos 2001). The figures for Aymara and Quechua have been corrected for the original exclusion of children aged between 0 to 4. The figure of Quechua II includes Amazonian Quechua speakers (c. 27,000)

Family, Languages	Speakers	Population	Trans- mission	Status
Aymaran				
Aymara	466,000		yes	a, a–
Jaqaru	725	2,000	yes	a–, b
Kawki	11		no	d
Yungan				
Mochica	extinct in the 1950s			e
Quechuan				
Quechua I	750,000		yes (locally not)	a, a–, b, c, d
Quechua II	2,675,000		yes (locally not)	a, a–, b, c, d

Table 6. Endangered Quechua varieties in Peru. Contains some examples of endangered Quechuan varieties in Peru (data from Pozzi-Escot 1998; Godenzzi 1998)

Variety	Speakers	Transmission
Alto Pativilca (QI)	no data	in decay
Cajamarca (QII)	10,000	locally
Chachapoyas (QII)	a few elder speakers	no
Huanca (QI)	35,000	only in a few districts
Lamas (QII)	15,000	locally
Pacaraos (separate)	a few elder speakers in group of 900	no
Yaru (QI)	38,000 (less than 10% of population)	very little transmission
Yauyos (QI)(QII): several dialects	no data	locally

Table 7. Indigenous languages of Ecuador: Highlands and Coast.
Data based on Juncosa (ed.) 1997; Haboud 1999

Family, Languages	Speakers	Population	Trans-mission	Status
Barbacoan				
Coaiquer, Awá, Awapit	all	2,000 ~ 3,000 (more in Colombia)	yes	a
Cayapa, Chachi, Cha'palaachi	all	7,600	yes	a
Colorado, Tsachila, Tsafiki	all	2,000	yes	a
Chocoan				
Emberá	all	60 (more in Colombia)	yes	a
Quechuan				
Quechua (Highlands)	1,405,000 ~ 2,000,000		yes	a, a–, b
Quechua (Amazonia)	14,000 ~ 30,000		yes	a

Table 8. Indigenous languages of Colombia: Highland, Coast and Llanos. Data provided by J. Landaburu and based on Arango and Sánchez 1998. Additionally, González and Rodríguez 2000

Family, Languages	Speakers	Population	Trans-mission	Status
Arawakan				
Achagua	most	280	yes	a–
Piapoco	all	4,470 (more in Venezuela)	yes	a
Goajiro, Wayuunaiki	all	140,000 (more in Venezuela)	yes	a
Barbacoan				
Coaiquer, Awapit	most	12,940		a–
Guambiano	most	18,000 ~ 20,780	yes	a–
Totoró	4	3,650	no	d
Cariban				
Opon-Carare	probably extinct			e?
Yucpa, Yuco	all	1,500 ~ 3,530	yes	a

Table 8. cont.

Family, Languages	Speakers	Population	Trans- mission	Status
Chibchan				
Barí, Dobocubí	all	3,530	yes	a
Chimila	most	900	yes	a–
Cuna, Tule	all	1,160 (more in Panamá)	yes	a
Ika, Arhuaco, Bíntucua	all	8,600 ~ 14,300	yes	a
Kankuamo, Atánquez		extinct in 1970s		e
Kogui, Kaggaba	all	7,000 ~ 9,770	yes	a
Tunebo, U'wa	all	3,000 ~ 7,010	yes	a–
Wiwa, Damana, Arsario, Malayo, Guamaca, Marocasero, Sanká	all	1,850 ~ 2,800	yes	a
Chocoan				
Emberá	most	71,000 (more in Panamá)	yes	a
Wounaan, Waunana	all	7,970	yes	a
Guahiboan				
Cuiba	all	2,270 (more in Venezuela)	yes	a
Guahibo, Sikuani	all	21,425 (more in Venezuela)	yes	a
Guayabero	all	1,060	yes	a–
Macaguane, Hitnu	all	184 ~ 542	yes	a
Makú-Puinave				
Puinave	all?	2,000 ~ 5,380	yes	a
Paezan				
Páez, Nasa Yuwe	40,000 or more	80,000 ~ 119,000	yes, locally	a, a–
Quechuan				
Inga(no)	all	17,860 ~ 26,000	yes	a

Table 8. cont.

Family, Languages	Speakers	Population	Trans- mission	Status
Salivan				
Piaroa, Dearuwa, Wo'tiheh	most	797 (more in Venezuela)	yes	a
Sáliba	in decay	1,304	no	c
Sebundoy				
Camsá, Sebundoy	most	4,020 ~ 4,736	yes	a
Tinigua				
Tinigua	2		no	d

Map 1. Hispanic South America

Added letters refer to specific dialects of Quechua I and Quechua II.

1	Mapuche	36	Chipaya
2	Gününa Yajich (Gününa Küne)	37	Iru-Itu (Uchumataco)
3	Ona (Selk'nam)	38	Chané
4	Tehuelche (Aonek'enk)	39	Paunaca
5	Mocovi	40	Chiquitano (Besïro)
6	Pilagá	41	Jaqaru
7	Toba	42	Kawki
8	Vilela	43	Mochica
9	Chorote (Chorotí)	44	Quechua I
10	Chulupí (Ashluslay, Nivaclé)	44a	Alto Pativilca
11	Mataco (Wichi, Weenhayek)	44b	Huanca
12	Quechua II (Collas)	44c	Yaru
12a	Santiago del Estero	45	Pacaraos Quechua
12b	Cajamarca	46	Coaiquer (Awá, Awapit)
12c	Chachapoyas	47	Cayapa (Chachi, Cha'palaachi)
12d	Lamas	48	Colorado (Tsachila, Tsafiki)
12e	Yauyos	49	Emberá (Catío, Chamí, Sambú)
12f	Ecuadorian Highlands Quichua	50	Achagua
12g	Ecuadorian Lowlands Quichua	51	Piapoco
12h	Inga (Ingano)	52	Goajiro (Wayuunaiki)
13	Chiriguano (Ava,Guaraní boliviano)	53	Guambiano
14	Mbyá	54	Totoró
15	Tapieté	55	Opon-Carare
16	Guaraní correntino	56	Yucpa (Yuco)
17	Kawesqar (Alacaluf)	57	Barí (Dobocubi)
18	Huilliche	58	Chimila (Ette Taara)
19	Atacameño (Kunza)	59	Cuna (Tule)
20	Aymara	60	Ika (Arhuaco, Bíntucua)
21	Yahgan (Yamana)	61	Kankuamo (Atánquez)
22	Emok-Toba	62	Kogui (Kaggaba)
23	Angaité	63	Tunebo (U'wa)
24	Guaná	64	Damana (Wiwa, Arsario, Malayo
25	Lengua		Guamaca, Marocasero, Sanká)
26	Sanapaná	65	Wounaan (Waunana)
27	Toba Mascoi	66	Cuiba
28	Mak'á	67	Guahibo (Sikuani)
29	Aché (Guayakí)	68	Guayabero
30	Guarayo (Guarani-eté)	69	Macaguane (Hitnü)
31	Chiripa (Nhandeva)	70	Puinave
32	Paí Taviterã (Kaiwá)	71	Páez (Nasa Yuwe)
33	Ayoreo	72	Piaroa (De'aruwa, Wotiheh)
34	Chamacoco	73	Sáliba
35	Callahuaya	74	Kamsá (Sebundoy)
		75	Tinigua

References

Adelaar, Willem F. H.
  1999   Unprotected languages: The silent death of the languages of north-
            ern Peru. In Herzfeld and Lastra (eds.) *Las Causas Sociales de la De-
            saparición y del Mantenimiento de las Lenguas en las Naciones de
            América* [Trabajos presentados en el 49°. Congreso Internacional de
            Americanistas, Quito, Ecuador, julio 7–11, 1997] Hermosillo, Sono-
            ra: Editorial Unison. 205–222.
Adelaar, Willem F. H., with the collaboration of Pieter C. Muysken
  2004   *The languages of the Andes.* Cambridge: Cambridge University Press.
Albó, Xavier
  1995   *Bolivia plurilingüe: una guía para planificadores y educadores*, vol. 1–
            3. La Paz: CIPCA and UNICEF.
Álvarez-Santullano Busch, María Pilar
  1992   Variedad interna y deterioro del dialecto Huilliche. *Revista de
            lingüística teórica y aplicada (RLA)* (Concepción–Chile) 30: 61–74.
Arango Ochoa, Raúl and Enrique Sánchez Gutiérrez
  1998   *Los pueblos indígenas de Colombia 1997.* Bogotá: Tercer Mundo and
            Departamento Nacional de Planeación.
Casement, Roger
  1988   *Putumayo: Caucho y Sangre* [Relación al Parlamento Inglés (1911)].
            Quito: Ediciones Abya-Yala.
Censabella, Marisa
  1999   *Las lenguas indígenas de la Argentina. Una mirada actual.* Buenos
            Aires: Editorial Universitaria de Buenos Aires.
Chirinos Rivera, Andrés
  1999   Lealtad o utilidad de las lenguas indígenas en el Perú y Bolivia. Mi-
            rando más allá del año 2000. Lecture presented at the symposium: *In-
            forme sobre las lenguas del Mundo. La situación latinoamericana.*
            Cochabamba: UNESCO and PROEIB Andes, March 1999.
  2001   *Atlas lingüístico del Peru.* Cuzco–Lima: Ministerio de Educación and
            Centro Bartolomé de Las Casas.
Cerrón-Palomino, Rodolfo
  1989   Language policy in Peru: a historical overview. In Hornberger (ed.)
            11–33.
Crevels, Emily and Willem F. H. Adelaar
  2001–04 South America (online reports on endangered languages of Argenti-
            na, Bolivia, Chile, Ecuador, French Guyana, Guyana, Paraguay, Peru
            and Suriname). In K. Matsumura (ed.), *UNESCO Red Book of En-
            dangered Languages.* Tokyo: The International Clearing House of
            Endangered Languages (ICHEL)
            (www.tooyoo.l.u–tokyo.ac.jp/ichel/archive/southamerica.html).

Escobar, Alberto (ed.)
1976   *Serie de seis Gramáticas referenciales y seis Diccionarios de consulta de la lengua quechua.* Lima: Ministerio de Educación and Instituto de Estudios Peruanos.
Godenzzi, Juan Carlos
1998   Transfondo: 'Cultura de paz, bilingüismo e interculturalidad.' *Coiné, Boletín informativo de temas lingüísticos del Departamento de Humanidades de la Universidad del Pacífico.* Año 1, No. 2. Lima: Universidad del Pacífico.
González de Pérez, María Stella and María Luisa Rodríguez de Montes
2000   *Lenguas indígenas de Colombia. Una visión descriptiva.* Santafé de Bogotá: Instituto Caro y Cuervo.
Gray, Andrew
1996   *The Arakmbut: mythology, spirituality, and history in an Amazonian community. (Arakmbut Indians of Amazonian Peru,* 1). Providence: Berghahn.
Gundermann Kröll, Hans
1994   Cuántos hablan en Chile la lengua aymara? *Revista de lingüística teórica y aplicada (RLA)* (Concepción-Chile) 32: 125–139.
Haboud, Marleen
1999   La situación lingüística de las lenguas en Ecuador. Lecture presented at the symposium: *Informe sobre las lenguas del Mundo. La situación latinoamericana.* Cochabamba: UNESCO and PROEIB Andes, March 1999.
Hornberger, N. H. (ed.)
1989   *Bilingual education and language planning in Indigenous Latin America. (International journal of the sociology of language,* 77). Berlin, New York: Mouton de Gruyter.
Juncosa, José E. (ed.)
1997   *Monografías mínimas del Ecuador. Tsachila – Chachis – Cholo – Cofán – Awá-Coaiquer.* Serie Pueblos del Ecuador Nº 14. Quito: Abya-Yala.
Klein, Harriet E. Manelis and Louisa R. Stark
1985   Indian languages of the Paraguayan Chaco. In Klein and Stark (eds.) *South American Indian languages. Retrospect and prospect.* Austin: University of Texas Press. 802–845.
Martínez Sarasola, Carlos
1992   *Nuestros paisanos los Indios. Vida, historia y destino de las comunidades indígenas en la Argentina.* Buenos Aires: Emecé.
Martinic, M.
1989   Los canoeros de la Patagonia occidental. Población histórica y distribución geográfica (siglos XIX y XX). El fin de una etnia. *Journal de la Société des Américanistes* (Paris) 75: 35–61.

Marzal, Manuel M.
  1992   *Utopia posible. Indios y jesuitas en la América colonial (1549–1767)*.
          2 Vols. Lima: Pontificia Universidad Católica del Perú, Fondo Edito-
          rial.
Melià, Bartomeu
  1997   *Pueblos indígenas en el Paraguay*. Fernando de la Mora, Paraguay:
          Dirección General de Estadística, Encuestas y Censos (DGEEC).
Pi Hugarte, Renzo
  1993   *Los indios de Uruguay*. Colección Pueblos y Lenguas Indígenas 3.
          Quito: Ediciones Abya–Yala [Originally Madrid: Ediciones MAP-
          FRE].
Poblete M., María Teresa and Adalberto Salas
  1997   El aymara de Chile (fonología, textos, léxico). *Filología y Lingüística*
          (San José: Universidad de Costa Rica.) 23,1: 121–203; 23,2: 95–138.
  1999   Fonemas yamana (yagan). Estructura fonológica de la palabra. *Re-
          vista de lingüística teórica y aplicada (RLA)* (Concepción-Chile) 37:
          107–122.
Pozzi-Escot, Inés
  1998   *El Multilingüismo en el Perú*. Cuzco: Centro de Estudios Regionales
          Andinos "Bartolomé de Las Casas" and PROEIB Andes.
Rodríguez Bazán, Luis Antonio
  2000   Estado de las lenguas indígenas del Oriente, Chaco y Amazonía bo-
          livianos. In Queixalós and Renault-Lescure (eds.) *As Línguas Ama-
          zônicas Hoje* [The Amazonian languages today] São Paulo: Instituto
          Socioambiental. 129–149.
Rowe, John Howland
  1947   The Distribution of Indians and Indian languages in Peru. *The Geo-
          graphical Review* (New York) 37: 202–215.
Santos, Fernando
  1992   *Etnohistoria de la Alta Amazonía, Siglos XV–XVIII*. Colección 500.
          Años Nº 46. Quito: Abya-Yala, Movimientos Laicos para América
          Latina (MLAL).
Torero Fernández de Córdova, Alfredo
  1964   Los dialectos quechuas. *Anales Científicos de la Universidad Agraria*
          (Lima: Universidad Agraria de La Molina.) 2: 446–478.
Triana y Antorveza, Humberto
  1987   *Las lenguas indígenas en la historia social del Nuevo Reino de Gran-
          ada*. Biblioteca "Ezequiel Uricoechea" Nº 2. Bogotá: Instituto Caro
          y Cuervo.
Viegas Barros, J. Pedro
  n. d.   *La lengua de los Chonos del sur de Chile. Una comparación con el
          Qawasqar y el Yagan*. Buenos Aires. (unpublished manuscript)

Chapter 3
Endangered Languages of Lowland Tropical South America[1]

Denny Moore

The languages discussed in this chapter are found in a vast region which roughly corresponds to lowland South America: the Amazonian regions of Bolivia, Peru, Ecuador, and Colombia, as well as all of Brazil, Venezuela, Guyana, Suriname, and French Guiana. Present figures indicate the presence of about 300 indigenous and creole languages in this region, though the number would be less if mutually intelligible dialects were not listed as separate languages. The available figures (and those presented here) are unreliable, but give some idea of the situation of these languages which can be compared to the situation in other world areas.

South America is noted for linguistic diversity. Nichols (1990: 479) estimates the continent has about 90 linguistic stocks, conservatively defined, compared to 14 stocks in Africa. Kaufman and Golla (2001: 48) estimate 50 language families and 50 isolates in South America. Lizarralde (2001: 266) estimates that there were "possibly 1,200 indigenous groups" in native South America before European contact, and that 65 percent of the native languages became extinct. Kaufman and Golla (2001: 48) estimate 550 native languages in pre-Columbian South America, of which 300 survive. The Andean highlands are rather different from the lowlands culturally, linguistically, and even genetically (Simoni et. al. 2001). The earliest pottery in the New World (8,000 to 6,000 B. P.) is in Amazonia (Roosevelt 1994: 5). According to Roosevelt (1994), the floodplains of Amazonia supported dense populations organized in chiefdoms which were quite different from the surviving indigenous cultures in the present-day tropical forest. The arrival of the Europeans ultimately decimated the chiefdoms, though there was a long and eventful period of interaction between them and the Europeans.

The surviving native lowland societies are mainly in the hinterlands, where sustained contact has been relatively recent. In Eastern Brazil, for example, few native groups still speak their language. Rodrigues (1993) estimates that 75 % of the native languages of Brazil have already disappeared. There are still indigenous groups in Amazonia who live with no contact with national society. Even today these groups usually lose two-thirds of their population from diseases when they enter into sustained contact. This mass death is completely unnecessary since the diseases responsible for it are all preventable or treatable, but the necessary assistance measures are seldom carried out, and both the general public and specialists, such as anthropologists, often accept the deaths as routine and normal.

Scientific knowledge of the languages of lowland South America is still limited. In Brazil, for example, according to the estimates of Franchetto (2000: 171) there is good description for only 19 % of the native languages, some description for 64 %, and nothing for 13 %. The national capacity for linguistic research varies greatly from country to country, with Brazil, Colombia, and Venezuela seemingly the most developed in scientific linguistics (leaving aside French Guiana, which is formally a part of France and undergoing recent development). In Brazil the scientific investigation of indigenous languages only began in the second half of the twentieth century but is developing at an accelerating pace. In the last 15 years 23 doctoral dissertations involving indigenous languages were defended in Brazilian graduate programs (including one by a foreign missionary linguist). Of these, 16 included analysis of language structure. Aside from these, 17 doctoral dissertations involving indigenous Brazilian languages were defended in graduate programs abroad (including three by foreign scientists). Of these, 15 included analysis of language structure. Characteristically for the region, the number of linguists with only an M.A. is disproportionately high: about one hundred M. A. theses involving indigenous languages have been defended in Brazil in the last 15 years.

Progress in the development of national centers for linguistics in the region increases the national capacity for dealing with the question of endangered languages and their documentation, though much more remains to be done. At least in Brazil there has been too little respect for linguistic description, which is often disparaged, more prestige being attributed to partial descriptions with theoretical pretensions. The first published complete description of an indigenous language by a Brazilian linguist in decades is the grammar of *Kamaiurá* by Seki (2000). Real dictionaries (not wordlists) and text collections are still rare in Brazil. Recent support by the *Volkswagen Foundation* for projects documenting the *Kuikúro*, *Trumái*, and *Awetí* languages of the Xingu is having an excellent impact on the level of documentation being carried out.

In my experience, the nature of scientific underdevelopment is not generally understood. Underdevelopment is not the lack of something; rather it is a positive system which intends to maintain itself and which will react against developmental efforts which might threaten it. Those wishing to promote scientific development should anticipate possible resistance by those most heavily invested in the underdeveloped system. Where development does not occur it is the result of human decisions and not of mystical factors or lack of innate capacity.

Though it is often believed that the presence of missionary linguistic organizations will help develop linguistics in the Third World, the facts from Latin America prove the contrary. Of the non-missionary Brazilian linguists with a doctorate, none owes his training principally to missionary organizations. There is an inverse relation between missionary presence and the development of national scientific linguistics. In Brazil, for example, the position of missionary linguists has declined steadily as more and more well-trained Brazilian linguists have appeared. In Bolivia, by contrast, where there are relatively few national linguists specializing in indigenous languages, the great preponderance of linguistic investigation is carried out by missionary organizations, which have little interest in producing non-missionary Bolivian linguists.

There are relatively few non-missionary foreign linguists active in lowland South America, in spite of the many research opportunities and the possibility of interesting collaborations with national entities and indigenous organizations. With a few exceptions, such as the regions of Colombia involved in armed conflict, there is reasonably secure access to research sites in the region. In Brazil anyone conducting scientific research in a native community must have the authorization of the National Indian Foundation, which entails having the permission of the community and formal affiliation with a Brazilian scientific institution. Foreigners must also have a research visa, which in principle takes 120 days to obtain, though delays are common and at least a third of foreign applicants fail to follow instructions and must repeat steps. In the other countries of the region the authorization process is probably less regulated than in Brazil. In Bolivia, for example, it is possible to conduct research on indigenous languages without special authorization. Linguists who have worked in other world areas are often surprised that in Brazil there is a firm expectation that the linguist will do something of practical use for the community and will collaborate with national linguists. In my experience, foreign linguists and Latin American linguists have very different attitudes toward missionary organizations. For most North American linguists, if these organizations eliminate native religions and do not develop national scientific linguistic capacity in the countries where they work, that is acceptable and even natural, especially if the missionaries are "nice" and do some "good linguistics" and perhaps offer data or other favors. By contrast, for most Brazilian linguists the elimination of native religions and the lack of interest in national scientific development are simply unacceptable-period.

Given the small size of most of the surviving groups of the lowlands, it is not surprising that many of their languages are in serious danger of extinction within one or two generations. This is especially true where history and social forces remove the contexts in which the language was always used. Intermarriage, dispersion in search of work or training, and minority status in relation to other indigenous languages in the same community tend to undermine transmission of the language over time. At least in Brazil the native communities are interested in documentation of their language and culture and usually welcome scientists willing to assist them in that respect. Methods for language revitalization are not generally known or employed yet in lowland South America, though there is considerable activity in literacy in the native language. In Brazil many such literacy efforts are hampered by orthographies which do not reflect the phonology of the language, by competing multiple orthographies, and by a lack of objective evaluation of results. In such cases the written materials developed will be of doubtful value to future generations since the pronunciation cannot be recovered from the written form.

In the tables that follow, an attempt is made to review the status of each of the languages of lowland South America. However, most of the data presented is questionable, since in this region few efforts are specifically aimed at collecting the information relevant for determining the degree of endangerment of languages, which are often spoken in remote locations. One general problem is the confusion of population size with the number of speakers, the latter being more important for possible endangerment. For example, Rodrigues (1986: 72 and 1993) estimates the number of speakers of *Yawalapití* as 135, whereas according to Seki (1999) only 13 people are really fluent in the language, due to encroachment by neighboring languages. The number of speakers of *Torá* is estimated as 256 by Rodrigues (1986: 81, 1993), and as 250 by Aikhenvald and Dixon (2000: 343), but according to a website for the *Torá* (www.socioambiental.org/website / epi/tora/tora.htm), they only speak *Portuguese*. The effect of this confusion is to underestimate the degree of endangerment. Data on the transmission of languages is generally missing, though this is one of the most important facts for endangerment. With time and the cooperation of specialists in various regions, it would be possible to obtain a more realistic and detailed picture of the status of the lowland languages, and this should be a priority.

A further difficulty in the data presented below is the confusion of ethnic or political groups with languages. For example, within the *Mondé* family *Gavião* and *Zoró* are listed as separate languages, though they speak slightly different dialects of the same language. Some of these confusions are corrected, especially if they are relevant for endangerment and there is no doubt about the correction. The data in each table is country-specific; that is, the population of a group is the population in that one country, which will be different from the total population if the group exists in other countries. The amount of study on each language, which is also country-specific, is a very rough estimate of doubtful reliability, based on available information. Languages with little or no significant scientific description are rated 0; those with a M.A. thesis or several articles are rated 1; those with a good overall sketch or doctoral thesis on some aspects of the language are rated 2; and those with reasonably complete descriptions are rated 3. Because of the fragility of the data, the only languages for which an endangerment status is attributed are those which are obviously in very severe immediate danger. These (77 in all) are marked as "d", "d, e" or "e". These letters refer to the Krauss definitions on the degrees of language vitality in chapter 1, this volume: "d" – "critically endangered" and "e" – "extinct". This obviously does not imply that the other languages are not endangered. The languages status was generally not marked if another dialect with a sizeable number of speakers or a fair-size community of speakers in another country exists. Notice that the most endangered languages tend also to be the languages with the least description. In some cases the language so marked may already be extinct, but it is better to indicate the language since it sometimes happens that a language thought to be extinct may have a few speakers somewhere, if a careful search is made. An attempt was made to retain the language names (variants are in parentheses) commonly used in each country, together with the classification usually recognized, though with occasional modifications. Principal and supplementary sources of information are indicated in each table. For countries other than Brazil, where my knowledge is very limited, considerable reliance was placed on *As Línguas Amazônicas Hoje* (= *LAH*) (Queixalós and Renault-Lescure 2000) and data kindly supplied by Willem Adelaar and Mily Crevels from their database on languages of the region. The map displaying the approximate locations of urgently endangered languages was created by Reinaldo Shinkai.

Table 1. Brazil

Language Dialects, Groups	Speakers	Popula- tion	Trans- mission	Studies	Status
Tupí Stock					
Tupí-Guaraní Family					
Akwáwa					
Parakanã	most	624	high?	0	
Suruí do Tocantins	most	185	high?	1	
Asurini do Tocantins	most	233	high?	2	
Amanayé	any?	66	none?	0	d, e
Anambé	6	105	none?	1	d
Apiaká	0?	43	?	0	d, e
Araweté	most	230	high	0	
Asuriní do Xingu	most	81	high?	0	
Avá-Canoeiro	most?	14		0	d
Guajá	all	370	high	1	
Guaraní		25,000		2	
Kaiowá		total			
Mbyá (in Ar, Pa)					
Nhandéva (in Ar, Pa)					
Kaapór / Urubu-Kaapór	most	500	high	2	
Kamayurá	most	364	high	3	
Kayabí	most?	1,200	high?	1	
Kawahíb				2	
Parintintin		130			
Diahkói		30			
Juma		7			
Karipúna					
Tenharin		360	med		
Uru-Eu-Wau-Wau	all	106	high		
Kokáma					
Kokáma (in Co, Pe)	320	5	low?	2	d
Omágua / Kambeba	[240]	few?	low?	0	d, e
Língua Geral Amazônica / Nheengatú					
= coastal Tupi-Guarani altered by contact (Co, V)		>6,000?	med	1	
Tapirapé	380			1	

Table 1. Brazil (cont.)

Language Dialects, Groups	Speakers	Popula- tion	Trans- mission	Studies	Status
Tenetehára					
Guajajara	10,200			1	
Tembé	800		variable	1	
Wayampí / Waiãpi / Oiampi (FG)	498	most?	high?	2	
Xetá	[8]	3			d
Zo'é / Puturú	152	all	high	1	
Arikém Family					
Karitiana	all	171	high	2	
Awetí Family					
Awetí	all	100	high	1	
Juruna Family					
Juruna / Yuruna / Yudjá	all	212	high	1	
Xipaia / Shipaya	2?	15?	none	2	d
Mawé Family					
Mawé / Sateré-Mawé	most?	5,825	good	2	
Mondê Family					
Aruá	12?	36	low	0	d, e
Cinta-Larga	all	643	high	1	
Cinta Larga, Zoró, Gavião dialects of one language					
Gavião	all	360	high	2	
Mondê	3 semi?	?	none?	0	d, e
Suruí / Paitér	all	586	high	1	
Zoró	all	257	high	0	
Puruborá Family					
Puruborá	?2 semi	20?	none	0	d, e
Mundurukú Family					
Kuruáya	3?	10?	none?	0	d, e
Mundurukú	most	3,000	high	3	
Ramarama Family					
Karo / Arara	most	130	good	2	
Tuparí Family					
Ajurú / Wayoró	10?	38	low	0	d, e
Makuráp		129	med?	1	

Table 1. Brazil (cont.)

Language Dialects, Groups	Speakers	Popula- tion	Trans- mission	Studies	Status
Mekém / Mekens / Sakirabiár	25	70	low	2	d
Tuparí	most?	204	med-low	1	
Akuntsu	7	7	high	0	d
Macro-Jê Stock					
Boróro Family					
Boróro		914		2	
Umutina / Omotina	1	100	low		d
Krenák Family					
Krenák	10?	99	low	1	d
Guató Family					
Guató	5 [40]	700	low	2	d
Jê Family					
Akwén					
Xakriabá	0?	4,952	none		e
Xavánte	most	7,100	high?	1	
Xerénte	all?	1,552		1	
Apinayé		718	high?	2	
Kaingáng		20,000 total		2	
Kaingang do Paraná					
Kaingáng Central					
Kaingáng do Sudoeste					
Kaingáng do Sudeste					
Kayapó		4,000 total	high	1	
Gorotire					
Kararaô					
Kokraimoro					
Kubenkrankegn					
Menkrangnoti					
Mentuktíre / Txukahamãe					
Xikrin					
Panará / Kren-akore / Kren-akarore	all	197	high	2	
Suyá					
Suyá	all	223	high	1-2	
Tapayúna / Beiço-de-Pau		63			

Table 1. Brazil (cont.)

Language Dialects, Groups	Speakers	Population	Transmission	Studies	Status
Timbíra					
Canela Apaniekra		336	high	2	
Canela Ramkokamekra		883	high		
Gavião do Pará / Parkateyé		333		1	
Gavião do Maranhão / Pukobiyé		150			
Krahô		1,198	high	1	
Krenjê / Kren-yé		?			
Krikatí / Krinkatí		420			
Xokléng		1,650	low	1	
Karajá Family					
Karajá					
Javaé	most	750	good	2	
Karajá	1,860	1,900	high	1	
Xambioá	10	250	none	0	
Maxakalí Family					
Maxakalí	most	594		1	
Ofayé Family					
Ofayé / Opayé / Ofayé-Xavante	25	87		0?	d
Rikbaktsá Family					
Rikbaktsá / Erikpaksá		690	med?	1	
Yathê Family					
Yathê / Iatê / Fulniô / Carnijó	most?	2,788	med?	1	
Arawá Family					
Banawá-Yafí		120	high	1	
Deni		570	high	1	
Jarawára		160	high	3	
Kulína (Pe)		2,500	high	1	
Paumarí		539	low	3	
Yamamadí / Jamamadí / Kanamantí		250	high	1	
Suruahá / Zuruahá		143	high	0	

Table 1. Brazil (cont.)

Language Dialects, Groups	Speakers	Population	Transmission	Studies	Status
Aruák Family (Arawak, Maipure)					
Apurinã / Ipurinã		2,800	med	2	
Baníwa do Içana / Kurripako (Co, V)		3,189 [5,000]	high	3	
Baré (V)	0?	2,170	none	1	
Kampa / Axíninka (Pe)		763		0	
[Mawayana] (Gu, Su)	>10	>10	none?	0	d
Mehináku					
close to Waurá	all	160	high	1	
Palikúr (FG)		722		1	
Paresí / Arití / Haliti		1,200		1	
Píro		[530]		0	
Manitenéri (Pe)					
Maxinéri (Bo)		[345]		0	
Salumã / Enawenê-Nawê		253	high	0	
Tariana					
Yurupari-Tapúya / Iyemi (Co)	100	1,630	very low	2	d
Terena / Tereno		15,000		1	
Wapixana (Gu)		5,000	variable	1	
Warekena (Co, V)		476		2	
Waurá					
close to Mehinaku	all	226	high	1	
Yawalapití	8	184	none	1	d
[Bora Family]					
[Miranha]					
dialect of Bora (Co)	few?	400		0	
[Guaikurú Family]					
[Kadiwéu]	most	[900]	high	2	
Jabutí Family					
Djeoromitxí / Jabutí	30?	67	low	1	d
Arikapú	3	6	none	0	d
Karib Family					
Aparaí / Apalaí (FG)	most	[150?]	high	2	
Arara do Pará / Ukarãgmã	all?	165	high?	1	

Table 1. Brazil (cont.)

Language Dialects, Groups	Speakers	Population	Transmission	Studies	Status
Bakairí	most	570	good	2	
Galibí do Oiapoque (Gu, Su, FG, V)		37	low?	0	
Hixkaryána	most?	[550]	high	3	
Ingarikó / Kapóng / Akwaio (Gu, V)		1,000	good	1	
Kalapálo					
Kalapalo, Kuikúro, Matipú, Nahukwá are dialects of one language	most	353	good	1	
Kuikúru	most	364 [500]	good	2	
Makuxí (Gu)	most	15,000	high?	3	
Matipú					
very close to Nahukwá?	few	62	low	0	
Mayongong / Makiritáre / Yekuána	most?	180	high?	0	
[Nahukwá]	most	86	good	1	
Taulipáng / Pemóng (V, Gu)	most	200	high?	1	
Tiriyó / Tirió / Trio (Su, Gu?)	all	380 [900]	high	3	
Txikão / Ikpeng	all	189	high	2	
Waimirí / Waimirí-Atroarí	all	611	high	1	
Wayána (FG, Su)	most?	[150?]	med?	1	
Wai-Wai (Gu)	all?	1,366	high	2	
Katukína Family					
Kanamarí	most?	1,300		1	
Katawixí	10?	250		0	d
Katukina do Rio Biá / Pedá Djapá	few?	250		0	d, e
Txunhuã-Djapá / Tsohom-Djapá	30?	100		0	d
Makú Family					
Bará / Kakua (Co)	220				
Dow / Kamã	83			1	
Húpda (Co)	1,800	1,800	high	1	

Table 1. Brazil (cont.)

Language Dialects, Groups	Speakers	Population	Transmission	Studies	Status
Nadëb / Guariba	400			1	
Yuhúp (Co)	400			1?	
Mura Family					
Mura	?any	1,400	none	0	d, e
Pirahã	all	179	high	3	
Nambikwára Family					
Nambikwára do Norte / Mamindê / Latundê / Nakarotê	323	[346]	med	1	
Nambikwára do Sul	all	[721]	good	2	
Sabanê	7 active	[30]	none	1	d
Pano Family					
Amawáka (Pe)		[220]		0	
Arara / Shawanauá					
Arara, Shanenawá, Yamináwa, Yawanawá dialects of one language	9?	300		1	
Katukina do Acre / Katukina Pano		400		1	
Kaxararí		220		0	
Kaxinawá (Pe)		3,387		2	
Korúbo		40		0	d
Marúbo		960	high	2?	
Matis	all	178	high	1	
Matsés / Mayoruna (Pe)		640	high	1	
Nukini	any ?	400	none ?	0	d, e
Poyanáwa	2	385	none	0	d
Shanenawá		[300]		1	
Yamináwa / Jaminawa (Pe)		270		0	
Yawanawá		200			
Tukano Family					
Arapaço		317		0	
Bará / Barasána (Co)		40		0	
Desána (Co)		1,458		1	
[Juriti] (Co)		[50?]			

Table 1. Brazil (cont.)

Language Dialects, Groups	Speakers	Popula- tion	Trans- mission	Studies	Status
Karapanã (Co)		40		0	
Kubewa / Kubeo (Co)		219		0	
Makúna / Yebá-masã (Co)		34		0	
Pira-Tapuya / Waíkana (Co)		926		0	
Siriáno (Co)		[10]		0	
Tukano (Co, V)		2,868		3	
Tuyúka (Co)		518		0	
Wanano (Co)		506		0	
Txapakúra Family					
Kujubim	2	[50]	none	0	d
Oro Win	few?	40			d, e
Torá	0?	25 [250]		0	e
Urupá	?	[150]		0	e
Warí / Pakaanova		1,300		3	
Yanomami Family					
Ninam / Yanam	466		high	2	
Sanumá (V)	462		high	2	
Yanomám / Yanomae (V)	[4,000]		high	2	
Yanomami (V)	6,000	9,000	high	3	
Isolated Languages					
Aikaná / Masaká / Kasupá		175	med?	1	
Iránxe very close to Mynky		250		2	
Kanoê	8	61	low	1	d
Kwazá / Koaiá	25	15 [40]	low	3	d
Máku	1	[1]	none	1	d, e
Mynky		69			
Trumái	51	94	low	2	d
Tikúna (Co, Pe)		23,000		3	
Creole languages					
[Galibi Marwono]		[860]		0	
[Karipuna do Norte]		[672]		1	

Language names and classification in table 1. are adapted from Instituto Sócio Ambiental 2001a. Population figures are generally taken from Instituto Socio Ambiental 2001b. Modifications and additional information, indicated in brackets, are taken from Rodrigues 1993, Centro de Documentação Indígena 1987, Dixon and Aikhenvald 1999, and various other sources, including personal communications. Amount of study estimates are taken from Rodrigues 1993, Dixon and Aikhenvald 1999, and a miscellany of other sources.

Table 2. Colombia

Family, Languages	Speakers	Population	Transmission	Studies	Status
Arawak Family					
Baniva (V, Br)		6,948 with Curripaco			
Cabiyari	few?	277	low?	0	d
Curripaco (V, Br)		6,948		2	
Guarequena (V, Br)	few	25			
Tariano (Br)	few?	255	none?		d
Yucuna		381		1	
Bora Family					
Bora (Pe)		388		1	
Maraña dialect of Bora (Br)		457			
Muinane		263		1	
Caribe Family					
Carijona	30 passive	234		1	d
Huitoto Family					
Nonuya	3	199		0	d
Ocaina (Pe)	few	126			d
Uitoto / Minica (Pe)		6,604		3	
Macú					
Cacua / Bara (Br)		300?	high		
Hupda (n Br)		few 100	high		
Nukak		700-1,000	high	1	
Yuhup (Br)		200	high	1	

Table 2. Colombia (cont.)

Family, Languages	Speakers	Popula-tion	Trans-mission	Studies	Status
Tucano Family					
Barasána (Br)		939 [1,891]		3	
Carapana (Br)		412		1	
Coreguaje		1,731		1	
Cubeo (Br)		4,616		1	
Desano (Br)		2,216		2	
Guanano / Wanano (Br)		1,113		1	
Macuna (Br)		571 [922]			
Piratapuyo (Br)		474			
Pisamira	25	54			d
Siona (Ec)		468 [700]		1	
Siriano (Br)		715			
Tanimuca / Retuarã		277 [1,149]		1	
Tatuyo		294		2	
Tucano (Br, V)		7,305		2	
Tuyuca (Br)		570		1	
Yuriti (Br)		610			
Tupi-Guarani Family					
Cocama (Pe, Br)	few	285 [767]			d
Geral / Nheengatu (Br, V)		some 100s			
Peba-Yagua Family					
Yagua (Pe)		279			
Isolated Languages					
Andoke		304	low?	3	
Cofán (Ec)		1,061	high?	1	
Ticuna (also Pe, Br)		5,578		2	

Language names and population estimates are adapted from Montes Rodrigues 2000 and Centro Colombiano de Estudos de Lenguas Aborigenes (C.C.E.L.A.) 2000. Other population estimates, in brackets, are from website "Etnias Indígenas de Colombia" 2001.

44   *Denny Moore*

Table 3. Venezuela

Family, Languages	Speakers	Population	Transmission	Studies	Status
Arawaka					
Añu / Paraujano (Co?)	[very few]	13,000		1	d, e
Baniwa (Br, Co)		1,129	low	2	c
Baré (Br)	[few]	1,209	low	1	d
Kurripako (Co, Br)		2,760[?]		1	
Piapoko (Co)	[100]	1167		1	
Warekena (Co, Br)		409		2	c
Wayuu / Guajiro (Co)		[179,31]	[high]	[2]	
Caribe					
Akwayo (Gu, Br)		few?			
Eñepa / Panare		[3,133]	high	3	
Kariña / Galibi (Br, Gu, FG, Su)		[45,000]		1	
Mapoyo	[semi]	[178]	none	1	d
Pemon (Br, Gu)		21,000	good	1	
Yabarana		318	low?		c
Yekuana / Maiongong / Maquiritari (Br)		2,619		2	
Yukpa (Co)		[4,174]		1	
Cibchan Family?					
Barí / Motilón		1,503	good		
Guajibo Family					
Guajibo / Sikuani		9,221		2	
Kuiva / Cuiba (Co)		[856]			
Puinave-Makú Family					
Puinave (Co)		774 [240]			d
Sáliva Family					
Mako (Co?)		345			d
Piaroa (Co)		8,938	good	1	
Sáliva (Co)		79			
Tukano Family					
Tukano (Co, Br)		731		1	

Table 3. Venezuela (cont.)

Family, Languages	Speakers	Popula-tion	Trans-mission	Studies	Status
Tupi-Guarani Family					
Yeral / Nheengatu (Co, Br)		100s?			
Yanomami Family					
Yanomami (Br)		7,069	good		
Sanema (Br)		373 [1,500]	good		
Isolated Languages					
Jodi / Yuwana		257	good	1	d
Pumé / Yaruro		6,000		2	
Uruak / Awaké (Br?)	few	[45]			d
Warao (Gu)		25,000		2	

Adapted from González Ñañez 2000 and Ruette 2000. Other informa-tion, in brackets, is mostly from the Database on Endangered Latin American Languages, compiled by Crevels and Adelaar. The status "en-dan" (endangered) is attributed by González Ñañez to Baré, Baniva, Jodí, Máku, Mapoyo, Puinave, Sáliva, Warekena, Yabarana.

Table 4. Peru

Family, Languages	Speakers**	Popula-tion**	Trans-mission	Studies	Status
Arawá Family					
Culina (Br)	[400]	[400]	[yes]	3 [3]	
Arawak Family					
Asháninca (Br)	52,232 [26,000]	[30,000]	[yes]	3[3]	
Campa Caquinte	229 [250-300]	[250-300]	[yes]	[1]	c
Chamicuro	126 (100-150) [2]	[10-20]	[no]	[1]	d
Iñapari	4 [4]		[no]	[1]	d, e
Machiguenga w/out Cogapacori	[5,700-13,000]	[6,400-13,000]	yes	2 [2]	

Table 4. Peru (cont.)

Family, Languages	Speakers**	Popula-tion**	Trans-mission	Studies	Status
Nomatsiguenga	[2,300-4,500]	[2,300-4,500]	[yes]	[1]	
Piro/Yine w/out Mashco-Piro (Br)	[2,150]	[2,150]	[yes]	3 [3]	
Resígaro	11 [11]	with Bora, Ocaina [5,500-10,000]	[some]	[2]	d
Yanesha / Amuesha	[1,750-8,000]		[locally]	2 [2]	
Bora Family					
Bora (Co)	[260-2,000]	[260-3,000]	[locally]	2 [2]	
Cahuapana Family					
Chayahuita	[7,900-12,000]	[7,900-12,000]	[yes]	[2]	
Jebero	few [elders, interest in revival]	[2,000-3,000]	[doubt-ful]	[1]	d
Harkmbut-Katukina Family					
Harakmbut	[830-1,000]	[900-1,000]	[yes]	[3]	
Huitoto Family					
Huitoto [Murui] (Co?)	[1,100-3,000]	[1,100-3,000]	[some]	[2]	
Huitoto [Muinane] (Br? Co?)	[50-100]				d
Ocaina (Co)	188 (150-250) [54-150]	150	few	[1]	d
Jíbaro Family					
Achuar (Ec)	[2,800-5,000]	[2,800-5,000]	[yes]	1 [2]	
Aguaruna (Ec)	45,137 [34,000-39,000]	[34,000-39,000]	[yes]	3 [3]	
Candoshi [-Shapra] [*Candoshi Family*]	[1,120-3,000]	[1,120-3,000]	[yes]		
Huambisa	[4,000-10,000]	[4,000-10,000]	[yes]	[2]	
[Munichi Family]					
[Munichi]	[3 in 1988]		no	[2]	e
Pano Family					
Amahuaca (Br)	247 [190-1,000]	[190-1,000]	[locally]	[3]	c

Table 4. Peru (cont.)

Family, Languages	Speakers**	Popula-tion**	Trans-mission	Studies	Status
Capanahua	[50-120]	[400]	no	1 [3]	d
Cashibo-Cacataibo	[1,150-1,500]	[1,150-1,500]	[yes]	[2]	
Cashinahua (Br)	[750-1,000]	[750-1,000]	[yes]	[3]	
[Chitonahua]?	[35]				d
[Mastanahua]?	[100]				d
Mayoruna / Matses (Br)	[890-2,500]	[890-2,500]	[yes]		
[Sharanahua]?	[350-450]	[350-450]	[yes]		
Shipibo-Conibo	20,168 [13,200-16,085]	[13,200-16,085]	[yes]	1 [2]	
Yaminahua (Br)	[380-1,000]	[380-1,000]	[yes]	[1]	
[Yora(nahua)]?	[200]	[200]			
Isconahua*	28 [30]				d
Moronahua*					
Remo*					
Peba-Yagua Family					
Yagua (Co)	[760-4,000]	[5,000]	[locally]	3 [3]	
Shimaco Family					
Urarina	[170-3,500]	[170-3,500]	[yes]		
Tacana Family					
Ese Eha [/Huarayo]	[225]	[225]	[most]		
Tucano Family					
Secoya (Ec, Co)	[250-600]	[250-600]	[yes]		
Orejón	190-300 [225-260]	[225-260]	[some]	1	
Tupi-Guarani Family					
Cocama-Cocamilla (Co, Br)	few [260]	[15,000]	[no]	[3]	d
Omagua (Ec?)	[nearly extinct]	[627 in 1976]	[no]		d, e
Záparo Family					
Arabela	[50-150]	[300]	few	1 [1]	d
[Cahuarano]	[5 in 1972]				d, e

Table 4. Peru (cont.)

Family, Languages	Speakers**	Population**	Trans-mission	Studies	Status
Iquito	150 [elder]	[150]	[no]	0 [0]	d
Taushiro [/Pinche] [Taushiro Family]	7 [7 in 1975]	[20]	[no]		d, e
Isolated Languages					
Ticuna (Co, Br)	[700-6,000]	[700-40,000]	[yes]		

* Unknown if dialect or different language.
** Numbers in brackets are from the Database on Endangered Latin American Languages, compiled by Crevels and Adelaar. Numbers in parentheses are from Solis Fonseca 2000 and represent the 1975 census. Other numbers are from García Rivera 2000 and it is unclear if they indicate population or speakers.

Information is also adapted from the map of Pozzi-Escot, Solis, and García Rivera 2000, which considers the following languages "in the process of extinction" ('c' or 'd' above): Campa Caquinte, Iñapari, Resígaro, Jebero, Ocaina, Amahuaca, Omagua, Iquito, and Taushiro.

Table 5. Bolivia

Family, Languages	Speakers	Population	Trans-mission	Studies	Status
Arawak Family					
Baure	40 elders	631	none	sil/1	d
Machineri (Br)	140	155	high	0	
Mojeño	22% use	20,805	med	mis/sil/1	
Mataco-Maka Family					
Chulupi (Ar, Pa)	none?	dispersed		0	e
Pano Family					
Chacobo	550	767	good	sil/1	
Pacahuara	9	9		sil/1	d
Yaminahua (Pe, Br)	137	161	good	0	
Tacana Family					
Araona	81	90	high	sil/1	

Table 5. Bolivia (cont.)

Family, Languages	Speakers	Population	Trans-mission	Studies	Status
Cavineña	1,180	1,736	med	sil/1	
Esse Ejja (Pe)	502	584	med	sil/1	
Reyesano	few elders?	4,118	none		d, e
Tacana	1,821	5,058	med/low	sil/1	
Tupi-Guarani Family					
Guarasugwe	0?	46	none	0	e
Guarayo	5,933	7,235		mis/sil/1	
Siriono	399	419		mis/2	
Yuqui / Bia Ye	125	156		0	
Isolated Languages					
Canichana	3 semi	583	none	sil/1	e
Cayubaba	2 semi	794	none	sil/1	e
Itonama	5 elder	5,099	none	sil/1	d, e
Leco	20	80		1	d
More	76	200		2	d
Moseten	585	1,177		sil/1	
Movima	2,000	6,516		mis/1	
Tsimane	5,316	5,907		mis/1	
Yuacare	2,675	3,333			

sil = study by SIL. mis = study by other mission. Adapted from Rodríguez Bazán 2000, Rodriguez Bazán and Ayreyu Cuellar 2000, and the Database on Endangered Latin American Languages, compiled by Crevels and Adelaar, which includes Albó 1995, Diez Astete and Murillo 1998, and the Censo Indígena Rural de las Tierras Bajas of 1994.

Table 6. Ecuador

Family, Languages	Speakers	Population	Transmission	Studies	Status
Jívaro Family					
Achuar Chicham (Pe)	4,000	[5,000]		1	
Shuar Chicham (Pe)	35,000			3	
Quíchua Family					
Runa Shimi	1,800			2	
(Western) Tucano Family					
Pai Coca / Siona / Secoya (Co, Pe)	600			1	
Zaparoan Family					
Záparo	24 [1-5]	24 [170]		1	d
Isolated Languages					
A'ingae / Cofán (Co)	800	[800]		1	
Wao Tiriro	1,200	[1,200]		2	

Based on Gnerre 2000, Ushiña S. 2000, Juncosa 2000, and the Database on Endangered Latin American Languages, compiled by Crevels and Adelaar. Numbers in brackets are from this last source.

Table 7. Guyana

Family, Languages	Speakers	Population	Transmission	Studies	Status
Arawak Family					
Arawak / Lokono (FG, Su)	<10%	15,500		2	
Mawayana (Br, Su)		?		0	e
Wapixana (Br)		6,900			
Carib Family					
Akwaio Kapon is auto-desig (V, Br)		5,000		1	
Carib / Kariña, Galibi / Kali'na (V, Br, FG, Su)		3,000			

Table 7. Guyana (cont.)

Family, Languages	Speakers	Population	Transmission	Studies	Status
Makushi (Br)		7,750			
Patamona Kapon is auto-desig		5,000			
Pemon / Arekuna (Br, V)		500			
WaiWai (Vr)		24			
Isolated Languages					
Warrau (V)				1	
Creole Languages					
Guyanese English base					
Berbice Dutch base				1?	c
Skepi Dutch base					c

Adapted from Forte 2000, Carmago and Boven 2000b, and the Database on Endangered Latin American Languages, compiled by Crevels and Adelaar. Carmago indicates an "endangered" status for Mawayana, Berbice, and Skepi.

Table 8. Suriname

Family, Languages	Speakers	Population	Transmission	Studies	Status
Arawak Family					
Arawak / Lokono (Gu, FG)	[700]	[2,000]	low	2	
Mawayana (Br, Gu)	[5]	[60]	none		d
Carib Family					
Akurio	[10]	50	low	0	d
Carib / Kariña (Br, Gu, FG, V)	[800-1,000]	3,000	med	3	
Sikïyana	[15]		none		d

Table 8. Suriname (cont.)

Family, Languages	Speakers	Population	Transmission	Studies	Status
Trio / Tiriyó (Gr?, Br)	[1,000-1,200]	1,000[-1,200]	high	1	
Tunayana close to Waiwai	[10]		none		
Wayana (FG, Br)	[500]	500	high	1	
Creole Languages, English based					
Alaku / Boni					
Guyanese					
Kwinti					d
Matawari					
Ndjuka					
Paramaca					
Sranan Tongo / Taki Taki					
Saramaccan English & Portuguese based					

Adapted from Boven and Morroy 2000, Camargo and Boven 2000, and the Database on Endangered Latin American Languages, compiled by Crevels and Adelaar. Camargo and Boven give indicate Akurio and Kwinti as in danger of extinction.

Table 9. French Guiana

Family, Languages	Speakers	Population	Transmission	Studies	Status
Arawak Family					
Arawak / Lokono (Gu, Su)		350		1?	
Palikur (Br)		500		1	

Table 9. French Guiana (cont.)

Family, Languages	Speakers	Population	Transmission	Studies	Status
Carib Family					
Aparaí (Br)					
Kali'na / Galibi / Carib (Br, Gu, Su, V)		2,000		2	
Wayana (Su, Br)		1,000		1	
Tupi-Guarani Family					
Émérillon	200	400+		1	c
Wayãpi (Br)		500		3	
Creole Languages					
Ndyuka English base					
Aluku / Boni English base					
Paramaka English base					
Saramaka English & Portuguese base					
Guyanais French base					

Adapted from Grenand 2000, Queixalós 2000 and Camargo and Boven 2000c. Camargo indicates Émérillon as endangered.

Map 2. Lowland and Tropical South America

Ecuador	26	Baré	48	Puruborá
1 Záparo	27	Uruak (Awaké)	49	Kujubim
Peru	*Guyana*		50	Mondê
2 Arabela	28	Mawayana	51	Akuntsu
3 Cahuarano	*Suriname*		52	Kwazá (Koaiá)
4 Taushiro [/Pinche]	28	Mawayana	53	Sabanê
5 Jebero	29	Akurio	54	Umutina (Omotina)
6 Chamicuro	30	Sikïyana	55	Guató
7 Munichi	*Brazil*		56	Apiaká
8 Iñapari	13	Kokáma	57	Yawalapití
9 Mastanahua?	15	Omágua (Kambeba)	58	Trumái
10 Chitonahua?	23	Tariána	59	Xipaya (Shipaya)
11 Isconahua?	26	Baré	60	Kuruáya
12 Capanahua	28	Mawayána	61	Anambé
13 Cocama-Cocamilla	31	Máku	62	Amanayé
14 Iquito	32	Poyanáwa	63	Avá-Canoeiro
15 Omagua	33	Korúbo	64	Akwén/Xakriabá
16 Ocaina	34	Txunhuã-Djapá	65	Krenák
17 Resígaro	35	Nukini	66	Ofayé (Ofayé-Xavante)
18 Huitoto [Muinane]	36	Katukina do Rio Biá	67	Xetá
Colombia		(Pedá Djapá)	*Bolivia*	
13 Cocama	37	Katawixí	68	Pacahuara
16 Ocaina	38	Mura	69	More
19 Nonuya	39	Torá	70	Cayubaba
20 Carijona	40	Oro Win	71	Reyesano
21 Cabiyari	41	Kanoê	72	Leco
22 Pisamira	42	Djeoromitxí (Jabutí)	73	Canichana
23 Tariano	43	Arikapú	74	Baure
Venezuela	44	Aruá	75	Itonama
24 Añu (Paraujano)	45	Mekém (Sakirabiár)	76	Guarasugwe
25 Mapoyo	46	Urupá	77	Chulupi
	47	Ajurú (Wayoró)		

Notes

1. I wish to thank the people who contributed information on languages: Francisco Queixalós, Odile Renault-Lescure, Willem Adelaar, Mily Crevels, Sérgio Meira, Gail Gomez, Raquel Guirardello, Yonne Leite, Henri Ramirez, Filomena Sandalo, Bruna Franchetto, Sebastian Drude, Elder Lanes, Spike Gildea, Leo Wetzels, Eithne Carlin, and Hein van der Voort. Errors are my own.
   The information presented here is that which was available in 2001. The situation has changed since then. For example, much more reseach has been done on the native languages of Bolivia. A more recent accont of the study of native Brasilian languages is given in Moore 2005.

References

Etnias Indígenas de Colombia – website
  2001   *Grupos Indígenas de Colombia* www.indígenascolombia.org/pueblos.
           htm/#Grupos. List of native groups adapted from *Los Pueblos Indí-
           genas de Colombia 1997*, by Raúl Arango and Enrique Sánchez. Bo-
           gatá: Tercer Mundo Editores. Departamento Nacional de Planea-
           ción. 1998.
Aikhenvald, Alexandra Y. and R. M. W. Dixon
  1999   Other small families and isolates. In Dixon and Aikhenvald (eds.)
           341–384.
Albó, Xavier
  1995   *Bolivia plurilingüe:* Una Guía para Planificadores y Educadores, 3
           vols. La Paz: UNICEF-CIPCA.
Boven, Karin and Robby Morroy
  2000   Indigenous languages of Suriname. *LAH* 377–384.
Camargo, Eliane, and Karin Boven
  2000   Indigenous languages of Suriname. Map accompanying *LAH*.
  2000b   Indigenous languages of Guyana. Map accompanying *LAH*.
  2000c   Langues Amérindiennes de Guyane Française. Map accompanying
           LAH.
Centro Colombiano de Estudios de Lenguas Aborígenes (C.C.E.L.A.)
  2000   Lenguas Indígenas de la Amazonia Colombiana. Map, adapted by
           Francisco Queixalós and Odile Renault-Lescure, accompanying *LAH*.
Centro de Documentação Indígena
  1987   Povos Indígenas no Brasil. Map. São Paulo: CEDI.
Díez Astete, Álvaro and David Murillo
  1998   Pueblos Indígenas de Tierras Bajas: Características Principales. La
           Paz: PNUD.

Dixon, R. M. W. and Alexandra Y. Aikhenvald (eds.)
1999   *The Amazonian languages.* Cambridge: Cambridge University Press.
Forte, Janette
2000   Amerindian languages of Guyana. *LAH* 317–333.
Franchetto, Bruna
2000   O Conhecimento Científico das Línguas Indígenas da Amazônia no Brasil. *LAH* 165–182.
García Rivera, Fernando Antonio
2000   Estado de las Lenguas en el Perú. *LAH* 333–342.
Gnerre, Maurizio
2000   Conocimiento Científico de las Lenguas de la Amazonia del Ecuador. *LAH* 277–286.
González Ñañez, Omar
2000   Las Lenguas del Amazonas Venezolano. *LAH* 385–418.
Grenand, Françoise
2000   La Connaissance Scientifique des Langues Amérindiennes en Guyane Française. *LAH* 307–316.
Instituto Sócio Ambiental.
2001a   Línguas Indígenas. www.socioambiental.org/website/povind/ linguas/index.html.
2001b   Lista de Povos Indígenas. www.socioambiental.org/website/povind/povos/morinfo.html. (1997 revision of information from Rodrigues 1986.)
Juncosa, José E.
2000   Lenguas Indígenas de la Amazonia Ecuatoriana. Map accompanying *LAH*.
Moore, Denny
2005   Brazil: Language situation. In Brown, Keith (ed.) *Encyclopedia of languages and linguistics.* Vol. 2: 117–127.
Kaufman, Terrence and Victor Golla
2001   Language groupings in the New World: their reliability and usability in cross-disciplinary studies. In Renfrew (ed.) 47–58.
Lizarralde, Manuel
2001   Biodiversity and loss of Indigenous languages and knowledge in South America. In Maffi, Luisa (ed.) *On biocultural diversity:* Linking language, knowledge, and the environment. Washington: Smithsonian Institution Press. 265–281.
Montes Rodrigues, María Emília
2000   Informe sobre el Conocimento Científico de las Lenguas Ameríndias Habladas em la Región Amazônica Colombiana. *LAH* 193–210.
Nichols, Johanna
1990   Linguistic diversity and the first settlement of the New World. *Language* 66.3: 475–521.

Pozzi-Escot, Ines, Gustavo Solis Fonseca and Fernando García Rivera
  2000   Lenguas Indígenas de la Amazonia Peruana. Map accompanying *LAH*.
Queixalós, Francisco and Odile Renault-Lescure (organizers)
  2000   *As Línguas Amazônicas Hoje* (= *LAH*). São Paulo: Instituto Sócio
           Ambiental.
Queixalós, Francisco
  2000   Les Langues de Guyane Française. *LAH* 299–306.
Renfrew, Colin (ed.)
  2001   *America past, America present:* Genes and languages in the Americas
           and beyond, Cambridge: The McDonald Institute for Archeological
           Research.
Rodrigues, Aryon D.
  1986   *Línguas Brasileiras:* para o Conhecimento das Línguas Indígenas.
           São Paulo: Edições Loyola.
Rodrigues, Aryon D.
  1993   Endangered languages in Brasil. Paper presented in the "Symposium on
           Endangered Languages of South America," Rijksuniversiteit, Leiden.
Rodríguez Bazán, Luis A.
  2000   Estado de las Lenguas Indígenas del Oriente, Chaco y Amazonia Bo-
           livianos. *LAH* 129–149.
Rodríguez Bazán, Luis A. and Herlan Ayreyu Cuellar
  2000   Lenguas Indígenas de la Amazonia Boliviana; Región de las Cuencas
           de los Rios Amazonas y de la Plata (Oriente, Chaco y Amazonia).
           Map accompanying *LAH*.
Roosevelt, Anna C.
  1994   Amazonian anthropology: Strategy for a new synthesis. In Roosevelt,
           Anna C. (ed.) *Amazonian Indians from prehistory to the present.* Tuc-
           son: The University of Arizona Press. 1–29.
Ruette, Krisna
  2000   Lenguas Indígenas de la Amazonia Venezolana (y otras Regiones del
           País). Map accompanying *LAH*.
Seki, Lucy
  1999   The Upper Xingu as an incipent linguistic area. In Dixon and
           Aikhenvald (eds) 417–430.
  2000   Gramática do Kamaiurá. Campinas: Editora da UNICAMP.
Simoni, Lucia; Tarazona-Santos, Eduardo; Luiselli, Donata and Davide Pettener
  2001   *Genetic differentiation of South American Native populations In-
           ferred from classical markers*: from explorative analyses to a working
           hypothesis. In Renfrew (ed.) 125–138.
Solís Fonseca, Gustavo
  2000   La Lingüística Amerindia Peruana de la Selva. *LAH* 343–360.
Ushiña S., Pedro H.
           Identificación de las Nacionalidades Indígenas del País. *LAH* 287–298.

Chapter 4
Endangered Languages of Mexico and Central America

Colette Grinevald

1. Introduction

The region to be talked about in this paper is hard to label, although it is clearly identifiable as lying between the United States to the north and Colombia to the south, and comprising the following eight countries: Mexico, Guatemala, Belize, El Salvador, Honduras, Nicaragua, Costa Rica and Panama. This area between North and South America partly overlaps with them both culturally and linguistically. It is subdivided into different specific political, economic and cultural subgroupings that have variously been labelled Middle America, Mesoamerica, Central America, or the Intermediate Area. This presentation will follow a straightforward country by country order, from Mexico in the north to Panama in the south, and underline the startling contrasts that characterize these countries in terms of the density of indigenous populations, the vitality of their languages and the development of programs for the linguistic training of native speakers.

It is a region where major centers of civilization flourished during the 2,500 years before the Spanish Conquest, like those of the of Teotihuacan, of the Toltec and the Aztec in Central Mexico, the Olmec on the Gulf Coast of Mexico, the Monte Alban of Oaxaca, and the Classic Maya of Chiapas in Mexico and the Peten in Guatemala (Longacre 1967).

One of the major characteristics of this area as a whole is that it was the most densely populated area of the continent before the arrival of the European conquerors and colonizers. It is estimated that the indigenous population of the region reached 25 million in 1519. The city of Tenotchtitlan, for instance, had 500,000 people, at a time when Rome had only 100,000 and Paris, the largest city of Europe had only 300,000 (Garza Cuarón and Lastra 1991:107). It is also one of the regions of the world that has suffered one of the greatest sudden losses of indigenous population: less than a century after the initial European contacts, the population had been reduced to one million people. This happened as the result of numerous converging dynamics, such as the physical elimination of ethnic populations, ethnic suicide by the populations themselves (through a combination of low birth rates and high rates of infanticide and adult suicide, of the kind witnessed today with some indigenous groups of the Amazonian region of South America), loss of population from incapacity at adapting to the inhospitable lands to which the indigenous populations were relegated, and deadly impact of diseases brought in from the Old World.

Today the proportion of indigenous population and of speakers of indigenous languages in this region is much higher than that of its neighbors to the north (the United States and Canada) and is only equalled by that of the Andean countries to the south. This region is home to some of the largest Amerindian language communities, with several languages having over a million speakers, such as *Nahuatl* (*Aztec*) and *Yucatec* in Mexico and the *Quichean* complex (*Kiche'-Tzutujil-Kaq'chikel*) in Guatemala, and more than two dozen languages with more than a 100,000 speakers. But, as is the case throughout the Americas, all of the indigenous languages of the region, large languages included, are to be considered endangered.[1]

2. Mexico[2]

The major actors at Mexican institutions involved in the study of the languages of Mexico all point to the fact that ALL Mexican languages are endangered if one includes the threat of potentially swift language shift in some major *Nahuatl* speaking communities (see Hill and Hill 1986; for instance). The same Mexican actors are also generally concerned that speakers of the languages to be documented and studied be trained to do linguistics whenever feasible, through the programs that will be mentioned below.

2.1. Overview of the languages of Mexico

The wealth of Mexico in terms of its number of indigenous languages and its diversity of language families is well known. Actual accounts give about 58 to 200 languages, depending on which criteria are used to determine languages. It is estimated that about 113 languages have disappeared in Mexico since the 12th century: this figure includes 48 languages that have remained unclassified and 65 classified languages, 33 of which were Uto-Aztecan and many of those on the Mexican-US border (Garza Cuarón and Lastra 1991: 97).

As expounded on numerous occasions by Kaufman, there is a great need to keep in mind the state of relatedness of the languages in all discussions of the genetic classification of the languages of this region of the world and of the simple count of languages spoken in the country. Kaufman distinguishes between dialects, language complexes, language groups (or branches or families if there is no superordinate category), language families and stocks or phyla. In this perspective for instance, Kaufman signals that the names *Nahua, Otomí, Zapoteco, Mixteco, Mazateco, Chinanteco, Tlapaneco, Popoloca, Pame, Zoque* actually refer to language groups, and not to individual languages, as each one contains two or more languages. The range of variation found in calculations of the number of languages of Mexico comes from linguists with different purposes, such as linguists focusing on the classification of languages like Kaufman, or linguists of the Summer Institute of Linguistics (SIL), who focus primarily on estimating the desirability of Bible translation. One can, for instance, contrast Kaufman's division of *Zapoteco* into 10 languages with the list of 57 *Zapoteco* entries given in the SIL Ethnologue.

Another characteristic of Mexico is its very large population of speakers of indigenous languages. According to the 2000 census, there are 1,448,936 speakers of *Náhuatl*, 452,887 of *Zapoteco*, and 444,498 of *Mixteca*.[3] Five of the *Mayan* languages total more than 1,5 million speakers.[4]

2.2. The endangered languages of Mexico[5]

Garza Cuarón and Lastra (1991) is one of the most reliable sources of information for the country: it combines the necessary wariness of figures from the official 1990 census and information from many field accounts.[6]

Table 1. The most endangered languages of Mexico (Garza Cuarón and Lastra 1991: 97)

Stock	Language	Speakers
Uto-Aztecan	Pima-Papago	236
	Varohio	300
Otomanguean	Ocuiltec (Tlahuica)	93
	Ixcatec	119
	Northern Pame	30
Mixe-Zoqueta	Oluta Popoluca	121
Mayan	Lacandon	200
	Acatec	100

Table 1. (cont.)

Stock	Language	Speakers
Yuman-Seri	Paipai	24
	Kiliwa	90
	Cochimi	220
	Cucapa	178
	Seri	500
Algonquian	Kickapoo	400

The following languages must be considered to be the most endangered because of their few speakers: *Oluta*: 14 (Zavala 2000), *South Zoque* of Tuxla: 0–5 and *Ayapa mixe zoque* 2–10 (Roberto Zavala, p. c.). To those can be added some *Mayan* languages spoken on the border with Guatemala, some spoken by immigrants from that country. The figures from the 2000 census are 90 for *Ixil*, 23 for *Aguacateco*, and a few each for *Mocho, Teco* and *Tuzanteko*.

In general, one must keep in mind several obstacles to the task of evaluating which languages need most attention such as great variation in the counting of languages, in the counting of speakers left, as well as in the assessment of which languages of Mexico are the most un(der)-documented.[7] What is certain is that the last ten years have seen a surge of interest in the indigenous languages and in fieldwork projects, as described in the next section.

2.3. Present day work on the languages of Mexico

This section will focus on various national programs attending to the study and documentation of the languages of Mexico, including the training of Mexican linguists, and for a few of particular interest here, the training of indigenous native speakers. A number of programs focusing on the study of indigenous languages have existed for a while in Mexico, but this last decade has seen a noticeable surge in linguistic studies that take advantage of the latest developments in the discipline. There is an increasingly active network of national and foreign linguists, national and foreign institutions, international conferences and workshops.

Linguistic training in Mexico City
- The *Escuela Nacional de Antropologia e Historia* (ENAH) is the oldest institution. It had been offering B.A. and M.A. (licenciatura y maestria) degrees and has just started offering a doctoral degree as well. The degree is in general linguistics, but there is training available for the study of Middle American Languages.
- The *Seminario de Lenguas Indígenas* is a research institute of the University of Mexico (UNAM).
- The *Instituto de Investigaciones Antropológicas* is another research institute of the University of Mexico (UNAM). It has a Ph.D. program in Anthropology and students can obtain training in linguistics by tutoring.
- The *Colegio de México* (COLMEX) has research programs and training of Ph.D. students.
- The *Universidad Autónoma Metropolitana* has a B.A., an M.A. and a Ph.D. in general linguistics
- The *Universidad Nacional Autónoma de Mexico* (UNAM) has also B.A., M.A. and Ph.D. in general linguistics with specialization in *Spanish*.

Other Mexican university and research centers focusing on Indian languages
- The *Universidad de Sonora* offers a B.A. and an M.A. in linguistics and specializes in the study of the Indian languages of this northern part of Mexico. They have been running well attended international conference in recent years and have produced collections of proceedings of these conferences (Encuentros de Hermosillo).
- The *Universidad de Guadalajara* through its Departamento de Lenguas Indígenas specializes in the languages of the northwest of Mexico. It has an MA in general linguistics.
- The *Universidad de Yucatán* in Mérida offers a B.A. in linguistics with a specialization in *Yucateco*.
- The *Centro de Investigación y Estudios Superiores en Antropología Social* (CIESAS) is a research institute and a training center delivering an M.A. degree in linguistics for native speakers in Amerindian languages. Beyond Mexico City it has several branches in different parts of the country. CIESAS-Sureste, based in San Cristobal de Las Casas, is actively attending to the languages of Chiapas and Southern of Mexico.

Program for the documentation of Mexican languages
  – The *Proyecto para la Documentación de las lenguas de Meso America*
    (PDLMA), co-directed by Kaufman (University of Pittsburgh), Juste-
    son (University of Albany) and Zavala (CIESAS-Sureste), is a major
    project for the documentation of Mexican languages. In the last de-
    cade it has been attending to a large number of Mexican languages, in-
    cluding all *MixeZoquean*, some *Zapotecan*, some *Totonacan*, some
    Nahua, one *Popoloca*, three *Mayan*, and both *Matlatzincan* languag-
    es.[8] The functioning of this program is described in Kaufman (2001).

A new government institute for the languages of Mexico
  – The *Instituto Nacional de Lenguas Indígenas de México* (INALI) was
    created in 2003 as a part of the General Law of Linguistic Rights for
    the Indigenous populations. It is dedicated to basic and applied re-
    search on the languages of Mexico, the standardization of writing
    systems and the production of teaching and education materials,
    elaborating maps and catalogs of languages. It is also meant also to
    organize campaigns for the diffusion of indigenous languages, to or-
    ganize conferences on the languages, to train and grant certification
    of translators. In addition it should promote language policies aimed
    at a greater use and development of indigenous languages. Much
    hope has been placed in this new institute and it is hoped that it will
    not be too bureaucratic and will fulfill some of the hopes it raises.[9]

2.4. Perspectives on Mexico

Mexico is the largest country of the region considered here and the one
with the greatest number of languages and diversity of languages. A significant amount of work has already been done on the languages but
much remains to be done. No family of languages in Mexico has been as
well studied as the *Mayan* languages spoken in Guatemala, for which the
level of linguistic knowledge is probably unparalleled in America. And a
number of languages are indeed in need of urgent documentation as their
speaker figures are alarming, although the general state of endangerment
of all the Indian languages, including the major ones like *Nahuatl*, is always to be kept in mind. Comprehensive documentation relying on modern linguistic analyses is still needed for a very large number of languages,
making Mexico a major center of linguistic activities in the future. If one

region was to be pointed at for an urgent need of attention to its languages, it would be the region of Baja California.

Most notable is the fact that the last 10 years have seen major developments aimed at advancing and coordinating linguistic studies in the languages of Mexico with which any outside linguist interested in Mexico would do well to become familiar. Regional centers such as the ones in Hermosillo in the North and San Cristobal de las Casas in the south are becoming active centers of linguistic studies relying on field studies of the local languages. A major part of their actitivies, at least in CIESAS-Sureste, is the training of native speakers. The success of such training is key if the new INALI institute is to be able to carry out its planned programs for the promotion of indigenous languages.

3. Guatemala[10]

As was the case with Mexico, the outline of the present state of language endangerment to be given will be followed by important information on the intense linguistic activities being carried out on the languages, in particular on how the study and development of *Mayan* languages is being more and more carried out by native *Mayan* speakers, as discussed in Grinevald 2002.[11]

The striking feature of *Mayan* languages is their omnipresence in the country. Mayas form absolute majorities in almost all of the communities where they presently live in Guatemala. The great majority of Mayas speak one of the twenty nine extant *Mayan* languages, almost always as a first language, and many Mayans are still monolingual in a *Mayan* language, especially among the older population. In spite of these demographic signs of vitality, however, language shift and loss among Mayas is growing at an alarming rate, and Mayan community leaders are increasingly concerned about the future viability of their languages and community structures.[12]

3.1. Guatemalan endangered languages

Most *Mayan* languages are potentially threatened but are not actually disappearing. The signs of potential threat are large populations of bilinguals, the beginning of *Spanish* monolingualism among children, particularly in urban areas, and the transfer (for some time now) of functions that were once filled in *Mayan* to *Spanish*, particularly literacy and public speech. The level of vitality of the different languages varies remarquably, as does the level of vitality of a particular variant.

3.1.1. Fast language shift

All *Mayan* languages show signs of active shift, including the largest one, *K'ichee'*, which has close to a million speakers. Speaker populations that range from around 20,000 to well over 100,000 – *Akatek, Chuj, Poqomchi', Ch'orti', Ixil, Tz'utujil* and *Q'anjob'al* – seem to be viable for the moment but shift could set in very fast. Such a fast shift has been detected with *Jakaltek* (*Popti'*), which today is considered one of the most endangered languages in Guatemala, although here, too, the community seems conscious of the danger and is preoccupied with finding ways of stemming the loss.

Although neither *Kaqchikel* (one of the majority languages with almost half a million speakers) nor *Q'anjob'al* (a minority language with less than 100,000 speakers) is severely threatened today, *Kaqchikel* is obviously more so than *Q'anjob'al*, but this could change in a generation. The striking difference is that in many (most?) Kaqchikel towns, it is increasingly common to hear *Spanish* in public areas (like the street), but in *Q'anjob'al* towns one still almost never hears *Spanish* (except, of course, Barillas, where the urban population is heavily Ladino).

3.1.2. Seriously endangered languages

Languages may be in this category for one of two reasons: either the number of speakers is very low or dropping fast or there is now only one community of speakers. *Mopan* is gravely endangered, as it is now spoken by relatively few people in Guatemala (and in Belize). *Poqomam*, although not as small or as immediately endangered, needs listing here too because it has been steadily losing speakers. Meanwhile *Uspantek, Sikapakense, Sakapultek*, and *Awakatek* are cases of languages that are endangered by the fact that they are all spoken in only one municipality.

3.1.3. Moribund languages

Itzaj has about 30 fluent speakers today, none of them children, which places it in the moribund category. This is a situation where the community has expressed interest in reviving the almost lost language and has enrolled the help of the linguist specialist of the language (Hofling 1992, England p. c.). It remains now to be seen how many of the sixty or so semispeakers, some of whom are still relatively young, might become fluent speakers. *Teko* in Guatemala may have younger speakers, including children, but it should still probably be classified as moribund. There also seem to be six speakers of *Xinka* (a non-Mayan language) left of the three *Xinka* languages that were still spoken in the 70's.

3.1.4. Revival possible?

In the particular context of Guatemala, where the strength of Maya identity has been on a sharp rise in the last two decades, buttressed by intense language planning and active promotion of *Mayan* languages by new Mayan institutions, England (p. c.) reports that some languages seem to be undergoing revival. While older children are *Spanish* dominant, younger children are becoming *Maya* dominant, because of a conscious effort on the part of parents to reverse the shift. For example with *Poqomam* of Palin, the imminent demise of which was predicted some 15 years ago by Guillermina Herrera and which today has more children speaking it than there were then. Something similar may be happening with *Ch'orti'*, where revival is found in some families. There is no telling how widespread this phenomenon might be today.

3.2. Institutions dealing with the preservation of Mayan languages

Academic and institutional attention to the *Mayan* languages of Guatemala has few parallels in other American countries today. The presentation of the institutions to be considered here follows a double line of logic: on the one hand it respects a chronological order and on the other it highlights the long term contributions of the two foreign linguists mentioned, Terrence Kaufman and Nora England, for the expected academic readership of this paper. This conscious bias towards highlighting the doings of foreign academics is meant to give an account of an interesting and unfortunately rare example of the constructive impact of outsiders on the development of national and local programs that create, promote and strengthen basic and applied linguistic research programs for native speakers.

– The *Proyecto Lingüístico Francisco Marroquin* (PLFM) was founded by Terrence Kaufman in 1970 with the purpose of advancing knowledge on the *Mayan* languages of the country. The operation consisted of matching doctoral students from universities in the United States

with teams of *Mayan* speakers in a mutual teaching program. 14 languages and 26 dialects received attention. About 80 *Mayan* speakers were taught the basics of descriptive linguistics and dictionary making procedures between 1972 and 1977, and about 40 more were taught descriptive linguistics and *Mayan* grammar in 1988 and 1989.[13]
- The *Academia de Lenguas Mayas de Guatemala* (ALMG) was approved as an autonomous state institution in 1991. In 1987, it had established a "unified" alphabet for *Mayan* languages. Several of its cofounders were previously members of the PLFM. Today it has branches for all *Mayan* languages of Guatemala, and it promotes their use and study through activities such as radio programs or translations of grammars originally written in *English* (England 1998).
- *Oxlajuuj Keej Maya' Ajtz'iib'* (OKMA) was founded in 1990 by Nora England, one of the original linguists of the PLFM, with *Mayan* speakers of *K'ichee', Achi, Kaqchikel, Q'anjob'al* and *Poqomam*. The goals of OKMA are to pursue the intensive study of *Mayan* linguistics, to attend to the production of grammatical and scholarly materials about *Mayan* languages and, to that end, to further train teams of native *Mayan* linguists. Recently it has become involved in documentation and archiving projects for severely endangered languages of Guatemala. This institution is unique in its being totally in the hands of native speakers and in producing high quality linguistic work recognized on the international academic scene. See a review of its work in Barret (2005). An OKMA member is finishing a doctoral program at Austin Texas, and an OKMA team has secured funding from the Hans Rausing Endangered Language Documentation Program (HRELDP) in London.

Guatemalan universities and other programs dealing with
Mayan Languages
- The *Universidad Rafael Landivar* (URL), in Guatemala City, offers bachelor's degrees in linguistics with a specialization in *Mayan* linguistics, and professional degrees in bilingual education and in legal interpreting.[14] A program called Edumaya has supported hundreds of *Mayan* students with full scholarships from US-AID.
- The *Universidad Mariano Galvez* (UMG) has applied linguistics and sociolinguistics programs, in which the great majority of the students are Mayas.
- Many other institutions for education and for writers' groups deal with *Mayan* languages and concentrate on linguistic training for

Mayan speakers. Many of the major writers for the National Program in Bilingual Education (PRO-NEBI, now DIGEBI) established in 1985 have been graduates of the PLFM and the University programs mentioned above.

3.3. An exemplary situation in Latin America

Guatemala has been an intense language planning laboratory that has attracted much attention in the past two decades. The 1996 Peace Accords have responded substantially to demands of the "Mayan Movement" for the recognition and development of the *Mayan* languages of the country (see Grinevald 2002).

The documentation of *Mayan* languages in Guatemala today is largely in the hands of native linguists. The linguists of OKMA are, for instance, presently documenting *Teko, Sakapulteko* and *Uspanteko* with support from the Hans Rausing Programme. The *Mayan* languages Kaufman still considered underdocumented are two variants of *Q'eqchi'* (*Cahabón* and *Lanquín*) and one variant of *K'iché* (*Cunén*). *Ch'orti* in the east of the country also remains in need of attention. The non-Mayan *Xinka* language is now being attended to as part of a three language documentation project supported by the new Documentation of Endangered Languages program (DEL) of the USA.[15]

4. Belize

The languages of this small country are an *English-based Creole* which serves as lingua franca, and several indigenous languages that are also spoken in neighboring countries. The figures on Belizean languages given below were all taken from *Ethnologue* (Gordon 2005).

Belize Creole English is the first or second language of the vast majority of the population of about 190,000. This creole is historically an extension of *Miskitu Coast Creole*, which is also spoken in Honduras and Nicaragua. The attitude of its speakers towards it is positive.

The *Garifuna* language of the Carib-Arawakan family is spoken by a population of 12,000 and is also spoken in Honduras. The Garifunas, who speak creole as a second language, are concerned with the loss of their ethnic language and interested in language revitalization.

Three *Mayan* languages are spoken by small communities: *Yucatec, Mopan* and *Kekchi*. The *Yucatec Maya* in Belize account for only 5,800 of the

700,000 total Yucatec population of the Yucatan peninsula. The Belizean Yucatec community is preoccupied with the loss of its language, as all speakers are now older than 40. Some classes in *Yucatec* are being started.

The Belizean community of *Mopan Maya* numbers about 7,000 and is larger than the Guatemalan one of 2,700. No indication of the level of vitality of *Mopan* in Belize is available, though it is known that the language is seriously endangered in Guatemala.

The community of Kekchi' in Belize is only 9,000 strong, while that of Guatemala has a population of 340,000. The *Kekchi* of Belize is a slightly different dialect from the dialects of *Guatemalan Kekchi'*.

5. El Salvador

Very few languages and speakers of indigenous languages have survived in El Salvador which had severe policies of elimination for those languages in the early part of the 20th century. Three ethnic groups of sizable numbers are still identified but the three languages – *K'ekchi (or Q'eqchi)*, *Lenca* and *Pipil* – are all nearly extinct.

The K'ekchi people are Mayan and are in a smaller number in El Salvador than in Belize, with only 12,000.

The *Lenca* language has remained unclassified, although it is considered by some to be *Macro-Chibchan*. The Lenca number 36,000 as an ethnic group in El Salvador, but the language is nearly extinct there, as it is in Honduras. The varieties of *Lenca* in El Salvador and Honduras are considered to be different dialects.

The third and largest ethnic group of El Salvador is the *Pipil*, with 200,000. Their language belongs to the *Nahuat* family and is the best known language of the country. This language once thought extinct, has been described in Campbell (1985), who unexpectedly found about twenty speakers thirty years ago, in the course of a survey of dying languages of Central America. Today, *Pipil* is the object of coordinated language revitalization efforts.[16]

6. Honduras[17]

6.1. The languages of Honduras

There are six indigenous languages spoken in Honduras, three of which have speaker populations in neighboring countries and are considered to have a reasonable level of vitality (within the confines of the general situation of endangerment of all the indigenous languages in the region already mentioned), and two other languages endogenous to Honduras and considered to be severely endangered. Two ethnic communities are said to have no speakers left. The Lenca people are about 50,000. They are thought to be the original occupants of Honduras and to have constituted its base population. Their language is unclassified, and is considered extinct, although there might be a few speakers left. The variant of Honduras is said to be a different dialect from the one of El Salvador.[18]

6.1.1. Less endangered languages of Honduras

The *Garifuna* language, already mentioned in the profiles of Belize and Guatemala, has about 22,000 speakers. It is spoken by a black population that is bilingual in *Garifuna* and either *Miskitu Coast Creole* or *Spanish*. The *Garifuna* language remains understudied and there is a clear need for some projects that would involve the interested communities of the region.[19] The other substantial speaker population is that of the *Miskitu*, which has about 23,000 speakers in Honduras, and many more in neighboring Nicaragua. There is also a community of *Tawahka* (*Sumu*) speakers of several hundreds, with also more speakers on the Nicaraguan side of the border.

6.1.2. Most endangered languages of Honduras

The *Paya* or *Pech* language belongs to the *Chibchan* family of languages and is spoken on the North Central Coast of Honduras by 869 out of a population of 2,000–2,500 people (Ramon Rivas 1993). The Paya community has expressed interest in preserving its language and some work has been carried out to that end.[20]

Tol (or *Tolupan*) is also called *Jicaque*. It is a language isolate that had two dialects, the western branch of which is extinct and the eastern one of which is spoken by around 1,000 (between speakers and semi-speakers) out of a population of 20,000. The speaker community best known is that of the Montaña de la Flor of the Francisco Morazan Department in North Central Honduras. The group is said to be hardly accessible and the field conditions very difficult. There remain 300 to 350 speakers out of a population of 600, including some children, all bilingual in *Spanish*.

6.2. Language planning in Honduras

The indigenous population of Honduras is rather small and the majority are actually mestizados indigenous peasant (indigenous people acculturated to the *mestizo-Spanish* speaking culture), but they have organized and have presented clear demands for the defense of land titles and for the defense of their indigenous languages. There are representatives of the indigenous population in the Ministry of Education for instance, although they are not always speakers of an indigenous language.

Towards the late 90's, some language planning took place, and the Bilingual Education program brought in linguists specialists of some of the local indigenous languages (Holt for *Paya*, Hale for *Miskitu* and *Sumu*, and Salamanca for *Miskitu*). But the programs encountered a number of difficulties, including the resistance of the financing institution, the World Bank, to invest in endangered languages (considered economically not viable), and a serious problem of manpower, not uncommon in development projects. It would seem that after several years of lethargy activity is beginning again.

7. Nicaragua

The fate of the indigenous languages of Nicaragua has been very different on the Pacific and the Atlantic sides of the country. No language has survived on the Pacific side, as in the interior: *Monimbo* (unclassified), *Matagalpa* (*Misumalpan*) and *Subtiava* have been extinct for some time. Meanwhile, several indigenous languages are still spoken in the eastern half of the country, now known as the Caribbean Coast (and previously the Atlantic Coast), where the lingua franca is in fact an *English-based creole* called *Miskitu Coast Creole* (or now *Kriol*). Creole and indigenous languages started receiving special attention twenty years ago as part of the process of establishing autonomy for the region during the Sandinista's government. The Autonomy Statute of the Nicaraguan Constitution of 1987 officially recognized all the languages of the region, and the point was specifically made that every language deserved recognition and protection, no matter how small its population and speaker base.

7.1. The indigenous languages of the Caribbean Coast of Nicaragua

Three languages are still spoken on the Caribbean Coast with varying degrees of vitality, with a fourth ethnic group claiming interest in language revitalization effort, in spite of having no speakers left.

Miskitu is the largest indigenous language of the region. It belongs to the *Misumalpan* family, the name of which is a blend of the languages of that family: MI for *Miskitu*, SUM for *Sumu*, ALPA for the extinct *Matagalpa*. The figures of the ethnic group are uncertain, but range between 75,000 and 120,000. To a great extent, the *Miskitu* language serves as a marker of identity for people of mixed background, many of whom were not declaring themselves Miskitu before the Sandinista Revolution, preferring to be identified as Creoles (i. e., of black descent). The language is also the second language of many Sumu people. It is secure in most Miskitu communities, where there is a high proportion of speakers and the language is taught to the children. The *Miskitu* language is set apart from most of the indigenous languages of this part of the world because of its status as a written language, as missionaries of the Moravian church developed materials for it in the mid-nineteen century and used it as a lingua franca in the region. The language is relatively well documented and a high proportion of its speakers are literate in it. It consists of several mutually-intelligible dialects.

Up until the Sandinista Revolution of the 1980's, one talked of the *Sumu* language as another Misumalpan language with three distinct dialects and with an ethnic population of about 6,000. And as the Sumus were dominated by the Miskitus, in whose language they were bilingual, many did not identify themselves as Sumus, and even less as *Sumu* speakers. Both *Sumu* and *Miskitu* are also spoken in Honduras to the north.

Rama is the only Nicaraguan language to be spoken only in Nicaragua. It belongs to the large *Chibchan* family of languages that ranges from Honduras to Costa Rica, Panama and the northern part of Colombia. *Rama* is the smallest of the indigenous languages of Nicaragua and is in fact a moribund language with no more than a few dozen speakers, the majority of whom are isolated jungle dwellers. A major language documentation project and language and cultural revitalization, to which the community is still committed, took place in the 1990's during Sandinista times.

There is an immigrant Garifuna community in Nicaragua but none speak the language, although the Garifunas participated in the discussion of the Autonomy project and claimed interest in language and culture revitalization efforts.

7.2. Linguistic rights and language development in Nicaragua

Today, programs of bilingual and multicutural education have been established for all the ethnic communities of the Atlantic Coast and operate with more or less success, given the limited support they have received in post-Sandinista times.

7.2.1. A team of professional linguists

A team of linguists self-identified as *"Linguists for Nicaragua"* has been working for over twenty years now on the various languages of Nicaragua for which communities have requested support. The work was carried out through the Center for Research and Documentation of the Atlantic Coast (CIDCA), now affiliated with the University of Central America (UCA-Managua).[21] The languages, linguists and work involved have included: for *Miskitu*, Danilo Salamanca, who worked on a grammar and a dictionary and who is promoting literary production; for *"Sumu"* Ken Hale, who demonstrated that *Mayangna* (or *Northern Sumu*, worked on by Susan Norwood first and now Helena Benedicto), and *Ulwa* (or Southern Sumu, worked on by Hale and later by Tom Green and Andrew Koontz-Garboden) were different languages. Those languages needed basic linguistic descriptions and the projects emphasized the development of literacy and the training of community linguists.[22]

On the other hand, the *"Rama* Language Project" was a combination of salvage linguistics and language revitalization of a moribund and profoundly devalued language. A team of linguists (Grinevald Craig, Tibbitts, Assadi), helped by volunteer students from the University of Oregon, worked through CIDCA with the Rama community for several years (Craig 1992, Grinevald 2003). Today, a second phase of the project concentrates on archiving documentation materials and supporting the language revitalization program, including support for the land claims of Ramas whose territory is being invaded.[23]

7.2.2. Institutions dealing with language revitalization

The *University of the Autonomous Regions of Caribbean Coast of Nicaragua* (URACCAN), a recently opened regional university, is committed to the development of programs for the maintenance and revitalization of the languages and cultures of the Caribbean Coast of Nicaragua through an Institute for researching and promoting the languages and cultures of the coast region (IPILC), while WANI, the magazine of CIDCA-UCA continues to be the main source of information for the Caribbean Coast.

Although the country still sorely lacks resources, personnel and know how for this line of work, IPILC at URACCAN nevertheless constitutes the type of local institution through which such work should be channeled. It is clear that by now all the indigenous populations of the region are mobilized to defend their linguistic rights and look to it for support and training.

8. Costa Rica[24]

8.1. Languages of Costa Rica

Among the native languages of Costa Rica, four are still vital (again within the limits of the general endangerment and precariousness of all the languages of the region), two are considered moribund, and two are definitely extinct. All the languages still spoken today belong to the same *Chibchan* family of languages.

Table 2. Languages of Costa Rica (Rojas Chaves 1997)

Language	Population	Speakers	Status
Bribri	12,172	75 % speakers	vital
Cabecar	9,308	95 % speakers	vital
Guaymi (or Moveres)	5,360	95 % speakers	vital
Guatuso (or Malecus)	1,074	70 % speakers	vital
Boruca (or Bruncas)	5,012	10 speakers (Rojas FW)	*moribund* and 30 semi-speakers
Terraba (Terribe in Panama)	1,253	1 or 2 speakers, 5 semi-speakers (Constenla p. c.)	*moribund* in Costa Rica
Huetar	816	none	extinct end of 18th century
Chorotega	795	none	extinct end of 18th century (lasted in Nicaragua into 19th century)

8.2. Institutions dealing with Costa Rican languages

By Executive Decree a "Subsystem of Indigenous Education for the Preservation and Revitalization of Indigenous Languages" was created in 1993. The reform of the Constitution in 1999 included an article stating that "the State will watch over the maintenance and development of the national indigenous languages".

The study of the languages of Costa Rica is linked to the name of Adolfo Constenla Umaña, of the University of Costa Rica, founder and coordinator (1985–1996) of a Program for Linguistic Research on the Languages of Costa Rica and Neighbouring Areas (PIL) and editor of the linguistic journal Estudios de Lingüística Chibcha.

9. Panama

9.1. Languages of Panama

All the languages of Panama demonstrate a greater vitality than the languages of neighbouring countries. The major danger to these languages is that of language shift induced by a growing urbanization of some of the populations.

Table 3. Languages of Panama (Ethnologue)

Family	Language	Population	Other contries
Chibchan			
	Guaymi	128,000	(also in Costa Rica)
	Kuna	50-70,000	
	Teribe	3,000	(also in Costa Rica as Terraba)
	Buglere	2,500	
Chaco			
	Emberá	7-8,000	(also in Colombia)
	Waumeo	3,000	(also in Colombia)

9.2. Documentation of Kuna by Kunas at AILLA

Panama is the site of an interesting case of extensive documentation being produced directly by speakers of the population concerned. After decades of research on the oral traditions of the Kunas by anthropological linguist Joel Sherzer, a situation has developed whereby *Kuna* speakers themselves are now actively documenting their traditions and archiving their recordings at the Archives of Indigenous Languages of Latin America (AILLA) in Austin Texas (founded by Sherzer himself). This is an interesting example of the contribution of new technologies and academic work being made available to a speaker population that demands it and uses it.

10. Conclusion

This report has emphasized the dynamics of the attention being given to indigenous languages of this central region of the American continents. The situations vary greatly from country to country, from very large and heavily populated countries like Mexico with major programs to very small and newly independent countries like Belize with little infrastructure for the study of its languages. It is a region with very large indigenous languages that have more than a million speakers, a phenomenon unknown in the countries to the north, but at the same time with numerous moribund languages and undocumented languages in need of urgent attention.

Mexico and Guatemala have major indigenous populations and large numbers of languages, some of which may have large speaker populations but are nevertheless endangered because they are at the mercy of powerful and potentially swift shifts to *Spanish*. The main characteristic of those two countries is the institutionalization of the systematic study of the local languages and the recent development of linguistic training programs for native speakers. Particularly striking are the ambitious language planning activities involving the *Mayan* languages of present-day Guatemala, including extensive bilingual education programs and language standardization and development programs.

Of the smaller and less populated countries to the south, one should remember the following aspects of their indigenous languages. Three languages have a large population base and a solid community of speakers. *Miskitu* is spoken across two countries (Honduras and Nicaragua) and benefits from a literate past. *Garifuna* is also spoken across two countries (Belize and Honduras) and may be in more dire need of linguistic attention. The large *Guaymi-Movere* and *Kuna* groups of Panama also constitute vital languages. Four relatively small *Chibchan* groups of Costa Rica nevertheless have a strikingly high proportion of speakers, which contrasts with the much more threatened languages of Honduras and the practically extinct languages of El Salvador. Meanwhile, the Sandinista Revolution, particularly through its project of Autonomy for the Atlantic/Caribbean Coast, attracted much attention to the indigenous languages of Nicaragua, big and small, and in the last decade of the 20th century turned the country into a major linguistic field laboratory that combined linguistic and applied linguistic research with language revitalization community programs. Major linguistic research and development work was also carried out in the emerging *Nicaraguan Sign Language.*

One of the main goals of this presentation was to highlight regional institutions of these countries and to underline the importance of acknowledging their existence. It emphasized in particular the important efforts being developed in several of these countries to provide their citizens with proper linguistic training in order for Amerindian linguistics to develop in situ in a self-sustainable way, the optimum scenario being of course the training of speakers of indigenous languages wherever and whenever possible. If properly thought through, the approach to the study of the indigenous languages of this region of the world ought to have a significant impact on how we conceive the relation of field linguists to the field, to linguistic communities, as well as to local and regional institutions. It means systematically integrating local concerns in the future planning of language-related academic efforts, which include standard linguistic research, newly developing language documentation and language maintenance projects, as well as situations of salvage linguistics for the moribund languages.

Mexico		*El Salvador*	
1	Pima-Panago 236 (speakers)	19	Pipil 200.000
2	Varohio 300		
3	Ocuiltec Tlahuica 93		*Honduras*
4	Ixcatec 119	20	Paya Pech 869
5	Northern Pame 30	21	Tol Jicaque 1.000
6	Olutla Popoluca 121		
7	Lacandon 200		*Nicaragua*
8	Akatek 100	22	Sumu Mayangna, Ulwa¿?
9	Paipai 24	23	Rama 25
10	Kiliwa 90		
11	Cochimi 220		*Costa Rica*
12	Cocopa 178	24	Teribe 1 or 2
13	Seri 500	25	Boruca 10
14	Kickapo Kikapu 400		
Guatemala			
15	Mopan few		
16	Itza 30		
17	Teko ¿?		
18	Xinka ¿?		

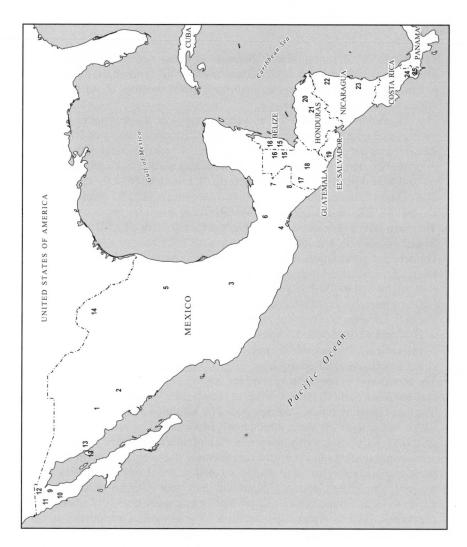

Map 3. Mexico and Central America

Notes

1. The fact that the community of linguists of these Amerindian languages is acutely aware of this state of affairs accounts for the tone of alarmism and the posture of activism that runs through most of the writings about the state of Amerindian languages today.
2. The material to be presented in this section relies on various publications and on personal communication with Terrence S Kaufman and Roberto Zavala. Reliable and detailed information on the state of endangerment of the languages of Mexico may be found in several publications, such as Bartholomew, Lastra and Manrique 1994, 1995 (henceforth B, L and M 1994, 1995), Campbell 2000, Garza Cuarón and Lastra 1991 (henceforth GC and L), Suarez 1983.
3. Otomí 291,722; Totonaca 240,034; Mazateco 214,477
4. They are Maya Yucateco with 799,696, Tzotzil with 297,561, Tzeltal with 284,826, Chol with 161,766 and Huasteco with 120,739.
5. For detailed information about the endangerment situation of specific families, the reader is referred to reports listed below:
   - B, L and M 1994 Vol. I: Yutoazteca (Dakin), Totonacan (MacKay), Tabasco (Perez-Gonzalez), Mixe-Zoquean (Wichmann), Maya (Hopkins and Josserand), Otopamean (Bartholomew).
   - B, L and M 1995 Vol. II: Mixtecano y Zapoteco (Smith-Stark), Chinanteco (Merrifield), Popolocan (Veerman-Leichsenring), Tlapaneco (Carrasco Zuñiga) and Huave (Hollenbach).
6. The situation is, of course, very complex, a good example of it being the detailed case the *Mixtec* and *Zapotec* families of languages by Smith-Stark (1995).
7. The list of languages below, also provided by Kaufman, includes "the languages which lack one of the three components of an adequate documentation (G = grammar, T = texts, L = dictionary). In each of the groups listed below there are some communities where children are learning the language, but in all groups, there are languages or large important dialect areas where children are no longer learning the language". Kaufman does "not consider most SIL dictionaries to be adequate because of [a] incomplete specification of phonological properties, [b] incomplete specification of grammatical properties of morphemes and stems. Mostly they are also too short."

Language	*Lacks*
Chinanteco [6+ languages]	t, g, l
Zapoteco [10+ languages]	t, g, lt
Trique [3 languages]	t, g, l
Mixteco [6+ languages]	t, g, l
Amuzgo [2 languages]	t, g, l
Cuicateco	t, g
Sierra de Puebla Nahuat	t, g, l
Tarasco	t, g?, l

Language	Lacks
Tojolabal	t, g
Chontal, Yokot'an [Mayan]	t, g, l?

8. This list reflects the knowledge accumulated by Kaufman over thirty years of field-work in the region and corresponds to the work to be done to meet his standards of documentation, not that there does not exist more documentation than he acknowledges here. The list does not reflect either the issue of how available accumulated documentation is at this point, as much more than is available to the newcomer to Mexican linguistics remains in the form of personal archives of linguists.

9. There are, however, still some *MixeZoquean*, many *Zapotecan*, many *Nahua*, some *Totonacan*, and several *Popolocan* languages for which no work has been scheduled so far.

10. There have been, for instance, televized political discussions in *Purépecha* with subtitles in *Spanish*, sponsored by INALI. The Institute's main challenge is going to be the lack of appropriately trained speakers, hence the importance of the training programs mentioned earlier.

11. The principal source of information for this report on the endangered languages of Guatemala is from personal communication with Nora England (see England 1992, 1996, 1998), and personal communication with OKMA members, Eladio Mateo Toledo (B'alam) in particular. Additional specific information on language endangerment and under-documentation was also provided by Terence Kaufman and Roberto Zavala (p.c. 2002).

12. Although the attention will be focused on the large Mayan family of languages which predominates in Guatemala, it is worth noting that another indigenous language of another family of languages is spoken on the Caribbean Coast of the country. The Garifuna, whose language is of the Carib-Arawak family of languages number about 16,000 in Guatemala. Other Garifuna communities are found in Belize and Honduras.

13. As mentioned earlier, there are more than 1,5 million speakers of *Mayan* languages in neighboring Mexico, with both large and very small languages. The most endangered language communities there are border communities.

14. The following North American linguists became *Mayan* specialists in the course of three two-year phases of funding:

Mayan specialists

1972 and 73 (phase I)	Nora England and Norman on *Mam*, *K'ichee'*, *Kaqchikel*.
1974 and 75 (phase II)	Tom Larsen on *Awakatek*, Steve Stewart on *Q'eqchi'*, Karen Dakin on *Q'anjob'al* and *Akatek*.
1976 and 77 (phase III)	Margaret Datz on *Popti'*, Glenn Ayres on *Ixil*, Linda Munson on *Mam*, Robin Quizar on *Ch'orti'*, Tom Larsen on *K'ichee'*.

The activities of the PLFM were curtailed by the ongoing state of insecurity that reigned in the country and peaked in the early 1980's (the years of civil war euphemistically talked about as "la violencia"). When it was possible to resume activities, England offered *Mayan linguistics courses* for native speakers through the PLFM. The languages involved were the following:

Mayan linguistic courses

1988	Mam, K'ichee', Kaqchikel, Q'eqchi', Wastek, Tz'utujiil, Q'anjob'al, Poqomam, Ch'orti' (16 Mayan students)
1989	Mam, K'ichee', Kaqchikel, Q'eqchi', Poqomam, Chuj, Achi, Ixil, Tz'utujiil, Popti'. (25 Mayan students)

The graduates of these courses were never made members of the PLFM, but many are still active and several are in OKMA (see 3.3.).

15. The programs were created and developed under the direction of Guillermina Herrera, Dean of Humanities, a graduate of the University of Iowa, where she studied under Nora England.
16. A new DEL program was started in 2005 by a consortium of the National Science Foundation, the National Endowment for the Humanities and the Smithsonian Institute. The DEL project includes the following three languages and linguists: *Pipil* of El Salvador (Lyle Campbell), *Mocho* of Mexico (Laura Martin) and *Xinca* of Guatemala (Roberto Zavala).
17. The revitalization project includes multimedia support for the teaching of the language (Lemmus 2003) and the creation of computer assisted language learning materials (Ward 2002).
18. The information for Honduras was obtained through Danilo Salamanca, specialist of *Miskitu* of Nicaragua and Honduras, who located the sources used.
19. The inventories of ethnic groups of Honduras often include *Chortis*, for which there is no figure available, and no speakers left.
20. Some linguistic study of the language has been carried out by P. Monro at UCLA with *Garifuna*-speaking residents of Los Angeles, California.
21. Dennis Holt, who did fieldwork on the language twenty years ago (Holt 1986) was called back to the country to be consultant for the Ministry of Education in the early 2000 and a Honduran university professor is said to have been working with the community, too.
22. In addition, a major research program of Linguists for Nicaragua has focused on *Nicaraguan Sign Language*. It has been directed by Judy Kegl. Although the challenge there is to attend to the development and standardization of a language rather than to the opposite work of documenting a moribund indigenous language, it is worth mentioning for being work on another precarious type of language.
23. The first phase (1985–93) was supported by NSF, NEH, and the Wenner Gren Foundation for Anthropological research. The second phase (2004–2006) is being financed by the HRELDP of SOAS, London.

24. The sources of information on the actual situation of the indigenous languages of Costa Rica come from Rojas Chaves (1997) and personal communication with Adolfo Constenla, professor of linguistics at the Universidad de Costa Rica, major figure of *Chibchan* Studies (Constenla 1989, 1991).

References

Barret, Rusty
    2005   Review of "Five Oxlajuuj Keej Mayab' Ajtz'iib' (OKMA) grammars. *International journal of American linguistics (IJAL)* 71,2: 215–220.

Bartholomew, Doris and Yolanda Lastra
    1994   Panorama de los estudios de las lenguas indígenas de Mexico. Tome 1. Colección Biblioteca Abya-Yala 16. Quito: Ediciones Abya-Yala.
    1995   Panorama de los estudios de la lenguas indígenas de Mexico. Tomo 2. Colección Biblioteca Abya-Yala. Quito: Ediciones Abya-Yala.

Benedicto, Elena
    2004   Linguistics rights in the Nicaraguan Atlantic Coast: Actions on the ground within the legislative framework of the Estatuto de Autonomia. In Argenter, J. and R. McKenna Brown (eds.) *Endangered languages and linguistics rights: on the margins of nations.* Proceedings of the Eigth FEL Conference. Barcelona, 1–3 October 2004. Bath: The FEL. 73–76.

Campbell, Lyle
    1979   Middle American languages. In Campbell L. and M. Mithun (eds.) *The languages of Native America historical and comparative assessment.* Austin: University of Texas Press. 902–1000.
    1985   *The Pipil language of El Salvador.* Berlin: Mouton.
    2000   *American Indian languages.* The historical linguistics of Native America. Oxford studies in anthropological linguistics, 4. Oxford University Press.

Campbell, Lyle; Kaufman, Terence and Thomas Smith-Stark
    1986   Meso-America as a linguistic area. *Language* 62,3: 530–570.

Constenla, Adolfo Umaña
    1989   La subagrupación de las lenguas chibchas: Algunos nuevos indicios comparativos y lexicoestadísticos. *Estudios de lingüística Chibcha* 8: 17–72.
    1991   *Las lenguas del Area Intermedia.* Introducción a su estudio areal. Editorial de ka Universidad de Costa Rica, San José.

Craig, Colette
    1992   A constitutional response to language endangerment: The case of Nicaragua. *Language* 68,1: 11–16.

England, Nora
  1992   *Autonomía de los idiomas mayas: historia e identidad.* Guatemala Chol-samaj.
  1996   *Introducción a la lingüística maya.* Antigua/Guatemala PLFM-Chol-samaj.
  1998   Mayan efforts towards language preservation. In Grenoble, L. and L. Whaley (eds.) 99–116.
Garza Cuarón, Beatriz and Yolanda Lastra
  1991   Endangered languages of Mexico. In Robins, R. H. and E. M. Uhlenbeck (eds.) *Endangered languages.* Eds. Oxford/New York: BERG. 93–134.
Gordon, Raymond G, Jr. (ed.)
  2005   *Ethnologue: Languages of the world.* Fifteenth edition. Dallas, Tex.: SIL International. Online version: http://www.ethnologue.com
Grenoble, Leonore and Lindsay, Whaley (eds.)
  1998   *Endangered languages: Current issues and future prospects.* Cambridge University Press.
Grinevald, Colette
  1998   Language endangerment in South America: a programmatic approach. In Grenoble, L. and L. Whaley (eds.) 124–160.
  2002   Linguistique et langues mayas du Guatemala. In Landaburu, J. and F. Queixalos (eds.) *Méso-Amérique, Caraibes, Amazonie* Vol 1. Faits de Langues no 20. Paris: Ophrys. 17–25.
  2003   Educación Intercultural y Multilingüe: El caso de los Ramas. In *WANI*, 34: 20–38. Managua.
Hale, Kenneth; Craig, Colette; England, Nora; Masayesva-Jeanne, LaVerne; Krauss, Michael; Watahomigie, Lucille and Akira Yamamoyo
  1992   Language endangerment. *Language* 69,1: 35–42.
Herranz, Atanasio
  1996   Estado Sociedad y Lenguaje – La política lingüística de Honduras. Editorial Guaymuras, Tegucigalpa.
Hill, Jane H. and Kenneth C. Hill
  1986   *Speaking Mexicano: Dynamics or syncretic language change in Central America.* Tucson: University of Arizona Press.
Hofling, Andrew
  1982   Itza Maya morphosyntax from a discourse perspective. PhD. Washington University.
Holt, Dennis G.
  1986   The development of the Paya sound system. Ph.D Dissertation. UCLA.
Kaufman, Terence
  1974   Meso-American Indian languages. Languages of the world. *Encyclopaedia Britannica*, 15th Edition. 22: 767–774.

Kaufman, Terence
  1990   Language history in South America: What we know. In Payne, D. L.
          (ed.) *Amazonian linguistics: Studies in Lowland South American lan-*
          guages. Austin: University of Texas Press. 13–74.
  2001   Two highly effective models for large-scale documentation of endan-
          gered languages. In *Lectures on endangered languages: 2 – from Kyo-*
          to conference 2000 – Endangered languages of the Pacific Rim.
          ELPR C002. 269–284.
Lemus, Jorge
  2003   *Revitalizing indigenous languages: The case of Pipil in El Salvador.*
          Expert meeting – Endangered languages – Unesco Paris 2003
Rivas, Ramón
  1993   *Pueblos Indígenas y Garífuna de Honduras.* Editorial Guayamuras,
          Tegucigalpa.
Rojas Chaves, Carmen
  1997   Revitalización lingüística de las lenguas indígenas de Costa Rica. In
          Estudios de Lingüística Chibcha 16–7, 97–246.
Smith-Stark, Thomas C.
  1995   El estado actual de los estudios de las lenguas Mixtecanas y Zapote-
          canas. In Bartholomew, D. and Y. Lastra (eds.) *Panorama de los estu-*
          dios de las lenguas indígenas de México, tomo I, II. Colección Biblio-
          teca Abya-Yala, 16, 17. Quito: Ediciones Abya-Yala. 5–186.
Suarez, Jorge
  1983   *The Mesoamerican Indian languages.* Cambridge: Cambridge Uni-
          versity Press.
Zavala, Roberto
  2000   A grammar of Oluta Popoluca. Ph.D Dissertation. University of Or-
          egon.
Ward, Monica
  2002   Using new technologies to produce language material for minority
          and endangered languages. Paper presented at the World Congress
          on language policies. Barcelona 16–20 April 2002.

Websites

AILLA
   www.ailla.utexas.org/site/welcome.html
   The Archives of the Indigenous Languages of Latin America.
CIESAS
   http://www.ciesas.edu.mx
   Centro de Investigaciones y Estudios Superiores en Antropología Social.
ENAH
   www.inah.gob.mx/docencia/enah/inicio/
   Escuela Nacional de Antropología e Historia.
HRELP
   www.hrelp.org
   Hans Rausing Endangered Languages Program.
OKMA
   www.okma.org
   Oxlajuuj Keej Maya' Ajtz'iib'.
URACCAN-IPILC
   www.uraccan.edu.ni/spanish/institutos/Spn-ipilc.php
   Institute for Linguistic Research and Cultural Recovery.

Chapter 5
Endangered Languages in USA and Canada[1]

Akira Yamamoto

1. Introduction

Various linguists have estimated that there were 300 to 600 indigenous languages in North America at the time of the first European arrival. Mithun (1999: 2) also observes:

> Some of the languages are still spoken skillfully by people of all ages, such as Navajo with well over 100,000 speakers. The overall situation is critical, however. Almost all of the languages still in use are endangered: fewer children are learning them every year, as in the case of Navajo, or children are no longer learning them at all. Well over a third of the languages spoken at contact have already disappeared. Another quarter are now remembered by only a small number of elderly speakers. Nearly all are likely to be gone by the end of the twenty-first century.

Goddard (1996: 1–16; with an excellent updated map), surveying major works in linguistic studies of North America, identifies 34 language families and 28 language isolates:

> Language Families (number of languages): 1. Algic (45 languages), 2. Alsean (2), 3. Atakapan (2), 4. Caddoan (6), 5. Chimakuan (2), 6. Chinookan (3), 7. Chumashan (6), 8. Cochimí-Yuman (15), 9. Comecrudan (3), 10. Coosan (2), 11. Eskimo-Aleut (13), 12. Iroquoian (11), 13. Keresan (2), 14. Kiowa-Tanoan (7), 15. Maiduan (3), 16. Muskogean (7), 17. Nadene (47), 18. Otomanguean (1), 19. Palaihnihan (2), 20. Plateau Penution (4), 21. Pomoan (7), 22. Salinan (2), 23. Salishan (23), 24. Shastan (4), 25. Siouan-Catawban (17), 26. Takelman (4), 27. Timucuan (2), 28. Tsimshianic (2), 29. Utian (15), 30. Uto-Aztecan (26), 31. Wakashan (6), 32. Wintuan (2), 33. Yokutsan (6), 34. Yukian (2), and 35–63. Language Isolates (Adai, Aranama, Beothuk, Calusa, Cayuse, Chimariko, Chitimacha, Coahuilteco, Cotoname, Esselen, Guaicura, Haida, Karankawa, Karok, Kootenani, Maratino, Natchez, Naolan, Quinigua, Seri, Siuslaw, Solano, Tonkawa, Tunica, Washoe, Yana, Yuchi, Zuni).

Of these 329 languages, 46 have significant number of children as their speakers, 91 are spoken by adults but no or very few children, 72 by only a few of the oldest people and 120 are extinct (Goddard 1996: 3 citing Krauss 1991).

Mithun (1999) expertly discusses indigenous languages of North America. Especially useful for our purpose is Chapter 7 (326–616). Languages are presented by family with a historical overview, and each language is discussed with a brief description of language situation (location, number of speakers) and major published work. At the end of her discussion of a family, Mithun shows major structural characteristics of the family.

Although the information contained in the survey data is incomplete, it gives us a general picture of the language situations in the US and Canada, and we will be able to raise important questions about the nature of endangerment. In the following, we show different stages of language shift situations (see *note 1*, and for the full survey data, the website of the Indigenous Language Institute at ⟨www.indigenous-language.org⟩).[2]

2. Canada

In Canada, there were some 60 languages prior to the sixteenth century when Europeans arrived there (Kinkade 1992: 158), and currently 36 languages are remembered or spoken. There are eight language families and four language isolates (also Goddard 1996: 1–16). Kinkade (1992: 158–167) categorizes the original languages of Canada into five groups:

1) Already Extinct (*Extinct*);

2) Near Extinction (*NExtinct*) are those languages that have a very few elderly persons who either remember or speak their ancestral languages, and "probably beyond the possibility of revival" (p. 161);

3) Endangered (*Endangered*) are languages which "are still spoken by enough people to make survival an outside possibility, given sufficient community interest and concerted educational programmes" (p. 162);

4) Viable with small population base (*Viable*) are those languages that have more than 1,000 speakers. Some of these language communities live in relatively isolated regions with fewer pressures of language shift, and others are well-organized communities with strong self-awareness. Here the ancestral language "is one of the important marks of identity" (162-163); and

5) Viable (*TrulyViable*) are those languages which have a large base of speakers of all ages. Kinkade identifies four such languages in Canada (Cree, Ojibwa, Dakota, and Inuktitut) (p. 163).

Kinkade (1992: 163) comments that 32 languages of Near Extinct and Endangered groups are in urgent need for more thorough documentation. He further states that "most have received (and continue to receive) study, often by one or two, sometimes by some half a dozen, linguists, *but not in ways that will lead to language preservation*" (emphasis added). I have summarized Kinkade's survey in Appendix I (Summary of Kinkade's survey of Indigenous Languages of Canada).

There are several other excellent reports on indigenous languages in Canada: "Sociolinguistic Survey of Indigenous Languages in Saskatchewan" by the Saskatchwan Indigenous Languages Committee (1991). The Committee found that the indigenous languages in nine communities were facing an extremely critical situation; two in critical condition, four in serious condition, two in fair but deteriorating condition, and three in good health but with a few symptoms of ill-health (also New Economy Development Group 1993: 10).

Heather Blair (1997) completed her report, "Indian Languages Policy and Planning in Saskatchewan," for the Saskatchewan Department of Education, Indian and Métis Education Unit. Before presenting our survey result, a brief description of one of Blair's sample communities will be given below.[3]

Case study: La Ronge Band Cree of Stanley Mission (Blair 1997: 25–38)

This is a Cree community of the La Ronge Band of about 1,600 people, initially established in 1851 by the Anglican church, becoming a central meeting and gradually a settlement place. The Anglican missionaries used the *Cree* language adopting the use of a syllabic orthography of other Cree missions. The establishment of a school and introduction of the printing press by John A. MacKay (*Cree*-speaking minister) were instrumental in the spread of Cree pride and literacy. When, however, a public school opened in 1952, the language of the school was *English*, no longer *Cree*, because educators believed indigenous languages were a hindrance to *English* language development and the development of children. In 1976, the band controlled the school and established a bilingual education policy. At this time, it was noted that all children came to school speaking *Cree* reflecting the *Cree* as the dominant language of the community. The *Cree* dominance was also noted in the 1988 sociolinguistic study by the Saskatchewan Indigenous Languages Committee, but the Committee expressed its concern over the increasing number of children who speak *English* more often than *Cree* to their friends and others. In her 1996 study, however, Blair notes that the nature of language use in Stanley Mission has changed dramatically to the extent that the *English* language has become the dominant language of school age children. Teachers reported that only 10 to 15% were *Cree* dominant speakers.

Table 1. Stages of language decline, Canada
Numbers preceding language names refer to the maps

Language (Family)	Speakers/ Population	Speaker %	Language programs	Documentation
Critically endangered (5):				
1. Delaware/ Munsee (Algic)	10/1,500	0.67	exst	morphology, dictionary
2. Onondaga (Iroquoian)	34/18,173	0.19	grade school, adult classes	aspects of grammar (monograph)
3. Saanich (Coast Salishan)	20/a few 1,000	0.067	exist	grammatical sketch, word list
4. Sekani (Athabascan)	30~40/600	5~6.7	school program	draft dictionary, sketches
5. Samish (Coast Salishan)	10/a few 1,000	3.3	none	sketch, grammars of other dialects
Severely endangered (2):				
6. Cayuga (Iroquoian)	130 ~ 150/ 3,000	4.3~5	school, community (all ages)	teaching grammar, various papers
7. Cayuga (Iroquoian)	100/17,000	0.59	elementary & middle school	teaching grammar, various papers
8. Oneida (Iroquoian)	190/1,500 ~ 2,000	9.5~ 12.67	exist	morphology, various papers
	(Ontario) 50/3,000	1.7	exist	morphology, various papers
Definitively endangered (1):				
9. Babine/ Witsuwit'en (Athabascan)	500/2,200	22.72	school programs	phonology, grammar sketch
Endangered (1):				
10. Mi'kmaq (Algic)	3,000/25,000	12	band-school program	dictionary, teaching grammar

Table 1. cont.

Language (Family)	Speakers/ Population	Speaker %	Language programs	Documentation
Stable (5):				
11. Inuktitut (Eskimo-Aleut)	Arctic Quebec, NWT 6,000/6.000 NW Territories 17,000/?	100	college classes	grammars, various articles
12. Slavey (Athabascan)	4,500/5,000	90	exist	grammar
13. Dogrib (Athabascan)	2,700/3,000	90	literacy activities at schools	grammars, dictonary
14. Naskapi (Algic)	650/650	100	exist	grammar, dictionary
15. Ojibwe (Algic)	most/ 19,510	100?	exist	grammar, texts, dictionaries

3. USA

Leanne Hinton and Yolanda Montijo (1994: 25) reported the result of their sociolinguistic survey of *California Indian languages* (*Appendix II*). They state:

The number of speakers of California languages might seem depressingly low, and it is sad to note that the speakers of these languages are almost all elders ... not a single California language is being learned by children as the primary language of the household. But Native Californians are waging a battle to keep their languages alive.

Their survey is excellent for several reasons. They provide three figures for the number of speakers: 1) the people's best estimate of the number of fluent speakers; 2) an estimate of the number of individuals of different degree of fluency, including those who are considered semi-speakers and second language speakers; and 3) the self-reported number of speakers in the 1990 US census. They also include information on community-based language activities such as singing, language programs, and materials development. In California, there are 107 federally recognized tribes and close to 50 languages. The picture of language situations in most of the California communities are indeed grim, and, unfortunately, these situations are not unique to California.

In general, the American Indian and Alaska Natives numbered 1,959,234 in 1990, that is 0.08% of the total population of the United States, and that was about a 40% increase since 1980. The size of the Native American population is increasing but the number of speakers of these indigenous languages is decreasing. This is also true of Canada.

Table 2. Stages of language decline, USA
Numbers in the first column refer to the maps

Language (Family)	Speakers/ Population	Speaker %	Community programs	Documentation
Exinct (10):				
16. Wiyot (Algic)	0/800	0	none	grammar, texts, dictionary
17. Wyandotte (Iroquoian)	0/3,200	0	none	grammar, texts
18. Chimariko (Lg Isolate)	0/0	0	none	various publications
19. Salinan (Salinan)	0/100s	0	none	published & unpublished documents
20. Kechayi (Yokuts)	1?/with other Yokuts	0?	none	some sketches
21. Costanoan lgs (Utian)	0/0	0	none	grammar
22. Yuki (Yukian)	0/80?	0	none	vocabulary list, some sketches
23. Nooksack (Salishan)	0/1,600	0	?	phonemics
24. Ioway-Otoe/ Missouria (Siouan)	a few semi/ 3,650	0?	high school classes	grammar, lexicon, various publications
25. Miluk/Kusan (Penutian)	1 semi/2,200	0?	none	grammatical sketch, pedagogical material

Table 2. cont.

Language (Family)	Speakers/ Population	Speaker %	Community programs	Documentation
Almost extinct (3):				
26. Haida (Lg Isolate)	a few/3,000	0.01?	none	sketches of grammar, dictionary
27. Lenape (Algic)	2 (+9 semi)/ 13,500	0?	exist	academic and pedagogical materials
28. Pit River (Palaihnihan)	10 semi/ 1,000	1?	exist & school classes	sketches
Critically endangered (27):				
29. Loyal Shawnee (Algic)	14/8,000	0.17	exist	lexicon, sketches
30. Potawatomi (Algic)	50/25,000	0.2	daycare, preschool, community	grammar, dictionary, various publications
31. Osage (Siouan)	5 ~ 10/ 15,000	0.03 ~ 0.06	exist	grammar, dictionary, teaching materials
32. Chiwere (Siouan)	5?/several hundred	0.5 ~ 1.0?	exist?	sketches and various publications
33. Tuscarora (Iroquoian)	4 ~ 5/ 1,200	0.4	exist	grammar, texts, various sketches
34. Arikara (Caddoan)	20/3,000?	0.67	elementary school, college	texts, some sketches, teaching grammar
35. Caddo (Caddoan)	25/3,371	0.74	sporadic meetings	some sketches
36. Pawnee (Caddoan)	20/2,500	0.8	none	texts
37. Yuchi (Lg Isolate)	10 ~ 12/ 1,500	0.66 ~ 0.8	exist	various sketches, grammar
38. Central Pomo (Pomoan)	2 ~ 5/ 4,766	0.1?	none	articles
39. Karuk (Lg Isolate)	10/4,800	0.2	exist, very active	grammar, dictionary

Table 2. cont.

Language (Family)	Speakers/ Population	Speaker %	Community programs	Documentation
40. Waksachi (Yokuts)	1?/750?	0.1	none	some wordlists?
41. Wintu (Wintuan)	5 ~ 6/ 2,244	0.2	none	some
42. Klamath/Modoc (Penutian)	1 ~ 2/ 2,000	0.05 ~ 0.1	exist & master-apprentice	grammar, texts
43. Monachi (Uto-Aztecan)	2 ~ 5/ 1,155	0.4	none	some
44. Klallam (Coast Salishan)	10/several 1,000s	0.3	exist	in progress
45. Holkomelem (Salishan)	25/5,267	0.5	exist, very active	ethnography, phonology
46. Yavbé (Yuman)	4 ~ 5/ 130	3 ~ 3.8	exist	grammar, dictionary
47. Chinimne (Yokuts)	6/300	2	none	sketch, lexicon
48. Chukchansi (Yokuts)	6/100	6	preschool program	grammar, sketches
49. Miwok (Utian)	40/3,381	1.1	none	sketch, texts, dictionary
50. Mandan (Siouan)	10 ~ 20/ 400	2.5 ~ 5.0	none	in progress
51. Luiseño (Uto-Aztecan)	15/500	3	exist	grammar, dictionary, articles
52. Montana Salish (Salishan)	70/5,000	1.4	school programs	grammar, dictionaries
53. Snchit su'umshstsn (Salishan)	10 ~ 20/ 1,213	0.8 ~ 1.6	exist & high school classes	abundant
55. Louisiana French Creole	3,000/ 4 million	0.008	none	vocabulary list

Severely endangered (8):

56. Assiniboine (Siouan)	250/5,000?	5.0?	limited instruction	none

Table 2. cont.

Language (Family)	Speakers/ Population	Speaker %	Community programs	Documentation
57. Hok (Winneba go) (Siouan)	230/6,000	3.8	exist, very active	extensive
58. Yanktonai (Siouan)	250/5,000	5	limited instruction	none
59. Oneida (Iroquoian)	30/700?	4.3	exist & school classes	morphology, other articles
60. Seneca (Iroquoian)	150/6,241	2.4	bilingual programs	morphology, dictionary, articles
61. Sahaptin (Sahaptian/ Penutian)	500?/12,000	4.2	exist & college classes	sketches, texts
62. Mississippi Gulf Coast French	50/5,000	1	none	none
63. Isleño (Romance)	50 (+ 450 semi)/2,000	2.5	social gatherings	good
Definitively endangered (4):				
64. Absentee Shawnee (Algic)	250/2,500	10	exist	good
65. Eastern Band Cherokee (Iroq)	1,000/9,800	10.2	school programs	good
66. Nez Perce (Sahaptian/ Penutian)	100 ~ 300/ 2,700	3.7 ~ 11.1	exist, very active	good
67. Alabama (Muskogean)	100/800	12.5	exist	sketches, dictionary
Endangered (13):				
68. Mohawk (Iroquoian)	3,000/6,000 (NY State)	22.5	exist, very active	great
69. Maliseet-Passa- maquoddy (Algic)	1,000/2,500 ~ 3,000	33.3 ~ 40.0	exist	morphology, dictionary, articles
70. Lakota (Siouan)	6,000/ 20,000	30	exist	?
71. Kawaiisu (Uto-Aztecan)	20/35	57.1	none	grammar, texts, vocabulary

Table 2. cont.

Language (Family)	Speakers/ Population	Speaker %	Community programs	Documentation
72. Iñupiatun (Eskimo-Aleut)	3,000/5,500	54.5	school programs	articles
73. Choctaw (Muskogean)	4,000/6,000	66.7	exist	sketches, dictionary
74. Hwalbáy (Yuman)	1,000/1872	53.4	school program	good
75. Zuni (Lg Isolate)	6,413/9,000	71.2	school programs	excellent documentation
76. Laguna (Keresan)	2060/6865	30	exist & school classes	some sketches, texts
77. Acoma (Keresan)	1930/3860	50	school program	sketches, texts
78. Cochiti (Keresan)	525/1050	50	exist & school classes	some sketches, teaching materials
79. Santa Ana (Keresan)	384/640	60	exist	some sketches
80. Zia (Keresan)	504/720	70	preservation projects	none

Stable (3):

81. Havasupai (Yuman)	530/565	93.8	active school program	sketches, vocabulary
82. San Felipe (Keresan)	1985/2205	90	exist	some sketches
83. Santo Domingo (Keresan)	2965/3120	95	exist	grammar, texts, various sketches

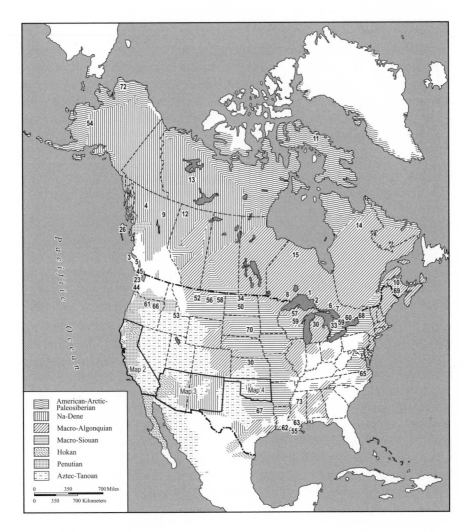

Map 4: North America

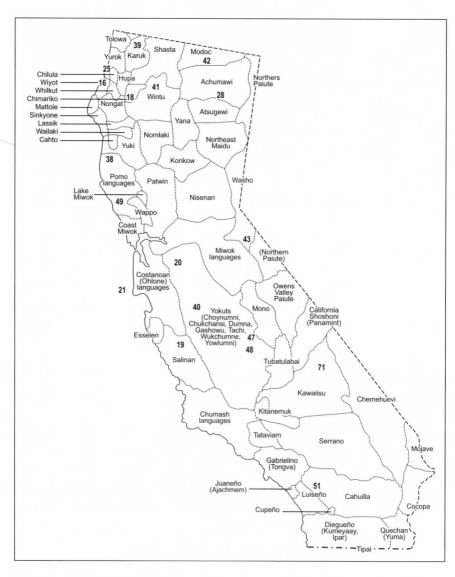

Map 5. California

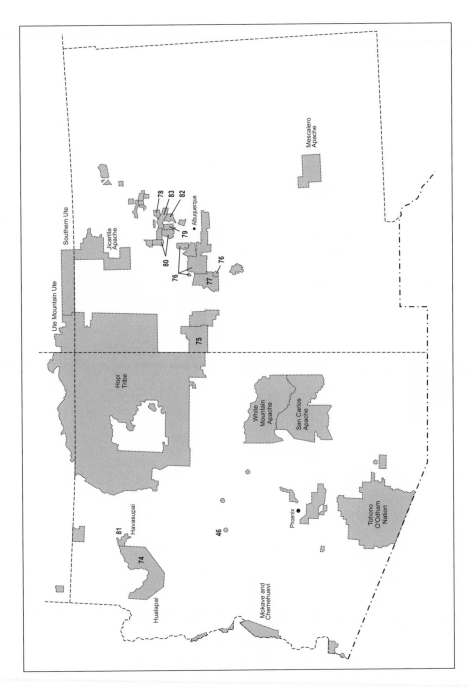

Map 6. Arizona and New Mexico

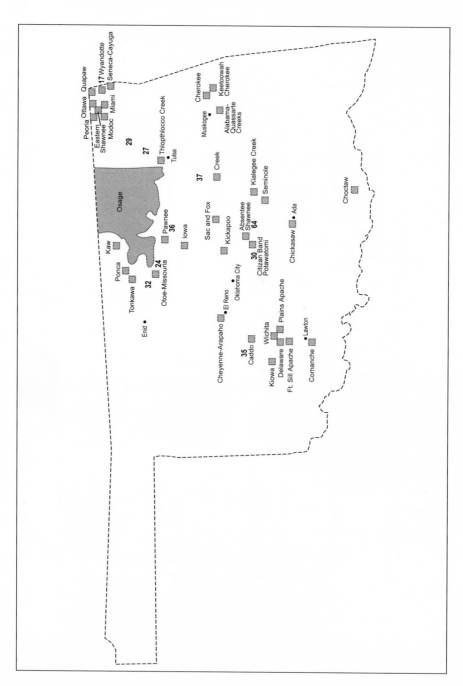

Map 7. Oklahoma

4. Languages in different stages of endangerment: some examples

4.1. General observation

When we examine the survey data, what is immediately suggested is that the number of speakers may be an immediate index for its endangered situation. However, it alone is not an accurate indicator of the language situation of the given population. For example, in the Supai community in the Grand Canyon (*Map 6, #81*), there are over 530 speakers of *Havasupai* of all ages. The number 530 seems very small, but the total population of this group is 565. Thus, 93.8% of the population speaks *Havasupai* as their first language. Most of the Supai children acquire *Havasupai* as their first language, and later they learn *English* as their second language. Is this an endangered language community? In Prescott, in the central part of Arizona (*Map 6, #46*), we find a close relative of *Havasupai*-speaking people, the Prescott Yavapai. There, the language *Yavbé* is spoken by five people of advanced ages; the total population is 130 and no children are acquiring the language. One of the speakers and the language teacher passed away in January 2000. That is, about 3.8% of the population speaks the language. In Peach Springs (*Map 6, #74*), there is another closely related language, *Hwalbáy*. There, about 1,000 out of the total population of 1,872 Hualapai people speak the language, i.e. about 66.7%. Some children still acquire the language as their first language. It seems clear that *Yavbé* is the most endangered among the three. But which one is more endangered, *Hwalbáy* or *Havasupai*?[4]

4.2. Upland Yuman groups: a sketch

Havasupai, Hualapai, and *Yavapai* are closely related languages of the Upland *Yuman* family and they are referred to as the Upland *Yuman* languages.

4.2.1. Havasupai

Although the descendants of the 13 bands of the Upland *Yuman*-speaking Pai ('People'), the Havasupai were separated from the other Pai bands, and in 1880 they received a reservation of 518 acres at the bottom of Havasu Canyon, adding to their reservation in 1975 another 185,000

acres. Traditionally they engaged in hunting and gathering, but now in
their present-day village of Supai, they have abundant water to irrigate
their gardens. Since the 1960s, government agencies, a contract school (K
– 6), and tourism began to bring cash income to the people ($2,800.00/per
capita income in 1994). Martin (1994: 233) observes the following:

Transformed from a loosely related collection of families and winter camp groups,
the population is growing into a small (565 people) corporate, politically aggressive community, with a resurgent and creative religious and cultural life.

Their major contact with the outside world is the tourists. There are some
non-Havasupai teachers at the school; their life as a teacher there is about
one year. The school is controlled by the Havasupai School Board members and staffed by the local members and certified teachers from outside.
Television has not taken over their entertainment, and they engage in intergenerational interactions. They continue to practice bilingual/bicultur-
al education programs.

4.2.2. Hualapai

The Hualapai currently occupy 991,680 acres of range and forest lands in
the northwestern section of Arizona. Like Havasupai people, they engaged in hunting and gathering. They now live in and around their tribal
capital of Peach Springs, which lies along the mainline of the Santa Fe
Railroad and along Highway 66. There is a public school (K – 8) and a
high school (9 – 12), a health clinic, a post office, a general store, and various tribal offices. Since the 1970s, a number of modern houses were built
with the help of the federal government (HUD), changing the traditional
extended families to nuclear families. In addition, the spread of radio and
television is extensive and these have taken over as entertainment, resulting in disruption of traditional cultural and linguistic transmission within
and across generations. Watahomigie (1994: 247) observes:

The Hualapai language and culture are very much a part of the older Hualapai
people's everyday life. Among the young the traditional lifestyle has lost its primary role but the young still consider the knowledge of the traditional lifestyle to
be crucial for their identity as Hualapai. The school has played an important role
in the maintenance of the language and culture among the young ....

The school is becoming the place for transmitting linguistic knowledge to
the younger generations.

4.2.3. Yavapai

The Yavapai have three reservations in central Arizona constituting three separate governments: the Fort McDowell Mohave-Apache Indian Community (640 people), the Yavapai-Prescott Tribe (130), and the Camp Verde Yavapai-Apache Indian Community (650). Like the Havasupai and the Hualapai, the Yavapai were also hunters and gatherers with small-scale farming. The 24,967 acre Fort McDowell is only 26 miles away from metropolitan Phoenix, and every possible modern convenience is immediately accessible. In 1984, the tribe opened a gaming center and it provides funding for a wide range of activities, including language and culture programs. Camp Verde is a 1,092 acre reservation and it has begun their gaming center operation. They developed, in agreement with the National Park Service, a visitor center associated with Montezuma Castle National Monument and a cultural center. These attract a large number of tourists. Cultural preservation activities are carried out at the cultural center, and some language activities take place in an informal basis.

The Yavapai-Prescott Tribe is in the middle of the city of Prescott, and more than three generations of the Yavapai have been educated in the public school systems. The tribe leases land for a shopping center and a resort hotel, and it operates a gaming center. The tribe is actively engaged in cultural preservation but the language-related activities are not their priority.

4.2.4. Degree of endangeredness

Thus, among the Upland Yuman groups of Havasupai, Hualapai, and Yavapai, the Havasupai is the most physically isolated in the depth of the Grand Canyon only accessible on foot, by horse, or in an emergency case by helicopter. The major industry there, however, is tourism, and they face constant exposure to non-Havasupai elements.

The Hualapai live along US Highway 66. Flagstaff is 120 miles to the east and Kingman is 50 miles to the west, making modern conveniences easily accessible to the people. Primarily because of the role of the school, there is a strong awareness of the traditional language and culture.

The Yavapai communities all have their gaming centers and continue to focus their efforts on economic development. Unlike the Havasupai and the Hualapai, the Camp Verde and Prescott children attend public schools outside their own communities. Fort McDowell community began their language program in 1998 with support from their school and the tribe.

The following table shows the % of speakers within the population; the children acquiring the language; the communities' attitudes towards their language; level of documentation.

Language	Speakers %	Children	Domains	Attitudes	Documentation	Comments
Havasupai	93.8	majority	all	supportive	good	limited contacts
Hualapai	53.4	half	most	very supportive	good	frequent contacts
Yavapai	3.8	none	none	supportive	good	high contacts

4.2.5. Characteristics of Upland Yuman languages: Hualapai (Watahomigie et al. 2001)

Possession expressions

Nouns are classified in four ways: kinship terms, domesticated animals, properties, and things associated with what one does. This classification is shown by the ways possession relationships are expressed.

1. Hak∂gwi:ve *nya∂ála*ch ∂adaha:dkwi.
    Hak∂gwi:v-e   nya ∂al-a-ch   ∂adaha:d-k-wi
    Peach Springs- 1   father-Def-Subj 3.work-SameSubject (SS)-
    around   Aux/do
    'My father is working in Peach Springs.'

2. Ma m∂álach *waksí ma mnyihá∂a* he:dkwi.
    ma m-∂al-a-ch   waksi ma   m-nyi-ha∂-a   he:d-k-wi
    you 2-father-Def-Subj cow   you 2/3-the.one.that- 3/3.rope-SS-
                                        pet-Def   Aux/do
    'Your father is roping your cow.'

3. *Anbil nya wi:*hch hankyu.
    anbil nya wi:-h-ch   han-k-yu
    car   1   1/3.own-that-Subj 3.be good-SS-Aux/be
    'The car I own is good.'

4.   *Gwe nya hwál*ohch hánkyu.
     gwe   nya   hwal-o-h-ch   han-k-yu
     thing 1   1/3.cultivate-Loc/place-   3.be good-SS-
                  Dem/that-Subj   Aux/be
     'My garden (= the place that I cultivate) is good.'

Auxiliary verbs and verb categories

In *Hualapai*, four major auxiliary verbs are derived from the independent
full verbs: *wi* 'to do', *yu* 'to be', *i* 'to say,' and *yi* 'to feel.' Accordingly, verbs
are classified into verbs of vocalization (marked with –*i*), verbs of emo-
tions (-*yi*), intransitive verbs (–*yu*), and transitive verbs (-*wi*).

5.   Nyihách Hwalbáy gwa:wki̱.
     nyi-ha-ch   hwalbay   gwa:w-k-i
     Specific-that.one-Subj Hualapai 3/3.speak-SS-Aux/say
     'That one is speaking Hualapai.'

6.   Hwal̲báy gwa:w gwala yi:ky̲i.
     Hwalbay   gwa:w   gwal-a   yi:-k-yi
     Hualapai 3.speak.Def   want-Def   3.feel-SS-Aux/feel
     'She wants to speak Hualapai.'

7.   Nya ∂álach viyámky̲u.
     nya   ∂al-a-ch   viyam-k-yu
     my   father-Def-Subj   3.run-SS-Aux/be
     'My father is running.'

8.   Nya nuwa:hach gweviyám gwa:mkw̲i.
     nya nuwa:h-a-ch   gweviyam   gwa:m-k-wi
     my   friend-Def-Subj   car   3/3.drive-SS-Aux/do
     'My friend is driving a car.'

Switch reference

When there are two or more predicates in a sentence, the sameness or difference of the subjects of predicates must be indicated: -*k* 'SameSubject'
(the subjects of the predicates are the same) or -*m* 'DifferentSubject' (the
subjects are different):

9. Hma:nych yima:j<u>k</u> handávj<u>m</u> a'diyé'yu.
   hma:ny-ch   yima:-j-k   han-dav-j-m   a'-diye'-yu
   child.Pl-Subj 3.dance-Pl-SS 3.be.good-very-Pl-   1-be.happy-
                                  DifferentSubject (DS) Aux/be
   'Children dancing well makes me happy.'
   (Literally, "*Children* dance, and *they* are very good, and **I** am happy.")

4.3. *Yuchi (Euchee)*: a sketch

The Euchee people lived in what are now the states of Georgia and Ala-
bama, and northward into eastern Tennessee, but they were removed
with the Creek (Mvskoke) to Indian Territory (Oklahoma) in 1832. Although they had an opportunity to separate themselves legally from the
Mvskoke Creeks in 1938, they did not do so. Under the leadership of their
traditional chief, they maintained strong linguistic, cultural, and ceremonial traditions until the 1950s. They maintain the ceremonial tradition
with their three ceremonial grounds, but the speakers of the language diminished to a mere dozen in recent years. Since the late 1980s, however,
there have been efforts to revive and revitalize the language (Moore
1994: 716; Linn 1997: 189).

Language	Speakers %	Children	Domains	Attitudes	Docu- mentation	Comments
Euchee	0.8	none	none	supportive	good	high contacts

4.3.1. *Characteristics of Yuchi (Euchee) (Linn 2001)*

Euchee is a language isolate. The earliest European explorers noted that
Euchee held no affinity with any of its neighboring languages, namely the
Creek dialects (*Muskogean*), *Shawnee* (*Algonquian*), and *Cherokee* (*Iroquoian*). One of the interesting characteristics of the language is their
unique way of classifying nouns.

Noun classification

There are three inanimate classes and five animate classes. The inanimate
classes correspond to the inherent positions: sitting *-çi*, standing *-fa,* and
lying *-'e.*

10.a. te-*çi*   ßoßo
       mulberry-Cl rotten
       'That mulberry is rotten.'

10.b. k'ójįne-ti   se-nó
       store-inside she(E)-be
       'She's inside the store.'

10.c. s'äa-yo-gwa-'*e*   nä-di-'ne
       field-Dir-you-talk-Cl not-I-see
       'I can't see the field you're talking about.'

The five animate classes are: 1) non-Euchee living things; 2) Euchee male; 3) Euchee female; 4) related Euchee female of ascending generation; and 5) Euchee male or female of spousal status or ascending generation.

11.a. dzene yomp'ä yotʰo-'ę́-wenó
       dog   tai   short-Verbalizer-Cl
       'the short-tailed dog'

11.b. Henry he-tʰoß'ine-henó
       Henry his-hat-Cl
       'Henry's hat' (men's speech)

11.c. Henry s'e-tʰoß'ine-s'nó
       Henry his-hat-Cl
       'Henry's hat' (women's speech)

11.d. Jo se-gowäne-senó
       Jo her-blanket-Cl
       'Jo's blanket'

11.e. di-laha   Lou-'enó
       my-grandmother Lou-Cl
       'my grandmother Lou'

11.f. Bill-'onó age   'o-nó
       Bill-Cl   here he-is
       'Bill (my husband) is here.'

Linn (1997: 190) also states that the *Euchee* "noun class system requires concord with other parts of the sentence. The third-person pronominal prefix to the verb must agree with the class marker suffix on the noun."

12.a. Henry-s'enó,   s'e-di-n'ejé
       Henry-Cl/Euchee 3-2-saw
       'I saw Henry (Euchee man, a woman speaking).'

12.b. Mary-wenó,   we-di-n'ejé
       Mary-Cl/non-Euchee 3-1-saw
       'I saw Mary (Non-Euchee, a woman speaking).'

5. Discussion: Language communities and linguists

For the fieldworkers, the research situations have drastically changed during the past several decades. Grinevald (1998: 156) succinctly summarizes the concept of fieldwork frameworks that Cameron *et al.* (1983) examined. In the tradition of the American linguistics, the period up to the early 1960s may be characterized as working "*on* the language and for the sake of science," the late 1960s and 1970s as work "*on* the language and *for* the people," and the 1980s and 1990s as developing the framework of "work *on* the language, *for* its speakers and *with* its speakers." It has also been our goal to ultimately "promote work *on* the language *by* the speakers." This shift in our fieldwork frameworks induces and also reflects the changes in the language communities in which we do our work.

At the language community level, "people have begun to speak out about the urgent situation of their ancestral languages. In many indigenous communities there was awareness that only a handful of individuals still remembered or spoke the language, yet few realized the long-term significance of this" (Yamamoto 1999: 12). Now, they have begun to re-examine the language situation in their own communities. Even in communities where there are a relatively large number of speakers, they have discovered that the language is no longer transmitted to children in their own homes.

Many communities began to look inwardly and to formulate strategies for reversing the language shift from the ancestral language to the dominant language. Strategies include community language programs and school programs. They may take the form of the total immersion program, master-apprentice program, soft immersion program, ancestral language as a second language program, and short-term language camp.

In this context, community people began to appreciate the significant contribution of academic professionals in having documented their languages and making materials available to them. Academic professionals, however, were made aware that, although documented language data are appreciated as valuable by the communities, many of the documented materials are extremely difficult, if not impossible, for nonprofessionals to use for the language revitalization purpose.

5.1. Characteristics of successful programs: Types of collaboration

When Rough Rock Community School (Dick and McCarty 1996), Rock Point Community School (Holm and Holm, 1995), and *Hualapai* Bilingual/Bicultural Program (Watahomigie and McCarty 1994) demonstrated their successful Native language programs, both the native communities and professional academicians hailed the programs as responsive to community needs, academically sound, and pedagogically effective and innovative. They have become known as the Arizona Models. They all have in common the following:

a. The members of the larger linguistic culture, although contains contradictory beliefs, has at least tentatively showed their support of small-language communities.
b. With different degrees of difficulties and persuasion, each of these communities have convinced the members of their communities that their languages are crucial for their children's future.
c. Although they have not been able to establish educational programs for members of all ages, they have succeeded in establishing strong bilingual/bicultural programs.
d. In the process of creating bilingual/bicultural programs, they have effectively recruited parents and elders of their communities into the educational processes.
e. While they practice the bilingual/bicultural programs, they have also engaged in aggressive teacher training activities for the members of their own communities.
f. Each of the programs has produced in a variety of manners both oral and written materials for children.
g. They were not afraid of involving outside professionals. They have recruited them and worked with them.
h. These model programs' goal is to create and strengthen the environment where the ancestral languages are the language of communication, thinking, creation, and belief.

Stimulated by these and other programs, academic professionals also initiated a variety of ways to provide their services to the language communities. We have seen different ways to do this, and I will present a few examples. One is "doing linguistics" at a distance and the other "doing linguistics" on the spot (see Linn et al. 1998 for a related discussion).

5.2. Linguists and Other Academic Professionals: from academic settings to communities

5.2.1. Linguistics-at-a-distance approach

In this approach, it is the speakers, teachers, and community people who come to an academic setting away from their communities. Since the summer of 1978, the American Indian Language Development Institute (AILDI) has been active in training teachers of Native American languages (McCarty *et al.* 2001). For several years now, AILDI has been held at the University of Arizona. It has attracted teachers of Native American languages throughout Arizona, California, Alaska, Maine, Canada, and during the summer of 1996 from Brazil and Venezuela as well. The University of Arizona saw the important role of AILDI to the State of Arizona and the rest of the country, and in 1996 it committed permanent funding for the institute. AILDI continues to train Native American language teachers, ESL teachers, multicultural teachers, curriculum developers, materials developers, as well as linguists.

5.2.2. Linguistics-on-the-spot approach

In this approach, it is the linguists who go to the communities – the academic setting is moved to the community site.

a. Linguists-in-residence

These activities that I have mentioned above are the teacher training institutes where community people come to the institute location to work on their languages. The following two examples demonstrate a potential bridge between academic institutions and language communities.

The *Euchee* project in which Mary Linn has been involved initially had dual goals: one was to conduct her dissertation research project (documentation of an endangered language) and at the same time to create a cooperative project with the Euchee community (language revitalization and preservation project). Working with the Euchee people, Linn had to take into consideration the following: first, Euchee people are not a federally recognized tribe and live under the jurisdiction of the Creek Nation, the situation of which has threatened the Euchee ethnolinguistic vitality; second, they recently became intensely aware of their language endangerment, and are successful in mobilizing the older speakers to re-establish the environment for using the language; third, they began to seek outside professional assistance in recording their language and in describing the language; fourth, *Euchee* has been studied to some extent by professional linguists but the description is by no means satisfactory in terms of the details and the range of information; fifth, *Euchee* is a language isolate and it has to be examined without any other closely related languages for reference or comparison; and sixth, the *Euchee* speakers and Linn must feel comfortable working together. Linn was careful and patient in locating herself in the community. She became adopted by one family, and through them, she established an excellent working relationship with the elders and language revitalization project members of the community. This work was and continues to be important not only for the intellectual community but also more immediately for the language community she works with. Traditionally, the academic people have "studied" varieties of peoples without returning useful materials to those very peoples they have studied. This was also true with academic people's work in the Native American communities. Only recently, academic societies such as the Linguistic Society of America and the Society for the Study of the Indigenous Languages of the Americas have begun to promote vigorously their responsibilities to the language communities, and Linn is among yet a small number of young scholars who are engaged in the new collaborative approach to linguistic research in Native American communities.

b. Linguists-on-call

The second case is an example of linguists-on-call, and this is the work by another University of Kansas graduate student, Marcellino Berardo. During the spring of 1996 when he completed his oral comprehensive examination, Berardo had already begun his work with the Loyal Shawnee people in and around White Oak, Oklahoma. The Loyal Shawnee was not a federally recognized tribe and had been a part of the Cherokee Nation. As a part of their cultural revitalization efforts, Loyal Shawnee people began to engage in the language documentation project and they wanted to recruit academic linguists to help them. They had a series of meetings with Berardo and other University of Kansas linguists to "feel" each other out and to establish common goals for the project. Loyal Shawnee people and the University of Kansas linguistic team agreed that Berardo would work with them to document the language and to prepare language teaching materials. It was also agreed that Berardo would utilize the language data in the writing of his Ph.D. dissertation (Berardo 2000).

Berardo conducted several months of intensive fieldwork with a few speakers left in the Loyal Shawnee community. In the process, the *Loyal Shawnee Language Committee* of which Berardo became a member prepared language lessons with audiotapes. Berardo was instrumental in designing the class: the format, content, techniques, and materials. On many weekends during 1997–98, Berardo drove several hundred miles to be at the language classes and made sure that the classes were well organized and interesting so they would continue to thrive.

One of the most important effects of the collaborative projects is that it provides the members of the language community the means to evaluate how the academic professionals work, and to form a new perception of academic linguists. The linguists in collaborative projects are no longer looked at as people who would tell Native Americans what their language is like, how they should be documented and analyzed, how they should write, and how they should teach their languages. They welcome the linguists as co-workers and team members of the language maintenance and revitalization projects.

5.2.3. Issues in the linguists-on-call approach

Time:
In the case of teacher training workshops, time is relatively flexible and we can adjust our workshop time, more or less. But, in case of a program-specific request, we must be ready to adjust our schedule to theirs.

Travel:
Usually each trip may be several hundred miles, a full day trip, or sometimes a longer time spent for travelling. Thus, this reduces the time to work with other team members.

Expenses:
We try to go to the site with other team members (who are oftentimes students). For reasons of avoiding reinforcing the myth that linguists are making money off Indians, we may accept only words of "thanks." Thus, we need to obtain funding in other ways than from the people we work with.

Continuity:
The work tends to be sporadic and non-continuous. Often the participating members change and this often means to begin a new cycle of team training. Thus, long range planning is essential so that we do not repeat the same process over and again.

5.2.4. Issues in the linguists-in-residence approach

Funding:
The length of stay in the language community ranges from a week at a time to several months. This requires securing funding from such sources as Native American Languages Act funding through the Administration for Native Americans, National Science Foundation, National Endowment for the Humanities, Endangered Language Fund, Ford Foundation, etc.

Family Approach:
Louanna Furbee and her students (Davidson 1999) found it most effective to become a part of a family, sort of an apprentice to a group of language experts in the community. This, however, implies that we may be involved in the "family" chores and responsibilities: driving them to stores and to clinics; doing cooking and laundry with them; or working in the vegetable garden. On the other hand, becoming a part of the family may mean doing basket weaving, bead work, and singing and dancing in the language – learning the real living language.

Community politics:
It seems that the smaller the community, the more intense the political conflicts become. Whose way of speaking is "correct," whose way of talking is more authentic, who should be the teacher, who should work with whom, and the list goes on. Here, too, the formation of the language team is crucial; otherwise we may have to depend on ceremonial leaders and a primary family with whom we associate for our survival – if they are willing to defend the kind of work we do.

5.2.5. Steps for planning a cooperative project

A cooperative project entails steps that we need to follow (Yamamoto 1998b):

1. Meeting of the community people and outside researchers to "feel each other out" and begin to form a working team.

2. Identification of problems and/or issues.
3. Long-range planning and commitment both by the community group and outside researchers.
4. Short-term planning, establishing immediate goal and objectives.
5. Data collection procedures and methods.
6. Actual data collection.
7. Analysis of the data. (Repeat steps 4–7.)
8. Description/presentation (e. g. a grammar, a dictionary, a language curriculum, stories, texts, etc.): methods and means.
9. Storing the documents (where, by whom, how). (Repeat the whole process for a continued or new project.)

In this process, the linguist gains knowledge of the language and culture from the local community team members, and the community members gain linguistic and research knowledge and skills from the linguist. Training in this context is always reciprocal. Empowering the community must be a part of the goal of the team so that ultimately the community will be able to continue research on community issues and find solutions on their own. In this sense, the linguist is helping the team members to become researchers themselves, but it has a meaning very different from the "one-sided helping." Cooperative projects begin with the people and end with the people.

Notes

1. I am grateful to Norma S. Larzalere, Mary S. Linn, and Kimiko Yaska who carefully and critically read an earlier version of this chapter and provided insightful comments and valuable suggestions. Very special thanks are due to those who participated in the Endangered Language Survey Project.
2. We began our preparation for a survey of endangered languages at the 1995 meeting of the Committee on Endangered Languages and Their Preservation in New Orleans, Louisiana. This survey was to be done with the members of the Linguistic Society of America (LSA) who had worked or were working with endangered languages. Consulting other linguistic societies and organizations (e. g., German Linguistic group, International Clearing House for Endangered Languages, Society for the Study of the Indigenous Languages of the Americas (SSILA)), the Endangered Languages Survey Questionnaire was prepared. The LSA Bulletin and the SSILA Newsletter circulated the questionnaire in their late summer issues. At their 1996 meeting in San Diego, California, the Committee decided to continue the survey and the information is now placed

on the web site of the Indigenous Language Institute (ILI) at <www.indige-nous-language.org>.
3. My task here is to utilize the survey data and present a critical discussion of the situation of the indigenous languages in the USA and Canada although Canadian data is limited. Because of the limited nature of the data, my discussion is necessarily incomplete. It is obvious that for any linguistic work, whether it be for a sociolinguistic project or for language planning, we need to have at least some idea of numbers of speakers, size of the total population, their communities, and degrees of bi- or multi-lingualism. But, as the authors of chapters in this book acknowledge, it is very difficult to obtain an accurate figure or even an educated guess of these facts. Some of the reasons for this difficulty are simple and others complex. For example, in many communities, the population is shifting constantly – many leave the indigenous communities for education, for marriage, or for economic opportunities. Some may come back to their communities but many may not unless there is a special reason for them to return (e.g. for better economic situations thanks to the establishment of gaming industries).
4. See, for a detailed discussion on the crucial factors that impact language vitality, "Language Vitality and Endangerment" (<www.unesco.org>, then *Culture -> Intangible Cultural Heritage -> Endangered Languages -> Language Vitality and Endangerment*), the 2003 document of the Intangible Cultural Heritage Unit, UNESCO.

References

Berardo, Marcellino
    2000   *Animacy hierarchy and Shawnee verb inflections.* Doctoral dissertation. Lawrence, Kansas: Department of Linguistics, University of Kansas.
Blair, Heather
    1991   *Sociolinguistic survey of Indigenous languages in Saskatchewan: On the critical list.* Saskatoon, Saskatchewan: Saskatchewan Indigenous Languages Committee.
    1997   *Indian languages policy and planning in Saskatchewan: Research report.* Saskatchewan department of education. Saskatchewan Indigenous Languages Committee.
Cameron, Deborah; Frazer, Elizabeth; Harvey, Penelope; Rampton, Ben and Kay Richardson
    1993   Ethics, advocacy and empowerment: issues of method in researching language. *Language and communication* 13: 81–94.
Canadian Studies New Economy Development Group
    1993   *Evaluation of the Canada – NWT: Cooperation agreement for French and Aboriginal languages in the NWT* (Part I pp. 155, Part II pp. 220,

Appendices (11 appendices), Technical Paper: A literature review, maintenance and revitalization of aboriginal languages pp. 89). Final Report for the Government of the Northwest Territories prepared by New Economy Development Group, Ottawa, Ontario. December 1993. Contact person: Elizabeth (Sabet) Biscaye, Assistant Deputy Minister, Department of the Executive, Official Languages Unit, Government of the Northwest Territories, P.O. Box 1320, Yellowknife, N.W.T., Canada NT X1A 2L9.

Davidson, Jill D.
1999   Reflections on fieldwork in two Native American communities. *Practicing anthropology* 21: 28–33.

Davis, Mary B. (ed.)
1994   *Native America in the twentieth century: An encyclopedia.* New York: Garland Publishing.

Dick, Galena Sells and Teresa L. McCarty
1996   Reclaiming Navajo: Language renewal in an American Indian community school. In Hornberger, Nancy H. (ed.) *Indigenous literacies in the Americas.* Berlin: Mouton de Gruyter. 69–94.

Dorian, Nancy
1998   Western language ideologies and small-language prospects. In Grenoble and Whaley (eds.) 5–21.

Furbee, N. Louanna; Stanley, Lori and Tony Arkeketa
1998   The Roles of two kinds of expert in language renewal. In Ostler (ed.) 75–79.

Goddard, Ives (ed.)
1996   *Handbook of North American Indians, Volume 17: Languages.* Washington DC: Smithsonian Institution. Grammatical sektches include Central Alaskan Yupic (Miyaoka), Hupa (Golla), Cree (Wolfart), Lakhota (Rood & Taylor), Zuni (Newman), Eastern Pomo (McLendon), Seneca (Chafe), Wichita (Rood), Thompson (Thompson, Thompson & Egesdal), Coahuilteco (Troike), Sahaptin (Rigsby & Rude), Shoshone (Miller). This contains an excellent updated map (*Native languages and language families of North America*, compiled by Ives Goddard).

Grenoble, Lenore A. and Lindsay J. Whaley
1998   Toward a typology of language endangerment. In Grenoble and Whaley (eds.) 22–54.

Grenoble, Lenore A. and Lindsay J. Whaley (eds.)
1998   *Endangered languages: Language loss and community response.* Cambridge: Cambridge University Press.

Grinevald, Colette
1998   Language endangerment in South America: a programmatic approach. In Grenoble and Whaley (eds.) 124–159.

Hale, Kenneth; Krauss, Michael; Masayesva-Jeanne, LaVerne; Watahomigie, Lucille J.; Yamamoto, Akira Y.; Craig, Colette G. and Nora England
   1992   Endangered languages. *Language* 68(1): 1–42.
Hinton, Leanne
   1994   *Flutes of fire: Essays on California Indian languages.* Berkeley, California: Heyday Books.
Hinton, Leanne and Yolanda Montijo
   1994   Living California Indian languages. In Hinton 21–33.
Holm, Agnes and Wayne Holm
   1995   Navajo language education: Retrospect and prospects." *Bilingual research journal* 19,1: 141–167.
Kinkade, M. Dale
   1992   The decline of Native languages in Canada. In Robins, Robert H. and Eugenius M. Uhlenbeck (eds.) *Endangered languages* Oxford: Berg. 157–176.
Krauss, Michael
   1998.   The condition of Native North American languages: the need for realistic assessment and action. *International journal of the sociology of language* 132: 9–21.
Linn, Mary S.
   1997   Yuchi and Non-Yuchi: A living classification. *The Florida anthropologist* 50,4: 189–196.
   2001   A grammar of Euchee. Doctoral dissertation. Lawrence, Kansas: Department of Linguistics, University of Kansas.
Linn, Mary; Berardo, Marcellino and Akira Y. Yamamoto
   1998   Creating language team in Oklahoma Native American communities: a process of team-formation. *International journal of sociology of language* 132: 59–78.
Mariella, Patricia and Violet Mitchell-Enos
   1994   Yavapai. In Davis (ed.) 710–712.
Martin, John F.
   1994   Havasupai. In Davis (ed.) 213–233.
Matsumura, Kazuto (ed.)
   1998   *Studies in endangered languages* (Papers from the international symposium on endangered languages, University of Tokyo, November 18–20, 1995). Tokyo: Hituzi Syobo.
McCarty, Teresa L., Akira Y. Yamamoto, Lucille J. Watahomigie, and Ofelia Zepeda
   2001   School-Community-University collaborations: The American Indian Language Development Institute. In Hale Ken and Leanne Hinton (eds.) *Green book of language revitalization practice.* New York: Academic Press. 371–383.
McCarty, Teresa L.; Watahomigie, Lucille J. and Akira Y. Yamamoto (eds.)
   1999   Reversing language shift in Indigenous America: Collaborations and views from the field. *Practicing anthropology* 21,2: 1–47.

Mithun, Marianne
  1993   Introduction to symposium preservation of North American Indian
          Languages. The annual meeting of the Linguistic Society of America.
          Los Angeles, California. January 7, 1993.
  1999   *The languages of Native North America.* Cambridge: Cambridge University Press.
Moore, John H.
  1994   Yuchi. In Davis (ed.) 716.
Nakagawa, Hiroshi and Yoichi Ohtani
  1995   The present status and problems of the Ainu linguistic study. *Gengo Kenkyu* 108:115-135.
Ostler. Nicholas (ed.)
  1998   *Endangered languages – what role for the specialist?* Bath, England:
          Foundation for Endangered Languages.
Schiffman, Harold F.
  1996   *Linguistic culture and language policy.* London: Routledge.
Tamura, Suzuko
  1996   Endangered languages: the issues and researchers tasks. *Gengo kenkyu* 109: 140–148.
Tsunoda, Tasaku
  1996   Fieldwork on Australian Aboriginal Languages. *Gengo kenkyu* 109: 149–160.
Watahomigie, Lucille J.
  1994   Hualapai. In Davis (ed.) 246–247.
Watahomigie, Lucille J.; Bender, Jorigine; Watahomigie, Philbert Sr. and Akira Y.
Yamamoto with Elnora Mapatis, Malinda Powskey and Josie Steele
  2001   *Hualapai reference grammar (Revised and expanded edition).* (ELPR
          Publications A2-003). Kyoto: Endangered Languages of the Pacific
          Rim.
Yamamoto, Akira Y.
  1998a   Linguists and endangered language communities: Issues and approaches. In Matsumura (ed.) 213–252.
  1998b   Retrospect and prospect on new emerging language communities. In
          Ostler (ed.) 113–120.
  1999a   Review of *Endangered languages* Lenore A. Grenoble and Lindsay
          J. Whaley (eds.) 1998. *International journal American linguistics* 65,2:
          233–240.
  1999b   Training for fieldwork in endangered-language communities. *Practicing anthropology* 20,2: 12–15.

Appendix I:

Summary of Kinkade's survey of Indigenous Languages of Canada (the asterisk marked numbers of speakers are taken from Statistics Canada, 1996)

Eskimo-Aleut Family:

Inuktitut (16,000 ~ 18,000 speakers in Canada, 6,000 in northern Alaska, 41,000 in Greenland) TrulyViable

Algonquian Family:

Micmac (7,000; Nova Scotia, New Brunswick, Prince Edward Island, New Foundland) Viable

Malecite (*655; western New Brunswick and adjacent USA) Viable

Abenaki (southern Quebec and adjacent USA) NExtinct (10 in Canada, 5 in USA)

Delaware (southern Ontario, but primarily USA) NExtinct (7 ~ 8 in Canada, a few in USA)

Potawatomi (southern Ontario, but primarily USA) Endangered (100 in Canada, many more in USA)

Montagnais-Naskapi (*9,070; Labrador and northern Quebec) Viable

Cree (60,000+; from Quebec to British Columbia) TrulyViable

Ojibwa (southern Quebec to southern Manitoba and adjacent USA) Truly Viable (30,000 in Canada, 20,000 in USA)

Blackfoot (*4,145; southern Alberta and adjacent USA) Viable

Athabaskan Family:

Chepewyan (*1,455; northern Manitoba, Saskatchewan, Alberta and adjacent USA) Viable

Slave (southern Northwest Territories) and Hare, a major dialect of Slave (northwestern Northwest Territories) Endangered (600):

Dogrib (*2,085; west-central Northwest Territories) Viable

Beaver (300; northern Alberta) Endangered

Sarcee (less than 50; south-central Alberta) NExtinct

Kaska (200 ~ 500; northern British Columbia) Endangered

Sekani (100 ~ 500; central British Columbia and western Alberta) Endangered

Han (Yukon and adjacent Alaska) NExtinct (a few in Canada, 20 in USA-Alaska)

Gwich'in (*430; Yukon and adjacent Alaska) Viable

Tutchone (Yukon and adjacent Alaska) Viable

Tahltan (40; northwestern British Columbia) NExtinct

Tagish (less than 6; northwestern British Columbia, southern Yukon) NExtinct

Tsetsaut (north-central British Columbia coast) Extinct (early 20th century)

Babine (west-central British Columbia) Endangered?

Carrier (central British Columbia) Viable

Chilcotin (*705; south-central British Columbia) Viable

Nicola (south-central British Columbia) Extinct (20th century)

Beothuk Isolate. Extinct (well over 100 years)

Haida Isolate (Queen Charlotte Islands of British Columbia and adjacent USA) Endangered (225 in Canada, 100 in USA; language programs)

Iroquoian Family:

Huron (southern Quebec and Ontario) Extinct (well over 100 years)

Petun (southern Ontario) Extinct (well over 100 years)

Neutral (southern Ontario) Extinct (well over 100 years)

St. Lawrence Iroquoian (southern Quebec and Ontario) Extinct (well over 100 years)

Mohawk (*350; southern Quebec, Ontario, and adjacent USA) Viable

Seneca (southern Ontario and adjacent USA) NExtinct (25 in Canada, larger number in USA)

Cayuga (southern Ontario and adjacent USA) Endangered (360 in Canada, 10 in USA)

Oneida (southern Ontario and adjacent USA) Endangered (200 in Canada, 50 in USA)

Onondaga (southern Ontario and adjacent USA) Endangered (50~100 in Canada, 50 in USA)

Tuscarora (southern Ontario and adjacent USA) NExtinct (7~8 in Canada, more in USA)

Kootenay Isolate (southeastern British Columbia and adjacent USA) Endangered (250 or less in Canada, a few in USA; language programs)

Salishan Family:

Okanagan (500; south-central British Columbia) Endangered (language programs)

Shuswap (500; south-central British Columbia) Endangered (language programs)

Thompson (500; south-central British Columbia) Endangered (language programs)

Lillooet (300 ~ 400; southwestern British Columbia) Endangered (language programs)

Bella Coola (less than 200; central British Columbia coast) Endangered (language programs)

Comox-Sliammon (southwestern British Columbia) Endangered (400 or less of Sliammon dialect, 0 of the Island dialect of Comox)

Pentlatch (Vancouver Island) Extinct (20th century)

Sechelt (40; southwestern British Columbia) NExtinct

Squamish (20; southwestern British Columbia) NExtinct

Halkomelem (500; southwestern British Columbia) Endangered (language programs)

Straits (southwestern British Columbia and adjacent USA) NExtinct (30 or less; mostly the Saanich dialect in British Columbia, no speakers of Sooke or Songish dialects)

Siouan Family:
  Dakota (southern Manitoba, Saskatchewan, Alberta and adjacent USA) TrulyViable (5,000 in Canada, 15,000 in USA)
  Tlingit Isolate (*145; northwestern British Columbia and adjacent Alaska) Viable

Tsimshian Family:
  Nass-Gitksan (*1,200; north-central British Columbia coast) Viable
  Coast-Southern Tsimshian (north-central British Columbia coast) NExtinct (10 or less of Southern Tsimshian dialect); Endangered (200 or less of Coast Tsumshian dialect)

Wakashan Family:
  Haisla (central British Columbia coast) Endangered (200 or less of whom 25 are fluent)
  Heiltsuk (central British Columbia coast) Viable
  Kwak'wala (central British Columbia coast and Vancouver Island) Viable
  Nootka (less than 600; Vancouver Island) Endangered
  Nitinaht (30; southern Vancouver Island) Nextinct

Appendix II:

Hinton and Montijo (1994) Survey of *California Indian Languages*
I will include here an abbreviated version of their more thorough survey. I use their conservative estimate of *fluent* speakers adding the estimated total population figures whenever available from Davis 1994.

Algic
  Wiyot (0) Population 450
  Yurok (20 ~ 30) Population 3,500
Chumashan
  Chumash (0) Population 156
Cochimí-Yuman
  Diegueño [Kumeyaay (50), Ipai (25), Tipai (200)] Population 2,562
  Mojave [Fort Mojave Reservation (30 ~ 35), Colorado River Reservation (35 ~ 50)] Population 767
  Quechan (Yuma) (150) Population 3,000
Esselen Language Isolate (0) Population 80
Karuk Language Isolate (10~12) Population 1,900
Maiduan
  Maidu languages [Konkow (3 ~ 5), Nisenan (1), and Northeast Maidu (1 ~ 2)] Population 2,500
Nadene
  Hupa (12~25) Population 150
  Tolowa (4 ~ 5) Population 1,000

Palaihnihan
   Achumawi (5 ~ 10) and Atsugewi (3) together have the total population of 1,350.
Plateau Penutian
   Modoc (Klamath) (1 ~ 3) Population 2,000?
Pomoan
   Cahto (0)
   Pomo languages [Kashaya Pomo (45), Southern Pomo (1), Central Pomo (8),
   Northern Pomo (1), Eastern Pomo (5), Southeastern Pomo (5), Northeastern
   Pomo (0)] Population (all combined including Cahto Pomo) 4,766
Salinan
   Salinan (0) Population several hundred?
Shastan
   Shasta (0) Population 1,300
Utian
   Miwok languages [Coast Miwok (1), Lake Miwok (1 ~ 2), Bay Miwok (0), Plains
   Miwok (1), Northern Sierra Miwok (6 or less), Eastern Central Sierra (6), West-
   ern Central Sierra (6), Southern Central Sierra (7)] Population 3,000
   Ohlone languages (0) Population several hundreds~several thousands?
Uto-Aztecan
   Cahuilla (7 ~ 20) Population 2,300?
   Chemehuevi [Colorado river Reservation (10 or less), Chemehuevi Reserva-
   tion (3)] Population 900?
   Cupeño (1 ~ 5) Population 700
   Gabrielino (Tongva) (0) Population 1,000~2,000
   Juaneño (Ajachmem) (0) Population (see Luiseño)
   Kawaiisu (8 ~ 10) Population 35
   Luiseño (30 ~ 40) Population 2,500 (with Juaneño)
   Mono [North fork (10 ~ 12), Auberry (15), Big Sandy Mono (7 ~ 8), Dunlap
   Mono (5 ~ 6), Waksachi (0)] Population 600
   Paiute languages [Owens Valley Paiute (50), Northern Paiute (25 ~ 40 in Cali-
   fornia, 1,000 in USA), California Shoshoni (20)] Population?
   Serrano (2) Population 85
   Tubatulabal (3 ~ 5) Population 900
Washo Language Isolate (25?) Population 1,500
Wintuan
   Wintun languages [Wintu (6), Nomlaki (0 ~ 1), Patwin (1 ~ 2) Population 2,500
Yanan Language Isolate (0) Population ?
Yokutsan
   Yokuts languages [Choynumni (8 ~ 10), Chukchansi (12), Dumna (1), Tachi
   (3), Wukchumne (10), Yowlumni (25 ~ 27), Gashowu (1)] Population 2,500
Yukian
   Wappo (2) Population ?
   Yuki (0) Population 1,200

Chapter 6
Language Endangerment in Northern Africa

Matthias Brenzinger

1. Introduction

Standard Arabic is the "official language" not only in the Western states of the Maghreb region, i. e. Morocco, Algeria, Tunisia, and Mauritania, but also in Libya and Egypt. After independence, most African governments assigned official roles in modern sectors such as education and administration to the languages of the former colonial powers. The governments of the Maghreb states opted for the contrary policy: *Modern Standard Arabic* and the liturgical *Classical Arabic* receive governmental support by the pan-Arabist ruling elites in these countries. Since then their policy has been primarily directed to push back *French*, the language of the former colonizers, by fostering the use of *Modern Standard Arabic*. Schools are instrumental in homogenizing the populations of North Africa through the promotion of Islam and *Arabic* under the slogan "one religion and one language" (Almasude 1999: 120).

The official language policy of the Moroccan government, for example, aims at reestablishing the status and function of *Arabic* to the level it had before the French invasion in 1912.[1] To that end, government policy attempts to modernize *Modern Standard Arabic* for allowing its use in technology and science. The undervalued and stigmatized other languages, i. e. *Amazigh* and the colloquial *Arabic* languages have no place in such national language policies of the Maghreb states. In addition to that, *Amazigh* (*Berber*) has been and often still is regarded to be a threat to Arab Muslim identity (Boukouss 2001: 20–24). In recent years, however, the officially prevailing Arabo-Islamic ideology of "Arabization" has been challenged by a fast spreading international Amazigh renaissance. Some scholars, such as Guessoum (2002) express doubts on the underlying motives of and thus the outcomes desired by these movements. He assumes that the "Berber renaissance" is mainly a cover of the francophone Maghreb elite (in Algeria) to counter the Arab expansion. He suspects that the primary interest of those activists is the reintroduction of *French* in its former functions. According to Guessoum, the support of raising the status and use of *Amazigh* is only of secondary importance.

2. The *Amazigh (Berber)* languages[2]

The indigenous people of northern Africa and their languages are widely known as "Berber", but because this term goes back to "Barbarian", they prefer the name Amazigh (Imazighen), literally "free people". Most Amazigh seem to have agreed to call themselves and their language *Amazigh* or *Tamazight* when they use *English*. We will follow these conventions, with the exception of terms established in linguistic classification, such as "*North Berber*".

Little is known about pre-historic times, but nobody seems to question that the Amazigh are the indigenous inhabitants of Northern Africa before the "Islamic Conquest" of the Arabs. In the 7th and 8th centuries, *Arabic* started to spread along with Islam among former *Amazigh* speakers. This Arab expansion took several hundred years. However, it was not the aforementioned high prestige *Arabic* varieties that replaced the ethnic tongues of Amazigh. Instead, colloquial varieties, which today are often referred to by the names of the nations, such as *Moroccan Arabic, Algerian Arabic, Tunisian Arabic*, have become the mother tongues of many Amazigh. These mainly oral *Arabic* varieties – not *Standard Arabic* – are still the main threat to the ancestral languages of the indigenous populations of Northern Africa.

In order to foster a common identity and join their strength, Amazigh activists generally speak of one *Amazigh* language by acknowledging the existence of regional varieties. While most linguists agree on a close genetic relationship, they distinguish various *Amazigh* languages based on linguistic analyses. Only neighboring *Amazigh* speech varieties are mutually intelligible and linguistic dissimilarity increases with geographical distance. Studies have demonstrated that there is a considerable variation among the *Amazigh* languages, not only in the lexicon, but also in their morphology (Aikhenwald 1990, 1995). Figures provided for the number of *Amazigh* languages range from 'one' to more than a 100 and some even mention as many as 5,000 local forms (Irvine 1994: 270). The 24 *Amazigh* languages listed in table 1 (see also *Map 8*) are an attempt to present an overview of the distinct *Amazigh* languages. Update information on the languages is mainly derived from the Ethnologue 2001 in its electronic version of December 2004 (Grimes ed. 2001). The status of most *Amazigh* varieties with regard to their linguistic distance needs further investigation and a coherent linguistic atlas of the *Amazigh* languages is still lacking (Applegate 1970).

Amazigh languages are still spoken between Mauritania at the Atlantic coast and Egypt in the east, Tunisia in the north and Burkina Faso and Niger in the south. Before the Arab invasion, the entire northern part of the African continent might have been a vast contiguous area of an *Amazigh* dialectal continuum in which neighboring varieties were mutually intelligible.

A continuum still exists in Morocco, in which speakers of the southern varieties of *Tashelhit* can communicate with those speaking the central varieties, called *Tamazight*. The latter converse with the speakers of *Tarifit*, the northern varieties, whereas *Tashelhit* and *Tarifit* languages are mutually incomprehensible (Yamina el Kirat, pers. com.). To the east, *Tarifit* borders the *Kabyle* area of Algeria and these two varieties are closely related and mutually intelligible, regardless of the different national affiliations (Sadiqi 1998). The *Moroccan Amazigh* languages are grouped together with most *Algerian Amazigh* languages, such as *Shawiya, Shenowa, Tagargrent,* and *Tumzabt* as *"North Berber"*.

The westernmost *Amazigh* language is *Zenaga*, with only a few hundred speakers in an isolated pocket in the coastal border region of Mauritania and Senegal. Most scholars consider this language to be the only surviving member of *"West Berber"*.

Spanish has replaced the *Amazigh* language of the Guanche in the Canary Islands after a final defeat in 1496. Mainly because of lack of language data, the classificatory status of *Guanche* will remain a matter of dispute. Based on her analyses of grammatical features, mainly the case system, Aikhenvald (1990: 113) claims a first split of *Guanche* (*"proto-Berber-Guanche"*) from the ancestor language of all other *Amazigh* languages (*"proto-Berber"*).

The oasis of Siwa in Egypt is the most eastern Amazigh settlement. Their language, named *Siwi* is still spoken by about 10,000 people; however, since it became part of Egypt in 1920, *Arabic* vocabulary entered the language through formal education and military service (Vycichi 2005: 162). *Siwi* is related to *Amazigh* languages of Libya, such as *Awjila* and *Nafusi*. Dialects of the latter, namely *Djerbi* and *Tamezret* are also spoken in Tunisia. These languages together form *"East Berber"*.

Most *Amazigh* languages spoken in the southern parts of the Maghreb, such as *Tamasheq* and *Tamajaq* are classified as *"South Berber"*.

The sociopolitical environment for the *Amazigh* speech communities differs considerably in the North African States. Colonel Muammar Gaddafi, Libya's "Leader of the Revolution", neglects any distinct Amazigh identity and considers the "Berber" as being genuine Arabs. Gaddafi is not prepared to accept any promotion of *Amazigh* languages in his country. Their existence is widely ignored in Tunisia and Mauritania, because the Amazigh are few in number in these two countries (Souag 2004: 10).

After independence, many Amazigh in Algeria maintained their ethnic and linguistic identity and even became involved in armed struggle against what they considered an Arab imperialism. In May 2002, the Algerian government agreed on a constitutional amendment by which *Amazigh* receives the status of a "national language".

The most positive prospects for the future, it seems, have the *Amazigh* languages spoken in Morocco, not only because their speakers are the most numerous. King Mohammed VI of Morocco established "The Royal Institute of the Amazigh Culture" (IRCAM) with the *Dahir of Ajdir* in October 17th, 2001. This Royal Institute in Rabat has been created to preserve and promote *Amazigh* culture and language. The goal of IRCAM is to contribute to the implementation of the policies adopted by the King: "... which will allow for the introduction of the *Amazigh* language in the educational system and insure the spread of its influence in the social, cultural, media, national, regional and local contexts" *Royal Dahir, Art. 2.* (IRCAM 2004)

The most challenging tasks assigned to IRCAM by the king are the standardization of the so-called *Moroccan Amazigh* "dialects", and the establishing of a standard *Amazigh* orthography.

In dealing with the first problem, IRCAM decided to produce three separate manuals for the primary level, one for *Tashelhit, Tamazight* and *Tarifit* each. For the second level, they produced a common manual in what IRCAM claims to be a standard form of *Amazigh*. IRCAM proceeds in standardization *Amazigh* and aims at finally coming up with a *Moroccan Standard Amazigh*. This written *Amazigh* variety, however, may end up as being no one's mother tongue.

With regard to the second task, i. e. a writing system for *Amazigh*, there are basically two opposing positions. The Moroccan, like the Algerian government, has advocated the use of an *Arabic*-based script for *Amazigh* while most Amazigh themselves use and support a *Latin*-based script.

For hundreds of years, Amazigh fought against and resisted the Arab dominance, just as they did against the others, the European colonizers. Given these facts, Guessoum's account of the positive stance towards *Arabic* and the *Arabic* script by *Amazigh* sounds rather suspicious; it merely represents the official version of the history from the perspective of Islamist elites.

Nos ancêtres kabyles n'ont jamais posé le problème de l'amazighité en tant que tel ; au contraire, nos savants d'origine kabyle ont toujours utilisé le verbe et les caractères arabes pour transmettre le message kabyle, se sentant ainsi mieux dans leur milieu arabo-islamique. (Guessoum 2002: 197)

According to by far most other sources, there is no support for the introduction of the *Arabic* script among Amazigh. The Amazigh intelligentsia
in Morocco and Algeria is predominately educated in *French*, and they
strongly promote the use of a Roman alphabet. The governments of Mali
and Niger, like that of Algeria, accepted these aspirations and decided on
the use of the *Latin* script.

In Algeria, the government body in charge of the matter – the Haut Commision
pour l'Amazighté – appears to have settled on Latin after a period of vacillation;
if so, Latin (script, M. B.) will likely take hold irreversibly in the coming years as
Berber is introduced in the classroom. (Souag 2004: 4)

IRCAM, i. e. the King of Morocco, came up with a rather unexpected
third alternative, a Neo-Tifinagh. Given the ideological dimensions associated with the choice of *Arabic* or *Latin*, the King following the suggestion of IRCAM and opted for Neo-Tifinagh as a "neutral" choice. Each
language is written in its own script: *Arabic* in *Arabic* script, *French, Spanish* and *English* in *Latin* script and *Amazigh* in Tifinagh.

At first, IRCAM introduced a Tifinagh-alphabet for "*Standard Amazigh*" with 33 characters. In 2003, IRCAM added some 30 more characters,
which allow representing the distinctive phonemes in the now recognized
three major *Moroccan Amazigh* "varieties". The Moroccan government
decided on the use of this official Neo-Tifinagh script for producing educational materials.

The IRCAM script seems to attract Amazigh irrespective of where they
live and whether they speak *Amazigh* or not. Outside of Morocco, Tifinagh characters are used merely as symbols in letterheads and logos. More
than 2000 years ago, "the Numidians and other early Berber kingdoms developed a script now known as Numidic, Old Libyan, or Libyco-Berber."
(Souag 2004: 1) Various stone inscriptions testify to the long history of a
geometric script, which the Tuareg have preserved until today as Tifinagh.
Characters from rock inscriptions and a few manuscripts formed the basis
for the development of the Neo-Tifinagh script.

The Islamists support the *Arabic* script and claim that this script should
be adopted for *Amazigh* because Morocco is a Moslem nation. The use of
the Latin alphabet to them means the rejection of Islam through a Western secularism. It is seen as an unpatriotic support of the former colonizers and non-Moslem. Nevertheless, many Amazigh use and promote the
Latin script and feel that the Neo-Tifinagh script will segregate the
Amazigh language. Neo-Tifinagh is considered to be difficult to use by

most Amazigh and even experts, who work with and developed the script, are not yet at ease in using this "artificial" writing system.

Several newspapers, periodicals and magazines are published in *Amazigh,* predominantly in *Latin* script, but also in *Arabic* script and to a lesser extent in Tifinagh. National radio and TV programs are broadcasted in various *Amazigh* languages in Algeria and Morocco. However, the internet has developed into the most important medium for *Amazigh* (language) activists (Almasude 1999). Several organizations in the Diaspora maintain web pages, such as the Amazigh Cultural Association in America (ACAA) and Syphax Sociaal-culturele Verenniging (The Netherlands). Update information Amazigh issues is disseminated on web portals such as Amazigh-Voice, Monde Berbere, Amazigh World and Amazigh NL.[3] All these and many other networks want to help to promote and foster the *Amazigh* culture and language.

Language survival depends on the speakers, most importantly on their language attitudes and language behavior. Several *Amazigh* languages have already become extinct, such as *Sened* in Tunisia or *Ghomara* and *Sanhaja* of Srair in Algeria. Others, such as *Zenaga* in Mauritania and *Sawkna* in Libya are under serious threat. *Kabyle, Tamasheq* and *Tamazight* are among those languages, which spoken by large communities, seem to be safe.

More than 70% of North Africans of Amazigh origins speak no *Amazigh* languages, but *Arabic* languages only. In Morocco and Algerian about 80% of the citizens are considered to be of Amazigh origin, as are roughly 60% of those in Tunisia and Libya. Origin and identity does not necessarily match. In the latter two countries, few citizens have maintained their Amazigh identity. In contrast, increasing numbers refer to themselves as Amazigh in Algeria and in Morocco. With 11 to 14 million speakers of *Amazigh* languages in total, only about half of those who currently claim their Amazigh identity still speak an *Amazigh* language. Obviously, to call a person an Amazigh does no longer require any *Amazigh* languages competence. This is a most threatening fact for the vitality of *Amazigh* languages and serious indicator for its endangerment.

Recent studies on language vitality, such as those undertaken by Yamina El Kirat, demonstrate that not only small *Amazigh* languages in isolated pockets are under threat. El Kirat found that Beni Iznassen people are in large numbers abandoning their *Amazigh* language in favor of *Moroccan Arabic.* They no longer transmit their language to children, and formerly fluent speakers lose proficiency because they hardly use their ethnic language in everyday communication.

The Beni Iznassen people have developed a very negative attitude towards their mother tongue to the extent of rejecting it and denying their Amazigh identity. Most Beni Iznassen people consider their language as being a stigma and think Moroccan Arabic is more useful than Beni Iznassen Amazigh. (El Kirat 2001: 93)

Even though some of the *Amazigh* languages seem to be quite safe, unstable bilingualism is widespread and puts even larger *Amazigh* languages at risk. Unlike "their Riffi neighbors, Beni Iznassen people are not proud of their Amazigh identity and even try hard to hide it from outsiders." (El Kirat 2004: 44). In the rural areas, Beni Iznassen children acquire *Moroccan Arabic* as their first language and if they know any *Amazigh* at all, have only a limited proficiency. Most of their urban age-mates grow up with *Moroccan Arabic* and *French* with almost no contact with *Amazigh*. There is widespread language shift and an interruption of language transmission in northeastern Morocco.

It is doubtful whether current developments, in which the intellectual Amazigh elite is employing the language and script to raise political awareness, will have a positive impact on the actual language use of the rural Amazigh communities.

Brandissant la banderole de l'amazighité, ce mouvement «pour la culture berbère» n'est en réalité qu'une revendication francophone sous l'étiquette berbère. Sinon, comment expliquer cette hostilité des revendications de la berbérité à tout ce qui est arabe: culture, écriture, paroles, lettres, etc. (Guessoum 2002: 197)

Guessoum's interpretation according to which *Amazigh* is being taken advantage of by a movement, whose primary goal is to oppose *Arabic*, may be exaggerated. Nevertheless, when movements make use of languages merely as (political) symbols – and there are indications for that with *Amazigh* – they do not necessarily support the maintenance of a community's home language.

Many of the numerous Diaspora Amazigh communities in countries such as France, Spain, the Netherlands, Germany and United States retain a quite strong loyalty to their *Amazigh* languages. Amazigh children abroad may grow up as bilinguals, with the language of their host country and *Amazigh*, without speaking any *Arabic*. These immigrant communities play an important role in the revival and maintenance of *Amazigh* languages, and Salem Mezhoud even speaks of "Salvation through Migration" (Mezhoud 2005).

Several *Amazigh* languages have already disappeared and others are severely endangered. Only the usage in the family ensures the survival of a language. Most urban children in cities of the Maghreb, even those of elite Amazigh activists, do no longer acquire *Amazigh* languages and the break in the intergenerational transmission in most *Amazigh* languages is evident. The fate of those, which are still spoken by millions, relies on the implementation human and civil rights in the states of Maghreb region. The future of the *Amazigh* speech communities in the Diaspora will also depend on the national policies of the host countries towards immigrate languages.

3. Endangered and extinct languages of other non-Muslim communities

The most prominent "dead" language of North Africa is *Coptic*, which was one of the stages of *Egyptian*. The decline of *Coptic* started with the Arab conquest of Egypt in the seventh century. Until then, *Coptic* had been the spoken language of Egypt; written first in the hieroglyphic script, then in the hieratic and later in the demotic form of writing. About 2,300 years ago, the Egyptians adopted the *Greek* alphabet and added some letters to represent all the distinctive sounds of their language, then called "*Coptic*".

Soon after the conquest, *Arabic* became the only language used in administration and pressure to apostasy to Islam increased on the orthodox Christian communities. A main factor responsible for accelerating the process of abandonment of *Coptic*, i. e. the orthodox Christian language, by the indigenous populations was the introduction of a progressively heavier capitation tax known as *Jizyah* on non-Muslims.

The Dominican traveler J. M. Vansleb reported, in the account of his journey to Upper Egypt in 1672–73, that he had met a certain Mu'allim Athanasius. Vansleb refers to him as last Copt to be fluent in the *Coptic* language. From the seventeenth century onwards, only formal phrases of *Coptic* "survived" in the reduced functional spiritual domain as "language" of the liturgy (Ishaq 1991: 604–606). Today, approximately 4 million Copts in Egypt still know some liturgical phrases, but no one can conduct natural conversations on everyday issues in *Coptic*. The Copts, as orthodox Christians, play an important role by easily interacting with non-Muslim foreigners in the tourist industry. They maintain their Coptic identity as well as their religious faith. Copts marry among themselves, the *Coptic* language, however, no longer exists as their community's language.

Long before the spread of Islam and *Arabic*, Jewish communities were scattered along the North African coastline from Egypt in the east to Mauritania in the west. There is no proof, but "it is plausible to posit a Jewish migration from Palestine towards the West after the destruction of the first temple [586 B.C.E., M. B.]. That such a migration occurred after the fall of the second Temple [70 C.E., M. B.] is a well documented historical fact" (Udovitch and Valensi 1984: 10–11). Jewish communities in Europe and Middle East speak distinct languages and so did Jews in the Maghreb. These "*Jewish* languages" are in general based on the languages spoken by the host communities. They differ from these in a strong *Hebrew* interference and in being written in *Hebrew* script.

Jewish communities in North African spoke varieties of *Judaeo-Berber* for hundreds of years and only after the 12th century, most Jews shifted to those of *Judaeo-Arabic*. Today, the only Jewish communities of North Africa speaking *Judaeo-Arabic* live on the Tunisian island of Jerba. Berberophone Jewish communities left the African continent for Israel in the mid 1950s in large numbers. The Jerba Jews are the only community marked on the North African map (*Map 8*), because there was no update information on the present conditions of any other North African speech communities of *Jewish* languages.

Haïm Zafrani (1971: 307) claims that *Judaeo-Berber,* as a *Hebrew*-influenced *Amazigh* variety, was widely spoken by Jewish communities in Southern Morocco, but also by some who lived in parts of Algeria and Tunisia. According to Zafrani, North African Jews used *Judaeo-Berber* in all domains, within the family and in social and economic interactions. Cultural instructions as well as oral traditions were given in this *Amazigh*-based *Jewish* language and it was along with *Hebrew* even used in religious contexts. The scanty historical sources do not allow for reconstructing the history of this presumably first North African "*Jewish* languages". With the emigration of the Jews to Israel after the Independence of Morocco, a few elderly people seem to be the last with some competence in *Judaeo-Berber* (Zafrani 1971: 307).

In contrast to *Judaeo-Berber*, *Judaeo-Arabic* varieties spread throughout the *Arabic*-speaking world, including North Africa. National distinctions for these languages are frequent today, such as *Moroccan Judaeo-Arabic, Tunisian* and *Algerian Judaeo-Arabic* (see Grimes ed. 2001), while scholarly descriptions by linguists rather distinguish local varieties, such as *Judaeo-Arabic of Fès* (Brunot and Malka 1940) or *Judaeo-Arabic of Constantine* (Tirosh-Becker 1988, 1989).

Based on written sources, Benjamin Hary (2003: 1) distinguishes five *Judaeo-Arabic* periods:

Pre-Islamic Judeo-Arabic (pre-eighth century), Early Judeo-Arabic (eighth/ninth to tenth centuries), Classical Judeo-Arabic (tenth to fifteenth centuries), Later Judeo-Arabic (fifteenth to nineteenth centuries), and Modern Judeo-Arabic (twentieth century).

Before the 15th century *Judaeo-Arabic* was mainly the language of Rabbis and few other Jewish intellectuals. Written documents such as letters from this small Jewish elite suggest that no great regional variation of *Judaeo-Arabic* existed at that time (Tedghi 2002).

This situation changed, however, in the 15th century, when the so-called *Late*, i.e. *Later* and *Modern Judaeo-Arabic,* varieties developed and became the languages of Jewish communities. The regional varieties of *Judaeo-Arabic* that evolved in various parts of North Africa are unintelligible to *Arabic* speakers outside the Jewish communities. *Judaeo-Arabic* "contains elements of *Classical Arabic*, dialectal components, pseudo-corrections, and standardization of some features, as well as influences from *Hebrew* and *Aramaic*" (Hary 2003). In addition, influence from contact with other Jewish communities, such as *Ladino*-speaking ones from Spain is evident in North African *Judaeo-Arabic* varieties.[4] Since the *Hebrew* script is used to write *Judaeo-Arabic*, these languages are generally indecipherable to non-Jews.

In the mid-20th century, most Jews left the Maghreb to live in Israel, while some others migrated to France. In Israel, the situation for *Judaeo-Arabic* was quite hostile, and there was strong pressure on the North African immigrants to adopt *Hebrew*. *Judaeo-Arabic* varieties did not receive the same recognition as other *Jewish* languages, for example *Yiddish*. Following *Hebrew* and *English, Arabic* is the third most-spoken language in Israel today and most of the *Arabic*-speaking Jews originate from North Africa. There are initiatives, such as *Ot Brit Kodesh* of the *Association des Juifs de Mogador et du Maroc*[5] which support *Judaeo-Arabic* in Israel, as well as in North Africa (Morocco). However, these initiatives will not be able to reverse the decline of the *Judaeo-Arabic* varieties, neither in Israel nor in North Africa (Danielle Gamain, pers. com.).

In 1984, Udovitch and Valensi claim to describe the "The last Arab Jews" of North Africa. The number of these Jews on the Tunisian Island Jerba dropped from 4,500 in 1946 to 1,100 in 1984. After successive migration waves to Palestine only few Jews have remained in two villages, 300 in Hara Sghira and 800 in Hara Hebira (Udovitch and Valensi 1984: 5).

Joseph Tedghi compiled more than 2,000 *Judaeo-Arabic* texts from the *Medieval* to the *Modern Judaeo-Arab* period.

Mais, en raison de l'immigration massive des Juifs du Maghreb depuis près d'un demi-siècle – vers Israël et la France notamment – et du recul de la pratique du judéo-arabe au détriment de l'hébreu et du français, un tel objectif semble de plus en plus difficile à réaliser. Ces textes constitueront donc les seules sources pour l'étude des parlers judéo-arabes voués désormais à la disparition. (Tedghi 2002: 438)

Collections of written documents, such as Tedghi's compilation, may soon be the only source available for the study of *Judaeo-Arabic*, as the younger generations have already abandoned these languages.

Table 1. The Amazigh languages of Northern Africa

Map	Country	Language	Speakers	Population	Status
The Amazigh languages					
1	Canary Islands	Guanchen	0	0	e
2	Mauritania	Zenaga	?	200–300	b
3	Morocco	Tachelhit	3 m	3.5 m	a–
4	Morocco	Tamazight	3 m	3.5 m	a–
5	Morocco	Tarifit	1.5 m	2 m	a–, a
6	Morocco	Ghomara	0	?	e
7	Morocco	Sanhaja of Srair	0	?	e
8	Algeria	Shenowa	15,000–75,000	?	?
9	Algeria	Kabyle	2.5 m–3 m	?	a–
10	Algeria	Shawiya	1.4 m	?	a–
11	Algeria	Temashin Tamazigh	?	6,000	d, e
12	Algeria	Tumzabt, Mzab	70,000	70,000	a–
13	Algeria	Tagargrent, Wargla	5,000	5,000	a–
14	Algeria	Taznatit	40,000	40,000	a–
15	Algeria	Tidikelt Tamazigh	?	9,000	d, e
16	Mali, Burkina Faso, Niger	Tamasheq	270,000	270,000	a–
17	Niger, Mali	Tamajaq	650,000	650,000	a–
18	Algeria, Niger, Libya	Tamahaq	62,000	62,000	a–
19	Libya, Algeria	Ghadamès	4,000	4,000	a–
20	Tunisia	Sened	0	?	e

21	Libya, Tunesia	Nafusi	167,000	167,000	a–
22	Libya	Awjila	few ?	2,000	d, e
23	Libya	Sawkna	0 ?	?	e ?
24	Egypt	Siwi	10,000	?	a

Other languages

25	Egypt	Coptic	0	4 m–6 m	e
26	Tunisia	Judaeo-Arabic	1,100	1,100	d
	Israel	Judaeo-Berber	few ?		d, e

For defining status see Krauss Chapter 1, this volume:

"safe"	a+
stable	a–
instable; eroded	a
definitively endangered	b
severely endangered	c
critically endangered	d
extinct	e

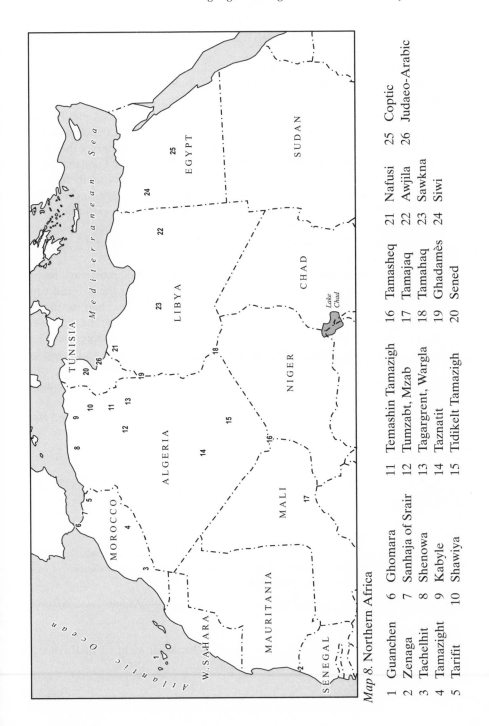

Map 8. Northern Africa

1 Guanchen	6 Ghomara
2 Zenaga	7 Sanhaja of Srair
3 Tachelhit	8 Shenowa
4 Tamazight	9 Kabyle
5 Tarifit	10 Shawiya

11 Temashin Tamazigh	16 Tamasheq
12 Tumzabt, Mzab	17 Tamajaq
13 Tagargrent, Wargla	18 Tamahaq
14 Taznatit	19 Ghadamês
15 Tidikelt Tamazigh	20 Sened

21 Nafusi	25 Coptic
22 Awjila	26 Judaeo-Arabic
23 Sawkna	
24 Siwi	

Notes

1. The lengths and thus the impact of French colonial presence varied considerably between the Maghreb states: Morocco 1912–56, Tunisia 1881–1956, Algeria 1830–1962 (Ayoub 2002: 40)
2. I would like to thank Yamina el Kirat (University Mohamed V – Agdal/Rabat) for valuable suggestions. I am also indented to Jilali Saib and Ahmed Boukouss from The Royal Institut of the Amazigh Culture in Rabat for sharing their first hand experience on Amazigh language development. Danielle Gamain (Nice) was kind enough to provide her academic as well as personal (family history) insights on Judaeo-Arabic. Thanks for comments to Ofra Tirosh-Becker (The Hebrew University of Jerusalem), Axel Fleisch, Jonathan Allen Brindle,
3. International Amazigh web portals: http://www.amazigh-voice.com, http://www.mondeberbere.com, http://www.amazighworld.com, and http://www.amazigh.nl.
4. Ladino, the Jewish language of the Sephardic Jews of Spain, must have had a strong presence also on the African continent, at least after the 15th century. Spanish Jews fled in large numbers also to the Maghreb after their expulsion from Spain in 1498. In urban settings, Spanish Jews soon became the new Jewish elite, which absorbed small, previously existing Judaeo-Arabic speaking Jewish communities (Marx 1990: 60). Very little facts are known on the use of Ladino in North Africa, but the dominance of Ladino speaking Sephardic Jews in urban centers of the Maghreb probably had an impact on the language used by North African Jews.
5. "Ot Brit Kodesh" publishes a bilingual review entitled "Brit" in *French* and *Hebrew*.

References

Aikhenvald, Alexandra Yu.
  1990   On Berber cases in the light of Afroasiatic languages. In Mukarovski, H. (ed.) *Proceedings of the Fifth International Hamito-Semitic Congress.* Wien: Universität Wien.
  1995   Split ergativity in Berber languages. *St. Petersburg journal of African studies* 4: 39–68.
Almasude, Amar
  1999   The new media and the shaping of Amazigh identity. In Reyhner; Cantoni; Clair and Parsons Yazzie (eds.) 117–128.
Applegate, Joseph R.
  1970   The Berber language. In Sebeok (ed.) 561–586.

Atiya, Aziz S. (ed.)
1991   *The Coptic encyclopedia.* New York: Macmillan Publishing Company.
Ayoub, Georgine
2002   La langue arabe entre l'écrit et l'oral. In Bistolfi (ed.) 31–52.
Bistolfi, Robert (ed.) (in collaboration with Henri Giordan)
2002   *Les Langues de la Métiterranée.* Paris:L'Harmattan.
Boukouss, Ahmed
2001   Language policy, identity and education in Morocco. *Languages and linguistics* 8: 17–27.
Brunot, Louis and Elie Malka
1940   *Glossaire Judéo-Arabe de Fès.* Rabat : Ecole du livre.
Caubet, Dominique; Chaker, Salem and Jean Sibille (eds.)
2002   *Codification des langues de France.* Paris : L'Harmattan.
El Kirat, Yamina
2001   The current status and future of the Amazigh language in the Beni Iznassen community. *Languages and linguistics* 8: 81–95.
2004   The lexical and morphological structure of the Amazigh of the Beni Iznassen in a context of language loss. Ph.D.-thesis. University of Rabat
Grimes, Barbara F. (ed.)
2001   *Ethnologue.* (15th Edition). Dallas: SIL International.
Guessoum, Abderrazak
2002   Problématique linguistique en Algérie. In Bistolfi (ed.) 187–202.
Hary, Benjamin
2003   Judeo-Arabic. Jewish language research website. Editor: Sarah Bunin Benor <editor@jewish-languages.org>
Ishaq, Emile Maher
1991   Coptic language, spoken. In Atiya (ed.) 604–607.
Irvine, A. K.
1994   The Middle East, North Africa and Ethiopia. In Moseley and Asher (eds.) 265–271.
Marx, Bettina
1990   *Juden Marokkos und Europas.* Das marokkanische Judentum im 19. Jahrhundert und seine Darstellung in der zeitgenössischen jüdischen Presse in Deutschland, Frankreich und Großbritannien. Frankfurt a. M., Bern, New York, Paris: Lang.
Mezhoud, Salem
2005   Salvation through migration: Immigrant communities as engine rooms for the survival and revival of the Tamazight (Berber) language. In Crawhall, Nigel and Nicholas Ostler (eds.) *Creating outsiders.* Endangered languages, migration and marginalization. Bath: Foundation of Endangered Languages. 109–116.

138   *Matthias Brenzinger*

Moseley, Christopher and R. E. Asher (eds.)
1994   *Atlas of the world's language.* London: Routledge.
Reyhner, Jon; Cantoni, Gina; Clair, Robert N. St. and Evangeline Parsons Yazzie (eds.)
1999   *Revitalizing Indigeneous languages.* Flagstaff, AZ: Northern Arizona University.
Royal Institut of the Amazigh Culture, The
2004   Information sheet on "The Royal Institut of the Amazigh Culture" (IRCAM). Rabat: IRCAM.
Sadiqi, Fatima
1998   Berber dialects/languages. Analysis of mutual intelligibility. *Notes and records* 6: 1–9.
Sebeok, Thomas A. (ed.).
1970   *Current trends in linguistics,* 6. The Hague, Paris: Mouton.
Souag, Lameen
2004   Writing Berber languages: a quick summary. (version 2.01.) http://www.geocities.com/lameens/tifinagh/
Tedghi, Joseph
2002   Usages de la graphie hébraëque dans la transcription des parlers ju-déo-arabes modernes au Maghreb. In Caubet; Chaker and Sibille (eds.) 415–441.
Tilmatinè, Mohand; el Molghy, Abdelghani; Castellanos, Carles and Hassan Ban-hakeia
1998   *La llengua rifenya. Tutlayt tarifit.* Bellaterra: Universitat Autònoma de Barcelona, Servei de Publicacions.
Tirosh-Becker, Ofra
1988   פונולוגיה ופרקים במורפולוגיה של תרגום תהילים בערבת-יהודית (אלג'יריה) מקונסטנט [The phonology and topics in the morphology of a Judeo-Arabic translation of the book of psalms from Constantine (Algeria)]. Master's Thesis, The Hebrew University of Jerusalem [in Hebrew].
1989   סוגיות לשוניות מן הערבית היהודית של קונסטנטון [A characterization of the Judeo-Arabic language of Constantine]. מסורות [Massrot] 3–4: 285–312 [in Hebrew].
Udovitch, Abraham L. and Lucette Valensi
1984   *The last Arab Jews.* The communities of Jerba, Tunisia. Chur, London, Paris, New York: Harwood Academic Publishers.
Vycichi, Werner
2005   *Berberstudien and a sketch of Siwi Berber* (Egypt). (Edited by Dymitr Ibriszimov and Maarten Kossmann) (*Berber studies,* 10). Cologne: Rüdiger Köppe.

Zafrani, Haïm
    1971   Judaeo-Berber. In Lewis, B., Ménage, V. L., Pellat, Ch. and J. Schacht
                (eds.) *The encyclopedia of Islam.* Leiden: Brill and London: Luzac and
                Co. 307–308.

Chapter 7
Endangered Languages in West Africa

Roger Blench

1. Introduction

1.1. Status of West African languages

Although the 1990s saw a substantial growth in concern for language endangerment, most notably in Asia and the Pacific, the African literature has been marked more by an expansion of comment than new descriptive materials. Wurm (1996) purportedly includes a map of endangered languages in West Africa, but since these are not identified by name, this is of limited value. Brenzinger (1998) represents a step towards identifying the gaps in the African literature and papers in that volume, such as Connell (1998) and Kastenholz (1998) provide case studies of threatened or moribund languages of West Africa. Typically, funding for fieldwork addresses issues of 'theoretical' interest rather than attempting to provide empirical data on endangered languages and suggest policies that might halt their decline.

Blench (1998) presents a summary of the status of the languages of the Middle Belt of Nigeria. The present paper[1] follows a similar format, but expands the canvas to cover the whole of West Africa, both listing endangered languages, analysing the sources of endangerment and likely impact of broadcast and literacy programmes on reversing endangerment trends. Dealing with a much larger database had made it necessary to extend and expand some of the categories used in the previous paper. The main changes are as follows;

a) The categories of language size have been extended at the upper end so that there is a category of 50,000–1,000,000 and then greater than 1,000,000.

b) Additional status categories of 'moribund' and 'declining' have been added

c) Because some languages are found in several countries, the database has been adapted to count the language when a national count is made, but to treat an individual language as a single record when other types of analysis are conducted.

1.2. The changing linguistic geography of West Africa

West Africa is considered to be all countries up to the border of Cameroon, including Mauretania, but excluding North African countries. The broad pattern of language distribution suggests that closer to the desert, the absolute number of languages is lower as is the numbers of their speakers. This cannot be entirely substantiated from the data used in this paper as languages such as *Berber* and *Arabic* are spoken principally outside West Africa. Unlike East Africa, where substantial numbers of pastoralists and hunter-gatherers persisted into recent times, there is a single group of hunter-gatherers in West Africa (the Nemadi) and essentially only two groups of pastoralists, the Fule and the Tamajeq. In addition, there are nomadic fishing peoples on the Niger River. Language distribution is thus overwhelmingly dominated by large and small farming groups. A consequence of this is that the constant shifting of subsistence strategy and thereby ethnic identity characteristic of small East African groups is largely absent in West Africa (see Tosco 1998 for a theoretical argument on this point). The most common causes of language endangerment are rather patterns of cultural and economic dominance.

The last decades of the 20th century have witnessed almost continuous warfare in some parts of the region, for example in the Casamance of Senegal, in Sierra Leone and spilling over sporadically into Liberia and Guinea-Bissau. The apparently stable Cote d'Ivoire has split North-South along ethnic lines leading to massive relocation of population and thus languages. Even minor skirmishes, such as that between Senegal and Mauretania, have resulted in the permanent departure of some ethnolinguistic groups and their replacement by others. Certain countries, such as Guinea, which has been relatively stable since the fall of the Sekou Touré government, have unwillingly become the semi-permanent home of refugees fleeing combat in neighbouring countries. The consequence is that numbers and locations are subject to change and survey data is best regarded as a timebound snapshot in unstable regions.

1.3. Data sources

The most important source of data is Ethnologue 2005[2] supplemented by the author's own fieldwork data in Nigeria, Mali and Ghana and by discussions with in-country scholars. The Ethnologue is regularly updated and draws extensively on unpublished field reports. However, it tends to accumulate spurious languages through individuals submitting unchecked or tendentious entries which once ensconced, become like persistent weeds, hard to eradicate. For example, the 1992 edition of Ethnologue attributed numerous languages to Nigeria which were in reality only spoken by small migrant communities in towns. I have thus tried to cross-check the data and eliminate uncertain entries as well as adding materials from other sources. *Table 1* shows the main non-Ethnologue sources drawn on for the data tables in this paper.

Table 1. Selected sources for additional data on West African languages

Country	References	Personal communications
Benin	Ceccaldi (1979)	Debbie Hatfield
Côte d'Ivoire	Ceccaldi (1978)	Bruce Connell,
		Jacques Rongier
Ghana		Tony Naden,
		Mary-Esther Kropp-Dakubu
Guinée		Tucker Childs
Mali		Robert Carlson,
		Lee Hochstetler,
		Denis Douyon
Nigeria	Temple (1922),	Bruce Connell,
	Shimizu (1983),	Kay Williamson (†),
	Crozier & Blench (1992)	Barau Kato,
	Kleinewillinghöfer (1996)	Andy Warren,
		Bernard Caron
Togo	Takassi (1983)	

Since the data analysed in Blench (1998) was collected, I have undertaken substantial new fieldwork in Central Nigeria, focussing on *Plateau* languages and on *Dogon* languages in Mali. In almost every case where a community was visited, published data on the population numbers, location and relative health of the language was found to be inaccurate. This rather suggests that standard references must be treated with a good deal of caution.

2. Language endangerment

2.1. The status of West African languages

To try and establish the distribution of endangered languages, a status was assigned to each language in the database. The Ethnologue rarely provides enough information to make such assignations unambiguously, and I have made a number of assumptions. These are;

a) Any language with over 50,000 speakers is 'not threatened'
b) Any language with under 400 speakers is 'definitely threatened'
c) Any language with fewer than 3,000 speakers without status data has been assigned to 'no information' on the grounds that it might well be threatened and should be made a priority for research.

Extracting sociolinguistic information from published sources is a problematic exercise; in some cases, where fieldwork is undertaken, it is possible to gain a sense of the reliability of the documentation. Thus the information in this paper for Ghana, Mali and Nigeria is probably more trustworthy than for the other countries, simply because I have conducted fieldwork in these countries and also talked to other researchers.

'Declining' and 'moribund' are categories introduced since my previous paper on Nigerian languages to try and capture languages that are apparently in decline despite having a viable number of speakers. The assumption is that there are many more languages in these classes and that further sociolinguistic surveys will clarify the status of individual speechforms. *Table 2* shows the numbers of languages assigned to each category on the basis of this revised categorization.

Table 2. Status of West African Languages

Status	*Number*
No information	304
Not threatened	683
Definitely threatened	55
Moribund	10
Probably extinct	16
Declining	7
Total	*1,075*

Perhaps the most depressing figure in *Table 2* is the large number of languages for which no reliable information is available. These are mostly small languages and therefore more likely to be threatened. The availability of information is extremely uneven, so the data was further analysed by country, as shown in *Table 3*. This illustrates yet again Nigeria's exceptional situation; its languages are less-known than any other country even in percentage terms.

Table 3. Distribution of languages with no status data by country

Country	Total languages	No data	% No data
Niger	11	0	0.0
Togo	39	4	10.3
Sierra Leone	21	1	4.8
Mali	44	5	11.4
Senegal	35	4	11.4
Guinea-Bissau	21	3	14.3
Ghana	66	9	13.6
Liberia	32	5	15.6
Mauretania	8	1	12.5
Burkina Faso	66	12	18.2
Côte d'Ivoire	78	15	19.2
Gambia	19	5	26.3
Guinea	28	8	28.6
Benin	50	16	32.0
Nigeria	553	216	39.1
Total and Mean	*1,071*	*304*	*28.4*

The explanation for this is simple; all other West African countries have had a fairly active programme of language survey conducted either by the French research establishment or by the SIL. In Nigeria, since the virtual cessation of SIL activities in 1976, very limited further survey work has been conducted.[3]

2.2. How accurate is existing data?

A curious consequence of the expansion of the endangered languages establishment is the adoption of unnecessarily pessimistic assessments. The apparent preconditions for language death set up negative expectations that may well be falsified by (rare) field surveys. For example, surveys of *Plateau* languages of Central Nigeria 1993–2006 showed that in almost every case, even languages with relatively small numbers of speakers appeared to be flourishing, despite gloomy prognostications of their disappearance (Blench, in press). By way of contrast, *Case study 1* gives an example of two related languages from the *Mambiloid* family of SE Nigeria which although they might appear prime candidates for endangerment are in fact thriving.

Case study 1: Mvanip and Ndunda
Roger Blench & Bruce Connell: Survey notes 1999

Meek (1931) gives a short wordlist of a language he calls Magu, spoken at Zongo Ajiya town in the northwest of the Mambila Plateau in southeastern Nigeria. While undoubtedly a Mambiloid language, it seems to be distinct from Mambila proper. In Crozier & Blench (1992) the population is given as 'less than 10,000' and called 'Mvano'. Following a field visit in 1999 we ascertained how incorrect this information was. The Mvanɨp people are only 100 (chief's estimate) consisting of a few households in one quarter of Zongo Ajiya. Almost all individuals seemed to be fluent in the other languages of Zongo Ajiya, Fulfulde, Mambila and Ndoro. Despite this, the language seems to be alive – the Jauro (chief) assured us that the children still speak it, and we observed this to be true. A long wordlist was taped and there is no doubt this is the same language given in Meek as Magu.

When we asked for the language closest to Mvanɨp, to our surprise we were given the name of the Ndunda people. Ndunda is a village some 5 km. from Yerimaru, past Kakara on the tea estate road south of Zongo Ajiya. And indeed, there proved to be a people and language of this name whose existence has so far entirely eluded the reference books. Their language resembles Mvanɨp but the two are sufficiently distinct as to be considered separate languages. There are probably 3–400 speakers of Ndunda and the language is also alive and well, although the Ndunda settlement is much more ethnically homogeneous than Zongo Ajiya.

Mvanɨp and Ndunda would appear to be prime candidates for language loss. Their numbers are very small, and the populations live in close proximity to prestigious and numerically dominant languages associated with Islam. However, they seem to have developed a situation of stable multilingualism and religious synthesis that allows them to conserve their traditions without seeming anomalous to outsiders. In contrast to the Yangkam (see *Case study 2*), the Mambila Plateau is off major trade routes and remains highly inaccessible even in modern Nigeria.

The conclusions to be drawn from this are that much of the published, repeated and re-analysed data on the numbers, location and status of minority languages is highly inaccurate. Secondly, our understanding and thus our ability to predict relative levels of language endangerment is very limited. The plethora of models to describe the theory of language endangerment that accompany every worried text have very limited applications to the survey and analysis of actual endangered languages.

3. Affiliation and distribution of West African languages

3.1. How many languages are spoken in each country?

Assessing the number of languages spoken in each country for analytical purposes is not quite the same as simply taking the Ethnologue figures at face value. Ethnologue tends to 'split' languages; in other words, language chains with high degrees of inter-intelligibility tend to appear as separate head entries. This is particularly the case with widespread languages such as *Arabic* and *Fulfulde*, which have two, three or more entries for each country in which they are spoken. Similarly, the Ethnologue includes sign or deaf languages and also colonial languages now used for national administrative purposes.[4] Ethnolgue (2005) now lists 'immigrant' languages separately in its national statistical tables. *Table 4* shows total language numbers for West African countries, but;

   a) Excludes languages spoken in most countries (*English, French, Arabic, Fulfulde*) but treats *Portuguese* as part of the inventory of the country where it is spoken
   b) Includes creoles as *Indo-European* languages the countries where they are spoken.[5]
   c) Registers cross-border languages for each country where they are spoken (the overall total thus includes significant double-counting)

Table 4. Total of languages spoken in each country (for this analysis)

Country	Number	Country	Number	Country	Number
Throughout	4	Mali	44	Ghana	66
Mauretania	8	Guinea	28	Burkina Faso	66
Niger	11	Liberia	32	Côte d'Ivoire	78
Gambia	19	Senegal	35	Nigeria	553
Guinea-Bissau	21	Togo	39		
Sierra Leone	21	Benin	50	*Total*	*1,075*

Eliminating multiple counts for widespread languages gives a total number of languages for West Africa of ca. 1,000. The predominance of Nigeria as a percentage of all languages will continue to skrew this analysis. Were the survey to include Cameroun with 279 languages and Chad with 132, the distribution would look more balanced. In analysing this type of data, much depends on where the boundaries are drawn.

On the basis of this, it seems useful to calculate approximately how many speakers a typical West African language has. Human population statistics are always highly controversial; some countries have only highly politicised speculative estimates while others have reasonably careful counts. The population figures in *Table 5* are from Ethnologue (2005) and are significantly more conservative than UN estimates. Countries are sorted in descending order, with those with the most speakers per language heading the table.

Table 5. Mean no. speakers per language in West African countries

Country	Population	Mean no. speakers per language
Niger	9,230,862	439,565
Mauretania	2,725,734	302,859
Ghana	20,119,660	242,406
Senegal	9,479,825	231,215
Sierra Leone	4,739,450	189,578
Guinea	6,747,526	174,935
Nigeria	90,026,548	174,470
Total and Mean	*185,322,189*	*172,125*
Mali	9,031,529	167,251
Burkina Faso	11,019,638	159,705
Benin	6,449,442	117,263
Côte d'Ivoire	9,220,274	100,220
Togo	3,978,381	94,723
Liberia	2,63,817	79,478
Guinea-Bissau	1,439,995	57,600
Gambia	1,113,325	50,606

For comparison, the figures for Cameroun and Chad are;

| Cameroun | 9,638,055 | 34,442 |
| Chad | 5,909,406 | 44,432 |

There is little doubt that we can identify broad ecological determinants for these differing language densities; desert countries such as Niger and Mauretania the highest number of speakers per language while countries dominated by humid coastal forest, the lowest. Nonetheless, nation-states are not generally divided into neat ecological units; countries such as Nigeria encompass tropical rain-forest and sand-dunes, and even Togo and Benin have a wide range of environmental conditions within their borders.

3.2. How many speakers do West African languages have?

West African languages were divided into a number of size classes, based on the most recent estimates available. Given the uncertainty as to the veri-similitude of these estimates it seemed appropriate to make the boundaries of each size-class quite generous. *Table 6* show the numbers and percentages assigned to each size class;

Table 6. Size classes of West African languages

Size class	Number
< 400	74
400–3,000	81
3,000–50,000	426
50,000–1,000,000	168
1,000,000 +	267
Unknown	59
Total	*1,075*

Without detailed sociolinguistic information it is hard to make an overall estimate of the numbers of endangered languages, but clearly any language with less than 3,000 speakers (i. e. 155) is potentially threatened.

3.3. Genetic affiliation of West African languages

Despite the linguistic diversity of West Africa, at the phylic level it is quite uniform. *Niger-Congo* languages dominate most countries and constitute 85 % of all languages spoken there. Only Nigeria has a substantial element of another phylum, *Afroasiatic. Table 7* presents a broad outline of the phyla and language families present in the West African region, with examples of specific languages;

Table 7. Genetic classification of the languages of West Africa

Phylum	Family	Examples
Niger-Congo	Mande	Mandinka, Busa
	West Atlantic	Fulfulde, Wolof, Bijogo, Kissi
	Dogon	Donno So, Tomo So
	Ijoid	Kalabari, Kolokuma
	Kru	Dan, Wobe, Seme
	Gur	Moore, Dagbane, Gulmancema, Bariba
	Adamawa	Chamba Leeko, Mumuye, [Kim, Mundang]
	Ubangian	Gbaya, [Zande, Ngbandi]
	Kwa	Akan, Ewe, Akebu, Gun
	Benue-Congo W.	Yoruba, Nupe, Igbo, Idoma, Bini
	Benue-Congo E.	Kamberi, Tyap, Birom, Jukun, Efik
	Bantoid N.	Mambila, Samba Daka
	Bantoid S.	Tivoid, Beboid
	Bantu	Jarawan, Ekoid
Afroasiatic	W. Chadic	Hausa, Angas, Mwaghavul,
	Central Chadic	Bacama, Huba
	Semitic	Shuwa Arabic
	Berber	Tamachek
Nilo-Saharan	Saharan	Kanuri, Teda
	Songhai	Zarma
Unclassified		Jalaa, Bagi Me

Languages in [] are not spoken in the sampled region

'*Dogon*' is not recognised in standard reference works. The *Dogon* languages are a separate branch of *Niger-Congo* and are highly internally diverse (Williamson and Blench 2000; Hochstetler *et al.* 2004). *Table 8* shows the numbers of languages in each major language family.

Table 8. Genetic affiliation of West African languages

Language family	Number	Language family	Number
Berber	5	Indo-European	9
Semitic	5	Unclassified	10
Saharan	7	Songhay	13
Ijoid	8	Dogon	19

Table 8. cont.

Language family	Number	Language family	Number
Kru	45	Mande	100
Adamawa-Ubangian	46	Chadic	125
West Benue-Congo	63	Gur	136
Atlantic	84	East Benue-Congo	305
Kwa	95	*Total*	*1,075*

Afroasiatic consists almost entirely of *Chadic* languages, including other-wise only *Arabic* and *Berber*. The category 'unclassified' usually implies simply a lack of data for a language known to exist. Data exists for two languages, *Jalaa* and *Bagi Me*, which appear to be truly unclassifiable.

3.4. Sources of language endangerment

In general, West African languages are in a healthy state. Compared to Eastern and Southern Africa, only a few languages are disappearing. The clear contrast with East Africa almost certainly reflects the dominance of smallholder farming systems. A lack of mobility and a relative inflexibility in reinventing subsistence strategies tends to conserve language and maintain classic patterns of diversification such as areal spread and dialect chains. Language endangerment in West Africa generally occurs through language shift, which usually reflects the rise of a dominant culture, former-ly military, but often nowadays commercial or religious. This is particularly the case with Islam; conversion to Islam was historically associated with the rise of highly militarised cultures and indeed the slave trade. Thus, *Hausa, Arabic, Mandinka, Bambara, Fulfulde* and *Kanuri* have all been associated with aggressive expansionism and the forcible conversion of enslaved peoples. In the colonial era, the convenience of these languages was such that they were frequently adopted as secondary languages of communication. Promoted by the administration they became ever more the vehicle of assimilatory forces pressing on minority languages.

Case study 2 illustrates the case of *Yangkam*, a language of Central Nigeria that is severely endangered through the association of its people with Islamic expansion during the nineteenth century.

Case study 2: Why is Yangkam is disappearing?
Roger Blench: fieldnotes 1997

The Yangkam people live in a region west of Bashar town, on the Amper-Bashar road, in Plateau State, Central Nigeria. They are known as 'Bashar' or 'Basherawa' (the Hausaised name for the people) in the existing literature (Greenberg 1963; Crozier & Blench 1992). The correct name of the Bashar language and people is YàNkàm, plural aYaNkam. Crozier and Blench (1992) give a figure of 20,000 speakers of the language located in and around Bashar town, some 50 km east of Amper on the Muri road. Fieldwork in 1997 showed this estimate turned out to be entirely erroneous. Yangkam society was transformed by nineteenth century slave raiding, perhaps by the Jukun as well as the Hausa. The Yangkam converted to Islam and a relatively powerful political and trading centre was established at Bashar. At the same time they began to switch to speaking Hausa, while still retaining strongly their Bashar identity. In the region of Bashar town in 1997, there were just two old men who remain reasonably fluent in the language, in the village of Yuli some 15 km northwest of Bashar. However, at the time of the raids, the population split into two and another group sought refuge in Tukur, west of Bashar. Yangkam is spoken in some four villages, Tukur, Bayar, Pyaksam and Kiram. Even here Yangkam is only spoken by people over fifty and all the young people speak Hausa. There seems to be no likelihood that Yangkam will be maintained as speakers are quite content with the switch to Hausa. The local estimate of the number of fluent speakers is 400, and falling every year. In many hamlets around Bashar town in Wase local Government the populations are ethnically Yangkam but they no longer speak the language.

Yangkam is something of a paradox; members of the ethnic group are very proud of their history and identity, but do not associate them with retention of the language. Hausa is not spoken as a first language by any populations nearby and Bashar is today well off major routes for long-distance trade. A typescript of the history of Bashar circulates in the district, larded with non-Hausa names and words but Yangkam do not draw the conclusion that there is any link between this identity and the language they formerly spoke. Although Yangkam has nearly disappeared as a language, the populations who formerly spoke it are likely to retain Basherawa and Basheranci as their name for the people and language as long as they retain a separate identity.

The expansion of *Hausa* represents a confluence of Islam, political and military power and a high level of proficiency in establishing trade networks. But not all large vehicular languages in West Africa were the products of Islamization; *Moore, Yoruba, Efik/Ibibio, Akan* and *Wolof* seem to have expanded, often in a military context, but prior to or unrelated to Islam. Interestingly, these languages have been less successful in the post-colonial phase of cultural expansion, suggesting that a less pluralistic engine of expansion made the transition to a trade language was more difficult than for the *Hausa* or *Bambara*. These languages had the resources to reinvent themselves when the military option was exhausted. Islam, as also Christianity, has always had long-distance trade as a second arrow in its quiver. Languages with a prior embedded trade and institutional vocabulary recommended themselves to colonial administrators. Cultures with less orientation towards commerce meant that their associated vehicular languages made more limited inroads in an era of relative peace.

4. Broadcasting, literacy programmes and their impact

One guilty party usually identified by morbilinguophiles is urbanization; as individuals and households move to the cities, they lose their languages and switch to dominant speech-systems.[6] There is no doubt that this is partly true, especially during the great afflux to cities in the third part of the twentieth century. However, city culture also has interesting countervailing tendencies. It provides access to communications technology, most recently FM radio, which can sometimes act to support language maintenance. In Mali and Northern Ghana, commercial broadcasting in minority languages has become a major growth area and has acted dramatically to increase the prestige of indigenous languages.[7] If a language can be adapted to 'modern' life it paradoxically gains more prestige in rural areas. Broadcasts then become a major channel for neologisms and syntax changes to reach rural areas. A likely consequence, as in Western Europe, is that broadcast media tend to eliminate local dialect variation,[8] but the experiment is too new in West Africa for any results to be measured.

Between overt government policy and ground reality huge chasms yawn invitingly. No government these days can be seen to be against minority languages, but few governments have the political will to actively support languages with small numbers of speakers. Most governments have some type of literacy bureau, proffering a few dusty pamphlets in major languages. One exception to this is Mali, which, through its agency DNAFLA, has tried to make use of a spectrum of funding sources to print primers, grammars, dictionaries for a wide variety of languages over several decades. Government involvement in literacy cuts both way; DNAFLA tried to establish a 'standard' *Dogon* that would effectively eliminate the other 20 *Dogon* languages from development (Hochstetler et al. 2004).

The reality is that literacy in minority languages is most likely to be driven by the resources of organizations, notably the SIL and its affiliates, who consider it a means to an end, in this case reading the Bible. For example, in Ghana, SIL (locally GILBTT) runs literacy programmes in some thirty-two languages and is actively researching the potential of the relatively few remaining minority languages. The Ghana Bureau of Languages, by contrast, offers one or two pamphlets in about ten languages, printed many years ago in now-discarded orthographies. An intriguing exception to this is Nigeria, where the size of the economy and the growth of ethnic consciousness among minorities has been responsible for a lively enthusiasm for local publishing, especially in the popular arena, focusing on proverbs, oral literature and reading and writing. Recent publications include Gochal (1994) on *Ngas*, Mamfa (1998) as well as Lar and Dandam (2002) on *Tarok* and Nyako (2000) on *Izere*. This type of publishing will probably continue to expand and take in more ethnolinguistic groups.

Whether externally-driven literacy programmes really do assist language maintenance is a moot point, as they can run into the sand with threatened languages. Almost by definition it is hardly worthwhile to spend limited resources on languages whose speakers seem to be deserting them; and most programmes thus focus on 'medium-scale' languages with a viable number of speakers. Nonetheless, the criteria for viability varies strikingly between continents. A language with less than 1,000 speakers in Africa looks seriously endangered and is unlikely to get literacy materials; such languages in New Guinea are regularly the subject of literacy programmes.

The definition of the unit of endangerment in language survey is often problematic and it is difficult to assess whether resources should be allocated to languages that are relatively close to vigorous speech-forms. The case of *Tchumbuli* in Benin is a case in point (*Case study 3*);

Case study 3: Tchumbuli

A report on the Tchumbuli language of Benin provides some information on a little-known and endangered speech-form (Schoch & Wolf 2001). Tchumbuli is a Northern Guang language spoken in three villages in the Departement de Collines between Savé and Ouessé. These villages are Okounfo, Gbede and Edaningbe and their total population is 3,500 individuals.

The origin of the Tchumbuli is complex; they are closely related to the Chumburung of NE Ghana and oral tradition suggests that they migrated to their present site in the mid eighteenth century. However, while in Ghana they absorbed the 'Cobecha', mercenaries from Benin (the precolonial state in Nigeria) who had come to fight in the Ashanti wars and halted on their way home. This ethnic distinction is maintained in the Tchumbuli communities in Benin Republic today, despite the homogeneity of the spoken language. To add to the confusion, in the 1950s an expedition led by their Paramount Chief returned with a number of families back to Ghana and settled in Anyinamae, near the present-day Chumburung community. Their language has effectively been relexified and absorbed back into Chumburung.

Tchumbuli is slowly dying as a result of contact with two major neighbouring languages, Maxi and Cabe. Maxi is part of the Fon group while Cabe is a type of Yoruba, closely related to that spoken across the border in Nigeria. In Okounfo village, the switch to Cabe has occurred, with pervasive bilingualism and Tchumbuli only known to the older generation. In Edaningbe, Maxi is replacing Tchumbuli although a more complex ethnic mixture in the village means that the process of replacement is less straightforward. In Gbede, Tchumbuli remains widely spoken although Cabe is used to communicate with outsiders and appears to be spreading among younger children.

The total number of speakers of Tchumbuli was estimated at 1838, and although this is relatively high compared with many other threatened languages in West Africa, it conceals the fact that the language is largely confined to the older generation. Paradoxically, the Tchumbuli are proud of their historical traditions and their links with Ghana. Tchumbuli illustrates the problem of how much weight to give to languages close to those that are not threatened. Tchumbuli is sufficiently close to Chumburung for linguists to classify it as a dialect. However, the results of complex interactions with Maxi and Cabe and the very different cultural traditions of the Tchumbuli have made the language quite distinct above the level of fundamental vocabulary.

Many of the factors responsible for language endangerment are contingent; they cannot necessarily be predicted from sociological variables nor prevented by well-meaning programmes. War and social disruption have been key forces displacing populations, fragmenting speech communities and prematurely ending the life of speech communities. But refugees are refugees, it would hardly be appropriate to suggest specialised assistance for those speaking threatened languages. The forces of globalization similarly depend on political stability and also the macro-economic order. It is hard to listen to the government radio station if you can't afford the batteries.

5. The research agenda

It would be pleasant to report, that West African languages, especially those endangered by language shift, were the focus of a lively research effort. But this is far from the case; indeed the opposite is true. Why should this be so?

First and foremost, because of the moribund research establishment in African universities. Political insecurity in many countries has made it difficult for universities and other institutions to function at all. Many West African universities are in decay and staff morale is low, in part because of

uncertain pay and conditions, but also because of a lack of support for research. The other body with a record of interest in research, the Summer
Institute of Linguistics, now tends to regard academic publication as a low
priority. Little has appeared in recent years, although the situation is
patchy; Mali for example, still tries to encourage academic publication of
results. The impact of the Euro-American research establishment is also
limited for rather different reasons. Research increasingly uses expatriate
and out-of-context informants, despite the oft-publicised danger of this
approach. The declining economies of the region and the more commercial approach of Euro-American universities has meant that many fewer
speakers of minority languages are visiting or studying in Europe and
America. This illustrates all too starkly the neo-colonial nature of fashion-
able linguistics, which takes no interest in languages for themselves, merely for their potential contribution to passing seminar-room fashion. Despite much talk, the institutions that purportedly encourage *Endangered
Languages* research have eccentric priorities, to judge by their profile in
Nigeria, which has by far the largest number of endangered languages in
Africa. Although fieldwork in Africa *is* still supported, the negative image
of Nigeria deters many fieldworkers and for a country that has more than
one-quarter of all African languages, research is at vanishingly low levels.

6. Conclusion

The situation of minority languages in West Africa can be summarised as
follows;

a) The information base remains extremely weak for many countries
b) Survey work is not a high priority for governments or academics
   within West African countries, while research by outside scholars is
   apparently declining
c) SIL surveys are useful but certainly do not focus directly on language
   endangerment issues, although policy is changing in this area.
d) Government policy usually has little to say about endangered languages although what policies exist are generally in favour of indigenous languages
e) However, government action in this area tends to be weak or non-ex-
   istent
f) Nonetheless, what evidence there is suggests that West African languages are generally holding their own in the face of globalization
   and the homogenising forces of the twenty-first century

Appendix: Endangered languages in West Africa

The following table does not include languages that are probably extinct.

Table 9. Annotated list of severely threatened languages in West Africa

Country Languages	Comment
Nigeria	
Akpondu	Moribund
Bade	Still a large number of speakers but giving way rapidly to Hausa. Probably also Duwai.
Bakpinka	No recent information
Defaka	About 200 speakers. Those in direct contact with Nkoroo are losing their language
Dulbu	Giving way to Hausa
Dyarim	Ca. 100 fluent speakers. Giving way to Hausa
Fyem	Giving way to Hausa
Geji cluster	Several hundred speakers of each member of the cluster. Giving way to Hausa
Gera	Giving way to Hausa
Gura	Giving way to Hausa
Gurdu-Mbaaru	Giving way to Hausa
Gyem	Giving way to Hausa
Ilue	Giving way to Efik/Oron
Jilbe	A single village (Tourneux p.c.)
Kiong	Giving way to Efik. Moribund
Kona	Giving way to Hausa
Kudu-Camo	42 speakers in early 1990s (Bross p. c.) Giving way to Hausa
Luri	Only 2 speakers remained in 2003
Mvanip	About 100 speakers in 1999.
Ndunda	<400 speakers in 1999
Ngwaba	Two villages in 1991
Odut	Only about 20 speakers in early 1980s
Polci cluster	Giving way to Hausa
Reshe	Still a vigorous speech community at present but giving way to Hausa

Table 9. cont.

Country Languages	Comment
Nigeria (cont.)	
Sambe	2 very elderly speakers in 2005. The language is giving way to Ninzo.
Country Languages	Comment
Somyev	About 20 elderly speakers in 1995 (Connell 1995 and p. c.).
Yangkam	About 2-300 older speakers in 1993.
Zeem/Tule/ Danshe	These languages are probably extinct (Caron p. c. 2005).
Cote d'Ivoire	
Ega	est. 1,000 speakers in 1999. The population is switching to Dida.
Eotile	200 speakers in 1999. The population is switching to Anyi.
Jeri Kuo	According to Kastenholz (1998: 259) there are 1,500 speakers from an ethnic population of 20,000. The Muslims are switching to Manding, the non-Muslim to Sienare Senufo. See also Kastenholz (1992).
Mali	
Banka	5,085 ethnic population in 1995, but the population is switching to Bambara.
Nemadi	The Nemadi migrate between Mauretania and Mali. There were 200 in 1977. Their language is reported to be Hassaniya Arabic with only some technical terms of unknown source and is probably not 'endangered'.
Sierra Leone	
Bom	250 speakers out of an ethnic group of 5,000 in 1991. The population is switching to Mende.
Mmani	Only a few speakers out of 6,800 in the ethnic group in 1988. The population is switching to Temne.
Krim	500 speakers or fewer out of an ethnic group of 10,000 in 1990. The population is switching to Sherbro and Temne.
Mauretania	
Imeraguen	534 speakers in 2000. No recent information.

Table 10. Unclassified languages in West Africa

Country Languages	Comment
Côte d'Ivoire	
Mbre	Niger-Congo language of unknown affiliation.
Mauretania	
Imeraguen	534 (2000). Near Nouakchott, the region stretching from Cape Timiris to Nouadhibou. Unclassified. The language is reported to be a variety of Hassaniyya structured on an Azer (Soninke) base.
Mali	
Bagi Me[9]	Ca. 2,000 speakers in 2005. Language isolate.
Nigeria	
Kofa	Unknown but possibly Chadic language spoken north of Yola.
Jalaa	Moribund. Language isolate.

Sources: either quoted directly from Ethnologue 2005 or personal observation in West Africa.

1	Imeraguen	18	Polci
2	Mmani	19	Dulbu
3	Bom Krim	20	Luri
4	Nemadi	21	Guruntum-Mbaaru
5	Banka	22	Dugusa
6	Jeri Kuo	23	Fyem
7	Ega	24	Yangkam
8	Eotile	25	Sambe
9	Tchumbuli	26	Kona
10	Reshe	27	Mvanp
11	Bade	28	Ndunda
12	Kudu-Camo	29	Somyev
13	Gura	30	Bakpinka
14	Gyem	31	Odut Kiong
15	Gera	32	Defaka
16	Ngwaba	33	Ilue
17	Jilbe		

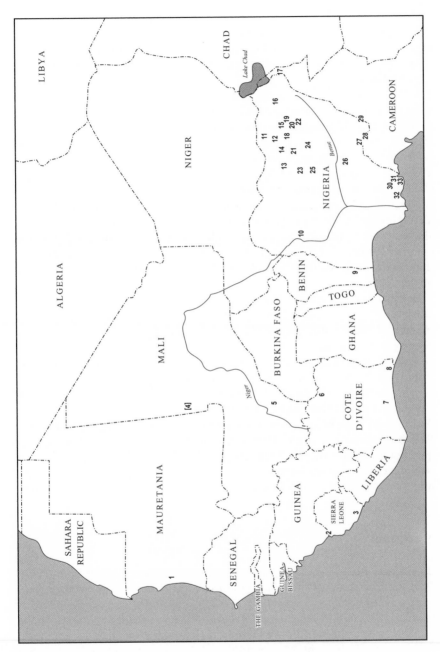

Map 9. West Africa

Notes

1. The original version of this paper was submitted prior to the Bad Godesborg meeting but has been amended in April 2005 to include five additional years' data from subsequent field trips. My thanks to all those in listed in Table 1 for unpublished field data.
2. The 15th Edition of Ethnologue online edition includes much of the new data from the period 2001–2005. However, this paper includes materials collected subsequent to the deadline for closure of submissions.
3. Regrettably an attempt to restart survey work in Nigeria in 2001 was stalled by policy problems in the relevant institutions.
4. This is not to say that *French, English* or *Portuguese* should be excluded, especially as they are clearly the first language of a large number of resident expatriates and are increasingly becoming the 'home' language of city families.
5. This is highly controversial linguistically, since many standard creoles are considered to be better analysed as African languages heavily relexified from the external (usually I–E) language. However, for the purposes of this analysis they can be excluded from the count of African languages assigned to specific phyla.
6. I use this term advisedly; in Nigeria at least, the would-be urban migrant usually has to contend with at least two 'duelling' languages, for example, *Hausa* or *Yoruba* and *English*. Effective communication skills usually involve rapid code-switching between these.
7. Nigeria has long had government broadcasts in numerous languages, especially from state capitals. However, these seem to have had much less impact than commercial stations, presumably because the desire of government to control content has made them much less interesting for listeners.
8. At the same time, broadcast media may well act to spread new speech-styles. Within England, *'Estuary English'* has undoubtedly been diffused as a consequence of its dominance in the media.
9. New data can be downloaded at:
   http://www.rogerblench.info/Linguistics%20papers%20opening%20page.htm

References

Blench, Roger M.
   1998   The status of the languages of Central Nigeria. In Brenzinger (ed.) 187–205.
   in press. *Plateau languages – state of the art.* Papers from the conference on the retirement of Ludwig Gerhardt, Hamburg 2004. T. Schumann (ed.) Available at: http://homepage.ntlworld.com/roger_blench/Unpublished %20papers%20 Languages.htm

Brenzinger, Matthias (ed.)
1998   *Endangered languages in Africa.* Köln: Rüdiger Köppe.
Ceccaldi, Pierrette
1978   *Essai de nomenclature des populations, langues et dialectes de Côte d'Ivoire.* Paris: EHESS, CEA, CARDAN.
1979   *Essai de nomenclature des populations, langues et dialectes de la république populaire du Bénin.* Paris: EHESS, CEA, CARDAN.
Connell, Bruce
1995   *Dying languages and the complexity of the Mambiloid group.* Paper presented at the 25th Colloquium on African Languages and Linguistics, Leiden. Abstract available electronically at: http://lucy.ukc.ac.uk/dz/index.html.
1998   Moribund languages of the Nigeria-Cameroon borderland. In Brenzinger (ed.) 207–225.
Crozier, David and Roger M. Blench
1992   *Index of Nigerian languages (edition 2).* Dallas: SIL. [N.B. an electronic third edition is available at: http://homepage.ntlworld.com/roger_blench/Language%20data/ composite%20Index%20of%20Nigerian%20Languages%20ed. %20III.pdf).
Gordon, R.
2005   *Ethnologue (15th edition),* Dallas: Summer Institute of Linguistics.
Grimes, Barbara F.
2000   *Ethnologue (14th edition),* Dallas: Summer Institute of Linguistics.
Hochstetler, J. Lee, Durieux, J. A. and E. I. K. Durieux-Boon
2004   *Sociolinguistic survey of the Dogon language area.* SIL International. Available at: http://www.sil.org/silesr/2004/silesr2004-004.pdf
Kastenholz, Raimund
1992   Une première note sur le jeri.kuo (langue mandé des Jeri): Repartition géographique et matériel lexical. *Cahiers Ivoiriens de Recherche Linguistique,* 29: 19–60.
1998   Language shift and language death among Mande blacksmiths and leatherworkers in the diaspora. In Brenzinger (ed.) 253–266.
Kleinewillinghöfer, Uli
1996   Die nordwestlichen Adamawasprachen – eine Übersicht. *Frankfurter Afrikanistische Blätter,* 8: 81–104.
Shimizu, K.
1983   Die Jarawan-Bantusprachen des Bundesstaates Bauchi, Nordnigeria. In Vossen Rainer and Ulrike Claudi (eds.) *Sprache Geschichte und Kultur in Afrika.* Hamburg: Buske. 291–301.
Takassi, Issa
1983   *Inventaire linguistique du Togo.* Abidjan: ILA/ACCT.

Temple, O.
  1922   *Notes on the tribes, provinces, emirates and states of the Northern Provinces of Nigeria.* Lagos: CMS Bookshop.
Tosco, Mauro
  1998   "People who are not the language they speak". On language shift without language decay in East Africa. In Brenzinger (ed.) 207–225.
Williamson, Kay and Roger Blench
  2000   Niger-Congo. In Nurse, Derek and Bernd Heine (eds.) *African languages.*. Cambridge: Cambridge University Press. 11–42.
Wolf, K. and G. Schoch
  2001   *A sociolinguistic survey of the Tchumbuli language area.* Unpublished report. SIL, Cotonou, Benin.
Wurm, Stephen A. (ed.)
  1996   *Atlas of the world's languages in danger of disappearing.* Canberra/Paris: Pacific Linguistics/UNESCO.

Chapter 8
Endangered Languages in Central Africa[1]

Bruce Connell

1. Introduction

Research done over the last 10–15 years and documented primarily in two collections edited by Brenzinger (Brenzinger 1992, 1998), as well as a number of individual papers scattered in the literature (particularly Brenzinger, Heine and Sommer 1991), appears to show that the situation regarding language endangerment in Africa may be less dire than that reported for a great many other parts of the world. This however is not to suggest that all is fine with African languages; one of the reasons for this perception may be that language shift in Africa often involves the adoption of another African language rather than that of a European colonial power, and as such may escape the eyes of many researchers whose primary interests are not in language endangerment *per se*.[2] A second, and more important, reason may be the relatively high degree of multilingualism found in many parts of Africa, which may tend to obscure the degree of language shift in progress. However perhaps most important, as other papers in this volume attest, to a large extent this perception may be no more than a reflection of our lack of knowledge of the linguistic situation in a great many parts of Africa; a lack of available information. In this chapter, I examine the question of language endangerment in Central Africa. The findings and conclusions presented here are based primarily on my own fieldwork, discussions with and contributions from colleagues and the small number of relevant published sources, in particular the online edition of the *Ethnologue* (Grimes 2000). Colleagues who have provided information through personal communications include Stephen Anderson, Keith Beavon, Roger Blench, Raymond Boyd, Ed Brye, Myles Leitch and Jim Roberts.

Several countries in the Central African region are not reported in the Ethnologue as having threatened languages, however, at the same time for these countries a great many languages are listed for which not even a population estimate is available. Many of these are revealed in the discussion below to be in what may be considered an endangered state. *Table 1* presents the countries which, for the purposes of this chapter, are considered

as comprising Central Africa, together with an estimate of the total population of the country, the number of languages spoken, the number believed
to be endangered, and those for which we have no relevant information. I
identify and include languages with fewer than 1,000 speakers as being endangered, though it should be pointed out that as a cut-off point this figure
is arbitrary. The number of known extinct languages is included in *Table 1*,
on the assumption that these represent relatively recent language deaths
and may therefore help give some indication as to the general situation in
each country. I tend to a pessimistic view with respect to those languages for
which there is no data: the absence of information in these cases may well
be indicative of the low status or prestige and small number of speakers that
lead to language endangerment. While this is obviously not always the case,
evidence confirming this view, at least in the case of certain languages in
Gabon and Congo, is given below. It is also possible that some of those languages for which no information is available may simply be alternative
names for languages for which data does exist, though it should be noted
that the Ethnologue does include alternative names where these are
known. Information in *Table 1* is drawn largely from Grimes (2000).

Before proceeding with the discussion of the current situation of language endangerment in Central Africa, it may be useful to have some
background on the geography and history of the region, since these factors are relevant to understanding the present situation and the vitality of
individual languages.

1.1. Geographical perspective

The area under consideration covers a large portion of the African continent, and the topographical and climatic variations found within this zone
are correspondingly diverse. The northern-most part of the region (i. e.
much of Chad and the extreme north of Cameroon) is desert; this gives
way to grasslands in Central African Republic (CAR), and then forest as
one approaches the equatorial zone. The southern part of Democratic
Republic of Congo (DRC) is mostly savanna. One also finds considerable
variation in altitude in Central Africa, from mountainous regions and dis-
sected plateaus, to lowland plains. Rivers have typically facilitated movement and defined trade routes in much of Central Africa, and populations
more distant from the trade routes have tended to be more isolated. Although there is no space to examine the issue in depth here, it is safe to
assume that geography has had a determining influence on the distribu-

tion of languages in the region, on their exposure to other languages, and consequently on their vitality. Evidence of this is presented below.

Table 1. Central African countries and basic language/population data. Population estimates from Grimes (2000)

Country	Population	Languages	Endangered languages	Data
Cameroon	14,305,000	286	7 with < 2,000 speakers; 31 with < 1,000 speakers (6 nearly extinct); 6 extinct	54
CAR	3,485,000	69	6 with < 2,000 speakers; 4 with < 1,000.	0
Chad	7,270,000	132	15 with < 2,000 speakers; 16 with < 1,000 speakers (5 nearly extinct); 2 extinct	15
Congo	2,785,000	61	None listed with < 2,000 speakers	30
DRC	49,139,000	219	3 with < 2,000 speakers; 4 with < 1,000 speakers; 1 extinct	65
Equatorial Guinea	431,000	13	1 with < 1,000 speakers	2
Gabon	1,167,000	41	2 with < 1,000 speakers	11

1.2. Historical perspective

It is well established that the Bantu languages have spread from a postu- lated homeland in the Nigeria-Cameroon borderland to the point where they now cover virtually all of sub-Equatorial Africa. There is also a con- sensus that this diffusion began at least 3,000 years ago, with some scholars arguing there is evidence to suggest the dispersal is more likely to have be- gun nearer to 4,000 years ago (e. g. Clist 1995). Much of the geographical area considered in this paper is now populated almost exclusively by *Bantu* languages (i. e. with the exclusion of Northern Cameroon, Chad, parts of CAR and northeastern DRC). Obviously then, the languages of the pre- Bantu inhabitants have been absorbed or replaced; a number of languages must have succumbed to the expansion of *Bantu*. In southern Africa, the *Khoisan* languages are generally considered to be remnants of languages that pre-existed the Bantu expansion. For Central Africa, most scholars of the region consider that the various hunter-gatherer (Pygmy) groups present constitute remnant populations, however there appear to be no real remnant languages, or indeed much evidence at all of those that must surely have existed. The Pygmies all speak the language of their immediate neighbours, whether *Bantu*, *Central Sudanic* or *Ubangian*. It is a matter of some controversy, though, whether distinct "Pygmy languages" ever existed, given this lack of evidence (see Blench 1999). It is beyond the limits of this paper to delve into this issue, so I simply note that the region in question would have been Bantu-ized early, possibly 2,000–4,000 years ago assuming a 4,000 year expansion, and that this time depth is quite probably sufficient for virtually all traces of pre-existing languages to have been obliterated, through obsolescence or absorption. Indeed it must be sufficient given that, as stated, there are no remnant languages in the region, Pygmy or otherwise, though there is no suggestion that the region was uninhabited prior to the *Bantu* expansion. This may be compared with southern Africa, where there are remnant languages, but which was only first touched by the *Bantu* expansion several hundred to a thousand years ago.

The *Bantu* expansion in a sense continues to have an effect on the linguistic make-up of Central Africa, particularly in the south-eastern region of this geographical zone, as *Swahili* spreads and replaces smaller languages. The effect *Swahili* has had on smaller languages in East Africa, in particular Tanzania, is already well documented (Batibo 1992; see also Wardhaugh 1987). Its influence continues to grow and spread.[3] A similar phenomenon is now in evidence in the western region of Central Africa, with the growth of *Lingala*.

Finally, a brief look at recent history, and the current situation. Many of the countries in the central African region have experienced serious conflict and warfare within the last two decades: Congo and the Democratic Republic of Congo are most notable among these, and the region has also been influenced by conflict in adjoining countries such as Angola, Burundi, Rwanda, and Sudan. It is not yet possible to assess the effect these conflicts have had on local languages. But it is apparent that a great many people – entire ethnic groups – have been driven from their homelands and dispersed, with the potential loss of group cohesiveness and consequent weakening of the linguistic base.

2. Linguistic structure of Central Africa

2.1. Distribution of languages by phyla

Four major language phyla are found in Africa, *Niger-Congo*, *Afroasiatic*, *Nilo-Saharan*, and *Khoisan*. Languages from three of the four are found in Central Africa, though only two, *Niger-Congo* and *Nilo-Saharan*, are widespread in the region, and only *Niger-Congo* is found in all countries. *Afroasiatic* languages are found in Chad and the northern part of Cameroon, while *Khoisan* doesn't extend far enough north to be included in the region under study though, as already noted, many scholars assume that the *Khoisan* languages were at one time more widespread. *Table 2* shows the number of languages per phyla in each of the countries under consideration.

Table 2. Languages in Central Africa by phyla and by country

Country	Niger-Congo	Afro-asiatic	Nilo-Saharan	Un-classified	Total
Cameroon	217	60	6	1	284
CAR	51	0	14	1	66
Chad	24	53	48	2	127
Congo	58	0	0	0	58
DRC	194	0	24	0	218
Eq. Guinea	8	0	0	1	9
Gabon	39	0	0	0	39
Total	*591*	*113*	*92*	*5*	*801*

Proportionally, Niger-Congo comprises two thirds of the total language population of Central Africa; most of these belong to two branches within *Niger-Congo, Adamawa-Ubangi* and *Benue-Congo*, and of these almost half are *Narrow Bantu* languages. Indeed all, or virtually all, the languages of Equatorial Guinea, Gabon, Congo, and Democratic Republic of Congo, are *Narrow Bantu*.

2.2. Demographic breakdown

It is also of interest to view the number of languages per country against the population of the country; that is, a breakdown in terms of average number of speakers per language, and the number of languages within a given range of speakers. *Table 3* shows this information. In considering the information in this table, it should be borne in mind that many languages are spoken on both sides of a national frontier, or even in three and sometimes four countries. It should be reiterated that although I have arbitrarily set fewer than 1,000 speakers as indicative of a language being

endangered, the number of speakers is by no means a sure way of evaluating the vitality of language – at least one case discussed below provides
evidence of this.

Table 3. Average number of speakers per language and number of languages
by size class for Central African languages

Country	Average	1,000	2,000	10,000	50,000	50,000+	Unknown
Cameroon	51,000	22	7	56	66	133	46
CAR	50,500	3	3	15	19	26	0
Chad	55,900	7	10	18	39	48	5
Congo	45,700	0	0	10	14	19	15
DRC	224,400	2	3	26	49	84	54
Eq. Guinea	33,150	0	1	4	2	1	1
Gabon	28,460	2	0	14	13	6	4

3. Language endangerment in Central Africa

It has often been assumed that the languages of much of Central Africa
are relatively stable, in part due to their relative isolation one from another. This view is reflected in the information gleaned from the *Ethnologue*
and examined above, which showed for several countries (Equatorial
Guinea, Gabon, Congo, and DRC) little or no indication of threatened
languages, and indeed few if any languages with less than 2,000 speakers.
Recently gathered information shows there is greater need for concern
than previously thought. The following subsections attempt to give an impression of language endangerment in selected Central African countries.
I emphasize the impressionistic nature of these reports.

3.1. Congo

Congo is one Central African country for which no endangered languages
have been reported. *Bonjo* is one of the Congolese languages for which no
population figures are given in the *Ethnologue*. It is presented here as being representative of what constitutes an endangered language in Congo.
Bonjo is a *Bantu* language (C10) spoken in and around the regional capital
of Impfondo (Likouala Region), on the Ubangi River. Recent reports

from the field (Myles Leitch, personal communication) suggest *Bonjo* has 2,000-3,000 speakers and that it is subject to severe competition from *Lingala*, a regional lingua franca and trade language. *Lingala* is spoken by an estimated 300,000 people in Congo, but its primary population base is in DRC; its total population, including second language speakers, numbers several million. It has had a preferred position in the region going back to early colonial times, if not farther, when its use was promoted by the Belgians in preference to other smaller local languages (or *French*). *Bonjo* is still spoken by the young generation of adults, though it is increasingly used for ceremonial and symbolic purposes only. *Lingala* is learned and used as primary language by children. Indeed, *Lingala* appears to be gaining the upper hand on a number of local languages; a similar shift, for example, is underway among *Teke* speakers near Brazzaville. (*Teke* is a relatively large language, with roughly half a million speakers in Congo; the dialect in question has approximately 5,000 speakers.) On the other hand, an example of a small language in Congo that is relatively stable is *Babole* (Bantu C20; population 3,000–4,000). Unlike *Bonjo*, *Babole* is holding its own against *Lingala*, despite the fact that all Babole also speak *Lingala*. *Lingala*, though, is not typically used in the Babole region among Babole, who maintain a high degree of pride in their own language. The differentiating factor between *Babole* and *Bonjo* appears to be location with respect to a strong center of trade language dominance; historically, and today, the major trade route in Congo followed the Congo and Ubangi Rivers. This is the region where *Lingala* and its influence are strongest.

Another Congolese language for which some information is available is *Mbosi* (Bantu C30). *Mbosi* is spoken by approximately 200,000 people – over 10 % of the population of Congo – and as such we would expect it to be not under threat at the present time. Reports are, however, somewhat to the contrary, as *Mbosi* appears to be giving way on two fronts. *Mbosi* speakers also know *Lingala, Teke* and *French*; now, multilingualism in itself does not constitute a threat (one might argue it is the solution to language endangerment), but in this case the youngest generation in the urban centers now tends not to use or learn *Mbosi*, though those in the villages still do. *Lingala* is again the local lingua franca and trade language, and *French* is of course used in government offices, schools, and churches (Ruth Chatfield, personal communication). While the situation in Congo is said not to be as worrisome as elsewhere in Central Africa, this assessment seems in need of revision: *Mbosi* is likely to be either typical of languages in Congo or on the 'healthy' end of the spectrum; evidence that it is in the early stages of decline does not bode well for the Congolese situation in general.

3.2. Gabon

The situation in Gabon appears to be worthy of greater cause for concern than that in neighbouring countries. The languages listed for Gabon for which no population figures were available in the *Ethnologue*, or which were said to have approximately 1,000 speakers, are: *Bwisi* (also spoken in Congo), *Kande, Mahongwe, Sake, Sighu*, and *Vumbu*. Recent reports (Leitch personal communication) reveal that of these all but *Bwisi* appear to be seriously threatened. All are underdocumented. Current population estimates for these are as follows:

Kande (B30): less than 1,000 speakers
Mahongwe (B20): less than 1,000 speakers
Sake (B20): very small group
Sighu (B20): several hundreds only
Vumbu (B20): several hundreds only

Another Gabonese language, *Benga* (A30), is identified by linguists in Gabon as the most advanced case of language contraction. While the *Ethnologue* lists this language as having 3,000 speakers, most of whom are in Equatorial Guinea, in Gabon there are said to be only small groups of older speakers remaining. Since the Benga areas in the two countries are contiguous, pending information to the contrary it is prudent to assume the language may not be faring much better in Equatorial Guinea.

The three main factors contributing to language endangerment in Gabon are identified as:

(i) Urbanization: there has been sizeable migration away from tribal homelands to the capital Libreville, resulting in the break-up of linguistic communities, increased use of lingua francas, and lower prestige of local languages.

(ii) The impact of French colonization: the strong and sustained influence of French culture, language and politics has contributed to a massive devaluing of local languages.

(iii) The oil-based economy: this underlies the other two factors, with all three working together to undermine respect for and use of local languages.

The encouraging news from Gabon is that local linguists, together with SIL workers, are beginning to take interest in the situation of indigenous Gabonese languages.

3.3. Cameroon

After Nigeria, Cameroon is the most linguistically heterogeneous country in Africa – in fact, if considered in terms of languages per capita, Cameroon is more complex than Nigeria. The *Ethnologue* information presents Cameroon as the Central Africa country with the most worrisome situation: 31 languages with fewer than 1,000 speakers, six of which are said to be nearly extinct, and another 54 for which there is no information. Most of those that we know to be endangered are situated in the borderland with Nigeria; most of those for which we have no data are also in the borderland. Indeed in this area we see entire sub-groups of languages disappearing. Sketchy information suggests this is the fate of the *Furu* subgroup, one of which is listed as having 600 speakers, another with 400, and a further three which are said to be nearly extinct and known to only a very small number of old people. The *Furu* languages have reportedly given way to *Jukun* and *Cameroon Pidgin*. However, these languages are so remote and so little is known of them that, while they are believed to be *Bantoid*, it is not certain what their genetic affiliations are and whether they actually do constitute a separate genetic grouping in themselves. Another language subgroup in the area, *Western Beboid*, may also be on the brink. Most of the languages believed to constitute this subgroup are among those for which the *Ethnologue* offers no population estimate. A recent survey by SIL members (Ed Brye, personal communication) indicates these languages to be spoken in a string of villages, each with its own language and a population of roughly 500 people. Until recently, perhaps, their isolation may have kept these languages relatively stable; however the isolation is now breaking down. The need for a lingua franca is obvious, and *Cameroon Pidgin* is now widely used in the area.

The situation of another subgroup of languages, still in the same general region, but somewhat less remote, is better known (Connell 1998). The languages *Cambap, Njerep, Kasabe* and *Yeni* formed a subgroup of *Mambiloid* languages, apparently a cluster within the large *Mambila* language complex. Today *Cambap* is the only one of these four that is still spoken on even a more or less daily basis (Connell 2002). It has approximately 30 speakers, while *Njerep* has four 'rememberers' (Connell and Zeitlyn 2000). *Kasabe* and *Yeni* are extinct, though for both of these there are people who recall songs in the language, and *Kasabe* was documented to some extent before its last speaker died (Connell, in prep). Two other languages in the immediate vicinity also bear mention: *Njanga*, a conservative dialect of *Kwanja* is now known by fewer than 20 people, while *Bung* is remembered best by one non-native speaker. A third, also on the brink, is *Somyev* the language of a former blacksmith caste, which has fewer than five speakers in Cameroon and approximately 15 in Nigeria.

The circumstances surrounding the demise of these languages, while perhaps not unique in the African context, do not fit commonly anticipated patterns. The speakers of these languages are all multilingual, typically having a repertoire of three or four languages though many knowing upwards of six. Detailed knowledge of the factors that precipitated the downfall of these languages is now lost to time, but it seems probable that invasion from the north – either the Chamba or later the Fulbe, or perhaps both in their turn – resulted in a decimation of the local populations. This led to a greater degree of intermarriage with neighbouring peoples than previously and a concomitant shift to the language of the neighbours. This has resulted in two characteristics which set this situation apart. First, *Fulfulde*, the language of the incoming Fulbe, has become the lingua franca in the area, but not the language of choice for any of the indigenous groups. Use of *Fulfulde* is, by and large, restricted to market situations and use with strangers and others with whom no common other language can be found. The other notable characteristic is that former speakers of these languages, having shifted to a neighbouring language rather than that of a colonial power or even a regional lingua franca, have adopted a language and culture not too different from their own. The sense of estrangement often found to accompany the disappearance of a language and its culture, seemingly has not played an overbearing role in this situation. Nevertheless, there is clearly a strong sense of loss, which is tempered to some extent by pragmatism; and while there is little interest in language revival ("Why do we need it?" "Who would we speak it with?"), among the Camba there is satisfaction in seeing their language documented for posterity. However, a more unfortunate side of the situation also exists. Use of both *Fulfulde* and *French* is gradually on the increase, especially among school-aged children, with a situation similar to, but by no means as advanced, as that reported by Schaefer and Egbokhare (1999) regarding use of *English* among the Emai in Southern Nigeria. And, lastly, the languages to which people have switched, particularly *Kwanja*, are small and they themselves may be under serious threat within two or three generations.

4. Summary and conclusions

There has been, and still is, an absence of detailed information regarding language endangerment in Central Africa. For some parts of this geographical zone, this has led to an assumption of relative linguistic vitality. Recent indications, though, are that even in these areas, a number of languages are severely endangered, and that this number is increasing. In other areas – Chad, Cameroon apart from the Nigeria borderland, and DRC, the situation may indeed be relatively stable, though we note again that little if any relevant survey work has been done in these areas. In addition, civil war in both Congo and DRC may well prove to have a devastating effect on a number of languages in these countries, just as it appears to be doing elsewhere in Africa, for example in Sudan.

At present, the number of languages in Central Africa known or believed to be endangered constitutes only a small proportion of the total number of languages in the region, though this may be no more than a reflection of our ignorance of the situation. It must also be noted that, with the possible exception of Gabon, little action if any appears to be taken by governmental or local organizations to preserve, protect, and promote indigenous languages. Considerable effort is needed simply to provide basic information as to numbers of speakers, language use in the home and other settings, and intergenerational transmission, to assess the real extent language endangerment in Central Africa.

Appendix: Endangered languages in Central Africa

The following *Table 4* includes languages in Central Africa known to be seriously endangered, or those spoken by fewer than 1,000 people. The list is not comprehensive, as there remains considerable work to be done to assess the viability of languages in many parts of Central Africa. Languages known to be extinct are not included. Population figures refer to estimated numbers of speakers rather than size of ethnic group. Languages for which no population assessment is available from any source are not included, unless the endangered status of the language is definitely known. It is possible, indeed likely, that many of these are also endangered.

Table 4. Seriously endangered languages in Central Africa

Country Language (Affiliationon)	Popula- tion	Comment
Cameroon		
1 Akum (Benue-Congo)	600	(Furu cluster) Cameroon Pidgin also used.
2 Bakole (Bantu A 20)	300	
3 Baldamu (Chadic, Mandara A5)	3	No longer used on a daily basis.
4 Bati (Bantu)	800	
5 Beezen (Benue-Congo)	400	(Furu cluster) Cameroon Pidgin also used?
6 Bikya (Benue-Congo)	1	(Furu cluster) Now speak Jukun. 1 speaker reported in 1986.
7 Bishuo (Benue-Congo)	1	(Furu cluster) Now speak Jukun.
8 Bubia (Bantu A 20)	600	Also speak Duala.
9 Bung (Bantoid?)	3	No native speakers; now use Kwanja.
10 Busuu (Benue-Congo)	8	(Furu cluster) Now speak Jukun; used only for reunions.
11 Cambap (Mambiloid)	30	Youngest speaker aged 45–50; now speak Kwanja.
12 Dimbong (Bantu A 50)		
13 Eman (Tivoid)	800	Pidgin, Ipulo also used.
14 Fungom (Grassfields Bantu)	1,000	
15 Hijuk (Bantu A 50)	400	Also use Yangben, Bassa, French, Yambasa.
16 Isubu (Bantu A 20)	800	Also use Mokpe, Duala.
17 Iyive (Tivoid)	< 1,000	
18 Kendem (Bantoid)	1,000	Kenyang, Pidgin also used.
19 Langa (Mambiloid)	< 500	Still used in the home; Fulfulde, other languages also spoken.
20 Mono (Adamawa Mbum)	1,000	
21 Ndai (Adamawa, Mbum)	few	
22 Ngong (Jarawan Bantu)	2	Possibly extinct.
23 Njerep (Mambiloid)	4	Youngest speaker aged about 60; now speak Mambila.

Table 4. cont.

Country Language (Affiliationon)	Population	Comment
Cameroon (cont.)		
24 Nubaca (Bantu A60)	800	Ewondo, Basaa, or French are used as second languages, French dominates among the younger generation.
25 Somyev (Mambiloid)	15–20	Former blacksmith language; mostly in Nigeria.
26 Tuotomb (Bantu A40)	< 1,000	Speakers bilingual in Tunen, Pidgin.
27 Yasa (Bantu A30)	1,500 total	Spoken in Cameroon, Equatorial-Guinea and Gabon.
28 Zumaya (Chadic, Masa)		Only a few speakers left (1987).
Central African Republic		
29 Birri (Central Sudanic)	200	Bilingual in Zande; assimilated by the Zande through marriage.
30 Bodo (Bantu D30)	15	Scattered throughout CAR.
31 Ganzi (Ubangi, Ngbaka)		Maybe intelligible with Baka.
32 Geme (Ubangi, Zande)	550	Sango used as second language.
33 Ngombe (Ubangi, Ngbaka)	1,400	Apparently not used by younger people
34 Ukhwejo (Bantu A80)	< 2,000	Population threatened by sleeping sickness increase.
Chad		
35 Berakou (Nilo-Saharan, Bagirmi)	2	Has given way to Shuwa Arabic and Kotoko; possibly extinct.
36 Boor (E. Chadic A)	< 100	Dialect of Miltu spoken in Dumraw village. Shifting to Bagirmi.
37 Buso (E. Chadic A)	40–50	Possibly now extinct.
38 Fongoro (Nilo-Saharan, Bagirmi)		Status unknown; possibly extinct.
39 Goundo (Adamawa-Kim)	30	Spoken only by older people in three villages; younger people shifting to Nancere, Kabalay.
40 Jonkor Bourmataguil (E. Chadic B)	< 1,500	Replaced by Chadic Arabic; may still known by children in one village.
41 Kendeje (Nilo-Saharan, Mabang)	< 2,000	Only in the home; Maba and Masalit used outside.

Table 4. cont.

Country Language (Affiliationon)	Popula- tion	Comment
Chad (cont.)		
42 Koke (Adamawa, Mbum)	600	Majority bilingual in Shuwa Arabic or Fania.
43 Kujarge (unclassified)	< 1,000	Status unknown, Possibly extinct.
44 Laal (Adamawa?)	< 500	
45 Massalat (Nilo-Saharan, Maban)	10	
46 Mbara (Chadic, Biu-Mandara, B)	< 1,000	
47 Miltu (E. Chadic A)	< 300	Speakers shifting to Bagirmi.
48 Noy (Adamawa, Mbum)	36	Speakers shifting to Sar; nearly extinct.
49 Toram (E. Chadic B)	< 4,000	Younger generation speaks Chadic Arabic.
Congo		
50 Bonjo (Bantu C10)	< 3,000	Speakers shifting to Lingala.
Equatorial Guinea		
51 Gyele (Bantu A80)	30 total	Also spoken in Cameroon.
Democratic Republic of Congo		
52 Beeke (Bantu D20)	< 1,000	Giving way to Ndaka.
53 Boguru (Bantu D30)	< 500 total	Spoken mailnly in Sudan.
54 Kari (Bantu D30)	< 1,000	Scattered groups.
55 Ngbinda (Bantu D30)	few	possibly extinct.
Gabon		
56 Benga (Bantu A30)		Spoken by small groups of old people.
57 Kande (Bantu B30)	< 1,000	Threatened, undocumented.
58 Mahongwe (Bantu B20)	< 1,000	Threatened, undocumented.
59 Sake (Bantu B20)	< 1,000	Threatened, undocumented.
60 Sighu (Bantu B20)	< 1,000	Threatened, undocumented.
61 Vumbu (Bantu B40)	< 1,000	Threatened, undocumented.

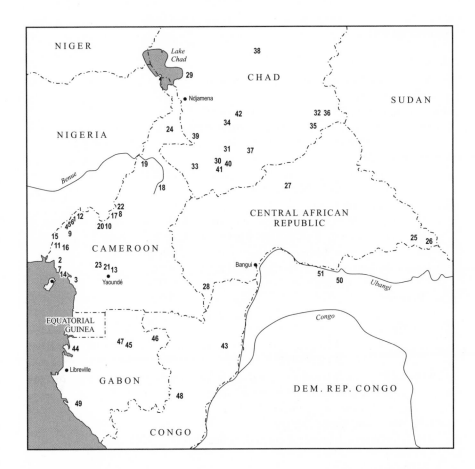

Map 10. Central Africa

Notes

1. Research contributing in part to this to this paper is funded by ESRC grant R000237450 "Language Death in the Nigeria-Cameroon Borderland" and conducted under the auspices of the Ministry of Technical and Scientific Research, Cameroon.

2. Indeed, this is precisely the case with certain languages discussed later in the paper. Linguists and missionary linguists alike failed to note either the existence or at least the precarious state of *Bung, Cambap, Kasabe, Njerep*, and *Somyev*, none of which are recorded in the *Atlas Linguistique du Cameroun*.

3. *Swahili* is not the only language in Tanzania which has come to replace other local languages. Batibo (1992) also discusses, in particular, *Maasai* and *Sukuma*.

References

Batibo, Herman
  1992   The fate of ethnic languages in Tanzania. In Brenzinger (ed.) 1992: 85–98.
Biesbrouck, Karen; Stefan Elders and Gerda Rossel (eds.)
  1999   *Challenging elusiveness:* Central African hunter-gatherers in a multi-disciplinary perspective, Leiden: Centre for Non-Western Studies.
Blench, Roger M.
  1999   Are the pygmies an ethnological fiction? In Biesbrouck, Elders and Rossel (eds.) 1999: 41–60.
Brenzinger, Matthias (ed.)
  1992   *Language death:* Factual and theoretical explorations with special reference to East Africa. Berlin: Mouton de Gruyter.
  1998   *Endangered languages in Africa.* Köln: Rüdiger Köppe.
Brenzinger, Matthias; Heine, Bernd and Gabriela Sommer
  1991   Language death in Africa. *Diogenes* 153, 19–44.
Clist, Bernard
  1995   *Gabon:* 100000 ans d'Histoire. Libreville: Sepia.
Connell, Bruce
  1998   Moribund languages of the Nigeria-Cameroon borderland. In Brenzinger (ed.) 207–225.
  2002   Phonetic/phonological variation and language contraction. *International journal of sociology of language* 157: 167–185.
  in prep. A Kasabe voice (working title).
Connell, Bruce and David Zeitlyn
  2000   Njerep: A postcard from the edge. *Studies in African linguistics.* 95–125.
Grimes, Barbara F. (ed.)
  2000   *Ethnologue* (14th Edition). Dallas: SIL International. CD-ROM edition.
Schaefer, Ronald P. and Francis O. Egbokhare
  1999   English and the pace of endangerment in Nigeria. *World Englishes* 18: 381–391.
Wardhaugh, Ronald
  1987   *Languages in competition.* Dominance, diversity, and decline. Oxford: Basil Blackwell.

Chapter 9
Language Endangerment in Southern and Eastern Africa

Matthias Brenzinger

1. Introduction

Southern and Eastern Africa are commonly referred to as the cradle of humankind. The autochthonous peoples in this part of the world most probably spoke *Khoisan* languages. The following sections will describe how *Khoisan* languages have vanished in each of these regions.

First, the decline of still spoken *Khoisan* languages will be the focus of the sketch on the Southern African region.

Secondly, we will turn to Eastern Africa where, unlike in Southern Africa, *Bantu*-speaking immigrants arrived only recently. The distribution of languages in Eastern Africa has been constantly reshaped by immigration over the past 5,000 years. Large-scale population movements, as well as recent migrations will be the main perspective in the description of language endangerment in Eastern Africa.[1]

2. Southern Africa and the decline of the Khoisan languages

Considerable confusion still prevails through an inconsistent use of the terms *Khoisan*, *Khoe* (Khoi) and San. This terminological obstruction apparently requires some clarification.

A short historical sketch of the colonial period will outline the oppressive rule as the main cause for the decline of *Khoisan* languages in the Cape.

While many *Khoisan* languages have already disappeared, the ones that still exist are either on the verge of extinction or at least endangered, even the "healthiest" one, which is *Khoekhoegowab*.

An overview of the present situation of language endangerment among the *Khoisan* languages will precede a map and the endangered language list, presented in the final section.

2.1. The terms *Khoisan, Khoe, Khoekhoe* and San

The physical anthropologist Leonhard Schultze Jena (1928) coined a new term *Khoisan*, by compounding "*Khoe*" (Khoi), the general term for "person" in the languages of the *Central Khoisan* branch and "Saan", "hunter-gatherers, foragers" in *Khoekhoegowab*[2]. Isaak Schapera introduced *Khoisan* as a classificatory term in social anthropology, by which he included the herding Khoekhoe, formerly known as "Hottentots" and the foraging San, often referred to as "Bushmen" (Schapera 1930). From the 1950s onwards, Joseph Greenberg tried to establish *Khoisan* as an exclusively linguistic term: *Khoisan* is one of the four phyla in his classification of the "Languages of Africa" (Greenberg 1966). Already Schapera stated that language is the most reliable single criterion for dealing with the "Khoisan people" (Schapera 1930). Referring to this assumption, Phillip Tobias in 1956 advocated the use of "the language criterion" as suggested by Schapera: "We could do no better than follow this authority on the Khoisan peoples" (Tobias 1956: 175). Until today, however, even linguists do not consistently follow this well-thought suggestion.

Geneticists, social anthropologists, and linguists use quite different definitions of the term *Khoisan*, but major problems arise in those usages of the term, in which features associated with these different research perspectives are fused.

Widespread perplexity prevails with the terms *Khoe* and San because many scholars mingle aspects of physical appearance and mode of subsistence together with linguistic affiliation. The term San has developed into the current self-reference among the activists of the former hunter-gatherers of Southern Africa, who increasingly reject the previously used label "Bushman". Not all the people and communities, who refer to themselves as San, share the stereotypical biological features set up for them by physical anthropologists, such as short size and fair skin color. People may call themselves simply San because they speak a *Khoisan* language or claim a hunter-gatherer past. In the Republic of South Africa, by far most San speak no *Khoisan* language, but *Afrikaans* instead. Without speaking a *Khoisan* language, accounts of a foragers past and features of physical appearance are the criteria by which these people claim San identity.

In the course of the adjustment to a politically correct naming of the people, the term San entered discussions as a reference for languages: "San languages" replaced the former term "Bushmen languages". Archeologists such as Garth Sampson (1988: 15 "San languages"), anthropologists such as Edwin Wilmsen (1989: 1, "San-speaking people, San-speakers") and Jiro Tanaka (1980: 9, "San language family"), and unfortunately, even linguists such as Anthony Traill (1996: 161, "the Khoe and San languages") widely employed these inappropriate notions.

"San languages" – or "Bushmen languages" in the old terminology – as a group of languages, which is exclusively spoken by hunter-gatherers or people of a certain physical type, do not exist. The phrasing "*Khoe* and San languages"[3] is particularly misleading, but also "*Khoekhoe* and San languages" fuels the extensive misconception, which links way of live with language. There is no grouping of *Khoekhoe* languages of pastoral societies as opposed to other so-called "San languages" of foragers, as for example, claimed by Diedrich Westermann (1949: 14).[4] *Khoekhoegowab*, the language of the pastoral Nama and Damara, is closely related to languages of former hunter-gatherers, such as *Khwe* and *Naro*. In linguistic terms, however, the latter languages of hunter-gatherers are only very distantly related to other languages spoken by hunter-gatherer communities, such as *!Xũ)* and *!Xóõ*). Finally, *Khoekhoegowab* is not the language of herders only, but also of the formerly hunting and gathering Haiǁ'om and ǂAuǁei.

In linguistic terms, *Khoe* languages refer to the entire *Central Khoisan* branch. To contrast *Khoe* languages (= *Central Khoisan*) and the notion "San languages" makes no sense, as most of the *Khoe* languages are spoken by former foraging peoples. *Khoekhoegowab* is the only surviving *Khoekhoe* language and, together with the *non-Khoekhoe* languages, forms *Khoe*, i. e. the *Central Khoisan* branch. Thus, languages spoken by various hunter-gatherer communities are fundamentally diverse while the language of *Khoekhoegowab*-speaking herders is closely related to some of the languages spoken by hunter-gatherers.

In our discussion, *Khoisan, Khoekhoe* and *Khoe* (= *Central Khoisan*) are terms used strictly in the linguistic classification of languages and they bear no cultural or racial implications for speakers. San, with its cultural and physical connotations, has no meaningful role to play in discussions on linguistic classifications. Linguists widely agree on which languages are *Khoisan* languages and which are not. This shared usage is rather surprising, as there is no substantiation of any genetic link between the major branches of *Khoisan* languages, as claimed by Joseph Greenberg (1966: 66–84), i. e. *Northern, Central* and *Southern South African Khoisan*, as well as the Tanzanian isolates *Hadza* and *Sandawe*. The established, pragmatic use of the term *Khoisan* includes all "click languages", with the exception of *Bantu* languages (such as *Xhosa, Zulu*) and the *Cushitic* language *Dahalo*, as these latter languages obviously borrowed their clicks from *Khoisan* languages.

The still limited knowledge on the *Khoisan* languages results in an inflated number of language names. Further studies will probably demonstrate that quite a number of names used to refer to distinct *Khoisan* languages, as listed in *Table 1*, are in fact names for different communities, some of which speak the same language. /*Gui* and //*Gana* speak one and the same language, and also /*Xaise* and !*Goro* claim to be one speech community with a common language, as do *Danisi* and *Tshara* (Hasselbring 2000).

Dialects of one language may have entered classifications as names for distinct languages, such as for example, *Buga. Khwe* (*Kxoe*) is a language with very little dialectal variation, and the two regional speech varieties are /*Xom-Buma* vs. /*Xo-Buga*. Buga-Khwe in Botswana and |Xo-Khwe in Namibia speak the same Eastern variety of the *Khwe* language.

Finally, languages may disappear from the list, because they have never existed, such as for example /*Ganda*. Rainer Vossen collected language data from Kwere Seriri, a famous Khwe elder who lived as the headman in Khwai till his death in 1995. Vossen (1997: 77) labeled the language /*Ganda*, even though Kwere Seriri himself insisted to speak /*Xo-Buga* variety.[5] Khwe call the *Bantu*-speaking *Nyemba* in Angola |Ganda. Khwe usually call community members from Angola either Buma-Khwe or Mbunda-Khwe, but they may also refer to them as Nyemba-Khwe or |Ganda-Khwe. Seriri's wife Tsoxee Leitho and his grandson Keitiretse Kwere both emphasize, however, that Seriri and his ancestors originated from the Okavango Delta area of Botswana. According to them and other residents of Khwai, Seriri spoke no distinct language, but the /*Xo-Buga* variety of *Khwe* from Khwai.

With the obstacles discussed in identifying the status of still spoken *Khoisan* varieties, we may assume a doubtful scientific value for most of the more than 100 language names, which exist for extinct *Khoisan* languages, especially those names noted in the early days of colonial presence in the Cape region. Unfortunately, the history of *Khoisan* language speech communities prior to the arrival of the Dutch in the 1650s seems to be out of reach for today's scholarly analysis.

The figures commonly provided for the number of *Khoisan* languages range from 30 to 35 (e. g. Güldemann and Vossen 2000). In excluding extinct and non-existing languages, however, we come up with only 20 language names. Among those, several are mutually intelligible and share a dialectal relationship. This means, that the total number of *Khoisan* languages is below 20.

2.2. ǀXam, a case of a physical and cultural genocide

In April 2000, a new coat of arms, was launched in the post-apartheid South Africa, and the motto of the state emblem is: *!Ke e: ǀxarra ǁke.* This sentence from *ǀXam*, a *Southern Khoisan* language, is translated as "diverse people unite". There are no speakers of *ǀXam* left today.[6] The phrase was coined on the basis of language documents, collected more than 90 years ago, and nobody knows if native speakers of *ǀXam* ever used these words to express such a notion.[7] Nevertheless, the documents of the *ǀXam* language form an important testimony of the autochthonous peoples of Southern Africa. The first words and some phrases of *ǀXam* where recorded by Hinrich Lichtenstein during his travels between 1803 and 1806. In 1870, Wilhelm Bleek and Lucy Lloyd (1911) began to document the *ǀXam* language, and the collection of extensive texts reveals that *ǀXam* at that time was still a vital language. Bleek and Lloyd worked in the Cape Town prison with *ǀXam*, who served sentences of imprisonment mainly for stock theft. In 1910-11, Dorothea Bleek visited remnant groups of *ǀXam* and found some bilingual in *ǀXam* and *Afrikaans*, while most others were already monolingual in *Afrikaans*. In the following years, the *ǀXam* identity and their language disappeared altogether (Traill 1996: 168).

What had happened to these people, their culture and language? Anthony Traill (1996) provides a description of the complex socio-historical context, which led to the decline of the *ǀXam* and their language. The strategies used by the intruding colonial powers to destroy the indigenous hunter-gatherer societies in the Cape area, as well as those employed by the San in their resistance, have been analyzed by Nigel Penn (1996).

The 'trekboers' were the first colonialist to push into the interior of South Africa, entering into a ruthless competition for natural resources. These frontier farmers appropriated watering places for their cattle and killed large numbers of game with their guns. The hunter-gatherer communities responded to this invasion into their land and to the massive destruction of their basis of subsistence with guerrilla tactics. San attacked kraals at night, frequently killed the guards and stole the cattle or sheep. When possible, they drove the livestock into hidden places to consume the meat, otherwise they simply killed the animals to destroy the farmers' property.

In the 1750s, the colonists decided to respond to the resistance with commandos. First, commandos were introduced to subjugate the pastoral Khoekhoe of the Western Cape. The Dutch intruders took their land and cattle and used the Khoekhoe as forced laborers (Penn 1996: 83). In the early missions against San, the commandos, that consisted now of Boers,

Bastards, Xhosa and Korana, had twin objectives: "crushing of resistance
and the capture of women and children for use as laborers" (Penn 1996:
83). The official policy at that time allowed the 'trekboers' to "sweep the
San out of their path or incorporate them into their economy as unfree
laborers" (Penn 1996: 85). Between 1770 and 1800, "the 'trekboers' and
the San were involved, literally, in a life or death struggle" throughout the
entire interior of the Cape escarpment (Penn 1996: 82).

   In 1774, a General Commando was set up to destroy any San resistance
on a large scale. Commonly, the various sections of the General Commando took off in surprise attacks at dawn, against individual kraals of sleep-
ing San. Against guns and horse-mounted enemies, the numerically small
San communities had no chance to strike back. The casualties among
members of the commandos were very few, if any at all, while Khoekhoe
fighting in the first lines were killed or injured. Very few Boers were
wounded or killed, while thousands of male San lost their lives. Instead of
capturing them, the commandos usually shot male San, because they considered them as being of no economic value.

   More than 70 years after the General Commando, between 1851 and
1869, commandos in Bushmanland again killed large numbers of |Xam
(Traill 1996: 165). The frontier farmers had given up attempts at 'civiliz-
ing' the San, at transforming their 'predatory existence' into the live of
pastoralists (Penn 1996: 81).

"By the 1870s the last remnants of the Cape San were being hunted to extinction
by the Boer and 'Bastaard' usurpers of Bushmanland. Those who were not shot
starved to death in the dusty margins of South Africa's most marginal land, whilst
a handful, mainly women and children, lived out their days as captive laborers on
their vanquishers' farms" (Penn 1996: 82).

Traill seems to contradict this interpretation of Penn and plays down the
role of physical violence in the demise of the *|Xam* culture and language.

"The genocide practiced on the |Xam for over a century was obviously an impor-
tant contributory factor, and it is quite likely that numbers of |Xam actually aban-
doned their language out of self-defense in response to this. But it is not accurate
to imply that it was the only (Brenzinger and Dimmendaal 1992: 3) or even the
main factor. The evidence that had been reviewed above also supports a more
conventional explanation based on the social disintegration of the |Xam and their
subjugation as a class of menial laborers" (Traill 1996: 183).

Traill further argues that through a process of 'taming', the |Xam identity
was extinguished. However, this 'taming' involved again killing of male

San and treatment of all San "with utter contempt" (Traill 1996: 183). Traill seems to have a somewhat apologetic understanding of what is commonly called genocide.

Colonial farmers eventually saw male San as a type of vermin or beast, "fit only for extermination, while San women and children were of not much economic interest" (Penn 1996: 89). Now, in addition to the commandos, also 'hunting parties' went out for the sole reason to kill San people. Thus, the war in the nineteenth century changed its objectives, as the farmers no longer aimed at breaking San resistance, but eradicating the San society.

"This conviction, deeply etched into the nineteenth century, even after the San had dropped their guard. The San perished not because it was so fatal but because of the legacy of violence inherited from the eighteenth century frontier" (Penn 1996: 85)

Penn (1996: 91) explains that the South African San perished because of the murderous ideas of the colonialists, who "never forgot the violent hatred which they had learnt in their struggle with the San during the eighteenth century". The colonial war against the |Xam, which finally led to the extinction of *|Xam* identity and their language, is one of the cruelest events of African history, a case of physical and cultural genocide.

2.3. The endangered Khoisan languages

While close genetic relationship among the languages of the *Central Khoisan* grouping has been attested (cf. Vossen 1997), the relationship between the major branches of *Khoisan* and the position of so far unclassified isolated *Khoisan* languages remains a major challenge to linguists. The following groupings of *Khoisan* languages do therefore not claim to represent genetic relationships between the language groupings at higher levels.

The only *Khoisan* language which seems to be "safe" is *Khoekhoegowab*, a *Central Khoisan* language spoken by pastoral Nama and Damara, as well as, by the Hai||om and ‡Aakhoe, formerly hunter-gatherers. Reports by Dutch settlers from the late 17th century indicate the existence of a dialect continuum of *Khoekhoe* languages from Cape Khoekhoe in the south far into Angola in the north (Haacke 2002: 1). The *Cape Khoekhoe* languages – still vital in 1652 – ceased to exist within three generations. The Khoekhoe pastoralists along the southern and eastern Cape shifted to *Afrikaans* or to *Xhosa*. *!Ora* and *Xiri*, two *Western Khoekhoe* languages, survived until recently. Today, however, all descendants of Ko-rana who spoke *!Ora* and the Griqua speakers of *Xiri* have lost these languages and taken *Afrikaans* as their first language (Traill 1996: 161).

With regard to *Kede*, the following observation made by Carlos Estermann recalls the state of the *Kede* and their language predating 1960, when he visited Angola for the last time.

"They are called *Kede* (Ovakede) by the Kwanyama, while in their own language, they are designated as *Sa Mu !Kwe*. This language is a Hottentot dialect, but may be considered dead today, at least on the Angolan side, for the few old people who once spoke it are no longer of this world." (Estermann 1976: 16).

No reports on *Kede* in Namibia exist, which makes in most likely, that the most northern *Khoekhoe* language is no longer spoken.

The last *Khoekhoe* language of *Central Khoisan*, i. e. *Khoekhoegowab,* is well documented and receives official recognition as a language of instruction in the Namibian educational system. Despite these facts, Wilfrid Haacke and Eliphas Eiseb consider even *Khoekhoegowab* to be an "endangered language" (Haacke and Eiseb 2002: iii). After *Oshiwambo*, with 713,919 speakers, *Khoekhoegowab* has the second largest speech community of the Republic of Namibia, with 175,554 speakers (cf. census figures of 1991 by language spoken, Haacke 1996: 32). Outcomes of several surveys demonstrate, however, that Nama and Damara take on a negative stand against the formal use of their language. *Khoekhoegowab* speakers are reluctant to enrol their children in schools in which their language is employed as medium of instruction (Laurentius Davids, p. c.). Even languages spoken by large communities may indeed disappear, as we know from other cases, if a negative attitude towards their language prevails among the speech community. The *Khoisan* languages as a whole, must therefore be considered to be endangered.

Among the *non-Khoekhoe* languages of the Central Khoisan grouping, *Naro*, spoken predominantly in Botswana and *Khwe*, with major speech communities in Namibia, Botswana and South Africa seem to be the most stable and vital.

Naro is spoken by roughly 9,000 persons as a first and by about the same number as second language. Long-term language work by religious missions has created a strong sense of linguistic identity among the Naro. *Naro* has been standardized and submitted to writing. Literacy in *Naro* is not restricted to the religious contexts, but has become an important feature of Naro identity. While *Naro* seems to be quite strong, the *Ts'ao* dialect of *Naro* as spoken in the Kuke region, is about to be replaced by "standard" *Naro* (Visser p. c.).

The Khwe amount to about 7,000 people in total, and up to 5,000 of them might be considered speakers of the *Khwe* language. The *Khwe* language seems to be safe in Namibia, at least for the time being, as all children speak *Khwe* as their first language in the Caprivi Strip. However, like many members of other minorities in Botswana, in this country also Khwe communicate increasingly in *Setswana*, even at home.

Since the early 1960s living conditions for San, i. e. Khwe and !Xũ (see below) and other inhabitants of Angola were primarily determined by war. Ill-educated San, who are widely considered as being an inferior people by Bantu-speaking neighbors, were easy to recruit into foreign armies with a regular income and promises of a higher status. From the early 1960s onwards, San were employed by the Portuguese to fight against the various liberation armies in Angola. In southeastern part of Angola about 30 % of the San population lost their lives in the first two years of the independence struggle. In 1974/75, after the defeat of the Portuguese colonizers, San soldiers fled from Angola in large numbers to Namibia. They got involved in another war by fighting for the South African Defense Force against the Namibian liberation fighters and the MPLA (Popular Movement for the Liberation of Angola). After the independence of Namibia in 1989, more than 1,300 Khwe withdrew together with the South African army to South Africa, where they live in the Diaspora since then and most children there grow up with *Afrikaans* as the first language.

/Xam ceased to be spoken in the early 1920s and last speakers of other Khoisan languages of the *!Ui* branch, such as *//Ng*, *//Kx'au*, *//Ku //'e*, and *!Gã !ne* passed away a decade later. One or two people spoke *//Xegwi* in the 1960s but the last of them died in 1988 (Traill 1996: 164). *!Ui* languages used to be spoken throughout the entire interior of Southern Africa, but today no intact speech community of any of the *!Ui* languages exist anymore. Among the 600 ǂKhomani (= Khomani), less than 20 old people still speak the *N/u* language. These few speakers of a language of the *!Ui* language group, are the most prominent last speakers on the entire African continent.

At the Namibia-Botswana border spread over a vast area, about 2,000 speaker of *!Xóõ* form the last speech community of a Southern Khoisan language. Despite their small number, Traill (1985) describes *!Xóõ* as a dialect cluster.

ǂHua has not yet shown any links to other *Khoisan* groupings. This language is spoken by less then 200 people in the northwestern part of Botswana, near Khutse. The language seems to bevanishing, as no chil-

dren speak *ǂHua* but acquire *SheKgalaghari* as their first language instead, along with the national language Setswana (Batibo (2005).

Kwadi is one of the most referred to extinct *Khoisan* languages. It was
spoken in southwestern Angola by only a few remaining individuals in the
1950s, and it became extinct before 1970. António de Almeida identified
50 Kwadi people as the only survivors of this ethnic group, back in 1960
(Almeida 1965: 29). With regard to their *Khoisan* language Almeida says,
"at present only four or five elder Kwádi can speak it" (Almeida 1965:
39). Father Carlos Estermann (1976: 42), who traveled extensively between 1924 and 1960 in the southwestern part of Angola, knew the Kwadi
area very well and only came across a few elderly speakers of *Kwadi* in
his later visits to the area. He quotes the first mentioning of what he identifies as *Kwadi* people. A. de Oliveira de Cadornega reported in the
História geral das guerrs angolanas in 1681 of people "who understood
nothing that he said; their language is like a clicking, ..." (Estermann
1976: 38). Finally, Ernst Westphal conducted fieldwork in 1965 with the
Kwadi and notes, "The language presents many problems and only three
people seem to use it regularly when together" (Westphal 1971: 396).

Tom Güldemann and Rainer Vossen analyze Westphal's scarce *Kwadi*
language data and find typological similarities of *Kwadi* to *Central Khoisan* and *Sandawe* in that they are all SOV languages with a head-final noun
phrase, and they also share sex-based gender suffixes (Güldemann and
Vossen 2000: 119–120). However, they claim no proof of a genetic relationship with these findings, and leave *Kwadi* unclassified.

According to Estermann (1976), *Kwadi* disappeared between 1920 and
1970. Most of the last members of this small speech community died of
diseases (tuberculosis) and the remaining few individuals gave up their
language. It is highly unlikely that persons with any competence in *Kwadi*
are still living today.

Table 1. The Khoisan languages of Southern and Eastern Africa

Language	Speakers	Population	Status[8]
Central Khoisan: Khoekhoe			
1 Khoekhoe-gowab	200,000	200,000	a–
2 Cape Khoe-khoe varieties	0	0	1700
3 Kede	0	?	1960
4 !Ora	0	?	? 1970s
5 Xiri	0	?	? 1970s

Table 1. cont.

Language	Speakers	Population	Status[8]
Central Khoisan: non-Khoekhoe			
6 Naro (Ts'ao)	9,000	9,000	a–
7 ǀGui	2,300	2,300	a–
8 ǁGana	1,500	1,500	a–
9 Khwe	6,000	7,000	a
10 ǁAni	1,100	1,300	b
11 ǀXaise	600	800	c
12 !Goro	1,200	1,200	a
13 Deti	few	few	d, e
14 Shua	1,700	1,700	a
15 Ts'ixa	400	400	b
16 Danisi, Tshara	670	670	b
17 Kua	2,500	3,000	b
18 Tshoa	380	380	c
Northern Khoisan			
19 !Xũ (Ju)	10,000	10,000	a–
Southern Khoisan			
20 ǀXam	0	0	1920s
21 Nǁu	0	600	1930s
22 ǁKx'au	0	0	1930s
23 ǁKu ǁ'e	0	0	1930s
24 !Gã !ne	0	0	1930s
25 ǁXegwi	0	0	1988
26 ŋǀu	10-20	500	d
27 !Xóõ	6,000	6,000	a–
Unclassified Isolates			
28 ǂHõã	200	?	d
29 Kwadi	0	0	1960
30 Hadza	800	800	a
31 Sandawe	? 70,000	70,000	a–

For defining status see Krauss Chapter 1, this volume:

"safe"	*a+*
stable	*a–*
instable; eroded	*a*
definitively endangered	*b*
severely endangered	*c*
critically endangered	*d*
extinct	*e*

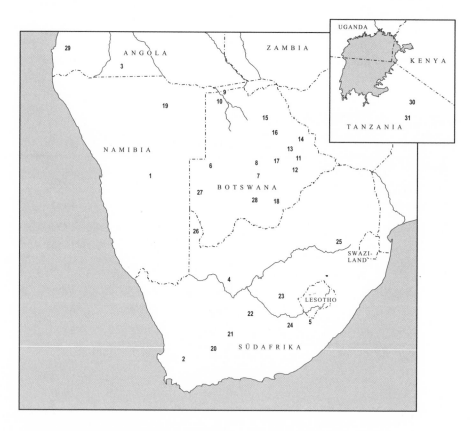

Map 11. The Khoisan languages of Southern and Eastern Africa

3. Eastern Africa and the scenarios of language endangerment

In most parts of the world, local languages are replaced by nationally dominant ones. In Africa, however, there are still various ongoing "traditional" language shifts, which take place in sub-national contexts. In the present review, brief case studies of such languages shifts experienced in Eastern Africa will illustrate types of language replacement that will soon be gone. The still existing variety of language endangerment settings in Eastern Africa will be presented in a typology of present-day shift scenarios.

3.1. Migrations in pre-colonial times

For Eastern Africa, as for most other parts of the continent, there is no information on specific language shifts that took place in the more distant past. Oral traditions generally do not cover more than a couple of centuries and there are no written accounts on African languages that were once spoken in the hinterlands. The reconstruction of the early history of language displacement, therefore, relies on assumptions based on the analysis of the current language maps, as well as on insights gained in the study of the ongoing "traditional" language shifts.

By applying methods of historical linguistics and by considering findings from other disciplines, the present language distribution in East Africa suggests the following interpretation: Dramatic changes in East African history have always been triggered by the arrival of waves of immigrants. For the last 5,000 years or so, various Nilotic, Cushitic, and *Bantu*-speaking populations spread, after arriving in East Africa, very often at the expense of previous arrivers and "indigenous" populations. These migrants departed from the central regions of present-day Sudan and from Ethiopia; others entered East Africa from the southern region of Angola.

These successive expansions of different cultures and languages caused language shifts and inevitably, many previously established "immigrant" languages of the region were replaced. In the course of these population dynamics, the number of "indigenous" languages decreased constantly and they were finally wiped out. Only seldom have scholars been able to detect traces of such now extinct languages. Christopher Ehret and Derek Nurse (1981) have identified remnants of the language of the so-called Taita Cushites in some *Bantu* languages, namely the Taita – Taveta, spoken in the southeastern part of Kenya. The "Taita" Cushites and their language vanished, but they left lexical traces in *Bantu* languages that might have become their new mother tongues. All ancestors of *Cushitic-* and *Nilotic*-language speakers came from the north and arrived in East Africa with their cattle at different times over the last 5,000 years. The "indigenous" hunter-gatherer population in Eastern and Southern Africa – prior to this influx of immigrants – spoke languages that were most likely related to present-day *Khoisan* languages.

The term "indigenous languages" has been widely employed in studies of language endangerment settings in other parts of the world. Very often, there is a contrast between "indigenous" endangered languages versus replacing languages of intruding colonial powers or spreading national languages of modern nation states. For the African continent, one needs to consider the relative connotation of "indigenous". With a rather *exclusive* use of the term, only *Khoisan* languages would qualify as "indigenous languages" for the African regions under discussion, as speakers of all other languages are immigrants. In a *wider meaning*, quite recently evolved languages, such as *Afrikaans* and *Fanagalo*, might be called "indigenous language", as they are spoken solely on the African continent. It seems to make not much sense to call, for example, *Southern Cushitic* languages more indigenous to East Africa than *Bantu* languages, only because the ancestors of present-day speakers of the former languages arrived a couple of thousand years earlier. Obviously, the blunt contrast "indigenous" versus "non-indigenous languages" does not capture the complexity and dynamics of language displacement scenarios on the African continent.

3.2. The decline of languages of the "last" hunter-gatherer communities

Some 12,000 ago all languages on earth were spoken by hunter-gather communities. Around that period, the number of human languages might have reached its peak, as the small bands of foragers were highly mobile and most probably spoke distinct languages. With the dawn of animal husbandry, the numbers of members of (speech) communities increased and contacts between communities were more regular. When men started farming and even more when they founded large settlements, the number of distinct languages on earth dropped dramatically.

Small hunter-gatherer communities might have assimilated to larger pastoral and agricultural societies not only in the mode of production and culture, but also by taking over the language of the pastoralist right from the invention of these new economies. Hunter-gatherer communities that had been living in balanced, symbiotic relationships with numerically dominant groups might have voluntarily decided or might have been forced to abandon their heritage language for various reasons, for example, at times of stress and disaster. Case studies of more recent language shifts of former hunter-gatherer communities reveal insights into the variance even of language shifts that took place in quite similar contact situations.

Maasai dominance and culture has spread over a wide area of East Africa and many hunter-gatherer communities have lost their distinct identity and language though pressure, but also due to the charms of a pastoral live stile. *Aasáx* and *Yaaku* are both *Cushitic* languages of former hunter-gatherer communities that were replaced by the Maasai variety of the *Maa* language that is classified as *Eastern Nilotic*.

The Aasáx, speakers of a *Southern Cushitic* language lived in the Maasai plains in northern Tanzania. *Aasáx*-speaking hunter-gatherers were affiliated with the then regionally dominant Maasai pastoralists, in what one may call a symbiotic relationship. The "Rinderpest" from 1891 to 1896 changed the contact setting dramatically. Most Maasai lost their cattle, the base of cultural, social and economic life to them, and about 50 % of the Maasai died during these years of hunger and of smallpox. The surviving, now cattle-less pastoralists had to rely on the help of agricultural neighbors and hunter-gatherers (see Winter 1979).

While larger agricultural communities were able to keep the impact of the Maasai refugees low, the weaker hunter-gatherer groups could not. Among them, in the course of time the help-seeking lodgers developed into occupation troops. In order to have total control of their new environment, the Maasai banned the use of the mother tongue of their hosts.

By the time the Maasai started to leave the Aasáx settlements to build up new herds, many Aasáx had established close ties with them. For a short period, the language was still used occasionally by men on hunting parties, but the final phase of decline of the *Aasáx* language started about 1910. Assimilated to agricultural communities as well as pastoralists, *Aasáx* ceased to be used in everyday communication in the following decade. After that time, only a few individuals retained some knowledge of the *Aasáx* language. In the early 1970s, Christopher Winter recorded the history of the Aasáx by the last speaker of the language. Kimíndet ole Kiyang'ú, the last *Aasáx* speaker, died in 1976 at the age of about 88 years. However, more than half a century before that, according to Winter, the language had ceased to exist as a communities' media in as much as most

Aasáx had already then shifted to the *Maasai* variety of *Maa* as their first and main language.

The members of the Mukogodo community settled in a mountainous area, just north of Mt. Kenya. They belong to the pastoral Maasai society and speak a variety of the *Maa* language. 100 years ago, their ancestors lived as hunter-gatherers in that same area, in rock shelters, and they spoke *Yaaku*. This *Cushitic* language was still mother tongue to some 1,000 people in the beginning of the 20th century. At that time, the neighboring communities that spoke several different languages began to shift to the Maasai culture and to take over the *Maa* language. Yaaku as well started to adopt the pastoral economy and along with that Maasai customs, such as female circumcision, the age-set system (in which groups of men go through initiation and other stages of life together) and marriage ceremonies. When Yaaku women began marrying neighboring pastoralists, their parents received livestock as bridewealth, not only beehives, as was the Yaaku custom. According to Cronk (1989) this was ultimately the main cause for abandoning the hunter-gatherer way of live, as Yaaku parents now demanded cattle as bridewealth, also from young Yaaku brooms.

In the beginning of the 1930s, the Yaaku community decided to stop teaching their own language to their children and to use Maa among themselves instead. In 1971, when Heine conducted his research and heard about this previous public decision on abandoning the heritage language, only 51 people had some language competence in Yaaku. At that time, some very few old people still used *Yaaku* in everyday communication. On a joint trip to Mukogodo with Bernd Heine in 1989, we did not come across any fluent Yaaku speakers. A few elders remembered only fragments of the old *Yaaku*. Recent attempts by some young community members to revive their heritage *Yaaku* language, althoug worthy of support, are most probably coming too late. Only a brief grammatical sketch (Heine 1975) as well as mainly botanical and honey-hunting terms of the vocabulary are the available language data of Yaaku (Brenzinger, Heine and Heine 1994).

Yaaku and *Aasáx* were once spoken by people that were called "Dorobo"; a derogative term of the *Maa*-speaking pastoralist for cattle-less people. Other East African languages of such small communities are the now extinct *Elmolo* in Northern Kenya and *K'wadza* in central Tanzania, as well as the threatened *Dahalo* language that is still spoken on the northern part of the Kenyan coast. These *Cushitic* languages, as well as several severely endangered *Nilo-Saharan languages*, such as *Akie* in Tanzania, *Okiek* and *Omotik* in Kenya and *Nyang'i* in Northern Uganda, are (or were) spoken exclusively by former hunter-gatherer communities. However, these languages belong genetically to language families with all other members being spoken by pastoralists. Possibly, hunter-gathering ancestors shifted to these languages, adapted from now extinct pastoral communities, or they themselves were pastoralist in the past and at time lost their cattle.

In Eastern Africa, the Hadza in Central Tanzania are the only hunter-gatherers who still speak a *Khoisan* language. The Hadza are less than 800 persons and their language and culture must be regarded as endangered, given the small number of community members.

The other East African language generally considered to belong to *Khoisan* is *Sandawe*. The Sandawe have lived as farmers with animal husbandry, at least for many hundreds of years, and their language seems to be safe.

3.3. Scenarios of language endangerment

On the African continent, the loss of speakers in one African language is typically the gain of speakers in another African language. *English* and *French*, the languages of the former colonial powers, are not replacing African languages, at least not for the time being. In other terms, these languages have not yet become mother tongues of communities. The fact that African languages replace other African languages, does not mean that language endangerment on the African continent is less severe than in other parts of the world, as distinct languages disappear.

In most parts of the world, namely Australia, the Americas, Europe and Japan, minority languages are increasingly under threat of being replaced by the official languages of national states. The scenarios, in which African languages are threatened, however, still range from sub-national settings to national contexts, while "globalization" has only started to have some impact on language use patterns. In analyzing language contact environments, three different contexts may be distinguished, that also reflect diachronically successive language shift settings: the recent global context, the established context of nation states, and the traditional sub-national context.

A few languages benefit from global merging, and at present mainly *English* and *Spanish* seem to be gaining speakers in the *context of globalization*. The "world economy" demands adjustment and reaches even the most remote rural areas in developing countries, in the same way as "world religions" do. A reduction of cultural diversity goes along with developments generally paraphrased as westernization, christianization, arabization, modernization, urbanization and industrialization. Global ideologies spread through modern mass media and formal education system, preparing also the way for a rapid expansion of a few "global" languages. These so-called "world languages", however, are so far acquired as additional, not as first languages and for that reason, languages have rarely been replaced in the context of globalization. Major East African languages, such as *Amharic*, *Swahili* and *Setswana*, are in competition with *English*, but of course they are not threatened to become extinct by the loss of domains and functions.

In the *context of national states*, governments rely on languages in which they run their countries. African governments predominantly use the languages of the former colonial powers for this purpose, and these are the prevailing languages in administration, in secondary and higher education, in modern literature, as well as in the mass media. The knowledge of these imported languages is still – after 50 years of independence – confined to the educated elite and to the urban centers, and for that very reason, *English* and *French* have not yet replaced African languages.

Swahili in the Republic of Tanzania and *Setswana* in the Republic of Botswana are among the few African languages that are official media of nation-wide communication. These languages are challenging the vitality of the other languages in their respective national context. The motives of speakers of minority languages for shifting to these nationally dominant languages are obvious; better prospects in social and economic mobility for themselves and their children. *Swahili* threatens more than 130 other Tanzanian languages, while *Setswana* does the same to about 30 languages spoken in Botswana. Governmental language policies in Botswana foster the use of the national language *Setswana* not only as a second, but also as a first language. Other East African languages with a nation-wide distribution, such as *Kinyaruanda* and *Kirundi*, do not dominate other languages, because they – maybe no longer – exist within the national boundaries. Twa communities in Rwanda and Burundi still maintain a distinct culture and identity. While they speak *Kinyaruanda* and *Kirundi* today, they might as well have had their own distinct linguistic heritage.

African languages of small speech communities, however, were threatened in the past exclusively and are threatened still today predominantly by languages of other African languages and in *sub-national contexts*. For minorities that speak severely endangered languages, the languages of the immediate neighbours are generally more attractive than the established national majority languages. Thus, very small languages are commonly threatened and replaced in local contact situations. In Southern Ethiopia, for example, *'Ongota* is replaced by *Ts'amakko* (*Tsamay*), *Kwegu* (*Koegu*) by *Mursi*, *Shabo* by *Majang* and *Harro* by *Bayso*. Speech communities of minority languages in all these cases abandon their languages for quite different reasons to adopt another minority language as a new mother tongue.

Ethno-linguistic minorities in Sub-Saharan Africa generally live in subnational contexts in multilingual settings, mainly because of marginalization. Bad government in many African states and policies of exclusion by the economically dominant countries of the world deny members of minorities, access to economic and social progress.

Poor infrastructure has kept many rural communities in isolation and some languages are spoken until today for that reasons. Quite a number of languages, for example, survived on islands in lakes of the East African Rift Valley such as *Elmolo* in Lake Turkana, *Gats'ame* in Lake Chamo, *Haro* in Lake Abbay, and *Zay* in Lake Zway. All these languages, however, either have disappeared (*Elmolo*) or are severely endangered, because the island-communities are leaving their isolated islands to live among other speech communities on the main land.

Sub-national settings, such as the ones mentioned in this chapter, are the most ancient scenarios of language displacement. Even when linguae francae spread as media in regional trade relations, these languages were commonly acquired as additional languages and for that reason did not challenge any mother tongues. With the rise of centralized power centers and the establishment of national states, ethnic languages have been increasingly threatened, very often through physical force. In Sudan, for example, an Arab elite has not only resettled entire communities, but also committed physical genocide in the Nuba mountains and other parts of the country. Since 1989, far more than a million people were killed and numerous communities where wiped out in the government's attempt to spread Islam and Arabic to the entire Sudan. Languages disappeared because the speech communities have been either dispersed or extirpated. The endangerment of communities, of course, must be the main concern in these cases of physical violence, however, the distinct cultures and languages of such people should not be ignored, because they are the reason for their suppression.

In most Nation states, national dominant majority languages threaten minority languages. In Sub-Saharan Africa, in contrast to other parts of the world, most languages of ethno-linguistic minorities have survived until today, *because* their speakers have been and are still being marginalized and neglected, that is excluded from national developments. As such barriers will fall, communities will also abandon their languages in order to participate in economic and social benefits.

Through mass media the charms of modern advertising and consumer goods reaches even local communities and world languages are spreading along with that. African languages will increasingly disappear, as communities will be allowed to participate in economic and social progress.

With about one third of the world's languages, the African continent is among the linguistically richest areas on our planet. Thus, a great deal of the future of linguistic diversity in general depends on what is going to happen to the African languages.

For a discussion of the terminology and designators used in the following tables, refer to Krauss Chapter 1, this volume:

"safe"	a+
stable	a–
instable; eroded	a
definitively endangered	b
severely endangered	c
critically endangered	d
extinct	e

The columns *Set A* and *Set B* refer to criteria for selecting and ranking of endangered languages most urgently in need for documentation (see *Introduction* to this volume). The four figures in *Set A* and two figures in *Set B* range from 1–4 ("–" no information) and they provide the following information (left to right):

Set A:
Speaker/population ratio: – = 0; 1 = < 5%; 2 = 5–10%; 3 = 11–50%; 4 = 51–90%.
Language transmission: 1 = no; 2 = <10%; 3 = 20–70%; 4 = close to 100%.
Language use: 1 = none; 2 = few, marginal; 3 = some key domains; 4 = all, most.
Attitude towards their own language: 1 = negative; 2 = neutral; 3 = not supportive to maintenance; 4 = strongly supportive.

Set B:
Scientific (linguistic) value): 1 = genetic status unknown; 2 = language isolate; 3 = specific aspects; 4 = closely related languages are described or vital.
Current extend of documentation: 1 = no data; 2 = poorly known; 3 = sketches; 4 = well documented.

Table 2. Endangered Languages in Eastern Africa

	Language	Speakers	Population	Set A	Set B	Status
1	Aasáx (T)	? 0	few	-,-,-,-	-,-	d, e
2	Aja (S)	200	–	-,-,-,-	3,-	c, d
3	Aka (S)	300	–	-,-,-,-	-,-	c, d
4	Akie (K, T)	50	> 500	2,1,1,-	3,2	c
5	Alagwa (T)	10,000	10,000	4,4,2,2	3,2	a
6	Anfillo (E)	> 100	1,000s	1,1,1,1	2,1	c
7	Arbore (E)	< 3,000	< 6,000	-,-,-,-	-,-	b
8	Argobba (E)	10,000	< 60,000	1,1,1,2	4,3	b
9	Baygo (S)	0	850	-,-,-,-	-,-	e
10	Bayso (E)	> 3,000	3,260	4,4,2,2	3,2	a
11	Berti (S)	0	–	-,-,-,-	-,-	e
12	Birkid (S)	0	< 100	-,-,-,-	-,-	e
13	Boguru (S)	494	–	-,-,-,-	2,-	c
14	Bong'om (K)	–	2,500	4,2,2,1	3,2	a
15	Bongo (S)	< 10,000	< 10,000	4,-,2,-	-,1	a
16	Boni, Aweera (K)	> 3,000	< 4,000	3,3,3,2	3,2	a
17	Buga, Mangayat (S)	400	–	-,-,2,-	3,2	b
18	Bussa (E)	> 4,000	> 6,000	–	-,-	a
19	Dahalo (K)	< 400	< 400	4,2,2,1	3,2	b
20	Dair (S)	1,000	–	-,-,-,-	2,-	c
21	Dilling (S)	5,000	–	-,-,2,-	3,2	a
22	Dimme (E)	> 4,000	> 6,000	3,3,1,-	3,2	a
23	El Hugeirat (S)	? 0	? 200	-,-,1,-	-,-	d, e
24	Elmolo (K)	0	> 400	-,-,-,-	3,1	e
25	Fongoro, Kole (S)	? few	? > 1,000	-,1,1,1	-,-	d
26	Gafat (E)	0	0	-,-,-,-	3,3	d
27	Ganjule, Gats'ame, Harro (E)	< 2,000	2,656	3,3,2,3	3,2	a
28	Gula (S)	few 100s	< 2,000	-,-,-,-	-,-	c
29	Gule/Anej (S)	< 10	1,000	1,1,2,1	3,2	d
30	Gweno (T)	few	1,000s	4,4,3,4	4,1	d
31	Hozo (E)	3,000	–	-,-,-,-	-,-	a
32	Indri (S)	700	–	–	-,-	b
33	Jebel Haraza (S)	0	–	-,-,-,-	-,-	e
34	K'emant (E)	1,500	170,000	1,1,1,1	3,3	c
35	Karo (E)	200	–	-,-,-,-	3,-	d
36	Keiga (S)	6,000	–	-,-,2,-	-,-	a
37	Kelo (S)	> 200	–	-,-,2,-	-,-	d

Table 2. cont.

Language	Speakers	Population	Set A	Set B	Status
38 Kidie Lafofa (S)	< 600	–	-,-,2,-	-,-	d
39 Kinare (K)	0	> 300	-,-,-,-	3,2	e
40 Ko (S)	< 5,000	–	-,-,-,-	3,-	a
41 Komo, Koma (E)	< 1,400	< 1,500	-,-,1,-	-,-	b
42 Kore (K)	0	< 250	-,-,-,-	3,3	e
43 Kw'adza (T)	0 ?	few	-,-,-,-	3,2	d
44 Kwegu (E)	> 200	< 500	1,1,1,1	3,3	d
45 Logorik (S)	2,000	–	-,-,-,-	-,-	b
46 Lorkoti (K)	0	< 10	-,-,-,-	3,3	e
47 Moda (S)	600	–	-,-,-,-	-,-	b
48 Molo (S)	> 100	–	-,-,1,-	3,2	d
49 Mursi (E)	3,200	3,200	-,-,-,-	-,-	a
50 Napore (K)	? 0	< 20	-,-,-,-	3,2	d
51 Na'o, Nayi (E)	3,000	< 4,000	-,-,1,-	3,2	a
52 Nyang'i (U)	< 10	< 100	1,1,1,1	3,2	d
53 Omo Murle (E)	few	425	1,1,1,1	3,3	d
54 Opuuo/Shita (E)	few	300	-,-,-,-	-,-	d, e
55 Omotik/Laamoot (K)	< 50	100s	2,1,1,1	3,2	c
56 Ongamo (K, T)	> 300	> 3,000	2,1,1,1	3,2	d
57 'Ongota/Birale (E)	> 10	> 100	2,1,1,2	2,2	c
58 Qwarenya (E)	? 4	> 30,000	1,1,1,1	3,2	d, e
59 Segeju (K)	? 0	few	-,-,-,-	3,3	d
60 Shabo (E)	< 500	> 600	3,2,1,1	2,2	b
61 Soo/Tepeth (U)	100	> 5,000	1,1,1,1	3,3	c
62 Sogoo (K)	? 0	few	-,1,1,1	3,2	d, e
63 Suba (K, T)	< 40,000	< 80,000	3,3,2,2	3,3	a
64 Tennet (S)	4,000	–	-,-,2,-	3,2	b
65 Ts'amakko (E)	< 8,000	–	-,-,-,-	3,2	a
66 Tumtum (S)	7,300	–	-,-,2,-	-,-	a
67 Wali (S)	< 500	–	-,-,-,-	-,-	c
68 Yaaku (K)	? 0/3	> 3,000	-,-,-,-	2,2	d, e
69 Yulu, Binga (S)	3,000	–	-,-,-,-	-,-	a
70 Zay, Zway (E)	< 1,000	? 5,000	4,3,1,2	3,2	d

Countries: E – Ethiopia, K – Kenya, S – Sudan, T – Tanzania, U – Uganda
Main source for Sudan: Gordon (ed) 2005. *Ethnologue.*

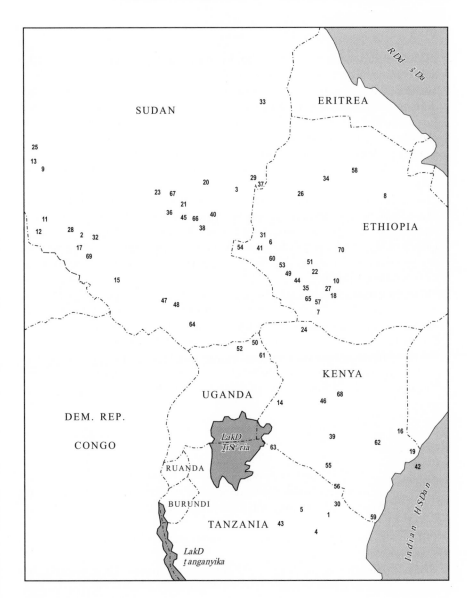

Map 12. Eastern Africa

Notes

1. I would like to thank Mats Exter, Jim Bennett, and Lenore Grenoble for valuable comments on a previous version of this paper.
2. Haacke (2002) suggested changing *Khoisan* to *Khoesaan* by referring to the underlying correct spellings of the source terms from *Khoekhoegowab*. As argued further below, *Khoisan* should only be used as a technical term of linguistic classification, and not in the meaning "herders" and "foragers". For that reason, we prefer the obviously artificial term and spelling *Khoisan*.
3. The people who are referred to by "Khoe" in this phrase call themselves Khoekhoe.
4. "Die Buschmannsprachen sind untereinander eng verwandt, haben aber zu anderen Sprachgruppen keine genetischen Beziehungen. ... Das Hottentottische (Khoekhoe, M. B.) steht ebenso isoliert wie die Sprachen der Buschmänner" (Westermann 1949: 14). "Es liegt auch kein haltbarer Grund vor, die Sprachen der Hottentotten und der Buschmänner als genetisch verwandt anzusehen" (Westermann 1949: 9).
5. "Mein Informant Siriri [Seriri, M. B.], der nur widerwillig zugab, ǀGandakhoe zu sein, bestand auf Búgákhòè auch als Selbstbezeichnung seiner Leute. Auch der Sprachname stimmte mit dem Búga-Namen überein" (Vossen 1997: 77).
6. It is highly unlikely that any ǀXam speakers are still living.
7. ǀxarra "different, separately", ǃke e: ǀxarra "people who are different, strangers" (D. Bleek 1956: 363), ǁke "to meet, be together with" (D. Bleek 1956: 566)
8. The years in this column refer to the time when the last fluent speakers passed away.

References

Almeida, António de (edited by Tobias, P. V. and J. Blacking)
  1965   *Bushmen and other Non-Bantu peoples of Angola.* Three lectures by António de Almeida. Johannesburg: Witwatersrand University.
Barnard, Alan
  1980   Khoesan Southern Africa as a culture area. *Namibiana* 2,2: 7–15.
Batibo, Herman
  2005   Hua: a critically endangered Khoesan language in the Kweneng District of Botswana. In Crawhall, Nigel and Nicholas Ostler (eds.) *Creating outsiders.* Endangered languages, migration and marginalization. Bath: Foundation of Endangered Languages. 87–93.
Bleek, Wilhelm Heinrich Immanuel and Lucy C. Lloyd
  1911   *Specimens of Bushmen folklore.* London: George Allen and Co.
Brenzinger, Matthias (ed.)
  1992   *Language Death.* Factual and theoretical explorations with special reference to East Africa. Berlin and New York: Mouton de Gruyter.

Brenzinger, Matthias and Gerrit J. Dimmendaal
  1992   Social contexts of language death. In Brenzinger (ed.) 3–7.
Brenzinger, Matthias; Heine Bernd and Ingo Heine
  1994   *The Mukogodo Maasai.* An ethnobotanical survey. Köln: Rüdiger
            Köppe.
Cassidy, Lin; Ken Good; Isaac Mazonde and Roberta Rivers
  2001   *An assessment of the status of the San/Basarwa in Botswana.* Wind-
            hoek: Legal Assistance Centre.
Cronk, Lee
  1989   From hunters to herders: Subsistence change as a reproductive strat-
            egy among the Mukogodo. *Current anthropology* 30,2: 224–234.
Ehret, Chrisopher and Derek Nurse
  1981   The Taita Cushites. *Sprache und Geschichte in Afrika* 3: 125–168.
Estermann, Carlos (edited by Gordon D. Gibson)
  1976   *The ethnography of Southwestern Angola. I: The Non-Bantu peoples.*
            The Ambo Ethnic Group. New York, London: Holmes and Meier.
Gordon, Raymond G. (ed.)
  2005   Ethnologue: Languages of the world. (15th edition) Dallas, Tex.: SIL
            International. Online version.
Greenberg, Joseph
  1966   *The languages of Africa.* Bloomington: Indiana University and The
            Hague: Mouton and Co.
Güldemann, Tom and Rainer Vossen
  2000   Khoisan. In Heine and Nurse (eds.) 99–122.
Haacke, Wilfrid H. G.
  1996   *Language and literature in Africa*, Study guide for Core Module HSL
            0111, part 1, Department of African Languages, University of Namibia.
  2002   *Linguistic evidence in the study of origins: The case of the Namibian
            Khoekhoe-speakers.* (UNAM Inaugural Lecture Proceedings) Wind-
            hoek: University of Namibia.
Haacke, Wilfrid H. G. and Eliphas Eiseb
  2002   *A Khoekhoegowab dictionary with an English-Khoekhoegowab In-
            dex.* Windhoek: Gamsberg-Macmillan.
Hasselbring, Sue
  2000   Where are the Khoesan of Botswana? In: Batibo, Herman M. and
            Birgit Smieja (eds.) *Botswana: The future of the minority languages.*
            Frankfurt a. M.: Peter Lang.
Heine, Bernd
  1974/75   Notes on the Yaaku language. *Afrika und Übersee* 58,1/2: 27–61 and
            119–138.
Heine, Bernd and Derek Nurse (eds.)
  2000   *African languages: An introduction.* Cambridge: Cambridge Univer-
            sity Press.

Penn, Nigel
    1996   "Fated to perish": the destruction of the Cape San. In Skotnes (ed.)
            81–91.
Schapera, Isaak
    1930   *The Khoisan peoples of South Africa: Bushmen and Hottentots.* Lon-
            don: George Routledge and Sons.
Schultze Jena, Leonhard
    1928   *Zur Kenntnis des Körpers der Hottentotten und Buschmänner.* Jena:
            Gustav Fischer.
Sampson, Clavil Garth
    1988   *Stylistic boundaries among mobile hunter-foragers.* Washington, Lon-
            don: Smithsonian Institute Press.
Skotnes, Pippa (ed.)
    1996   *Miscast: Negotiating the presence of the Bushmen.* Cape Town: Uni-
            versity of Cape Town.
Tanaka, Jiro
    1980   *The San, hunter-gatherers of the Kalahari.* A study in ecological an-
            thropology. (Translated by David W. Hughes). Tokyo: University of
            Tokyo Press.
Tobias, Phillip V.
    1956   On the survival of the Bushmen, with an estimate of the problem fac-
            ing anthropologists. *Africa* 26: 174–186.
Traill, Anthony
    1985   *Phonetic and phonological studies of !Xóõ Bushman.* Hamburg: Hel-
            mut Buske.
    1996   !Khwa-Ka Hhouiten Hhouiten "The rush of the storm": The linguis-
            tic death of |Xam. In Skotnes (ed.) 161–183.
Vossen, Rainer
    1997   *Die Khoe-Sprachen.* Ein Beitrag zur Erforschung der Sprachge-
            schichte Afrikas. Köln: Rüdiger Köppe.
Westermann, Diedrich
    1949   *Sprachbeziehungen und Sprachverwandtschaft in Afrika.* Sitzungsber-
            ichte der Deutschen Akademie der Wissenschaften zu Berlin. Philoso-
            phisch-historische Klasse, 1949, No. 1. Berlin: Akademie-Verlag.
Westphal, Ernst O. J.
    1971   The click languages of Southern and Eastern Africa. In Sebeok, T.
            (ed.) *Current trends in linguistics,* Vol. 7: *Linguistics in Sub-Saharan
            Africa.* 367–420.
Wilmsen, Edwin N.
    1989   *Land filled with flies.* A political economy of the Kalahari. Chicago,
            London: University of Chicago Press.
Winter, J. Christoph
    1976   Language shift among the Aasáx, a hunter-gatherer tribe in Tanza-
            nia. *Sprache und Geschichte in Afrika* 1: 175–204.

Chapter 10
Endangered Languages in Europe

Tapani Salminen

1. Introdution

In western Europe, the knowledge of endangered languages among lay-men and many linguists is limited to a small number of classic examples like *Basque*, the *Celtic* languages, *Frisian*, and *Romansch*, as well as, per-haps, *Saami* or *Sorbian*. It is the purpose of this article to show that, be-sides the best-known cases, there are many other languages in Europe that are, indeed, often marginalized or ignored by linguists and authori-ties alike. A related goal is to give a consistent and analytical assessment of the actual language divisions in a continent where literary traditions and other extra-linguistic factors tend to obscure language boundaries. Before entering strictly European matters, however, I try to present a glo-bal overview of what has been achieved by previous studies in classifying languages according to their levels of endangerment.[1]

2. Earlier studies in levels of language endangerement

While this book undoubtedly represents the first comprehensive and sys-tematic survey of endangered languages on a world-wide scale, it has several predecessors. Some of the earlier projects have had quite ambi-tious goals but their implementation has often left a lot to be desired. A few landmarks from the past decade follow.

The first collective work to contain broadly comparable data from various continents was *Endangered languages* (Robins and Uhlenbeck 1991), published under the authority of the Permanent International Committee of Linguistics (CIPL), which under Stephen Wurm's direc-tion became one of the central institutions in enhancing the study of en-dangered languages. It did not cover the world, one of the missing parts being, incidentally, Europe, but it gave a clear picture of the worldwide wave of language endangerment and extinction and thus boosted fur-ther research in the field.

More linguists became concerned and awakened to action when the
first issue of *Language* in 1992 published a collection of papers on language endangerment edited by Kenneth Hale. One of the contributions
included Michael Krauss's well-known predictions of rapid loss of language diversity (Krauss 1992) that were widely quoted in the media.

One of the immediate responses came from the 1992 International
Congress of Linguists in Quebec, which had endangered languages as a
special topic, and where Michael Krauss elaborated his views on the extent of language loss (Krauss 1993). Participants commonly agreed that
the maintenance and documentation of endangered languages should be
given the utmost priority.

In 1992, the Endangered Languages Committee of CIPL held a meeting in Paris under the auspices of UNESCO, where most leading linguists
active in the field were present. On the initiative of Stephen Wurm, the
meeting launched a major plan to collect and publish data on all endangered languages in the world, including a research project called the
UNESCO Red Book of Endangered Languages, and a research centre
called the International Clearing House for Endangered Languages
(ICHEL), whose establishment was entrusted to Shigeru Tsuchida.

The Red Book project was carried out by a number of regional experts, who by the end of 1993 prepared reports consisting of standard
one-page summaries of each endangered language, with information
about the state of the language (the presence of children speakers, mean
age of youngest speakers, total number of speakers, etc.) as well as relevant sources, in other words, the scope of the project was in many ways
similar to the present one.

The Clearing House was opened at the Department of Asian and Pacific Linguistics of the University of Tokyo in 1994, and with Tasaku Tsunoda as its director, it was officially inaugurated in 1995 in connection with
a symposium on endangered languages (Matsumura 1998). Already in
1994, the authors of the Red Book reports were requested to send their
contributions to the Clearing House, and over the course of the development of the Internet, some of reports were made available via the WWW.
Curiously, the Red Book project is only mentioned in passing in the symposium proceedings (Krauss 1998: 110, Wurm 1998: 195), so it seems that
at that time it did not have a priority status on the Clearing House agenda.
Consequently, the project has not received much publicity, and several reports, including all of the Americas and parts of Asia have been missing.
Recently, however, the first data on endangered languages in the Americas, those of Bolivia, appeared on the Red Book homepage at the ICHEL

site, so the Red Book is still alive and may one day become the extensive databank open to the public as it was intended to.

The only printed publication related to the Red Book project is the *Atlas of the world's languages in danger of disappearing*. This atlas was first published in 1996 (Wurm 1996) and revised, enlarged and updated in a second edition (Wurm 2001).

One of the problems with the UNESCO Red Book of Endangered Languages was that UNESCO itself effectively lost interest in it. For instance, there was no mention of it when the UNESCO Director-General in 1998 decided about a new project called the UNESCO Report on the World's Languages. It remains to be seen what comes out of the latter project, which is coordinated by the UNESCO Centre of the Basque Country, and has distributed questionnaires to language specialists and activists across the world. The general problem with this line of work is that incoming data is of uneven quality, which means that sorting out the data may take more time and energy than actively looking for information in published sources.

Another initiative to collect information of endangered languages was made by the Linguistic Society of America's Committee on Endangered Languages and their Preservation under the supervision of Akira Yamamoto. Information was gathered through special survey questionnaires (Yamamoto 1998), and an updated summary of the data is available at the LSA website. Since the participants are typically leading experts on the languages on which they have reported, the quality of the survey is high, but the coverage of the world is, by necessity, random. For instance, there are only three survey questionnaires on European languages, on *Gascon*, *Sorbian*, and *Faetar*, yet these contain very useful data.

A major source of information on all languages, irrespective of their endangerment status, the *Ethnologue* (Grimes 1996) should not be left without mention here. The main problem for a user interested in the least-known languages of the world is the frequent lack of exact and explicit source references, which makes it difficult to assess the background of occasional conflicts with other sources.

Other works with global data are the *Atlas of the world's languages* (Moseley and Asher 1994) and *The encyclopedia of language and linguistics* (Asher 1994). Some of the regional and country-specific publications that are largely devoted to the status of endangered languages are Collis (1990) for Arctic regions, Brenzinger (1992, 1998) for Africa, Solncev and Mikhalchenko (1992), Vakhtin (1993), and Neroznak (1994) for the Russian Federation, and Shoji and Janhunen (1997) for northern areas. Jenniges (1997) is a useful bibliography focusing on western Europe. It was published by the European Bureau for Lesser Used Languages, which has produced a great number of interesting publications on minority languages within the European Union. An earlier bibliography covering most parts of Europe is Pogarell (1983).

The history of language endangerment studies in Europe partly differs from the course of events in the rest of the world. Crucially, European minority language communities have not been politically subjugated and socially stigmatized to the same extent as indigenous communities in other continents, which means that they have been able to pursue their interests independently of each other. It is therefore not easy to formulate continent-wide generalizations. The roots of the field go further back in history than in other parts of the world, at least to the aftermath of the First World War. Nevertheless, the official policies of most European countries until recent decades were designed to eradicate minority languages.

Early publications dealing with language endangerment in Europe took a decidedly political view-point, for example *Lingual minorities in Europe* (Holmestad and Lade 1969), which consists of proceedings of a conference arranged by proponents of the *New Norwegian* literary language in Norway, and includes heated debate on the rights and the very existence of minority languages in areas which continue to be highly problematic for minority language communities, notably Greece.

Another line of publications – more closely related to language endangerment but from the angle of an outside observer rather than somebody directly concerned with the developments – is represented by *Welsh and the other dying languages in Europe* (Adler 1977). Several other, but generally more superficial presentations of the situation of endangered languages in Europe appeared in the 1970s and 1980s, but one book, *Minority languages today* (Haugen, McClure and Thomson 1981 [1990]), a collection of papers presented at the first International conference on minority languages in Glasgow in 1980, constitutes a clear landmark in its in-depth discussions and the first signs of what Lucille Watahomigie and Akira Yamamoto have aptly called 'action linguistics'. The same year saw the publishing of one of the most important case studies in the emerging field, namely *Language death: the life cycle of a Scottish Gaelic dialect* (Dorian 1981). Since then, the term 'language death' has been gradually replaced with 'language endangerment', as linguists have become aware of their possibilities not only to reflect on but also to take action in response to the threat of language extinction.

3. Special features of language endangerment in Europe

Europe is the home of most of the colonial powers in world history, and European languages are therefore well represented amongst those languages that are replacing others in every continent. In Europe itself, the picture of language endangerment is complex, but as a rule, the languages threatening the existence of others are the official languages of nation-states. With few exceptions, the leaders of these states have seen and largely still see linguistic and cultural pluralism as an unwanted historical relic undermining the so-called national unity of their countries, and have harnessed the government machinery for assimilating minority languages and cultures. Consequently, the large majority, more than two thirds, of European languages are endangered, while those languages that function as the official and dominant languages of European states, numbering less than fifty, can be regarded as very safe compared to languages with the same numbers of speakers in the rest of the world. It should be remembered, though, that a nominal official status does not necessarily secure the position of a language if it is not the factual dominant language of the country, as is well known from the case of *Irish Gaelic* in the Republic of Ireland.

There are several other features characteristic of the situation in Europe that affect the forecast of language survival in one direction or the other, some of which are dealt with here.

For one thing, it is obvious that languages with small numbers of speakers tend to be more endangered than those with much larger numbers. In Europe, however, the correlation between the number of speakers and the level of endangerment is remarkably poor. There are languages like *Faroese* with some 50,000 speakers but facing no immediate threat, while languages with several hundred thousand speakers, for instance *Breton* and *Erzya*, are definitely, or in the case of *Breton,* severely endangered. Similarly, *North Saami*, with its 30,000 speakers, while endangered, is perhaps less so than *Romani*, spoken by a couple of million people.

A high level of language maintenance among smaller peoples like the *Faroese* and the *North Saami* is the result of their relative isolation and their naturally evolved cultural autonomy which at least since recently has been supported by enlightened policies of the leadership of the states to which they are subjugated. By contrast, *Breton* and *Romani* are examples of languages treated with open hostility by the authorities in the countries where they are spoken. In most countries, political and administrative decision-makers take less extreme attitudes towards minority languages, but tend to be indifferent to their fate and reluctant to support them. A special case within Europe was the Soviet Union, where the official policies originally favoured linguistic pluralism but a dramatic change after the Second World War made a shift to *Russian* monolingualism among minority peoples the desired goal, if not in theory, at least in the implementation of educational and other cultural policies. The relatively strong position of larger minority languages such as *Erzya* is largely due to the ineffectiveness of the Soviet machinery in achieving its goal.

In recent years, the general atmosphere in most European countries, including the Russian Federation and to some extent France, has become more positive towards the maintenance of non-official languages. In many cases, however, the changes are cosmetic and, when more substantial, may have come too late to stop the gradual erosion of language communities. There are contrary examples to the recent positive trends as well, for instance, the position of *Sorbian* weakened after the unification of Germany from what it was in the German Democratic Republic. One country where hardly any positive changes have taken place is Greece, which contrary to its democratic traditions, continues to disregard the existence of minority languages and to suppress the freedom of expression of their speakers. The even more extreme case of Turkey, is beyond the scope of this article.

As the number of language families in Europe is low, it is common that the dominant and the minority languages are closely related. This situation tends to lead to, in Stephen Wurm's terms (this volume), both linguistic and sociolinguistic endangerment, which means that both the structures and the functions of the minority languages are being reduced. Furthermore, regional languages genetically close to the official language are often labelled 'dialect' or 'patois' by authorities and community members alike, which hampers their maintenance and development.

Another feature typical of Europe is the high level of political organization of minority language communities. In many cases, political activism has led to a fuller recognizition and occasionally to a genuine autonomy of a minority people, but there are examples of controversies, internal splits, and counterproductive actions within such movements as well. The recent history of the *North Saami* can be mentioned as an example of a success story: these communities have been able to secure a semi-autonomous area in northern Norway and to gain a better status in Finland and Sweden as well. The *North Saami* also functions as a model and a source of moral support to many other members in the so-called fourth world movement of indigenous peoples. On the other hand, *North Saami* activists tend to marginalize the other *Saami* language communities, which are much smaller and lack political weight. The *North Saami* also appear reluctant to allow a definitive survey of their own community presumably in fear of finding out that their number is smaller that expected which might have a negative impact on their further demands for political rights.

The *Occitan* movement of southern France is another characteristic example of cultural and political awakening in minority language circles. In France in particular, literary activities are standardly regarded as the highest level of culture, and *Occitan* activists have adopted this view in the propagation of a normative written use for several quite distinct language communities in the area. '*Occitan*' is therefore perhaps better understood as the name of a cultivated literary language than a label for all spoken varieties in the area. It can be noticed that while there is a productive albeit occasionally discordant network of individuals actively working on *Occitan* literature, the spoken use of *Occitano-Romance* languages in France is diminishing rapidly, and a cleavage between the 'pure' written *Occitan* and the 'mixed' vernaculars seems to be getting wider.

4. Technical and terminological issues

Before we can start putting languages on scales we must know what the languages are. Many linguists would start and finish the discussion on defining the distinction between 'language' and 'dialect' by saying that it is all too relative an issue and not really a linguistic one, and that no absolute criteria can ever be found for making it. I do not share that view and have grown quite tired of its endless repetitions. While there certainly are borderline cases, not least in Europe, it is usually quite easy to say which linguistic isoglosses amount to language boundaries and which do not, and the truly problematic cases are better regarded as challenges than obstacles. The problem is rather that the units recognizable as languages according to the most objective and consistent criteria do not correspond to the languages listed by authorities or linguists working from a traditional perspective.

Most misunderstandings in these questions arise when languages are equalled with literary traditions. While it is commonplace that one literary language is used per one language community, it is by no means a rule. There may be several literary traditions for a single language (*Norwegian* and *Serbo-Croat* being prime examples), or a language community may lack a literary language and use a literary tradition based on another, perhaps closely related language in a diglossic manner.

Another source of confusion is the normative usage of speech dictated by elite groups of nation-states. Most readers have probably heard that "a language is a dialect with an army and a navy". It seems that many people have not understood the critical and ironic nature of this slogan, but this becomes obvious from the fact that it was first stated in a language without an army or a navy, namely *Yiddish*.

Insofar as literary use or political boundaries do not define languages, it is possible to work within a strictly linguistic framework, as long as one strives for maximally consistent criteria when dealing with borderline cases. One has to choose between two policies, either a lumping procedure, where highly distinct varieties can at least historically be united and therefore regarded as dialects of one language, or a splitting strategy, which sees each straightforwardly identifiable distinct variety as an independent language. Since the latter policy is in much better accordance with ethnolinguistic pluralism, lumpers being typically those who want to subjugate smaller groups under larger ones without respecting their distinctiveness, I choose to be a splitter and would like to think that so do most people who are in direct contact and cooperation with language communities. In this framework, no question about the status of, for instance, *Frisian* or *Saami* arises, but they are undoubtedly language groups rather than single languages. There is, of course, a risk of taking the splitter approach too far, this is why employing consistent criteria across the continent, and the world, is so vital.

At the same time it must be readily acknowledged that there are different kinds of languages, and also different kinds of dialects, with regard to their affinities with other varieties. The concept of 'regional languages' as it is been used here refers to languages that are distinct from but sufficiently close to the dominant language of their area to live with it in a diglossic situation. Regional languages are typical of large areas of many European countries, notably Germany, France, and Italy.

There are also cases which I would like to call 'co-languages' (alternative term suggested by Christopher Moseley: 'twin languages'), meaning two (or more) varieties that are linguistically very close but whose few distinct features are nevertheless commonly seen as decisive, and whose borderline is vague or does not coincide with the officially defined language areas. Examples of co-languages in Europe would be *Galician* and *Portuguese*, or *Bulgarian* and *Macedonian*. The *Oc* languages of southern

France as well as *Campidanese Sardinian* and *Logudorese Sardinian* varieties might be called co-languages as well, but the use of the term should obviously not be inflated to the extent that it refers to all pairs and groups of closely related languages.

Furthermore, there are varieties that are geographically detached from a closely related larger variety, and these have been called either isolated or outlying or diaspora dialects, classic examples being *Channel Islands French* and *Cypriot Arabic*. At least in the context of language endangerment, it seems appropriate to call them languages rather than dialects, and the term that I adopt here is 'outlying languages'.

A few languages in Europe have a wide and discontinuous geographic distribution, often across several regions and beyond the boundaries of the continent. These 'non-territorial' languages include the *Jewish* languages *Judezmo* and *Yiddish*, as well as *Plautdietsch* and *Romani*. The most wide-spread language in Europe is easily *Romani*, and it may prove better to treat it as a group of perhaps seven languages rather than a single one, but this and related matters are aptly discussed in Matras, Bakker and Kyuchukov (1997). A major omission in this article are the so-called mixed languages with *Romani* influence, i. e. *Angloromani*, Traveller languages, *Caló*, and similar languages in the Balkans, but it is truly difficult to find information about their endangerment status. Needless to say, the same goes with secret in-group languages like *Hantyrka*, *Rotwelsch*, or *Shelta*. Both types of languages are dealt with in Bakker and Mous (1994).

Many other European languages are, because of a practical necessity, beyond the scope of this presentation, for instance sign languages, classical languages like *Latin*, and artificial languages like *Volapük*, although many of them may well be described as endangered. Languages spoken across the borders of Europe but with the majority of speakers outside Europe, notably *Kazakh*, *Tundra Nenets*, and *Turkish*, are not described below. Europe is defined as excluding all of Caucasia but including the island of Cyprus.

Map 13. Europe

1 Basque	36 Karelian	71 Resian Slovene
2 Galician	37 Lude	72 Romani
3 Asturian	38 Olonetsian	73 Judezmo
4 Leonese	39 Veps	74 Italkian
5 Aragonese	40 Livonian	75 Istriot
6 Gascon	41 Walloon	76 Aromanian
7 Languedocian	42 West Frisian	77 Istro-Romanian
8 Provençal	43 Saterlandic	78 Megleno-Romanian
9 Alpine Provençal	44 North Frisian	
10 Limousin	45 Low Saxon	79 Vojvodina Rusyn
11 Auvergnat	46 Lower Sorbian	80 Arvanite Albanian
12 Gallo	47 Upper Sorbian	81 Yevanic
13 Norman	48 Kashubian	82 Tsakonian
14 Channel Islands French	49 Burgenland Croatian	83 Csángó Hungarian
	50 Romansch	84 Cypriot Arabic
15 Picard	51 Algherese Catalan	85 Yiddish
16 Poitevin-Saintongeais	52 Gardiol	86 Plautdietsch
17 Francoprovençal	53 Faetar	87 Rusyn
18 Corsican	54 Gallurese Sardinian	88 Eastern Mari
19 Breton	55 Sassarese Sardinian	89 Western Mari
20 Welsh	56 Campidanese Sardinian	90 Erzya
21 Irish Gaelic		91 Moksha
22 Scottish Gaelic	57 Logudorese Sardinian	92 Udmurt
23 Scots	58 Piedmontese	93 Permyak
24 South Saami	59 Ligurian	94 Komi
25 Ume Saami	60 Lombard	95 Chuvash
26 Pite Saami	61 Emilian	96 Bashkir
27 Lule Saami	62 Romagnol	97 Crimean Tatar
28 North Saami	63 Friulian	98 Krimchak
29 Inari Saami	64 Ladin	99 Karaim
30 Skolt Saami	65 Cimbrian	100 Nogay
31 Akkala Saami	66 Mócheno	101 Gagauz
32 Kildin Saami	67 Töitschu	102 Trukhmen
33 Ter Saami	68 Arbëreshë Albanian	103 Kalmyk
34 Ingrian	69 Griko	
35 Vote	70 Molise Croatian	

5. Survey of endangered languages in Europe

In terms of genetic classification, European languages belong to the following units:

the *Basque* language,
the Albanian, Baltic, Celtic, Germanic, Hellenic, Romance, and Slavonic branches, and the Romani language of the Indo-Aryan subbranch of the Indo-Iranian branch of the *Indo-European* language family,
the Kalmyk language of the *Mongolic* language family,
the Cypriot Arabic and Maltese languages of the Arabic branch of the *Semitic* language family,
the Chuvash language, and several languages of the Kipchak and Oguz subbranches of the Common Turkic branch of the *Turkic* language family, and
the Finnic, Hungarian, Mari, Mordvin, Permian, and Saami branches of the *Uralic* (also known as *Finno-Ugrian*) language family.

Since the genetic classification of European languages, and the history of settlement of some of them, will be treated in more detail in the *Encyclopedia of the World's Endangered Languages* (Moseley, forthcoming), there is no further discussion on the subject here.

The following discussion attempts to evaluate the endangerment status of all autochthonous languages of Europe. Because of the wide ethnolinguistic and geopolitical variation characteristic of the continent, the discussion is divided into six geographic sections. In each section, most of the endangered languages of the area appear in tables following the general format employed in this book. For several of them, supplementary information is included in the preceding text.

In addition, several 'regional' languages, meaning those languages that are closely related to the dominant language of their area, are only mentioned in the text and do not appear in the tables. In most cases they are in a relatively stable diglossic relationship with the dominant language and therefore only 'potentially endangered', but often the situation is unclear, and these languages and their status are invariably in need of thorough documentation. Their exclusion from the tables is not to be understood as a statement against their importance or relevance, on the contrary, one of the reasons for their different treatment is that they have not been studied from the point of view of language endangerment to the extent that the number and age structure of speakers and other crucial data were available.

Languages that have become extinct in the modern era are briefly mentioned before each table.

European languages not included in the tables, whether dominant, regional, or extinct, appear in italics in the text. Endangered dialects of languages that on the whole appear safe are only added in parentheses, even when they are spoken by minority communities, like in the case of *Alsatian* in France, which, while very different from standard *German*, is close to the other *Alemannic* varieties spoken in Germany and Switzerland. In each case, readers are urged to study both the text and the tables before drawing far-fetched conclusions about the distribution and status of endangered languages.

Readers who want to quote figures and other language-specific data should keep in mind that this presentation is largely based on secondary sources, and is itself therefore a tertiary source. Since European languages are generally well-documented, finding suitable primary sources for individual languages is relatively easy, and always recommended. One must remember, though, that different sources may present conflicting data. This means that the figures and evaluations in this presentation are often based on educated guesses as to the reliability of the sources.

The geographic sections are the following: (i) Western Europe, i. e. the Iberian Peninsula, France, and the British Isles; (ii) Northern Europe, notably the Baltic and the Nordic countries; (iii) Central Europe, covering the Low Countries, Germany, Switzerland, Austria, and eastern Central Europe; (iv) Italy; (v) the Balkans; and (vi) Eastern Europe, largely corresponding to the European parts of the Commonwealth of Independent States. For practical reason, *Judezmo* and *Romani* are included in the Balkans section, and *Plautdietsch* and *Yiddish* in the Eastern European section.

For several languages, a relatively large proportion of current speakers reside outside Europe, but except for the non-territorial languages mentioned above, the figures generally refer to the communities that remain in Europe. Speakers who have learnt a language through formal teaching and only rarely have an active command of it are also not included in the figures. This makes a huge difference for *Irish*, but also influences the accounts of other languages with a strong position in the school system like *Basque* and *Welsh*. In their cases, quite a few young people become fluent in the standard forms of the languages but have little use for them in life outside school, especially because the language is often not used with relatives.

5.1. Western Europe

Dominant languages in the area are *English*, *French*, *Portuguese*, and *Spanish* (also called *Castilian*). *Lorrain* and *Champenois* may be better classified as separate *Oïl* languages but are here treated as dialects of *French*. Occasionally other names like '*Morvandiau*' appear in tentative lists of *Oïl* languages.

The only language without a state-wide official status that need not be regarded as endangered is *Catalan* (including *Valencian*), with 6 million speakers.

The only regional language not included in the table is *Extremaduran*, with reports about its distinctiveness, numbers of speakers, and endangerment status being conflicting.

The numbers of speakers of *Galician* (also called *Gallego*) and *Scots* (also called *Lowland Scots*) can be called into question, because it is difficult to estimate how many people in Galicia and Scotland use local varieties of *Spanish* and *English* instead.

Reliable estimates about the numbers of speakers of the *Oc* languages *Auvergnat*, *Languedocian*, and *Limousin*, and the *Oïl* languages *Gallo*, *Norman*, *Picard* and *Poitevin-Saintongeais* are difficult to come by. One could make calculations based on statements that 10 per cent of the population of their geographic areas are speakers. The one thing that is clear is that they are all severely endangered. The figure for *Alpine Provençal* in the table is based on the figure for Italy alone, and it must in reality be larger, and the *Provençal* figure correspondingly lower, insofar as they and the given *Gascon* figure are at all trustworthy. *Gascon* is marked "c+" in the table, thanks to the more vigorous language community on the *Spanish* side of the border where it is known as *Aranese*.

Asturian (also known as *Bable*) and *Leonese* are closely related and often regarded as one language. It seems, however, that original *Leonese* is largely extinct in Spain, while in Portugal, *Leonese*, locally known as *Mirandese*, is used actively. It is solely this group that the figure for *Leonese* is based on.

A well-known example of a language granted a nominal official status but which is not the factual dominant language of the country is *Irish Gaelic* (also called *Irish*) in the Republic of Ireland: the number of its every-day users continues to shrink, and this development can hardly be compensated by its ceremonial functions (Hindley 1990).

Extinct languages in the area include *Mozarabic*, the *Jewish* languages *Shuadit* (also called *Judeo-Provençal*) and *Zarphatic* (also called *Judeo-French*), as well as *Cornish*, *Manx Gaelic* (also called *Manx*), and *Norn*. *Cornish*, or rather a reconstructed version of it, and *Manx Gaelic* have speakers who have learnt them at language classes, but from the point of view of primary speakers they must be considered extinct, *Cornish* long since.

Table 1. Western Europe

Language	Speakers	A				B			Level
		a	b	c	d	a	b	c	
Basque	800,000	3	3	3	3	4	1	4	b
Galician	?	3	3	2	2	1	1	4	b
Asturian	100,000	2	2	2	2	2	1	4	c
Leonese	10,000	1	2	2	2	2	1	4	c
Aragonese	< 30,000	1	2	2	2	2	1	4	c
Gascon	250,000	2	2	2	2	2	1	4	c+
Languedocian	?	2	2	1	2	2	1	4	c
Provençal	< 250,000	2	2	1	2	2	1	4	c
Alpine Provençal	> 100,000	3	2	2	2	2	1	4	b–
Limousin	?	1	1	1	1	2	1	4	c–
Auvergnat	?	1	1	1	1	2	1	4	c–
Gallo	?	2	1	1	1	1	1	4	c–
Norman	?	2	1	1	1	1	1	4	c–
Channel Islands French	10,000	1	1	1	2	1	1	4	c–
Picard	?	2	1	1	1	1	1	4	c–
Poitevin-Saintongeais	?	2	1	1	1	1	1	4	c–
Francoprovençal	150,000	2	2	2	2	2	1	4	b
Corsican	200,000	3	2	2	2	2	1	4	b
Breton	250,000	2	2	2	2	3	1	4	c
Welsh	550,000	3	3	3	3	3	1	4	b
Irish Gaelic	60,000	1	2	2	3	3	1	4	b–
Scottish Gaelic	65,000	2	2	2	3	3	1	4	b
Scots	?	3	3	2	2	1	1	4	b

5.2. Northern Europe

Official languages in northern European countries are *Danish, Estonian, Finnish, Icelandic, Latvian, Lithuanian, Norwegian,* and *Swedish*. The area under discussion also includes adjacent parts of the Russian Federation, with *Russian* as the official language. *Faroese* is co-official in the Faroe Islands, and despite its relatively small number of speakers it cannot be regarded as endangered.

In my understanding, '*Nynorsk*', or *New Norwegian*, is a literary language based on non-endangered *Norwegian* dialects, and should not be dealt with in a discussion on endangerment of spoken languages.

Regional languages not found in the table are at least *Dalecarlian, Jutish, Latgalian, Scanian, Torne Valley Finnish* (including Finnmark Finnish), and *Võru Estonian*, of which at least *Dalecarlian* is likely to be endangered.

The case of *Torne Valley Finnish* is one that I know personally so I am able to give a brief description of the situation. *Torne Valley Finnish*, while usually known through literary activities in Sweden, is spoken on both sides of the Finnish–Swedish border, and on the Finnish side, its diglossia with standard *Finnish* is reasonably stable. *Torne Valley Finnish*, while having several characteristic features, is nevertheless so close to western *Finnish* dialects, including that of my own, that there are no obstacles to mutual understanding. Recognizing it as a separate language is therefore not quite consistent with the moderate splitter-type classification employed in this presentation, which after all that splitting still includes several languages with extensive dialect differences. This being said, it is probably instrumental to the speakers on the Swedish side that the language is cultivated in its local form, and in my view, similar actions would be very welcome in Finnish Torne Valley, and in similar settings everywhere.

Among the *Saami* (also spelled *Sámi*) branch, the language boundaries are generally quite clear, the overall differentiation being more extensive than, for instance, in *Romance* or *Slavonic* branches of the *Indo-European* family. *Akkala Saami* (also known as *Babino Saami*), being reasonably close to both *Skolt Saami* and *Kildin Saami*, is not always recognized but treated as a dialect of either of the neighbouring languages. Since the choice which language it should be a dialect of is basically arbitrary, the only unambiguous solution is to keep it separate from both.

Of the *Finnic* languages listed below *Lude* is not always and *Olonetsian* only rarely recognized as a separate language from *Karelian*. It is true that the neighbouring languages in the chain from Finnish through *Karelian*, *Olonetsian* and *Lude* to *Veps* are close to one another, but the language boundaries are nevertheless clear, and it is far from obvious that *Karelian* is actually closer to *Olonetsian* than to *Finnish*, or that *Lude* is closer to *Olonetsian* than to *Veps*. The only consistent solution is therefore to recognize fully the distinct position of both *Olonetsian* and *Lude*.

Hopefully, there are no major mistakes in the numbers of speakers published in this presentation, but it may be instructive to discuss briefly the background of the hugely erroneous figure of 500 speakers for *Ter*

Saami that I kept publishing several years ago, e. g. in Grünthal and Salminen (1993). First, I made an elementary mistake by counting all the 2,000 ethnic Saami in the Russian Federation as speakers while only less than half of them actually had claimed knowledge of the native language. Then I blindly assumed that the speakers were more or less evenly distributed among the eastern *Saami* languages while all other Saami communities except the Kildin Saami one had been forcibly removed from their home areas and consequently assimilated to Russians and partly to Kildin Saami. The figures given below should be as reliable as possible, and those of eastern *Saami* languages, in particular, are based on field observations of my knowledgeable colleague Leif Rantala.

The only language in the area to become extinct in the modern era is *Kemi Saami*.

While most endangered languages appear to be constantly losing speakers, it may be worthwhile to notice that at least in some *Lule Saami* communities, the language that had already lost its function as the means of communication among children was successfully introduced back to the playground through a concentrated collective effort.

Vote is an example of a language that does not seem to die easily. Already in the 1950s, the number of *Vote* speakers was given at approximately 50, and yet today, the same number is reported. The reason for this miraculous survival is rather mundane though. Several decades ago when linguists were still able to record 'pure' *Vote* they simply ignored speakers whose language, in their view, had been 'corrupted' by neighbouring languages. Today only the latter type of *Vote* is heard, so in the absence of anyone else, its speakers must qualify.

Table 2. Northern Europe

Language	Speakers	A				B			Level
		a	b	c	d	a	b	c	
South Saami	500	2	2	2	3	3	1	4	c
Ume Saami	10	1	1	1	2	3	3	4	d
Pite Saami	10	1	1	1	2	3	3	4	d
Lule Saami	2,000	2	2	2	2	3	1	4	c
North Saami	30,000	3	3	3	3	3	1	4	b
Inari Saami	300	2	2	2	3	3	1	4	c
Skolt Saami	300	2	2	2	3	3	1	4	c
Akkala Saami	8	1	1	1	2	3	3	3	d

Table 2. cont.

Language	Speakers	A				B			Level
		a	*b*	*c*	*d*	*a*	*b*	*c*	
Kildin Saami	700	2	2	2	2	3	1	4	c
Ter Saami	6	1	1	1	2	3	3	3	d
Ingrian	300	2	2	2	2	2	1	4	c
Vote	50	1	1	1	1	2	3	3	d
Karelian	40,000	3	2	2	2	2	1	4	b
Lude	5,000	2	2	2	2	2	1	4	c
Olonetsian	30,000	3	2	2	2	2	1	4	b
Veps	6,000	2	2	2	2	2	1	4	c
Livonian	10	1	1	1	3	2	3	4	d

5.3. Central Europe

Dominant languages in the area are *Czech, Dutch, German, Hungarian, Polish,* and *Slovak.* Not the first official language in Luxembourg, *Luxembourgian* (also called Moselle Franconian) nevertheless has a strong position in a triglossic society, and cannot be regarded as endangered.

Regional languages not included in the table are *Alemannic* (including *Swiss German* and *Alsatian*), *Bavarian* (including *Austrian German*), *Western Flemish, Limburgian, Ripuarian,* and *Eastern Slovak.* Most of these languages live in stable diglossia with official and standard languages and need not be regarded as endangered. There are further *Flemish* and *Franconian* varieties that may be labelled regional languages but are here treated as dialects of *Dutch* and *German,* respectively.

By contrast, *Kashubian* (also called *Cassubian*), which has functioned quite like a regional language in northern Poland, is now definitely and perhaps severely endangered. There are widely different estimates of the numbers of its speakers, ranging up to 150,000, but such huge figures probably refer to speakers of a local *Polish* dialect instead.

The number of speakers of *Low Saxon* (also known as *Low German*) is a few million, but no exact figures seem available.

The figure for *East Frisian* (also known as *Saterland Frisian* or *Saterlandic*) may be too optimistic, as some sources only give 1,000 speakers.

Extinct languages in the area are *Old Prussian* and *Polabian,* and *Slovincian* may be added as an extinct outlying language closely related to *Kashubian.*

Table 3. Central Europe

Language	Speakers	A				B			Level
		a	b	c	d	a	b	c	
Walloon	300,000	2	2	2	2	1	1	4	c
West Frisian	350,000	3	3	3	3	3	1	4	b
East Frisian	2,000	2	2	2	2	3	1	4	c
North Frisian	8,000	2	2	2	3	3	1	4	c
Low Saxon	?	3	3	3	3	2	1	4	b
Lower Sorbian	10,000	2	2	2	2	2	1	4	c
Upper Sorbian	20,000	3	2	2	2	2	1	4	b
Kashubian	< 10,000	2	2	2	2	2	1	4	c
Burgenland Croatian	< 20,000	3	2	2	2	1	1	4	b
Romansch	< 50,000	3	3	3	3	3	1	4	b

5.4. Italy

The dominant language in the area is *Italian* (also called *Tuscan*). *Maltese*, an official and non-endangered language in a small neighbouring country, may be mentioned here.

Regional languages not included in the table are *Venetan*, *Central Italian*, *South Italian*, and *Sicilian*. They seem to live in stable diglossia with Italian but would in all likelihood qualify as potentially endangered.

The figure for *Lombard* is subject to suspicion, and it seems impossible to say anything about the numbers of speakers of the other *Gallo-Romance* languages. *Ligurian* appears to be giving away to *Italian* much faster than the others.

Italiot Greek is locally known as *'Griko'*, to make a distinction from more recent *Greek*-speaking settlers.

The figures for the *Sardinian* languages are also rough estimates. It may be pointed out that *Gallurese* and *Sassarese* are more closely related to *Corsican* that to *Sardinian* proper, consisting of *Campidanese* and *Logudorese* (including *Nuorese*).

'Walser' conventionally refers to both *Germanic* varieties in Aosta Valley, one of which is a typical, rather independent outlying language called *'Töitschu'*, and the other one, known as *'Titsch'*, is very closely related to and in constant contact with cross-border *Alemannic* in Switzerland. The *Walser* data below is only supposed to cover *'Töitschu'*.

Table 4. Italy

Language	Speakers	A				B			Level
		a	b	c	d	a	b	c	
Algherese Catalan	20,000	3	2	2	2	1	1	4	b
Gardiol	?	2	2	2	2	2	1	4	c
Faetar	700	3	2	2	3	2	1	4	b–
Gallurese Sardinian	< 100,000	3	2	2	2	3	1	4	b
Sassarese Sardinian	< 100,000	3	2	2	2	3	1	4	b
Campidanese Sardinian	< 500,000	3	2	2	3	3	1	4	b
Logudorese Sardinian	< 500,000	3	2	2	3	3	1	4	b
Piedmontese	?	3	2	2	3	2	1	4	b
Ligurian	?	2	2	2	2	2	1	4	c
Lombard	4,000,000	3	2	2	3	2	1	4	b
Emilian	?	3	2	2	2	2	1	4	b
Romagnol	?	3	2	2	2	2	1	4	b
Friulian	< 500,000	3	2	2	2	3	1	4	b
Ladin	30,000	3	3	3	3	3	1	4	b
Cimbrian	2,000	2	2	2	3	1	1	4	b–
Mócheno	2,000	3	2	2	3	1	1	4	b
Walser	2,000	3	2	2	3	1	1	4	b
Arbëreshë Albanian	100,000	3	2	2	2	1	1	4	b
Italiot Greek	20,000	1	2	1	2	1	1	4	c
Molise Croatian	3,500	2	2	2	2	1	1	4	c
Resian Slovene	1,000	3	2	2	3	1	1	4	b

5.5. Balkans

Dominant languages in the area are *Albanian, Bulgarian, Greek, Macedonian, Romanian, Serbo-Croat, Slovene,* and *Turkish. Pomak* in Greece is currently treated as a dialect of *Bulgarian* but may be reclassified as an outlying language, undoubtedly an endangered one.

'Bosnian', 'Croatian', and *'Serbian'* are literary languages based on closely related central *South Slavonic* dialects. Many speakers resent the linguistic designation *'Serbo-Croat',* and any of the names of the literary languages can be used synonymously depending on the context.

The only language in the area to become extinct in the modern era is *Dalmatian.*

Of non-territorial languages, *Judezmo* (also known as *Judeo-Spanish*, *Ladino*, or *Haketía*) is still spoken in Bulgaria, Greece and European Turkey by a few thousand elderly people who survived the Holocaust and decided not to emigrate, but the vast majority of its speakers now live in Israel, and to a lesser extent in Western Europe and the United States. Of the other *Jewish* languages, *Italkian* (also called *Judeo-Italian*) is actively used only in a small community on the island of Corfu, and *Yevanic* (also called *Judeo-Greek*) may be extinct, the remaining speakers, if any, living in Israel.

The numbers of speakers of minority languages spoken in Greece are difficult to assess, and the figures for *Aromanian* (also known as *Macedo-Romanian*), *Megleno-Romanian* (also called *Meglenitic*), *Arvanite Albanian*, and *Tsakonian* may be far too high.

One outlying language, *Pontic Greek*, covered by the UNESCO Red Book report, is excluded from here because it is based in Anatolia, although most speakers have emigrated to Europe.

Vojvodina Rusyn, despite its name, appears to be more closely related to *Eastern Slovak* than *Rusyn*, but it has developed a few idiosyncratic features typical of an outlying language.

Gagauz (see Eastern Europe below) is spoken beyond its base area in and around Moldova in several small pockets in Bulgaria, Macedonia and European Turkey, collectively known as *Balkan Gagauz*, or slightly misleadingly, *Balkan Turkic*. The *Balkan Gagauz* varieties might deserve the status of outlying languages but very little information is available about them.

Table 5. Balkans

Language	Speakers	A				B			Level
		a	b	c	d	a	b	c	
Romani	?	3	2	2	2	3	2	3	b
Judezmo	300,000	2	1	1	2	3	1	4	c–
Italkian	?	1	1	1	2	1	3	4	d
Istriot	1,000	2	2	2	2	3	1	4	c
Aromanian	100,000	3	2	2	2	1	1	3	b
Istro-Romanian	1,500	2	2	2	2	1	1	4	c
Megleno-Romanian	5,000	2	2	2	2	1	1	2	c
Vojvodina Rusyn	25,000	3	2	2	2	1	1	4	b
Arvanite Albanian	50,000	2	2	2	2	1	1	2	c
Yevanic	< 50	1	1	1	2	1	3	3	d
Tsakonian	300	2	2	1	2	2	1	2	c
Csángó Hungarian	20,000	2	2	2	2	1	1	4	c
Cypriot Arabic	500	2	1	1	2	2	1	4	c–

5.6. Eastern Europe

Dominant languages in the area are *Russian* and *Ukrainian*. The *Belarusian* language, while co-official in Belarus, functions much like a regional language with regard to *Russian*, and can be called potentially endangered, the vagueness of such a designation notwithstanding. *Polissian* is a variety closely related to and currently treated as a dialect of *Belarusian* but it may become recognized as a regional language instead.

The only language with several million speakers but without statewide official status is *Tatar*, which as a whole cannot be characterized as endangered. Because of the geographic splintering of the language area, however, many distinct *Tatar* dialects are losing ground to *Russian*.

The only other *Slavonic*, hence regional language in the area is *Rusyn* (also known as *Carpatho-Ruthenian*), which has a large but unknown number of speakers in the Ukraine and a few in Poland (locally known as *Lemke*), where it is not recognized officially, and a substantial number of speakers in Slovakia where it is gaining recognition. However, everywhere it must be regarded as endangered.

There are communities traditionally speaking varieties of *Albanian*, *Bulgarian*, and *Greek* in the Black Sea area. It remains an open question to which extent these might be called outlying languages.

Komi (also called *Zyryan*) and *Permyak* are often regarded as one language and collectively referred to as *Komi* (in this broader sense, '*Zyryan*' is not synonymous). Their relationship can perhaps be described through the concept of co-languages. There is also a small isolated community whose traditional language is so-called *Yazva Komi*, or *Eastern Permyak*, which may qualify as an outlying language rather than a *Permyak* dialect.

The *Mari* languages are often known by the names of their principal dialects, *Meadow Mari* (for *Eastern Mari*) and *Hill Mari* (for *Western Mari*).

Most speakers of *Nogay* live in northern Caucasia, but there are two separate Nogay communities in Europe, one in Crimea, and another in Dobruja. The base area of Crimean Tatar was Crimea, but almost all speakers were evicted in the aftermath of the Second World War and relocated in Central Asia, from where some have returned to Crimea. There are also *Crimean Tatar* speakers in Dobruja, but little information is available about the situation of *Turkic* languages there.

Krimchak (also called *Judeo-Crimean Tatar*) may be on the verge of extinction. Its linguistic distinctiveness is not quite clear in the same way as that of other *Jewish* languages, notably *Judezmo* and *Yiddish*.

The only language in the area to become extinct in the modern era is *Gothic*. The *Iranian* language *Alan* was spoken in the Middle Ages in several pockets across eastern Europe, but while they have all disappeared, the language is continued as *Ossete* in Caucasia.

Most speakers of *Yiddish* (also called *Judeo-German*) live in the United States and Israel, but there are several tens of thousands of speakers in Western Europe, and over 100,000 speakers in eastern Europe. The drastic drop in numbers is evident when we compare the present figure 1,000,000 speakers with the estimated 4,000,000 speakers in the 1960s and the 11,000,000 speakers before the Second World War and the Holocaust. Young speakers are extremely few, except in a community in Antwerp, Belgium, where *Yiddish* functions as a school language for a group of children who thus learn it at least as a second language.

Plautdietsch is an outlying language closely related to *Low Saxon* spoken originally in Russia and from there translocated to Central Asia and Siberia and spread to the Americas.

Table 6. Eastern Europe

Language	Speakers	A				B			Level
		a	*b*	*c*	*d*	*a*	*b*	*c*	
Yiddish	1,000,000	2	2	2	2	3	1	4	c
Plautdietsch	100,000	3	2	2	2	1	1	4	b
Rusyn	?	3	2	2	3	1	1	4	b
Eastern Mari	500,000	3	3	3	3	3	1	4	b
Western Mari	50,000	2	2	2	3	3	1	4	c
Erzya	500,000	3	2	2	2	3	1	4	b
Moksha	250,000	3	2	2	2	3	1	4	b
Udmurt	500,000	3	3	3	3	3	1	4	b
Permyak	100,000	3	2	2	2	3	1	4	b
Komi	250,000	3	2	2	2	3	1	4	b
Chuvash	1,400,000	3	3	3	3	3	1	4	b
Bashkir	1,000,000	3	3	3	3	2	1	4	b
Crimean Tatar	< 250,000	2	2	2	3	3	1	4	c
Krimchak	< 100	1	1	1	2	1	3	4	d
Karaim	200	1	2	1	2	2	1	4	c
Nogay	80,000	3	3	3	3	2	1	4	b
Gagauz	< 200,000	3	2	2	2	2	1	4	b
Trukhmen	18,000	3	2	2	3	1	1	4	b
Kalmyk	150,000	3	2	2	3	2	1	4	b

6. Problems in assessing levels of endangerment in Europe

European languages have a reputation of being fairly well studied, at least from a purely grammatical point of view, and while this is generally true, there are quite a few contrary examples, notably in the Balkans. Endangerment status, by contrast, is insufficiently known for many if not most of the European languages. The main problem that remains is that the factors employed here and in similar studies in general are static rather than dynamic by nature. Since we are primarily interested in the future rather than the present state of the languages under scrutiny, the most crucial piece of information would be the rate of change in the level of endangerment. The present factors, however, do not immediately shed light on that. Another important factor that is not revealed by the above treatment is the variation within one language, which in Europe can be very extensive.

A related problem is how to weigh different factors. It goes without saying that the absolute number of speakers does not always indicate the strength of the language community. The definition of an ethnic group, in its turn, is very vague, in the European context in particular, so the percentage referring to that concept (set A, factor a) may tell little of the situation. Consequently, in the above treatment, this factor has been effectively replaced with the mean age of youngest speakers, which generally correlates with the proportion of the speakers and non-speakers in an ethnic group. Clearly the one factor that defines the level of endangerment in itself is the presence of children (set A, factor b) and young adults among speakers, and since a bundle of factors can be identified around this issue, one may want to think of ways to further elaborate evaluations based on it.

As to the functions (set A, factor c) and attitudes (set A, factor d) attached to languages, the static nature of the factors becomes pronounced. What we really need to know is whether these features are changing or have stabilized.

I would like to think that the question of how closely the language is related to another, perhaps non-endangered one (set B, factor a) is of little consequence. All languages represent a unique set of features, and without offering to study a particular language on the basis of its alleged lack of interest, its specific characteristics will forever remain unnoticed. I am also convinced that we do not want to save languages in isolation of cultures but rather wish to see languages survive as cultural media, and all cultures are, in my view, equal irrespective of linguistic affiliations. In this way, all languages would score 3, i. e. "a special case important to study", but above, I have tried to follow the standard guidelines.

The level of documentation (set B, factor b) is clearly important for prioritizing documentation projects, and further elaboration could be useful to get a balanced view of both the quantity and quality of previous works. At the same time, a project proposal should be evaluated against its own background, whether it brings forth new information of a language that may be well known from other viewpoints.

The final factor concerning the fieldwork conditions (set B, factor c) is generally irrelevant in Europe, because overwhelming obstacles are few, even in strongly anti-minority societies like Greece.

A few terminological discrepancies notwithstanding, a basic consensus of the levels or degrees of endangerment can be said to exist, at least with respect to languages, which have ceased to be spoken by children. For them, the scale 'definitely' vs. 'severely' vs. 'critically endangered' seems appropriate, and the last-mentioned term is clearly superior to both 'nearly extinct' and 'moribund', the latter one being both vague because languages without children speakers are all equally sure to die and offensive to many because of its unconditional nature.

The question of characterizing languages that are still learnt and used by some children but less commonly now than before, are the ones for which terminology may need sharpening. I occasionally use the term 'potentially endangered' but I do not find it satisfactory because all languages certainly have that potential. In the tables, I have lumped those languages that are merely 'eroding', i. e. rapidly losing speakers in young age groups, with those that are 'definitely endangered', supposed to have no speakers below the age of young adults, because from a practical point of view. Iinternal variation in each language community in question tends to obscure the difference in any case, and technically, "a–" simply looks too much like "a" while it factually is closer to "b".

Postscriptum: The author no longer considers *Basque, Galician, Welsh, Scots, West Frisian, Low Saxon, Rusyn, Chuvash* or *Bashkir* as strictly endangered, but their status should nevertheless be carefully monitored. An updated classification would have *Asturian-Leonese, Emilian-Romagnol, Limburgian-Ripuarian* and *Sorbian* (with the literary languages *Lower Sorbian* and *Upper Sorbian*) as single languages rather than groups of two languages. Furthermore, *Yevanic (Judeo-Greek)* appears to have been a literary variety of *Greek* instead of a separate spoken language. *Mócheno* as a Germanic variety is apparently extinct, and can at least historically be subsumed under *Cimbrian*. On the other hand, *Cypriot Greek* may perhaps be added to the list of regional languages in relatively stable diglossia. As anticipated in the text, *Yazva Komi* is currently treated as an

outlying language rather than a *Permyak* dialect. Outlying languages ignored in the text include *Gottscheerish* (originally spoken in Slovenia;
closely related to *Bavarian*), *Mariupolitan Greek* (in the Ukraine), *Crimean Turkish* (as distinct from *Crimean Tatar*; originally in the Ukraine),
and *Urum* (or *Greek Tatar*; in the Ukraine as well as in Georgia). *Channel
Islands French* can be better seen as a cover term for three separate outlying languages, *Alderney French*, *Guernsey French*, and *Jersey French*.
Three varieties of *Nogay*, known as *Alabugat Tatar*, *Karagash*, and *Yurt
Tatar*, are spoken in isolated communities in southern Russia and have
been influenced by *Tatar*, *Kazakh*, and *Kalmyk*, respectively, thus gaining
the status of outlying languages.

Notes

1. Acknowledgements: I have carried out this task while working as a researcher
   of the Academy of Finland. I thank all colleagues who have helped me finding
   and sorting through information, Paul Fryer for revising my *English*, and the
   editor of this volume for his unyielding patience.

References

Adler, M. K.
   1977   *Welsh and the other dying languages in Europe:* a sociolinguistic
           study. Hamburg: Helmut Buske.
Asher, R. E. (ed.)
   1994   *The encyclopedia of language and linguistics 1–5*. Oxford: Pergamon
           Press.
Bakker, Peter and Maarten Mous (eds)
   1994   *Mixed languages:* 15 case studies in language intertwining. Studies in
           language and language use 13; Amsterdam: IFOTT.
Brenzinger, Matthias (ed.)
   1992   *Language death:* factual and theoretical explorations with special ref-
           erence to East Africa. (*Contributions to the sociology of language*, 64)
           Berlin, New York: Mouton de Gruyter.
   1998   *Endangered languages in Africa*. Köln: Köppe.
Collis, Dirmid R. F. (ed.)
   1990   Arctic languages: an awakening. Paris: Unesco.
Dorian, Nancy C.
   1981   *Language death:* the life cycle of a Scottish Gaelic dialect. Philadel-
           phia: University of Pennsylvania Press.

Grimes, Barbara F. (ed.)
1996   *Ethnologue:* languages of the world. 13th edition. Dallas: Summer Institute of Linguistics.
Grünthal, Riho and Tapani Salminen
1993   *Geographical distribution of the Uralic languages* [a map with a legend]. Designed by Pirkko Numminen. Helsinki: Finno-Ugrian Society.
Haugen, Einar; McClure, J. Derrick and Derick Thomson (eds.)
1981   *Minority languages today:* a selection from the papers read at the first International conference on minority languages held at Glasgow University from 8 to 13 September 1980. Edinburgh: Edinburgh University Press. [2nd edition 1990].
Hindley, Reg
1990   *The death of the Irish language.* London, New York: Routledge.
Holmestad, Einar and Arild Jostein Lade (eds.)
1969   *Lingual minorities in Europe:* a selection of papers from the European Conference of Lingual Minorities in Oslo. Oslo: Det Norske Samlaget.
Jenniges, Wolfgang (ed.)
1997   *Select bibliography on minority languages in the European Union.* 2nd, revised edition. Brussels: European Bureau for Lesser Used Languages.
Krauss, Michael
1992   The world's languages in crisis. *Language* 68: 4–10.
1993   The language extinction catastrophe just ahead: should linguists care? In *Les langues menacées:* actes du XVᵉ Congrès international des linguistes, Québec, Université Laval 9–14 août 1992 = Endangered Languages: Proceedings of the XVᵗʰ International Congress of Linguists, Quebec, Université Laval, 9–14 August 1992. Sainte-Foy: Presses de l'Université Laval. 43–46.
1998   The scope of the language endangerment cricis and recent responses to it. In Matsumura (ed.) 101–113.
Matras, Yaron; Bakker, Peter and Hristo Kyuchukov (eds.)
1997   *The typology and dialectology of Romani. (Amsterdam studies in the theory and history of linguistic science* 4: Current issues in linguistic theory 156). Philadelphia, Pa.: J. Benjamins Pub. Co.
Matsumura, Kazuto (ed.)
1998   *Studies in endangered languages:* papers from the International Symposium on Endangered Languages Tokyo, November 18–20, 1995. (*ICHEL linguistic studies* 1). Tokyo: Hituzi Syobo.
Moseley, Christopher (ed.)
forthcoming   *Encyclopedia of the world's endangered languages.* Curzon Press.
Moseley, Christopher and R. E. Asher (eds.)
1994   *Atlas of the world's languages.* London: Routledge.

Neroznak, V. P. (ed.)
1994   *Krasnaja kniga jazykov narodov Rossii:* Ènciklopedicheskij slovar'-spravochnik. Moskva: Academia.
Pogarell, Reiner (ed.)
1983   *Minority languages in Europe:* a classified bibliography. Berlin: Mouton.
Robins, Robert H. and Eugenius M. Uhlenbeck (eds.)
1991   *Endangered languages.* Oxford: Berg Publishers.
Shoji, Hiroshi and Juha Janhunen (eds)
1997   *Northern minority languages:* Problems of survival. (Senri ethnological studies 44); Osaka: National Museum of Ethnology.
Solncev, V. M. and V. Ju Mikhalchenko (eds.)
1992   *Jazykovaja situacija v Rossijskoj Federacii: 1992* [with a detailed English summary: The language situation in the Russian Federation: 1992]. Moskva.
Vakhtin, Nikolaj
1993   *Korennoe naselenie Krajnego Severa Rossijskoj Federacii.* Sankt-Peterburg: Izdatel'stvo Evropejskogo Doma.
Wurm, Stephen A.
1998   Methods of language maintenance and revival, with selected cases of the language endangerment in the world. In Matsumura (ed.) 191–211.
Wurm, Stephen A. (ed.)
1996   *Atlas of the world's languages in danger of disappearing.* Paris: UNESCO Publishing. Canberra: Pacific Linguistics. [first edition]
2001   *Atlas of the world's languages in danger of disappearing.* Paris: UNESCO Publishing. [second edition, revised, enlarged and updated]
Yamamoto, Akira
1998   Linguists and endangered language communities: issues and approaches. In Matsumura (ed.) 213–252.

Chapter 11
Language Endangerment in the CIS

Olga Kazakevich and Aleksandr Kibrik

1. Introduction

Over two hundred languages are spoken in the CIS and about one third of them fall into the category of endangered languages. Three regions of different types and degrees of language endangerment might be easily distinguished on the territory of the CIS: Siberia and the Far East (the north of the European part of Russia with its four endangered languages might be also added), the Caucasus (Russia, Azerbaijan and Georgia), and Central Asia (Tajikistan and Uzbekistan). The Crimea peninsula (Ukraine) presents an additional islet of language endangerment (see *Table 1, Maps 14–16*). Though these areas were until recently parts of one state – the former USSR – their history, the traditional occupations of their indigenous populations and their language situations display significant differences. They should therefore be considered separately. The information presented below is taken from a number of publications of the last decade,[1] personal communication with colleagues working on the endangered languages of the region,[2] and some results of our own fieldwork experience. In addition we employed the materials from the database "Languages of indigenous minority peoples of Russia" developed at the Research Centre on Ethnic and Language Relations of the Institute of Linguistics (Russian Academy of Sciences).[3]

Before we discuss each area of language endangerment separately, a few remarks on their common history as part of one state, first the Russian Empire and then the USSR, are in order. We will pay special attention to educational issues since, among the various factors contributing to language endangerment and leading to language shift in different parts of the world, education appears to be one of the most significant, and the CIS is no exception in this respect.

Russia was proclaimed an empire at the beginning of the 18th century. During the 18th and 19th centuries its territory grew, and so did the number of languages spoken within its boundaries. Language loss, however, was also present. The list of languages which disappeared during this period is not too long (but we should keep in mind that our information on this issue might be incomplete). Languages which became extinct include *Assan, Arin, Kot, Pumpokol* (*Yenisei* language family); *Mator* (*Samoyed*); *Chuvan, Omok* (genetically related to *Yukagir*); *East* and *South Itelmen*. Some speakers of these languages died during the great epidemics of measles and smallpox brought to Siberia and the Far East by Russians, while others shifted to languages of their autochthonous neighbours or to *Russian*.

However, by the beginning of the 20th century very few members of indigenous minority groups on the territory of the Russian Empire were bilingual in *Russian* as their second language.[4] Most indigenous minorities still led their traditional way of life (semi-nomadic in Siberia and in the Far East and sedentary high up in the mountains of the Caucasus and of the Pamirs). They extensively used their ethnic languages and quite often also knew one or more of the languages of their neighbours, sometimes a regional lingua franca, which as a rule was not *Russian*. The overwhelming majority of the indigenous people were illiterate. Schools were scarce in the areas where they lived. But even if some of them, by chance, attended school, they were taught in *Russian* in Siberia and in the Far East, in *Arabic* in the Northern Caucasus, and in *Tajik* in the Pamirs. During the 14th century a few attempts were made to teach indigenous minority children in their mother tongues but most of those attempts came to nothing.[5]

After the October revolution, in the 1920s, the new government decided to make the entire population of the country literate. At first, adults and children were taught to read and write depending on the situation in each region, district, or even settlement and, of course, on the language competence of the teachers. For instance, at the beginning of the 1920s, *Azerbaijani* (or as it was called then, *Turkic*) was chosen as the language of education in Daghestan since it was a lingua franca for numerous ethnic groups of the area. The Selkups of the Tomsk region were taught in *Russian* as many of them could speak *Russian*, while in the Turukhansk district a young headmaster of a newly-opened boarding school for Northern minorities learned *Selkup* to be able to teach his pupils in their mother tongue since no children at his school were able to speak *Russian*. Since the latter was a typical situation for those years, no wonder that the best way to general literacy was thought to be through literacy in the mother tongue. However, most of the indigenous minority languages of the country did not have any written tradition, and this demanded special work aimed at creating writing systems for at least some of them. At the beginning of the 1930s writing systems had been developed for 20 minority languages; primers, readers, and textbooks in these languages were compiled and published, and the languages began to be used at primary school both as the medium of instruction and as a subject.[6] At that time, very few members of indigenous minorities were school teachers; so teachers of the so called "ethnic" schools had no competence in the mother tongue of their pupils and were obliged to learn the language of the children they taught. For this purpose summer courses were organised. It was during this time that the state policy of "indigenization" of schools was underway. The instructions for inspectors of Northern ethnic schools issued in 1935 contained the following recommendations: "Among the teachers of every Northern school there must be no less than two specialists who have been working at a Northern school for no less than two years and who are able to speak the mother tongue of the pupils", and "An 'indigenised' school should use the mother tongues of the pupils in the preparatory classes, in the first and also in the second grade if textbooks for the second grade in this language have already been published and sent to the school". Meanwhile, special teacher training colleges for representatives of minority ethnic groups were founded in various parts of the country. Starting from grade one, children were also taught *Russian*, and in the second grade they gradually switched to *Russian* as the main teaching medium. The school policy of "indigenization" changed abruptly in 1936-37 and so did the newly created writing systems: the *Latin* script was changed to *Cyrillic*.[7] It is worth mentioning that in the process of changing the writing systems from *Latin* to *Cyrillic* some languages just lost their writing systems and went back to being unwritten.[8]

These facts are well known and it would be no use repeating them here, but for one important issue not properly analysed up to now. At the dawn of the development of the language policy of the USSR, it was taken for granted that if a certain dialect of a language was chosen as the basis for a newly created written variety of the language and proclaimed as the standard, and if textbooks in the chosen dialect were issued, this standard and these textbooks were to be immediately accepted and employed by speakers of all the other dialects of that language.[9] Moreover, it was expected that speakers of some minor languages could be taught at school not in their vernaculars but in some related languages for which writing systems had already been produced.[10] In reality this solution did not work: not all indigenous communities were happy for their children to be taught in the language varieties suggested to them in the textbooks provided. This, together with the change in the state educational policy at the end of the 1930s, led to the rapid decay in the use of indigenous minority languages at school. Since then, school education has played and still plays a crucial role in the process of language shift. The state's teaching policy formed in the 1950s favoured the assimilation of native people: *Russian* became the main and, for most of minorities, the only language of teaching[11] on the territory of the Russian Federation. In Georgia the minorities were taught in *Georgian*, in Azerbaijan in *Azerbaijani*, in Tajikistan in *Tajik*, and in Uzbekistan in *Uzbek*. Though some minority languages (*Nenets, Khanty, Evenki, Even, Chukchee, Nanai*) have been continuously used at school since the beginning of the early 1930s, their role there was steadily decreasing. They gradually stopped being the medium of instruction and started being taught only as a subject. As more *Russian*-speaking bilinguals appeared among the indigenous minority population, less and less attention was paid to minority languages at school. The situation slowly began to change by the end of the 1970s and in the 1980s some indigenous minority languages returned to school. Alphabets were created for some previously unwritten languages and these languages began to be taught at school.[12] The beginning of the 1990s was a time of great expectations with respect to the development and possible protection of endangered languages. We will see what came of it by considering each separate area of language endangerment in the CIS. We will finish this introductory part with a list of languages which disappeared in the 20th century within the territory of the CIS: *Kamas* (*Samoyed*), *Ubykh* (*Abkhazo-Adyghean*), *Sirenik* (*Eskimo-Aleut*), *Yug* (*Yenisei*), *Ainu, Wanji* (*Pamir*).[13] It should be mentioned that many of the speakers of these languages shifted to neighbouring languages rather than to *Russian*.

2. Central Asia

All endangered languages in this area – with one exception – belong to the *East Iranian* language group and are concentrated in Tajikistan (see *Table 1, Maps 14, 16*). Most of them are spoken in the Gorno-Badakhshan autonomous region and are known as *Pamir* languages (*Yazgulami, Rushani, Khufi, Roshorvi, Bartangi* from the *Northern Pamir* group, *Vakhi* and *Ishkashimi*).[14] In the 1950s some groups of speakers of *Pamir* languages (*Vakhis, Bartangis, Yazgulamis*) were forcefully removed to the cotton-cultivating *Khalton* (*Kurgan-Tube*) region of Tajikistan.[15] The endangered *Pamir* languages are used as family and as community languages in rural communities – from one or two villages (Ishkashimi, Roshorvi) to over a dozen (Vakhi, Rushani). They are transmitted from parents to children.

These languages have from 1,000 to 20,000 speakers, and can be considered stable;[16] however, this stability is fragile. The very status of the *Pamir* languages has been problematic since 1937. In the period between 1937 and 1989, the *Pamir* languages were officially classified as dialects of *Tajik*. In 1989, the newly introduced Law on Languages of Tajikistan recognised the *Pamir* vernaculars as distinct languages. The law explicitly stated the necessity of providing favourable conditions for the "free development and use" of the *Pamir* languages. But in actual fact nothing (or almost nothing) has changed since then. Different versions of alphabets for all the *Pamir* languages (on the basis of the *Cyrillic*) are currently in preparation[17] and the introduction of the *Pamir* vernaculars into the school curriculum (both as the medium of instruction and as a subject) is under discussion. However, in present-day Tajikistan, *Tajik* remains the only language of education at all levels – from primary school to the university. *Yazgulami* is the only endangered *Pamir* language which is presently reported to be taught in primary schools as a subject (Edelman 2000). All the mother tongue speakers of the vernaculars are bi- or multilingual. Standard *Tajik*; the national language of Tajikistan; is the obligatory second language. For the entire population *Tajik* is the language of administration, legislature, courts, press and mass media. It is prestigious and is associated with good education and high social status. *Russian* is much less widespread, but it is still being taught as a subject in secondary schools, and one of the few TV programmes transmitted in the Gorno-Badakhshan autonomous region is a *Russian*-language programme from Moscow. The *Pamir* languages also differ in their status with respect to each other. *Shugnani* is the language of inter-ethnic communication in the regional centre Khorog, and may be called a lingua franca of the region. In the contact area of *Roshorvi* and *Bartangi* the latter is used as the language of inter-ethnic communication, and in the contact zone of *Ishkashimi* and *Vakhi*, *Vakhi* is spoken by the Ishkashimians and not the other way round. So, for instance, *Roshorvi* with its 2,000 speakers is currently under pressure not only from *Tajik* but also from *Shugnani* and *Bartangi*. Along similar lines, *Ishkashimi* with its 1,000 speakers is under pressure from both *Tajik* and *Vakhi*. According to Zarifa Nazarova, a linguist of Ishkashim origin, *Ishkashimi* might quite soon lose many speakers: in situations of economic crisis; rather many young people, especially men, leave the community in search for jobs. As a rule they get married outside the community, and their children almost always appear to be lost for the language.[18]

Two further languages in the area deserve mention. One of them is *Yagnobi*, a descendant of one of the Eastern dialects of *Sogdian*, the language of the Great Sogdian Empire. It has been spoken for centuries in the high-lands in the valley of the Yagnob river. Small groups of *Yagnobi* speakers who migrated from the valley in the 16th – 17th centuries now inhabit set-tlements on the Southern slopes of the Guissar mountain ridge. They have kept their language. Before 1970, the number of *Yagnobi* speakers was about 2,500 people. In 1970 the Yagnobis were forcefully removed from the Yagnob valley to the cotton-cultivating districts of the Lenino-bad region. This turned out to be detrimental for the language. Presently *Yagnobi* should be classified as instable. Today all Yagnobis are bilingual (their second language is *Tajik*). Though *Yagnobi* seems still to be trans-mitted within families (Vinogradova 2000) *Tajik*, the language of school education, dominates in practically all communicative spheres.[19] Recent-ly, *Yagnobi* has been introduced as a subject in primary schools. The *Cyril-lic* alphabet is used in the published school textbooks.

The only *Indo-Aryan* endangered language of the area, *Parya* is spoken in Tajikistan and in Uzbekistan. This language was first discovered by the academic community in the mid-1950s. The first and only book-length de-scription of it was published in 1977 (Oransky 1977; this also includes texts and a dictionary). The size of the Parya community is presently estimated at about 3,000 people. Their traditional occupation is agriculture (cotton cultivation), and they usually live closely together in villages and towns. Ac-cording to experts (Oranskaya 2001), all Paryas are bi- or multilingual; in addition to their mother tongue, they speak a dialect of *Tajik* brought from Afghanistan, along with standard *Tajik* in Tajikistan and standard *Uzbek* in Uzbekistan (these are the languages of school education); some also speak *Russian*. Until recently *Parya* was the language of the family even in mixed marriages. Now the situation is quickly changing: young people tend to get assimilated into the surrounding majority, and as a result, they abandon their ethnic language and switch to the majority language, even with their siblings and parents. It is not clear whether the language is still transmitted to children. The most pessimistic predictions (Oranskaya 2001) give *Parya* no more than 30 years. Even if this estimate is exaggerated, *Parya* appears to be the most endangered language of the area – definitely endangered. Urgent documentation of it is badly needed.

3. The Caucasus

The Caucasus is well known as one of the most multilingual regions of the world and it is often called 'the mountain of languages'. The number of endangered languages in this area is equally high. At least 24 languages spoken in the Caucasus should be classified as endangered. The majority of these (23) are so called autochthonous *Caucasian* languages from three language families: *Kartvelian* (*South-Caucasian*), *Abkhazo-Adyghean* (*West-Caucasian*), and *Nakh-Daghestanian* (*North-East Caucasian*).[20]

The only endangered *Indo-European* language in the Caucasus is *Tat*, from the *Iranian* branch. *Tat* is spoken in Daghestan (Russian Federation) where it is one of the national languages (this status was accorded to 10 autochthonous languages of the Daghestan Republic and to *Russian* by the Constitution of the Republic); it is also spoken in Kabardino-Balkaria (Russian Federation) and in Azerbaijan. The Tats live mostly in towns, where urban life does not contribute to preservation of minor languages. In Azerbaijan Tats are shifting to *Azerbaijani* (more than half of the Azerbaijan Tats are unable to speak their ethnic language), while in Daghestan and in Kabardino-Balkaria the Tats are tending to shift to *Russian*. In these two republics, the *Tat* language has been written down since 1925. In Daghestan it is taught in primary schools as a subject, it is used in radio and in TV broadcasting, and there is a weekly newspaper in Tat. In spite of all this, Tat tends to be less used in family and everyday communication; it should be classified as instable.

One of the *Abkhazo-Adyghean* languages, *Ubykh*, has recently become extinct. All the other languages of this group, spoken on the Caucasian coast of the Black sea and in the Northern part of the West Caucasus, can be regarded as safe, and so are beyond the scope of this paper.

Of the *Kartvelian* languages spoken in Georgia, only *Svan* is endangered. It is spoken by about 20,000 people in Georgia. The language has no official status. It is unwritten and has never been taught at school.

The *North-East Caucasian* languages are the most numerous. They are divided into two branches, *Daghestanian* and *Nakh*. The *Nakh* branch includes three languages of which two (*Chechen* and *Ingush*) are safe, whereas the third, *Bats*, spoken only in the village Zemo-Alvani in Georgia by no more than 1,500 people, is endangered. *Bats* does not have a writing system, and is predominantly used in family communication. The language of school education is *Georgian*. All Bats speakers know *Georgian* as their second language. Educated Batsbis can also speak *Russian*. *Bats* is to be classified as instable as the sphere of its use is steadily diminishing.

The *Daghestanian* branch is believed to comprise 26 languages, only five of which can be called safe with the remaining 21 endangered.

The *Daghestanian* languages fall into the following groups:

Avaric group:	Avar (the only safe language in the group);
	Andic subgroup: Axvax, Karata, Andi, Botlikh,
	Godoberi, Bagvalal, Tindi, Chamalal
	(all endangered);
	Tsezic subgroup: Khvarshi, Tsez, Hinukh, Bezhta, Hunzib
	(all endangered);
Lakic-Dargic group:	Lak, Dargwa (both safe);[21]
Lezgic group:	Lezgian, Tabasaran (the two safe languages in the group),
	Agul, Rutul, Tsakhur, Budukh, Kryz, Khinalug, Udi, Archi
	(all endangered).

The *Daghestanian* languages are spoken in the highlands of the Daghestan Republic in the Russian Federation; *Bezhta* and *Hunzib* are also spoken in Georgia; and *Axvax, Agul, Rutul* and *Tsakhur* in Azerbaijan. *Budukh, Kryz*, and *Khinalug* are spoken only in Azerdajan, and *Udi* speakers reside in two villages and one in Georgia one in Azerbaijan.

Many endangered *Daghestanian* languages are spoken in very restricted territories, some in only one village (e. g. *Archi, Tindi, Godoberi, Hinukh, Khinalug, Budukh*). These places are remote from centres of civilization, and the people preserve their traditional lifestyles, which contributes to the preservation of these languages. They are used as family and community languages in everyday life and are ideal to work on.[22] These languages could be characterised as stable, but the rather intense migration of the population to the lowland villages and towns (as well as sometimes to neighbouring countries) that has been observed during the last decade has created a real danger for language survival. For example, sociolinguistic research conducted by the *North Eurasian* Group of SIL International among the indigenous minority population of Azerbaijan in 1998–2002 showed low vitality of *Budukh* (Clifton et al. 2002a) and a shift to *Azerbaijani* of the Kryz population of some lowland villages (Clifton et al. 2002b).

Most of the *Daghestanian* languages are unwritten. Only six have writing systems: *Agul, Rutul, Tsakhur, Tsez, Khinalug*, and *Udi*. The writing system of *Udi* is based on the *Latin* alphabet (Clifton et al. 2002d); the rest are based on the *Cyrillic* alphabet. *Agul, Rutul, Tsakhur, Tsez*, and *Udi* are taught at school.[23] *Khinalug* was taught at school from 1993-1999, and then the *Khinalug* classes in the local school of the only Khinalug village were discontinued (Clifton et al. 2002c). *Agul, Rutul* and *Tsakhur* are taught at Makhachkala Teacher Training Institute. These three languages have the status of national languages of Daghestan. Outside the traditional communicative spheres (family life and communication within the villages), they are sporadically used in TV and radio broadcasts; some books

have been published in these languages during the 1990s (school textbooks, poetry, and fiction) (Kolesnik 2000).

4. Siberia, the Far East and the North of European Russia

In this area no less than 35 endangered languages[24] are still in use, though
the number of spheres of their usage and the frequency of use is steadily
and irrevocably diminishing. Indigenous languages of the area belong to
six language families (*Uralic, Turkic, Manchu-Tungus, Yenisei, Chukotko-
Kamchatkan*, and *Eskimo-Aleut*); in addition there are three isolates
(*Itelmen, Nivkh*, and *Yukagir*) (see *Table 1, Map 14*). The sizes of the corresponding ethnic groups range from 34,000 to 100, while the number of
actual speakers of the languages ranges from 25,000 (*Tundra Nenets*) to
just one to three people (*Kerek*). Some ethnic groups (such as the *Nenets,
Evenkis, Khantys, Mansis, Chukchees, Koryaks*, and *Dolgans*) have autonomous territories of their own: *Nenets, Yamalo-Nenets, Taimyr (Dolgano-
Nenets), Evenki, Khanty-Mansi, Chukot*, and *Koryak*. All these areas were
established in 1929–32 when indigenous minorities constituted the bulk of
the population there. As time went on, the industrial development of the
Northern territories and exploration of natural resources demanded a larger labour force. This was the reason for an extensive migration from the
central regions of Russia, and also from other republics of the former
USSR. Now indigenous peoples are the minority of the population on the
territory of their own autonomous areas (for instance, there are just 16%
Koryak in the Koryak autonomous area and less than 1% Khanty and under 0.5% Mansi in the Khanty-Mansi autonomous area). Nevertheless, the
languages of the autonomous areas appear to be in a better situation compared to languages in the regions which have no special status.

Practically all the speakers of endangered languages of the area also
speak *Russian*. People unable to speak *Russian* are only in the oldest generation or among pre-school children (under 7) in comparatively large
ethnic groups (*Nenets, Chukchee*) and within some small groups still preserving their traditional nomadic lifestyle (forest Nenets). It should be
mentioned that old people who do not know any *Russian* are hardly ever
monolingual. As a rule, they speak one or more of the languages of their
neighbours, as well as their mother tongue. Most ethnic groups of this area
were traditionally bi- or multilingual, due to long-term, intense contact with
their indigenous neighbours, long before they had come in contact with *Russian*. Inter-ethnic marriages were typical, especially for smaller groups.

No endangered language in this area can be called stable. The languages still transmitted within the family and thus spoken by children in at least some places of residence of the ethnic group are few. These include *Tundra Nenets, Chukchee, Koriak, Dolgan, Forest Nenets, Evenki, Even*, and *Khanty*. There are also some children (though rather few) speaking their ethnic language among *Mansis, Nganasans, Selkups*, and possibly *Shors*. All these languages, at least for some regions or settlements, can be called instable. But at the same time most of them are definitively endangered or even severely endangered in the other regions where they are still spoken.[25] All the other endangered languages of the area are no longer passed on to the next generation. Only a few have young speakers and thus can be ranked as definitively endangered at least in some areas where they are spoken (*Saami, Vepsian, Orok, Central Siberian Yupic*, and *Nivkh*). For many languages the age of the younger speakers ranges from 35 and 50, so they should be classified somewhere between definitively and severely endangered (*Ket, Orok, Enets, Chulym, Tofalar, Ulci*), or just as severely endangered (*Ingrien, Nanai, Negidal, Udihe, Oroch, Alutor, Naukan, Yukagir, Itelmen*). Some languages, such as *Kerek, Votic*, or *Aleut*, are at the brink of extinction[26] with the youngest speakers well over 60 years old (critically endangered).

The least threatened of the endangered languages of the area is *Tundra Nenets* (about 25,000 speakers). This is due partly to the relatively large size of the ethnic group (over 32,000) and partly to the fact that the majority of the Nenets still keep to their traditional occupation – reindeer herding – and hence lead a nomadic or semi-nomadic life. The fact that they live very far away from district centres and cannot easily be reached has also contributed to the preservation of the language. The only comparable situation is that of the Chukchee. The Dolgans preserve their language in the family and have been quite active in trying to broaden its spheres of use since it was officially acknowledged as a language some thirty years ago – it had previously been considered to be a dialect of *Yakut*. But the Dolgans are less numerous than the Nenets or the Chukchees – only about 7,000 with over 5,500 speakers.

The situation of *Evenki*, whose speakers (no more than 9,000 of the 30,000 strong ethnic group) are spread all over Siberia and the Far East, varies greatly from territory to territory and even from settlement to settlement.[27] Most of the Evenkis of Yakutia abandoned their ethnic language and shifted to *Yakut* or to *Russian*, whereas the Evenkis of the Amur and Chita regions and of the tiny village Sovetskaya Rechka, situated on the Western border of the Krasnoyarsk territory, use *Evenki* as a family and a community language and still transmit it to their children.[28] Thus, this language represents almost the whole spectrum of language endangerment, from merely 'instable' to 'critically endangered'. Dialect differentiation creates difficulties in teaching what is called 'standard *Evenki*' at school in regions where the local vernaculars differ radically from the adopted standard.

Unfortunately, the situation of *Ket* (the only still surviving member of the once rather large *Yenisei* language family) is much more typical. *Ket* is spoken in several villages of the Turukhansk district of the Krasnoyarsk territory and in one village of the Evenki autonomous area by no more than 200 people (the ethnic group numbers 1,100 people) A sociolinguistic survey carried out in seven Ket villages (in 1993, 1999, 2003 and 2004)[29] showed that speaking *Ket* has become most unusual and is now perceived as rather "unnatural" by the members of the Ket communities. The youngest speakers of Ket are over 35–40, but even those who are still competent in their ethnic language use *Ket* very seldom. No Ket parents speak *Ket* with their children; the natural intergenerational transmission of the language has stopped since the 1970s–1980s. Today, young Ket parents are simply unable to speak *Ket* themselves. In some families parents (or grandparents) try to teach their children (grandchildren) some *Ket*, but all they teach is a limited set of everyday words (e. g. nouns for body parts, animals, instruments, etc.). *Ket* speech recorded during the survey shows constant code switching with *Russian*. The attitude towards the ethnic language among the Kets is ambivalent: about 70 % of our informants expressed a positive attitude towards their ethnic language, saying they need it when they live in their native village, whereas 30 % said that *Ket* was absolutely useless. Most of those who proclaimed the uselessness of *Ket* were born in the 1950s and are to some extent competent in *Ket*. The economic situation in the Ket villages visited during the survey is most deplorable; most of the Kets live in poverty and are frustrated since they can see prospects neither for themselves nor for their children. Unfortunately for the Ket communities, the most active members of the Ket population just try to leave their villages and to settle down in the district centre where language shift and assimilation processes are much more rapid. In the Turukhansk district practically nothing is being done to preserve (or to revitalise) *Ket*. Teaching *Ket* as a subject started enthusiastically at the beginning of the 1990s at the local schools of some villages. By now in some schools it has stopped, partly because of the lack of encouragement from the regional and district education authorities, and partly because of the lack of language competence in *Ket* among local teachers as weel as the poor results achieved by the *Ket* classes.

In almost every Ket community surveyed, elderly people told us about the settlements of their youth. Surrounded by abundant hunting and fishing sites, there the community had led a happy life until they were "invited" to resettle "in a more comfortable place" and partly persuaded, partly forced to do so. The resettlements mostly took place in the 1970s. This was a period of liquidation of small villages all over the country, initiated by the central authorities. In the Turukhansk district this seems, however, to have had an additional pragmatic reason. During the Second World War, this district – along with some other districts of West and Central Siberia – was a place to which thousands of people were deported. Volga Germans, Armenians, Greeks, and Letts were brought to the banks of the Yenisey and its tributaries and forced to live and work there. At the beginning of the 1950s, they constituted the bulk of the population of some villages of the district. They did all sorts of work: fishing, hunting, cattle breeding, growing vegetables. They worked hard and the kolkhoses / sovkhoses (collective and then soviet farms) where they worked grew prosperous. By the beginning of the 1970s, the deported were at last allowed to leave the places of their banishment. Many of them left, and now the farms they had worked on were lacking labour force. It seems that the resettlement of the indigenous minorities from their small remote villages to the half-emptied villages at the banks of the Yenisey was sometimes aimed at supplying labour to those farms. The resettled people were torn out of their usual environment and found themselves in multiethnic, *Russian*-speaking surroundings, far away from their hunting and fishing sites. All this strongly affected the traditional ways of life and the minority languages of the indigenous population of the district and speeded up the process of their destruction.

When one gets to know the life of the small indigenous communities of Siberia and the Far East in the 20th century it is surprising that some of these communities still have the courage to keep to their traditions and their languages. Just to mention one example: the history of a small Selkup community of the village of Pur Tolka, situated in the Pur District of the Yamalo-Nenets autonomous area. The district is famous for its rich oil and gas fields discovered in the 1960s and intensively developed since the 1970s. Presently, the indigenous population of the district – Forest and Tundra Nenets, Khantys and Selkups – make up only 5 % of the total population, the majority of which consists of migrants from Central Russia and the former Republics of the USSR working for petrol companies.

The community of Pur Tolka is the only Selkup community of the district. It currently has about 100 people, only four of whom are newcomers whereas all the rest are native-born. During the 20th century, the community was twice forced to move away from its traditional territory, and twice people returned. The first "Babylonian captivity" happened at the beginning of the 1940s. It followed the "final liquidation of the shamans", in the district when about a dozen members of the community were accused of practising shaman rites, arrested and executed. The other inhabitants of the upper flow of the river Tolka were removed 500 km to the south, nearer to the district centre, so that the authorities could keep an eye on the relatives of the shamans. They were resettled in the basin of the river Sabun (the right tributary of the river Vakh) and organised into a collective farm. In their original place, they had had reindeer and they brought them to the new site. But neither the people nor the reindeer could get used to the new place: hunting and fishing sites and pastures were now far away. The children were taken to a boarding school where they soon began to suffer from scurvy and to die of unsuitable food (mostly bread, pasta and porridge instead of habitual fish and meat). Their parents couldn't hunt or fish properly and began to die of hunger. Reindeer could not find their way in the unknown surroundings and could not get enough food; many of them ran away and perished. During the Second World War, the men were drafted into the army. Many were killed; some came back crippled. After the war, the remainder of the community was allowed to return to the Tolka river basin. In 1947 on the right high bank of the Tolka people began to build a village with a school and a club. The river was full of fish and the forest full of game. They still had reindeer. Gradually life began to return to normal. In 1957, the village changed its administrative status: the territory passed from the Khanty-Mansi autonomous area to the Yamalo-Nenets autonomous area and became a part of the Pur district. By the early 1980s, the village appeared to be in the centre of an oil and gas prospecting area and the district authorities decided to clear the way for progress by removing the village population. This time, the community members were offered a choice: at a meeting they were told that a better life was waiting for them in the tiny fishing village Bystrinka, in the village Khaliasovaya or in the district centre Tarko-Sale. Still three families refused to leave and stayed in the deserted village, saying they had to take care of their reindeer. The early 1990s was a time of great expectations in the country, and for indigenous minorities it was a time of revival and strengthening of their ethnic and cultural consciousness and identity. The Selkups of Rur Tolka spread over the district decided to revitalise their native village. The idea was supported by the district authorities, and people began to return to the Upper Tolka banks.

"We were drawn here as if by a magnet", one of the community members told us. They are happy to be living in their native village, though their life here is hard and they are far from being prosperous. Currently the *Selkup* language is preserved and used in the community. It is spoken by all members over 35 years old and by about half of the young people (16-30).[30] Pre-school children do not speak *Selkup*.

Two demographic features of the community are typical of many other small indigenous communities of the area: among its members there are very few old people (over 60) and many unmarried men between 18 and 50. The life is hard in the north and people don't live too long in the north – these accounts for the first phenomenon. The second phenomenon may be explained by the fact that, currently, many indigenous women who face the choice between living in the traditional way and living in the modern world (with better living conditions) opt for the latter, that is, they prefer to live in district centres whenever possible, and quite often they marry newcomers. Among the descendants of the Pur Tolka community living in the district centre Tarko-Sale, women are the overwhelming majority.[31] In Pur Tolka, young families are rare, and children of pre-school age are few. In addition, there is no school in the village, so the children study in a boarding school in the district centre. Many of those who are in the boarding school still understand *Selkup*, some are even able to speak it, but will they remember their ethnic language after they graduate? Nobody knows if they will return to their village or will prefer to stay in the district centre. Will they one day speak *Selkup* with their children? There seems to be no reason for optimism.

Language loss in indigenous minority communities of the area was speeded up during the last two or three decades by the arrival of television in all corners of the taiga and tundra. Once we asked a young, 25 year old Selkup with a very high degree of competence in his ethnic language why the young generation in his small, practically monoethnic village, abandons *Selkup* and shifts to *Russian*. The young man pointed to the TV set in the corner of the only room of his house and replied, "It's because of that box!" He was right. Currently, mass media together with the educational system represent the two most powerful instruments working against minority languages.

There is a contradiction between what people say about their attitude to their ethnic language and what they actually do in practice as far as language use is concerned. The majority of the indigenous minority population of the area express a positive attitude to their ethnic languages. A series of sociolinguistic surveys carried out in the late 1990s[32] showed that most parents want their children to speak the language of their ancestors. At the same time the language actually spoken with children, even in most monoethnic families,[33] is *Russian*. If the ancestral language is regarded as desirable for children, it is *Russian* that is considered obligatory:[34] parents want their children to feel at ease at school.[35]

Thus we return to the role of school in language endangerment and language shift. As already mentioned, school is one of the most powerful instruments in language shift. Can it become an instrument of language preservation? In the early 1990s, it was believed that teaching indigenous minority languages at school could help to preserve them. Since then, there has been some positive – and quite a lot of negative – experience. The fact that a certain language is taught at school does not automatically contribute to its status in the community and to its preservation. A lot depends on the attitude of school authorities, on the personality of the teacher, on the quality of teaching materials, and, last but not least, on the language variety that is taught. The right choice of the language variety is crucial for a successful result. We argue that if teaching endangered minority languages at school is to be taken seriously as an instrument of language preservation, it is the language variety of each particular community that the children of that community should be taught. Only in this case will the children be aided by community members still competent in the language. All efforts to (artificially) construct a kind of inter-dialect (or perhaps "a mixed-dialect") norm or to use a chosen dialect in communities speaking other dialects have produced and are doomed to produce either no or negative results.

Producing teaching materials in various dialects is not as insurmountable as it would appear at first glance. Nowadays, practically all endangered languages on the territory of the CIS are documented to some extent: for each of them there exists at least a sketch of the grammar, and for many there is also a dictionary, as well as a collection of texts.[36] However, in view of the possibility of losing some of these languages within the next decade and of a large portion of the rest in no more than half a century, a systematic documentation of local varieties of every endangered language is most desirable. The internal processes in these languages, variously speeded up by external circumstances make them a perfect linguistic laboratory for typological studies of language development and language change. These studies would also allow for better understanding the past history of 'big' and 'absolutely safe' languages. Teaching materials for every documented local variety of a certain language should become an obligatory by-product of any language documentation programme.

Table 1. Endangered languages of the CIS

Family: Branch Language	Speakers	Mother tongue*	Population	School**	Status
European part of Russia					
Uralic: Baltic-Finnic and Saami					
Saami	500	797	1,890	Yes	b, c
Vepsian	5,000	6,355	12,501	Yes	a–, b, c
Ingrian	200	302	820	No	c
Votic	20	n.d.	200	No	d
Siberia and the Far East					
Uralic: Ugrian					
Khanty	10,000	13,615	22,521	Yes	a–, b, c, d
Mansi	2,000	3,140	8,474	Yes	a–, b, c, d
Uralic: Samoyed					
Tundra Nenets	25,000	26,730	32,665	Yes	a–, b
Forest Nenets	1,600		2,000	Yes	a–, b
Enets	50	95	209	No	b–, c
Nganasan	500	1,063	1,278	Yes	a–, b
Selkup	600	1,721	3,612	Yes	a–,b, c, d
Turkic					
Dolgan	5,000	5,676	6,945	Yes	a–
Shor	1,000	9,446	16,652	Yes	a–, b, c
Tofalar	200	314	731	Yes	b
Chulim	400	n.d.	500	No	b
Manchu-Tungus					
Even	7,000	7,543	17,199	Yes	a–, b
Evenki	9,000	9,175	30,163	Yes	a–, b, c, d
Neghidal	100	176	622	Yes	c
Nanai	2,000	5,298	12,023	Yes	c
Orok (Ulta)	35	124	402	Yes	b–, c
Ulchi	300	995	3,233	Yes	b–, c
Udihe	100	528	2,011	Yes	c
Oroch	50	113	703	No	c
Yenisei					
Ket	200	538	1,113	Yes	b–, c

Table 1. cont.

Family: Branch Language	Speakers	Mother tongue*	Population	School**	Status
Siberia and the Far East (cont.)					
Chukotko-Kamchatkan					
Chukchee	10,000	10,677	15,184	Yes	a–, b
Kerek	1–3	n. d.	100	No	d–
Koryak	2,500	4847	9,242	Yes	a–, b
Alutor	100–200	n. d.	2,000	Yes	c
Eskimo-Aleut					
Central Siberian Yupik	300	887	1,319	Yes	b
Naukan	70		400	No	c
Aleut	5	187	602	Yes (?)	d
Copper Is. Creol	10		100	No	d
Isolates					
Itelmen	100	487	2,481	Yes	c–, d
Nivkh	500	1,089	4,673	Yes	b, c
Yukagir	100	375	1,142	Yes	c, d
The Caucasus (Russia – R, Georgia – G and Azerbaijan – A)					
Ibero-Caucasian: Tsezic					
Tsez *R*	8,000	n. d.	8,000	Yes	a
Khvarshi *R*	1,500	n. d.	1,500	No	a
Bezhta *R, G*	7,000	n. d.	7,000	No	a
Hinukh *R*	700	n. d.	700	No	a
Hunzib	2,000	n. d.	2,000	No	a
Hunzib *R*	1,660		1,660		
Hunzib *G*	340		340		
Ibero-Caucasian: Andic					
Andi *R*	20,000	n. d.	20,000	No	a
Karata *R*	6,400	n. d.	6,400	No	a
Tindi *R*	5,000	n. d.	5,000	No	a
Axvax *R, A*	3,500	n. d.	3,500	No	a
Chamalal *R*	7,000	n. d.	7,000	No	a
Bagvalal *R*	7,000	n. d.	7,000	No	a
Botlikh *R*	5,000	n. d.	5,000	No	a
Godoberi *R*	2,500	n. d.	2,500	No	a

Table 1. cont.

Family: Branch Language	Speakers	Mother tongue*	Population	School**	Status
The Caucasus (Russia – R, Georgia – G and Azerbaijan – A) (cont.)					
Ibero-Caucasian: Lesgic					
Agul *R, A*	18,000	17,777	18,740	Yes	a
Rutul *R, A*	19,300	19,329	20,388	Yes	a
Tsakhur	19,000	19,007	19,972	Yes	a
Tsakhur *R*	6,000	6,165	6,492		
Tsakhur *A*	12,700	12,744	13,316		
Archi *A*	1,000	n. d.	1,000	No	a
Khinalug *A*	3,000	n. d.	3,000	No	a
Kryz *A*	8,000	n. d.	8,000	No	a–, b
Budukh *A*	5,000	n. d.	15,000	No	a–, b
Udi	6,500	n. d.	7,971	Yes	a–, b
Udi *A*			4,971		
Udi *G*			1,500		
Udi *R*			1,500		
Ibero-Caucasian: Nakh					
Bats *G*	1,500	n. d.	3,000	No	a–
Ibero-Caucasian: Cartvelian					
Svan *G*	20,000	n. d.	30,000	No	a–
Indo-European: Southern West Iranian					
Tat	22,000	22,041	30,669	Yes	a–
Tat *R*	16,000	16,208	19,420		
Tat *A*	5,000	5,266	10,239		
Central Asia (Tajikistan – T, Uzbekistan – U)					
Indo-European: East Iranian					
Yagnobi *T*	2,000	n. d.	2,500	Yes	a–, b
Indo-European: East Iranian: Pamir					
Vakhi *T*	20,000	n. d.	20,000	No	a
Ishkashimi *T*	1,000	n. d.	1,000	No	a
Rushani *T*	18,000	n. d.	18,000	No	a
Bartangi *T*	2,425	n. d.	2,425	No	a
Khufi *T*	2,380	n. d.	2,380	No	a
Roshorvi *T*	1,950	n. d.	1,950	No	a
Yazghulami *T*	3,000	n. d.	3,000	Yes	a

Table 1. cont.

Family: Branch Language	Speakers	Mother tongue*	Population	School**	Status
Central Asia (Tajikistan – T, Uzbekistan – U) (cont.)					
Indo-European: Indo-Aryan					
Parya *T, U*	2,000 (?)	n. d.	3,000	No	b
The Crimea (Ukraine – Uk, Lithuania – Lt, R – Russia)					
Turkic					
Karaim	300 (?)	502	2,602	No	c
Karaim *R*			680		
Karaim *Uk*			1,404		
Karaim *Lt*			289		

* Census 1989; ** Taught at School.

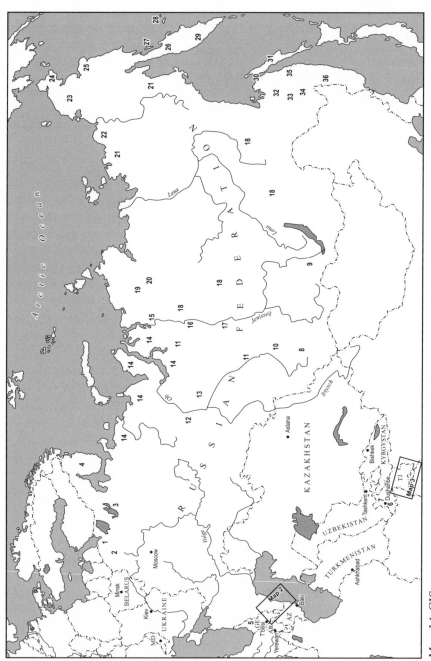

Map 14. CIS

Map 14		*Map 15*	
1	Votic	37	Batz
2	Ingrian	38	Andi
3	Vepsian	39	Botlikh
4	Saami	40	Godoberi
5	Svan	41	Axvax
6	Parya	42	Karata
7	Yaghnobi	43	Bagvalal
8	Shor	44	Tindi
9	Tofalar	45	Chamalal
10	Chulim	46	Tsez
11	Selkup	47	Khvarshi
12	Mansi	48	Inkhokvari
13	Khanty	49	Hinukh
14	Nenets	50	Bezhta
15	Enets	51	Hunzib
16	Keti	52	Agul
17	Yug	53	Rutul
18	Evenki	54	Tsakhur
19	Nganasan	55	Archi
20	Dolgan	56	Kryz
21	Even	57	Budukh
22	Yukagir	58	Udi
23	Chukchee	59	Khinalug
24	Siberian Yupik	60	Tat
25	Kerek		
26	Koryak	*Map 16*	
27	Alutor	61	Ishkashimi
28	Aleut	62	Shughni
29	Itelmen	63	Yazgulami
30	Nivkh	64	Vakhi
31	Orok	65	Rushani
32	Ulchi	66	Khufi
33	Negidal	67	Bartangi
34	Nanai	68	Roshorvi
35	Oroch		
36	Udihe		

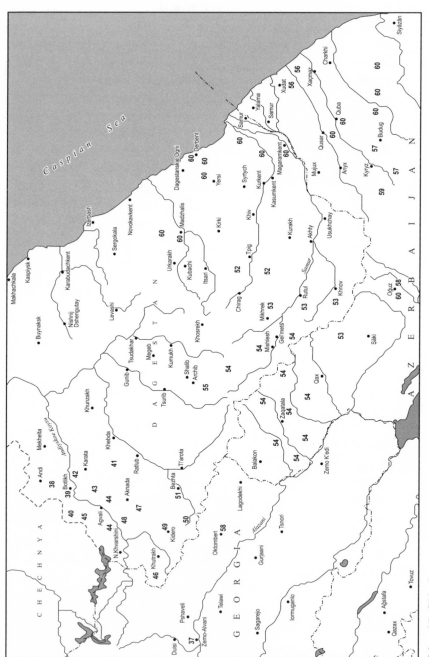

Map 15. CIS, Caucasus

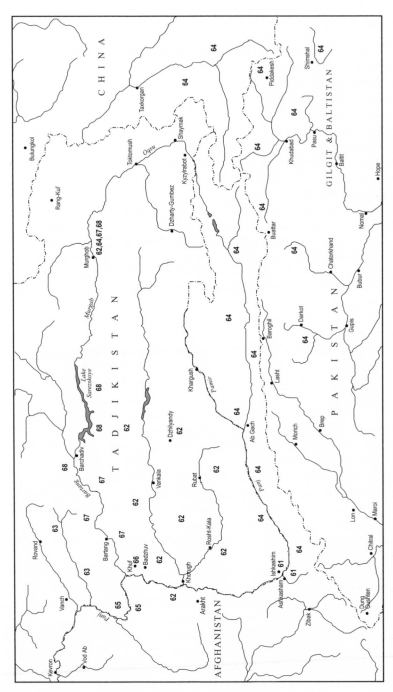

Map 16. CIS, Central Asia

Notes

1. Including publications of the authors of the present article, e. g. (Kibrik 1991a; 1991b; Kazakevich 1996a; Kazakevich 1998a; 2002).
2. We are especially grateful to our colleague Leila Dodykhudoeva who provided us with firsthand information on *Pamir* languages of Tadjikistan obtained during her fieldwork in the Gorno-Badakhshan autonomous region in the 1990s.
3. The bulk of the data base information has been published in (Sotsiolingvisticheskaya entsiklopedia 2000; 2003). Some information on the earlier stages of the Database development can be found in (Anoshkina and Kazakevich 1995; Mikhalchenko 1998). The *Russian* pilot version of the Database is accessible on the Internet: http://socioling.narod.ru.
4. The exceptions were a number of ethnic groups which had frequent contacts with the Russian population; these include the Vot and the Veps in the European part of Russia, the Southern Mansi and Southern Selkups in Western Siberia, and the Aleut and Itelmen in the Far East. Some representatives of these groups began to shift to *Russian* abandoning their mother tongue. At the same time in the early 20th century some groups of the Udihe and the Nanai in the Primorsky territory shifted to *Chinese*.
5. The Unalashka Aleut school education should be mentioned as a positive exception (see Golovko 1994).
6. The list of the languages used at school in the 1930s is as follows: *Chukchee, Even, Evenki, Ingrian, Itelmen, Khanty, Koryak, Mansi, Nanai, Nenets, Nivkh, Saami, Selkup, Shor, Siberian Yupik, Tat, Tsakhur, Udi, Udihe*, and *Vepsian*.
7. While in the early 1930s numerous articles were published arguing in favour of the *Latin* writing as most suitable for the newly created alphabets, after 1936 it was *Cyrillic* that began to be praised as the best means for reflecting specific features of newly written languages and the easiest script for children to learn at school.
8. Among them were *Ingrian, Itelmen, Saami, Tsakhur, Udihe*, and *Vepsian*.
9. The background for such an assumption was formed by standard languages with a long literary tradition. It was not taken into account that this long tradition had been formed under specific economic and political circumstances and that these factors must have influenced the choice of one variety as the standard.
10. Thus, it was expected that *Nanai* would be used as a teaching medium not only for the Nanais but also for the Ulcis and Oroks, and *Nenets* not only for all the Nenets but also for the Nganasans and Enets (see Yazyki i pismennost' 1937: 232).
11. The languages removed from school programmes in the 1950s are *Central Siberian Yupic, Koryak, Selkup, Shor*, and *Udi*.
12. The languages for which writing systems were developed (or whose writing systems were renewed) in the 1970s–1990s are *Agul, Dolgan, Itelmen, Ngana-*

san, Negidal, Ket, Orok, Rutul, Selkup, Tofalar, Tsakhur, Tsez, Ulchi, Yukagir,
see details in e. g. (Kazakevich 1996a; 1996b; 2002).

13. Some dialects of living languages could be added to this list, e. g. *Southern* and *Eastern Mansi.*

14. The list does not include the strongesr *Pamir* language – *Shugnani* spoken by more than 50,000 people as the mother tongue and by many of speakers of the other *Pamir* languages as their second or the third language. *Shugnani* is the language of inter-ethnic communication in some districts of the Gorno-Bada-khshan autonomous region and in the regional centre Khorog.

15. Some of the *Pamir* languages spoken in Tajikistan are also spoken outside the CIS: *Vakhi*, the strongest among them, is spoken in Afganistan, Pakistan and China, *Rushani* – in Afganistan, Ishkashimi – in one village in Afganistan.

16. We use here the schema for classifying languages according to degree of viability suggested by Michael Krauss (chapter one, this volume).

17. In the 1930s an alphabet was developed for *Shugnani* and *Vakhi*, and for some years (until the end of the 1930s) *Shugnani* was used at school, textbooks for primary school were published in it, and some books were translated into it. As for *Vakhi*, no information on its use at school is available.

18. The current language situation in the Gorno-Badakhshan autonomous region is described in Dodykhudoeva 1997.

19. See (Vinogradova 2000).

20. According to the Nostratic theory (Starostin 1999: 75), *Kartvelian* languages are regarded as members of the *Nostratic* family, while *Abkhazo-Adyghean* and *Nacho-Daghestanian* languages are united into the *North-Caucasian* family. The disintegration of the *North-Caucasian* family is supposed to date back into the 3rd – 4th millennium BC, and the split of the *Proto-North-East Caucasian* language is supposed to have taken place at the end of 3rd millennium BC (Alekseyev 1999a: 156).

21. *Dargwa* is represented by several dialects, four of which – *Kubachi, Kaitag, Chirag,* and *Urakhi* – are sometimes regarded as separate languages. Some argumentation concerning *Kubachi* is given in (Alekseev and Perekhvalskaya 2000).

22. During the last decades substantial work has been done by linguists of Makhachkala, Tbilisi, and Moscow, as well as by Western linguists. For some minority *Caucasian* languages there are detailed reference grammars, see, e. g., the grammars of *Khinalug, Archi, Godoberi, Tsakhur, Bagvalal,* prepared by Kibrik and his colleagues (Kibrik et al 1972; 1977; Kibrik 1996; 1999; 2001), and bibliography in (Alekseyev 1999a).

23. It should also be mentioned that within the borders of the Russian Federation, school education is based predominantly on *Russian*, and most of Daghestanians 20–50 years old speak *Russian* perfectly. Speakers of the languages of the *Avaric* group also speak *Avar* as for them *Avar* is the language of instruction in primary school; in secondary school the *Avar* language and literature are taught as subjects.

24. It is difficult to give the exact number of endangered languages in the area since many of these languages are split into dialects and some of these dialects are sometimes considered languages (see e. g. Salminen 1997; Krauss 1997). Compiling our list of languages we mostly followed the *Russian* linguistic nomenclature as it is represented in the publications of the last decade (e. g. Yazyki Rossiyskoy Federatsii 1997; Yazyki mira 1993–2000).

25. E. g. the Northern dialect of *Selkup* is instable in the village of Ratta, somewhat between instable and definitively endangered in the village of Pur Tolka, definitively endangered in the village of Tolka and Farkovo, severely endangered in the village of Krasnoselkup; all the Southern dialects of *Selkup* are critically endangered.

26. See (Volodin 1994; Agranat and Shoshiashvili 2000; Golovko 1994. The survival of *Kerek* now depends on the life of the last three speakers of this language who were elderly persons in 1991 (Volodin 1997). In the summer of 2000 at least one of them, a woman of about 80 years old, was still alive (information received from Michael Dunn), and (consequently) so was language.

27. Only 11.6% of the Evenkis of Russia live in the Evenki autonomous area whereas 48.3% of them live on the territory of Yakutia.

28. See (Bulatova 1994; Kazakevich and Parfenova 2000b).

29. See (Kazakevich 1994). The results of the survey of 1999 carried out as part of the project "Bi- and multilingualism and code-switching among indigenous population of the Turukhansk district" supported by the "Open Society" Reseach Support Scheme (grant N 801/1998), as well as the results of the latest surveys 2004 have not been published yet.

30. The ethnic language is considered a valuable heritage by many community members. A forty-year-old man told us how he used to talk and sing *Selkup* to himself during two years of military service for fear he might forget his mother tongue without practice. In his childhood, after having stayed two years first in the hospital and then in a sanatorium far away from his native village, he returned home and felt he couldn't speak *Selkup*. It took him some time to learn to speak it again, so he didn't want to lose his mother tongue once more.

31. In all indigenous minority ethnic groups of Siberia and the Far East, the educational level of women is much higher than that of men. Among those who received special secondary or tertiary education, women are an overwhelming majority.

32. See e. g. (Kazakevich 1997; 1998a; 1998b; Kazakevich and Parfenova 2000a; 2000b).

33. Over 50% of the marriages of the indigenous minority population in the area are inter-ethnic with one of the spouses being a newcomer (Russian, Ukrainian, Azerbaijani, Tatar, Mordvinian, Moldavian, etc.). The language of such families is usually *Russian*.

34. Since the mid-1990s, some parents say they also want their children to speak *English* or some other European language.

35. Some of them still remember their negative experience when they themselves went to school being incompetent in *Russian*.
36. See e. g. (Yazyki mira 1993–2000; Yazyki Rossiiskoy Federatsii 1997, 2001).

References

Agranat, Tatiana B. and Igor Shoshiashvili
    1997   Vodskiy yazyk: v kontse puti. In Kuznetsova, A. I.; Rayevskaya, O. V. and S. S. Skorvid (eds.) *Malyie yazyki Yevrazii: Sotsiolingvisticheskii aspect.* Moskva: Filologicheskiy fakul'tet MGU. 75–77.
Alekseyev, Mikhail E.; Klimov, G. A.; Starostin, S. A. and J. G. Testelets (eds.)
    1999   *Yazyki mira: Kavkazskiye yazyki.* Moskva: Academia.
Alekseyev, Mikhail E.
    1999   Nacho-Daghestanskiye yazyki. In Alekseyev, Klimov, Starostin and Testelets (eds.) 156–166.
Alekseyev, Mikhail E. and Elena A. Perekhvalskaya.
    2000   Kubachintsy i kubachinskiy (urbugskiy) yazyk. In Mikhalchenko, V. Yu.; Kriuchkova, T. B.; Kazakevich, O. A. and N. G. Kolesnik (eds.) *Yazyki Rossiyskoy Federatsii i novogo zarubezhya: status i funktsii.* Moskva: Editorial URSS. 211–218.
Anoshkina, Janna G. and Olga A. Kazakevich.
    1995   Bank sotsiolingvisticheskikh dannykh "Yazyki malochislennykh narodov Rossii (YAMAL)". In Mikhalchenko, V. Yu.; Bakhnian, K. V.; Kolesnik, N. G.; Kondrashkina, E. A. and L. P. Krysin (eds.) *Metody sotsiolingvisticheskikh issledovaniy.* Moskva: Institut Yazykoznaniya RAN. 7–26.
Bulatova, Nadezhda Ya.
    1994   Evenkiiskiy yazyk. In Neroznak (ed.) 68–70.
Clifton, John M. (ed.)
    2002   *Studies in Languages of Azerbaijan.* Vol. 1. Grand Rapids.
Clifton, John M.; Deckinga, G.; Lucht, L.; Mac, J.and C. Tiessen.
    2002a   The sociolinguistic Situation of the Budukh in Azerbaijan. In Clifton (ed.) 47–56.
    2002b   The sociolinguistic Situation of the Kryz in Azerbaijan. In Clifton (ed.) 57–70.
    2002c   The sociolinguistic Situation of the Khinalug in Azerbaijan. In Clifton (ed.) 77–98.
    2002d   The sociolinguistic Situation of the Udi in Azerbaijan. In Clifton (ed.) 107–123.
Golovko, Evgeniy V.
    1994   Aleutskiy yazyk. In Neroznak (ed.) 13–15.
Dodykhudoeva, Leila R.
    1997   Sotsiolingvisticheskaya situatsiya Gornogo Badakhshana. In Kuznetsova, Rayevskaya and Skorvid (eds.) 78–89.

Edelman, Joy I.
2000   Yazghulamiskii yazyk. In Rastorguyeva, Edelman and Moshkalo
          (eds.) 274–289.
Kazakevich, Olga A.
1994   Yazykovaya situatsiya u korennykh malochislennykh narodov Tu-
          rukhanskogo rayona: kety i sel'kupy. In Solncev, V. M.; Mikhalchen-
          ko V. Yu. and T. B. Kriuchkova (eds.) *Yazyk v kontekste obshiestven-
          nogo razvitiya.* Moskva: Institut Yazykoznaniya RAN. 110–123.
1996a   Yazyki malochislennykh narodov Rossii. *Chelovek* (Moskva) 4: 149–
          161.
1996b   The Education of the Selkups in Russia: Teaching the mothertongue as
          a foreign language. *International review of education* 42,4: 388–391.
1997   Yazykovaya situatsiya u korennykh narodov Severa v Yamalo-
          Nenetskom avtonomnom okruge. In Kuznetsova, Rayevskaya and
          Skorvid (eds.) 64–74.
1998a   Minor aboriginal peoples of Russia: Language and ethnic self-identi-
          fication. In Bombi, R and G. Graffi (eds.) *Proceedings of the interna-
          tional congress "Ethnicity and language community: an interdiscipli-
          nary and methodological comparison".* Udine: Forum. 307–323.
1998b   Northern Selkups, their language and identity. In V. Yu-Mikhal-
          chenko (ed.) *Social linguistics in the Russian Federation.* Moskva: In-
          stitut Yazykoznaniya RAN. 111–113.
2002   Education of indigenous minorities of Russia in the 1930s and in the
          1990s: mother tongue at school. In Matsumura, K. (ed.) *Lectures on
          Language Situation – Russia, Estonia, Finland.* Tokyo. 1–34.
Kazakevich, Olga A. and Olga S. Parfenova
2000a   Yazykovaya i etnokul'turnaya situatsiya v Krasnosel'kupskom ray-
          one Yamalo-Nenetskogo avtonomnogo okruga. In Mikhalchenko,
          Kriuchkova, Kazakevich and Kolesnik (eds.) 270–303.
2000b   Etnicheskiye i yazykovyie obshchnosti poselka Sovetskaya Rechka
          Turukhanskogo raiona. In Mikhalchenko, Kriuchkova, Kazakevich
          and Kolesnik (eds.) 304–308.
Kibrik, Aleksandr E.
1991a   Les langues en voie de disparition en U.R.S.S. *Diogenes* 153: 72–90.
1991b   The problem of endangered languages in the USSR. In Robins, R.
          and E. Uhlenbeck (eds.) *Endangered languages.* Oxford; New-York.
          257–273.
Kibrik, Aleksandr E. (ed.)
1996   *Godoberi.* München: Lincom Europa.
1999   *Elementy tsakhurskogo yazyka v tipologicheskom osveshchenii.* Mosk-
          va: Naslediye.
2001   *Bagvalinskiy yazyk.* Moskva: Nasledie.
Kibrik, Aleksandr E. and Sandro V. Kodzasov
1972   *Fragmenty grammatiki khinalugskogo yazyka.* Moskva: Izd. MGU.

Kibrik, Aleksandr E.; Kodzasov, Sandro V. and Irina P. Oloviannikova.
1977   *Opyt stukturnogo opisaniya archinskogo yazyka*, Vol. 1–3. Moskva: Izd. MGU.
Kibrik, Aleksandr E.; Kodzasov, Sandro V. and Irina A. Muraviova
2000   *Yazyk i folklor alutortsev.* Moskva: Nasledie.
Kolesnik, Natalia G.
2000   Funktsionirovaniye gosudarstvennykh yazykov v Daghestane. In Mikhalchenko, Kriuchkova, Kazakevich and Kolesnik (eds.) 219–241.
Krauss, Michael
1997   The indigenous languages of the North: a report on their present state. In Shoji and Janhunen (eds.) 1–34.
Kuznetsova, A. I.; Rayevskaya, O. V. and S. S. Skorvid (eds.)
1997   *Malyie yazyki Yevrazii: Sotsiolingvisticheskii aspect.* Moskva: Filologicheskiy fakul'tet MGU.
Mikhalchenko, Vida Yu
1998   Endangered languages of Russia: an Informational database. In Matsumura, K. (ed.) *Studies in endangered languages.* Tokyo: Hituzi Syobo. 115–142.
Mikhalchenko, Vida Yu; Kriuchkova, T. B.; Kazakevich, O. A. and N. G. Kolesnik (eds.)
2000   *Yazyki Rossiyskoy Federatsii i novogo zarubezhya: status i funktsii.* Moskva: Editorial URSS.
Neroznak, V. P. (ed.)
1994   *Krasnaya kniga yazykov narodov Rossii: Entsiklopedicheskiy slovar'-spravochnik.* Moskva: Academia.
Oransky, I. M.
1977   *Folklor i yazyk guissarskikh parya (Sredniaya Aziya) / Vvedeniye, teksty, slovar'.* Moskva: Nauka.
Oranskaya, T. I.
2001   Parya. In Vinogradov, V. A.; Tenishev, E. R.; Solncev, V. M.; Shakhnarovich, A. M.; Potseluyevskii, E. A. and G. A. Davydova (eds.) *Yazyki Rossiyskoy Federatsii i sopredel'nykh territoriy. Entsiklopediya.* Vol. 2. Moskva: Nauka. 413–426.
Prokofiev, G. N. (ed.)
1937   *Yazyki i pismennost' narodov Severa. Chast' 1.* Moscow/Leningrad: Uchpedgiz.
Rastorguyeva, V. S.; Moshkalo, V. V. and J. I. Edelman (eds.)
1997   *Yazyki mira Iranskiye yazyki. I. Yugo-zapadnyie iranskiye yazyki.* Moskva: Indrik.
Rastorguyeva, V. S.; Yefimov, V. A. and V. V. Moshkalo (eds.)
1999   *Yazyki mira: Iranskiye yazyki. II. Severo-zapadnyie iranskiye yazyki.* Moskva: Indrik.
Rastorguyeva, V. S.; Edelman, J. I. and V. V. Moshkalo (eds.)
2000   *Yazyki mira: Iranskiye yazyki. III. Vostochnoiranskiye yazyki.* Moskva: Indrik.

Salminen, Tapani
1997   Ecology and ethnic survival among the Nenets. In Shoji and Jan-
        hunen (eds.) 93–107.
Shoji, H. and J. Janhunen (eds.)
1997   *Northern minority languages: problems of survival.* Osaka: National
        museum of ethnology.
Simonov Mikhail D.
2000   Yazykovaya situatsiya u khorskikh udegeitsev. In Mikhalchenko,
        Kriuchkova, Kazakevich and Kolesnik (eds.) 315–317.
Solncev, V. M.; Mikhalchenko, V. Yu.; Kazakevich, O. A.; Kolesnik, N. G.; Kriuchkova, T. B. and I. V. Samarina (eds.)
2000, 2003   *Pismennyie yazyki mira: Yazyki Rossiiskoi Federatsii. Sotsiolingvis-
        ticheskaya entsiklopedia.* Vol. 1, 2. Moskva: Academia.
Starostin, Sergej A.
1999   Severokavkazskiye yazyki. In Alekseev, M. E.; Klimov, G. A.; Staros-
        tin, S. A. and J. G. Testelets (eds.) *Yazyki mira: Kavkazskiye yazyki.*
        Moskva: Academia. 75–79.
Tenishev, E. R.; Potseluyevskii, E. A.; Kormushin, I. V. and A. A. Kibrik (eds.)
1997   *Yazyki mira Tiurkskiye yazyki.* Moskva: Indrik.
Vinogradova, S. P.
2000   Yaghnobi. In Rastorguyeva, Edelman and Moshkalo (eds.) 290–310.
Vinogradov, V. A.; Tenishev, E. R.; Solncev, V. M.; Shakhnarovich, A. M.; Potseluyevskii, E. A.; Davydova, G. A. (eds.)
2001   *Yazyki Rossiiskoy Federatsii i sosednikh territoriy. Entsiklopedia.* Vol.
        2. Moskva: Nauka.
Volodin, Aleksandr P.
1994   Kerekskiy yazyk. In Neroznak (ed.) 30–31.
1997   Kerek. In Volodin, A. P.; Vakhtin, N. B. and A. A. Kibrik (eds.) *Yazy-
        ki mira: Paleoaziatskiye yazyki.* Moskva: Indrik. 53–60.
Volodin, A. P.; Vakhtin, N. B. and A. A. Kibrik (eds.)
1997   *Yazyki mira Paleoaziatskiye yazyki.* Moskva: Indrik.
Yartseva, V. A.; Vinogradov, V. A.; Solncev, V. M.; Tenishev, E. R.; Shakhnarovich, A. M. and G. A. Davydova (eds.)
1999   *Yazyki Rossiiskoy Federatsii i sosednikh territoriy. Entsiklopedia.* Vol.
        1. Moskva: Nauka.
Yeliseyev, Yu. S.; Maitinskaya, K. E. and O. I. Romanova (eds.)
1993   *Yazyki mira Ural'skiye yazyki.* Moskva: Nauka.

Chapter 12
Endangered Languages of the Middle East[1]

Jonathan Owens

The present chapter deals with endangered languages in the following countries: Afghanistan, Iran, Syria, Lebanon, Iraq, Saudi Arabia, Israel, Yemen and the various Gulf states, including Oman. The languages which are represented in this survey come from the *Afroasiatic*, *Indo-European* and *Altaic* language families.

The paper is divided into two main sections. In *section 1* I summarize the languages which are endangered by a narrow definition of the term, while in *section 2* are mentioned languages which, though falling outside the narrower definition, are either potentially endangered, or represent endangered dialects of otherwise larger languages.

The criteria defining endangerment are those suggested by Brenzinger in the organizational guidelines to the conference (p. x, this volume), supplemented by those of Krauss (pp. 1–8, this volume):

Number of speakers, minimally less than 10,000
Degree of transmission

These criteria are open to criticism from two perspectives. On the one hand, simply in terms of basic facts, recent, detailed information from one or both of these categories is often lacking, so effectively what is presented here frequently amounts to a call to conduct effective research on the languages presented. On the other hand, as was made clear during the presentations at the conference, the evaluation of endangerment ultimately is dependent not only on mechanistic criteria such as number of speakers, but crucially on social, cultural, economic, and political factors which exert differential effects on each individual language. A language with 15,000 speakers in one part of the world may be more threatened with disappearance than one with 500 speakers in another (see *Section 2*). Ultimately a detailed case by case inventory is needed to give an adequate regional profile.[2]

I would note that I do not include functional extension of use among the criteria. In today's global world, by definition endangered languages

are Languages of Restricted Communication (LRC's, opposed by terminological analogy to LWC's, languages of wider communication), largely
banned from usage in public places and official functions. For most of the
languages summarized in this chapter, more detailed knowledge is lacking, beyond the fact of restricted functional extension.[3]

1. Endangered languages

In comparison with the situation in other parts of the world, the total
number of languages in this geographical region is relatively small, as is,
correspondingly, the number of endangered languages:

Afghanistan: 11
Iran: ? (see below)
Syria: 1
Oman: 3
Yemen: (1)

These countries will be considered in turn.

1.1. Afghanistan

In terms of language diversity, the most interesting country in this region
is Afghanistan; in it are found nearly as many languages as are spoken in
the rest of the entire region, and it contains languages from 3 distinct language families, *Indo-European, Afroasiatic* (see discussion below), and
Turkic (see *Section 2*). Moreover, within the *Indo-European* family it
straddles the Indic and Iranic borderline, and contains yet a third major
Indo-Iranian sub-family, the *Nuristani* (*Kafiri*).

It is all the more unfortunate, therefore, that detailed studies on many
of these languages are lacking. In particular, for most of the languages spoken along the Afghan-Pakistan border there are only a handful of works,
more notably those published by the Norwegian linguist Georg Morgenstierne on the basis of various research expeditions he carried out from 1921
to 1960. There are nine endangered languages spoken in this area: *Sanglechi-Ishkashimi, Munji, Gawar-Bati, Prasuni, Tirahi* (probably extinct),
Woṭ (= *Wotapuri-Katarqalai* likely extinct) *Ashkun, Waigali,* and *Tregami.*
It is equally notable that for various logistical and political reasons, almost
none of the research done in this area was conducted in situ.[4] This is doubt-

lessly one of the reasons that detailed grammars of these languages are lacking. Another reason has to do with the essentially comparativistic aims of the researchers themselves. By modern standards many of the descriptions are very thin indeed. As early as 1972 Fussman (p. 4), who summarized the the language geography of the area on the basis of secondary sources, aptly remarked that, "Pour un linguiste de l'école moderne, les renseignements recueilles et publiées par Morgenstierne peuvent sembler dans bien des cas inutilisables. Pour qui a été forme á l'école de la linguistique historique, ils sont proprement irremplacables."

Two of the languages on the above list are probably extinct, namely *Tirahi*,[5] and *Woṯ* (*Wotapuri-Katarqalai*). Of the latter we can witness how the process of extinction has moved on inexorably in the course of the twentieth century. In the 1940's Morgenstierne reported that *Woṯ* was spoken in two villages in the Kaṯar valley, one at Wotapuri at the confluence of the Pech river with the streams coming from the valley, one further up the valley in Kaṯarqalai. 15 years later Budruss (1960) visited both villages, found no speakers of the language in the lower village, *Pashto* having completely replaced it, and in the upper one only a few passive speakers who remember having spoken the language in their earlier years.

Four of these languages belong to what is generally accepted as a third branch of the *Indo-Iranian* group, namely the *Nuristani* or *Kafiri*. The classificatory status of this group is not without its problems, and Morgenstierne himself presciently sketched theoretical issues relating to their classification in summarizing the status of *Dameli*, spoken just across the Afghanistan border in the Chitral area of Pakistan. "It is evident that there is a strong *Kafir* (*Nuristani*) element in *Dameli*, but we do not know whether an originally "*Dardic*" dialect has been influenced by *Kafir* or vice versa, nor is is possible to decide whether borrowing or mixture of languages would be the most adequate term for what has happened" (Morgenstierne 1945: 114). It is furthermore necessary to define the dialect situation among these languages, as it is reported (Morgenstierne 1954), for instance, that *Ashkun* and *Waigali* are very similar to one another.

Thanks to the work of Kieffer, among the better documented languages are *Ormuri* and *Parachi*. The latter, spoken in three valleys north of Kabul, is interesting in that in two of the valleys it serves as a LRC in the face of *Persian*, but in the third valley forms the middle link in a three-valued hierarchy, *Persian, Parachi, Pashai. Persian* is the LWC, *Pashai*, a larger *Dardic* language, the lowest member of the hierarchy, while *Parachi* holds a place in the middle inasfar as *Prasun* speakers may also learn *Parachi*, though not vice versa. This state of affairs (in the 1970's) was due to the relatively better economic status of the *Parachi*-speaking farmers (Kieffer 1986: 146). *Ormuri* is spoken in two villages separated by some 200 kilometers, Barakī-Barak in Afghanistan and *Kaaniigraam* in Pakistan.

The final endangered language in Afghanistan is what I term "*Central Asian Mixed Arabic*". In the 7th and 8th centuries Arab armies conquered eastern Iran (Khorasan), and much of what today is Afghanistan, Uzbekistan and Tadjekistan. Descendants of these speakers became largely cut off from the rest of the *Arabic*-speaking world by the 11th century. What developed thereafter is a mixed variety of *Arabic* whose phonology and morphology are basically *Arabic*, but whose syntax has been influenced by adstratal languages, particularly *Persian*, to such a degree that in important respects it no longer has the syntax of *Arabic*. Instead of the universal SVO word order of *Arabic* dialects, for instance, it has a consistent SOV sequence, like *Persian* (see Owens 1999).

I would note that I include this variety as an endangered language, not as an endangered dialect of *Arabic*. That is, its fundamentally mixed character provides prima facie linguistic reasons for considering it a separate language.[6]

1.2. Iran

Languages of Iran present two sorts of problems for present purposes. The first is a fundamental one, beyond resolution by an outside observer such as myself. It relates to the question of how many languages are to be recognized at all in Iran. On the one hand Windfuhr (1989: 251) notes that "The *New West Iranian* languages [including Iran, J. O.] exhibit a diversity on all linguistic levels as great as that of *Eastern Iranian*". The *Eastern Iranian* languages include those summarized above for Afghanistan. On the other hand, Redard (1970: 10) writing about *Central Persian* dialects (roughly, spoken north of Isfahan) remarks that "The actual dialects are close to varieties of *Persian*, and the distinction is not always easy to establish". Similarly, Yarshater (1969: 17) characterizes *Tati* as "*Iranian* dialects spoken in northwestern Persia…" Krahnke (1976: 47) notes the close linguistic resemblances between the Central dialects, *Tati*, *Semnani*, *Sivandi* and *Xuri*, to the extent that some of these (e. g. *Sivandi*, *Xuri*) are sometimes even classed among the Central dialects. The apparent lack of clarity regarding the boundaries between linguistic entities is reflected in terminological ambiguity as well. The "*New West Iranian* languages" spoken of by Windfuhr in the quote above become, on the same page (1989: 251, at bottom), "the *West Iranian 'dialects'* [my emphasis, J. O.]".[7] Voegelin (1965: 196) speaks in terms of an intelligibility chain stretching across Iran. It would, in any case, appear that many of those varieties which possibly qualify as independent languages (e. g. *Central Persian* dialects, *Fars* or SW dialects, *Semnani*) have a population of speakers above that of the danger line used here, as do a number of other languages of the *Western Iranian* family, such as *Gilaki* and *Tati*. The second problem awaits resolution of the first; should a decision regarding the language/dialect divide be possible, assigning endangered status would have to be carried out on a case by case basis. I leave this problem to specialists on the *Iranian* languages.

1.3. Syria

The remaining languages all belong to the *Semitic* family. In Syria there are three villages where modern *Western Neo-Aramaic* is spoken, Maʕlula, Baxʕa and Jubbʕadin. The population of speakers of this language appears to actually have increased during the course of the 20th century, due to natural population growth in the villages coupled with reduced emigration to the USA and Damascus (Werner Arnold p. c.). Arnold (see e. g. 1990, 2000) estimates the increase to have been in the range from 1,500 in 1900 to 10,000 today.

1.4. Oman and Yemen

In Oman and Yemen are found the six modern *South Arabic* languages. Three of these fall under the endangered rubric in the sense defined above. Two of the languages are spoken in Oman, which in recent years has been relatively inaccessible to research. The least is known about *Baṭḥari*, estimated to be spoken by about 300 speakers along the southern coast of Oman in an area hardly accessible except by boat. *Harsusi (Ḥarsuusi)* is spoken by about 600 individuals in the Jiddat al Ḥaraasiis area in south-central Oman. Simeone-Senelle (1997b: 8) reports that about 15 years ago Sultan Qaboos of Oman designated the Harsuusi's as the guardians of a nature park established in the area, a situation which has encouraged Harsuusis to remain in the area and effectively acting as a language maintenance program. Estimates for *Habyot (Habyoot)*, spoken on both sides of the Yemen-Oman border, run between 100 (Simeone-Senelle 1997a: 379) and 2,000 the latter figure one given to Werner Arnold (Arnold p. c.) by a native Habyot. Simeone-Senelle (p. c.) reports that there is some mutual intelligibility between *Habyot* and the larger *Mehri* language, particularly on the Yemen side of the Oman-Yemen border, which is at one and the same time a LWC adstrate for Habyot and a relative within the *South Arabic* sub-family of languages.

2. Further languages

Three further languages or language clusters may be mentioned which, though not falling within the criteria set here for endangered, nonetheless face a potentially perilous future in the region.

2.1. Eastern Neo-Aramaic

Eastern Aramaic is spoken in eastern Turkey, Azerbaidjan, NW Iran, Iraq and NE Syria. It is spoken by a people who identify themselves variously as Assyrians, Syrians, Chaldeans or Chaldeans (Athuuraye, Suryaye, Kaldanaye), and its varieties may be known by its various dialect names: *Urmi, Tkhumi, Ṭuroyo, Jilu, Baz, Mandaic*, etc. There also has developed a *pan-Eastern Aramaic koine*.[8]

It is not mutually intelligible with *Western Neo-Aramaic*, from which it is separated historically by well over 1,000 years. While the number of present-day speakers may be fairly large,[9] and in some areas, e. g. the *Tkhumi* dialects spoken in NE Syria, fairly well protected in their isolation, the twentieth century witnessed a rapid decimation of their numbers. It represents, perhaps, a textbook illustration of how a language can quickly move towards the endangered zone in reaction to unfavorable socio-political upheavals. It was the fate of eastern *Aramaic* speakers to choose the losing Russian side in their occupation of eastern Turkey during WW I, to be socially allied to the English during their occupation of Iraq, and to be Christians in a dominantly Islamic region of the world. These attributes brought ideological distrust upon this minority group, resulting in various forced exoduses at different times in the twentieth century. The ultimate exodus is that out of the region entirely, to Israel, the US (Chicago in particular) and Central Europe. Jastrow (1992: 1) estimates that there may be as many as 40,000 people of Ṭuroyo (Anatolia) descent in Germany and Sweden, as opposed to a few hundred still in Turkey. As Odisho (1993, 1999) has shown, residence in the West spells the certain demise of the language there within three or four generations. While there are still enclaves in the Middle East where the language is stable, should political events again turn against them, the number of *Eastern Neo-Aramaic* speakers could quickly sink to the danger zone.

2.2. Mogholi

Mogholi is basically *Mongol,* spoken by descendants of the Mongol invasions of the 13th century in a few villages south of Herat in Afghanistan. While Weiers (1972: 156) suggests that this variety of *Mongol* constitutes a mixed language (see above for *Central Asian Mixed Arabic*), he does not make a solid linguistic case for this judgment, and lacking such evidence the variety would not count as an endangered dialect of an otherwise non-endangered language (as with *Cypriot Arabic*, see n. 4). Already in the 1970's Weiers foresaw the imminent demise of the variety.

2.3. Languages with multiple lives

The Middle East is the repository of a rich variety of dead languages, attested through pergament, paper, cuneiform and stone inscriptions (see e.g Robin 1992). Lacking a living constituency, the survival of their documentation in all its forms is dependent on the benign and supportive policies of the countries where they are found.[10]

3. Tables

I divide the languages into two *tables,* the first geographically defined, Afghanistan, the second linguistically, all languages members of the *Semitic* family, with the problematic case of *Central Asian Mixed Arabic* included here.

Table 1. Afghanistan, Phase I

Language	Other names	LWC	Family	Speakers	Transmission	Status
1. Oormuṛi	Baraki (= autoname)	Persian[11]	IE\I-Ir\Ir\ eastern\ SE	I (Afghan.) (1986)[12]	I	a–, b
		Pashto		III (Pak.)	III	a–
2. Paraachii		Persian	IE\I-Ir\Ir\ eastern\ SE	IV (1986)	IV	a–
3. Sanglechi-Ishkashimi		Persian	IE\I-Ir\Ir\ eastern\NE\ Pamir	III (c. 1932, 1986)		a–

Table 1. cont., Phase I

Language	Other names	LWC	Family	Speakers	Trans- mission	Status
4. Munji- Yidgha	Munjani	Persian	IE\I-Ir\Ir\ eastern\NE\ Pamir	III (c. 1938, 1986)		a–
5. Gawar-Bati, with dialects Shumasti and Grangali	Gavaar- baatii- Gabari	Pashto	IE\I-Ir\ Indic\north- ern\ Dardic\ Kunar	III (?)		a– (?)
6. Tirahi	Tiro	Pashto	IE\I-Ir\ Indic\north- ern\ Dardic\ Kunar	I (prob- ably e)		e
7. Woṭ	Woṭapuri- Katarqalai	Pashto	IE\I-I\ Indic\north- ern\ Dardic\ Kunar	I (if not e)	I	d, e
8. Ashkun		Pashto	IE\I-Ir\ Nuristani	III (1932)		a– (?)
9. Prasun	Veron (= autoname), Wasi-weri	Pashto	IE\I-Ir\ Nuristani	III (1973)		a– (?)
10. Tregami	Gambiri	Pashto	IE\I-Ir\ Nuristani	III		a– (?)
11. Waigali	Kalaṣa- alaa	Pashto	IE\I-Ir\ Nuristani	III (1932)		a– (?)

Table 1. Phase II

Language	Endanger- ment	Docu- mentation	Feasibility	Conditions (Afghan./Pak.)
1. Oormuṛi	II (?)	B	A	X/?
2. Parachi	III (?)	B	A	X/?
3. Sanglechi- Ishkashimi	III (?)	A-B	A	X/?
4. Munji-Yidgha	III (?)	A-B	A	X/?
5. Gawar-Bati	III (?)	A-B	A	X/?
6. Tirahi	I	A	?	X/?
7. Woṭ	I	A-B	?	X/?
8. Ashkun	III	A-B	A	X/?
9. Prasun	III	A-B	A	X/?
10. Tregami	III	A-B	A	X/?
11. Waigalii	III	A-B	A	X/?

Table 2. Semitic, Phase I

Language	Other names	LWC	Language family	Speakers	Trans- mission	Status
1. Central Asian Mixed Arabic		Persian, Uzbek	? AA\Semitic\ West\Central + IE\I-Ir\Ir	III (Uzbek.)	III	a
				III (Afghan.)	?	?
				? (Tadj./Iran)	III	?
2. Habyoot	Habyoot Mahra	Arabic, Mehri	AA\Semitic\ West\South\ Eastern	II/III	III (?)	a
3. Ḥarsuusi		Arabic	AA\Semitic\ West\South\ Eastern	III (1977)		a
4. Baṭhari		Arabic	AA\Semitic\ West\South\ Eastern	II (1983)		a
5. Neo-West Aramaic		Arabic	AA\Semitic\ West\Central\ Northwest	IV	IV	a

Table 2. Phase II

Language	Endanger- ment	Docu- mentation	Feasibility	Conditions
1. Central Asian Arabic	III	B	A (Uzbek.)	A
	?	B	? (Afghan.)	X
	?	A	A (Iran)	A
		A	? (Tadj.)	?
2. Habyoot	II	A-B	A	A
3. Ḥarsuusi	III	A-B	A	X (Oman) A (Yemen)
4. Baṭhari	II	A-B	A	X (Oman) A (Yemen)
5. Neo-West Aramaic	IV	X	A	A

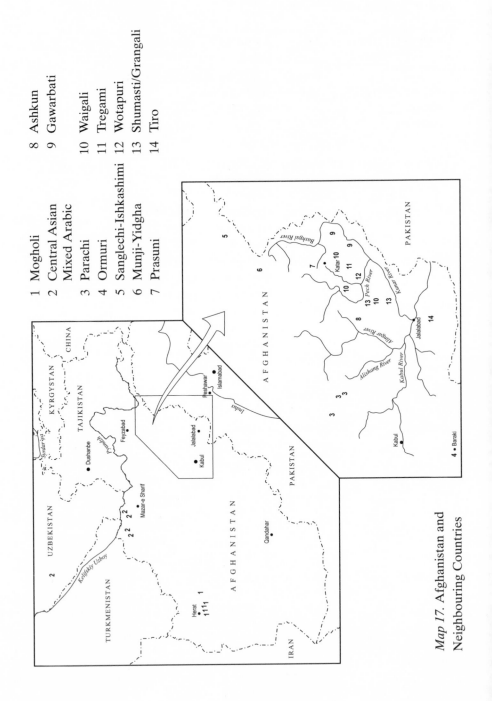

1 Mogholi
2 Central Asian
  Mixed Arabic
3 Parachi
4 Ormuri
5 Sanglechi-Ishkashimi
6 Munji-Yidgha
7 Prasuni
8 Ashkun
9 Gawarbati
10 Waigali
11 Tregami
12 Wotapuri
13 Shumasti/Grangali
14 Tiro

Map 17. Afghanistan and
Neighbouring Countries

15 Mahri
16 Habyot
17 Harsusi
18 Jibbali
19 Bathari
20 Soqotri

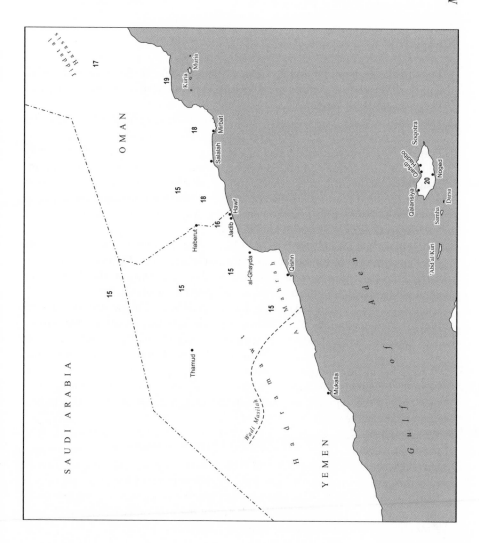

Map 18. Yemen and Oman

Abbreviations

AA = Afroasiatic,
IE = Indo-European,
I-Ir = Indo-Iranian,
Ir = Iranian,
Pak = Pakistan,
Afghan. = Afghanistan,
LRC = language of restricted communication,
LWC = language of wider communication

Notes

1. I would like to thank Dr. Marie-Claude Simeone-Senelle, Dr. Edward Odisho, and Prof. Dr. Werner Arnold for advice on various questions which emerged in the preparation of this article.
2. I should note that I have excluded from the study languages introduced into the region by relatively recent immigration.
3. Functional restrictedness is a fact of life for nearly all languages (*English* may be the only exception) and need not necessarily be construed as a sign of impoverishment, neglect, or discrimination. Functionally restricted languages may exhibit the vitality of less restricted ones in various ways (e. g. show dialectal and socially-based differentiation, and have distinct, institutionalized registers and para-varieties (e. g. secret languages).
4. Morgenstierne himself found most of his informants either in Kabul, or along the Pakistan side of the border in Chitral. Grierson (1925), a study of *Tirahi* carried out by a third party in Peshawar in Pakistan, confirms the difficulty of conducting research in the area. Budruss (1960) is one of the few exceptions.
5. Kieffer specifically searched out speakers of the language in the 1970's but found that it was remembered only in phrases by older speakers (Kieffer 1986: 106).
6. This case can be opposed to one such as *Cypriot (Kormakiti) Arabic*, a small and endangered variety strongly influenced by Greek, but not to the extent that its basic linguistic structure (phonology, morphology, syntax) has been 'de-arabicized'. I would not include *Cypriot Arabic* among endangered languages in the sense of this volume, as what is endangered is a dialect of a much larger, non-endangered entity.
7. Windfuhr 1989: 251 "Some recent studies towards the better understanding of the West Iranian *dialects...*" [my italics, J. O.].
8. Odisho (p.c.) distinguishes *Central Neo-Aramaic*, associated with SE Turkey (e. g. *Ṭuroyo*), from *Eastern Neo-Aramaic*, which includes the other varieties. I follow Jastrow (1997: 347), who opposes *Western* to *Eastern Neo-Aramaic* as the primary genetic split, while leaving open the possibility that *Eastern Neo-Aramaic* may include a number of distinct languages within it.

9. Odisho (p. c.) puts the number at 500,000, with 100,000 in the Chicago area alone.
10. Since my writing this article, Matras (1999) has appeared, which describes *Domari*, an Indic language related to *Romani* spoken mainly in urban areas in Israel, Syria, Lebanon, Palestine and Jordan. In Jerusalem, which Matras describes, it is spoken mainly by those over 50, so that of the 600–700 estimated ethnic Dom, only about 20% actively use the language.
11. Here, as elsewhere when reference is made to Afghanistan, *Persian* means the Afghan variety, known as *Daari*.
12. The years set in brackets are those for which the number of speakers cited was reported.

References

NJL = Norwegian Journal of Linguistics
JAOS = Journal of the American Oriental Society

Arnold, Werner
    1990   *Das Neuwestaramäische: Grammatik*. Erlangen.
    2000   The Arabic dialects in the Turkish province of Hatay and the Aramaic dialects in the Syrian Mountains of Qalamun: Two minority languages compared. In Owens (ed.) 347–370.
Budruss, Georg
    1960   *Die Sprache von Woṭapuur und Kaṭaarqalaa: Linguistische Studien im afghanistanischen Hindukusch*. Bonn: Orientalisches Seminar der Universität Bonn.
Fussman, Gerard
    1972   *Atlas Linguistique des Parlers Dardes et Kafirs*. Paris: Ecoles Francaise d'Extreme-Orient.
Grierson, George
    1925   On the Tirahi language. *Journal of the royal Asiatic society* 405–416.
Hetzron, Robert (ed.)
    1997   *The Semitic languages*. London: Routledge.
Jastrow, Otto
    1992   *Lehrbuch der Ṭuroyo-Sprache*. Wiesbaden: Harrassowitz.
    1997   The Neo-Aramaic languages. In Hetzron (ed.) 334–377.
Krahnke, John
    1976   *Linguistic relationships in Central Iran*. PhD Thesis, Univ. of Michigan.
Krauss, Michael
    2006   Classification and terminology for degrees of language endangerment. (Chapter 1, this volume).

Matras, Yaron
  1999   The state of present-day Domari in Jerusalem. *Mediterranean language review* 1–58.
Morgenstierne, Georg
  1932   *Report on a linguistic mission to North-western India.* Oslo: Instituttet for Sammenlignende Kulturforskning. (Journey in 1924).
  1938   *Indo-Iranian frontier languages.* Oslo: H. Aschehoug.
  1942   Notes on Dameli: a Kafir-Dardic language of Chitral. *NJL* 12: 115–197.
  1945   Notes on Shumashti: A Dardic dialect of the Gawar-bati type. *NJL* 13: 239–281.
  1950   Notes on Gawar-Bati. *Skrifter utgitt av Det Norske Videnskaps-Akademi i Oslo.* Oslo: I Kommisjon Hos Jacob Dybwad, 1–62.
  1952   Linguistic Gleanings from Nuristan. *NJL* 16: 117–135.
  1954   The Waigali language. *NJL* 17: 146–324.
  1974   Languages of Nuristan and surrounding regions. In Jettmar, Karl (ed.). *Cultures of the Hindukush.* Wiesbaden: Steiner. 1–11.
Kieffer, Charles
  1985   Afghanistan V, Languages. In Yarshater, Ehsan (ed.). *Encyclopedia Iranica.* London: Routledge and Kegan Paul. 501–16.
  1986   La maintenance de l'identite ethnique chez les Arabes arabophones, les Oormuṛ et les Parachi en Afghanistan. In Orywal (ed.) 101–164.
  2000   The Arabic speech of Bactria (Afghanistan). In Owens (ed.) 181–198.
Odisho, Edward
  1988   *The sound system of modern Assyrian.* Wiesbaden: Harrassowitz.
  1993   Bilingualism and multilingualism among Assyrians: A case of language erosion and demise. In Continiu, R.; F. Pennacchietti and M. Tosco (eds.). *Semitica.* Torino: Silvio Zamorani Editore, 189–200.
  1999   Assyrian language maintenance and erosion in U. S.: a World War I immigrant family case study. *Journal of Assyrian academic studies* XI-II: 3–14.
Orywal, Erwin (ed.)
  1986   *Die ethnischen Gruppen Afghanistans.* Wiesbaden: Reichert.
  1986   Erläuterungen zur Verbreitungskarten. In Orywal (ed.) 11–72.
Owens, Jonathan
  1999   Creole Arabic: the orphan of all orphans. Paper presented at the IX Colloque International des Etudes Créoles, Aix en Provence.
Owens, Jonathan (ed.)
  2000   *Arabic as a minority language.* Berlin: Mouton de Gruyter.
Redard, Georges
  1970   Other Iranian languages. In Sebeok, Thomas (ed.) *Current trends in linguistics,* Vol. 6, *Linguistics in South West Asia and North Africa.* The Hague: Mouton. 97–138

Robin, Christian (ed.)
  1992   *L'arabie antique de Karib'il a Mahomet.* Aix en Provence: Editions
          Edisud.
Ruhlen, Merrit
  1987   *A guide to the world's languages* Vol. 1. Stanford: Stanford Univ.
          Press.
Schmitt, Rüdiger
  1989   *Compendium Linguarum Iranicarum.* Wiesbaden: Reichert.
Simeone-Senelle, Marie-Claude
  1997a   The modern South Arabic languages. In Hetzron (ed.) 378–423.
  1997b   Les langues sudarabiques modernes, des langues sémitiques mena-
          cées? In Caron, B. (ed.) *Proceedings of the 16th international congress
          of linguists,* Paper No. 0449. Oxford: Pergamon.
Strand, Richard
  1973   Notes on the Nuristaani and Dardic languages. *JAOS* 93: 297–305.
Voegelin, C. and F. Voegelin
  1965   The Iranian sub-branch of the Indo-European branch of Indo-Euro-
          pean. *Anthropological linguistics* 7: 190–209.
Weiers, Michael
  1972   *Die Sprache der Moghol der Provinz Herat in Afghanistan.* Opladen:
          Westdeutscher Verlag.
Windfuhr, Gernot
  1989   New West Iranian. In Schmitt (ed.) 251–262.
Yarshater, Ehsan
  1969   *A grammar of southern Tati dialects.* The Hague: Mouton.

Chapter 13
Language Endangerment in China and Mainland Southeast Asia[1]

David Bradley

1. Introduction

In this chapter the discussion follows genetic classifications, starting with *Mon-Khmer* (hereafter *MK*) languages of the *Austroasiatic* family, then *Austro-Thai* languages: the few endangered *Austronesian* on the mainland, *Thai-Kadai*, and *Miao-Yao* (or *Hmong-Mien*). Following this are the *Sino-Tibetan* languages, including Sinitic and *Tibeto-Burman* (hereafter *TB*) with many branches. Finally the '*Altaic*' groups *Manchu-Tungus*, *Mongolic* and *Turkic* of northern and western China are discussed, with brief notes on *Indo-European* creoles and *Ainu*.

In China, Vietnam, Laos and Burma there is a rigid classification of all citizens into ethnic groups: a majority group speaking the national language and a number of minorities. In addition to the majority groups, China has 55 national minorities; in Laos there are 46, in Vietnam 53, and in Burma 134. All official statistics use these categories. In China closely related groups are usually lumped into one nationality; in Vietnam, Laos and Burma, the official categories tend to follow more localised ethnic categories. However, in Laos and Vietnam the ethnic groups most closely related to the majority group are lumped into one category: in Vietnam, the *Mu'o'ng*; and in Laos, the *Phu Tai*. Thus, ethnic groups speaking distinct languages may be classified within one nationality in China but as two or more ethnic groups in Vietnam, Laos or Burma.

Table 1. Ethnic Categories

	Ethnic groups	Percent majority	Minority categories
China	56	92	lumped
Vietnam	54	87	partly split
Laos	47	50.1	partly split
Burma	135	63?	split
Thailand	17+	over 95	split
Cambodia	–	over 95	none

Perhaps the most interesting category in China is the 'other – unclassified' national minority. This comprises small groups who have not (yet) been re-classified as members of some larger national minority. Since the 1950s the only additional nationality is the *Jinuo*, recognised in 1978. Most small groups who applied for nationality status since the 1970s have instead been amalgamated into an existing nationality; for example the *Laomian* and *Ku-cong* into the *Lahu*. The authorities now say that very small groups cannot get the status of a separate national minority, even though seven nationalities recognised in the 1950s now have fewer than 10,000 members. The *Gaoshan* nationality with 764 members in China is a special case; this is the nationality of the various Austronesian minority groups autochthonous to Taiwan.

The Thai list of Chaw Khaw 'hill tribes' has grown from 9 to 16 over the last thirty years; these are identified groups in the north and west of the country who get special assistance from the Public Welfare Department. In addition to these, there are many small scattered groups speaking *MK* languages in the northeast, a patchwork of speakers of different *Thai* lan-guages scattered across the central plain as a result of transportation of war captives from Laos and points north up to about a hundred years ago, also three groups speaking *Austronesian* languages and two groups speaking *MK* languages in the south.

Cambodia has no official list of minorities; in any case these are rela-tively small and mainly confined to peripheral areas, especially the north-east of the country. There is also a scattering of endangered *MK* languag-es of the *Pearic* subgroup with extremely small speaker populations in the western half of the country.

In Peninsular Malaysia the endangered languages are spoken by mem-bers of three categories of minority, the Orang Laut 'sea people' who speak various endangered *Austronesian* languages closely related to *Ma-lay*; the Orang Asli 'original people', the indigenous negrito groups with various endangered to extinct *MK* languages; and the creole Portuguese Kristang speakers of *Melaka*. A related creole is also spoken in Macao.

For more details, fuller references and exact locations of the languages cited below, see my contributions in Wurm and Hattori (1981), Wurm et al. (1987), Moseley and Asher (1994) and particularly Moseley (2006).

2. Austroasiatic languages

Apart from Vietnamese, Cambodian and Khasi of northeast India, all *MK* languages are endangered to some degree; only the more endan-gered among them are discussed here.

Of the *Monic* languages, although *Mon* is the state language of the Mon State in southeastern Burma and is said to be spoken by about 800,000 people, mainly in Burma, it has been receding under *Burmese* pressure for nearly 800 years and is now in decline.

Earlier Dvaravati kingdom *Mon* dominance in what is now central Thailand was broken more than a millenium ago. Vestiges of Dvaravati *Mon* are spoken by the Nyahkur in northeastern Thailand; fewer than 10,000 speakers of three dialects remain, but younger speakers are fewer and less fluent, and most young people have only passive or no knowledge.

The *Palaungic* subbranch of the Northern branch of *MK* includes many subgroups of the *Bulang* nationality in China and other tiny groups which have not achieved nationality status and whose languages are endangered, such as *Hu, Buxia, Buguo, Paijiao* and so on. In northeastern Burma are some 2,000 Tai Loi, with a few in northwest Laos and nearby in China. Burma also has various additional groups including the Danau (endangered). *Palaungic* languages of Thailand include *Phalok* (moribund or extinct) and *Lavua* (about 10,000 but decreasing). In Laos are the *Pasing* (1,530); there is also one *Pasing* village in China with 202 people. In Laos they are called *Bit* officially and *Khamit* locally, and *Kami* in China; the language is quite endangered.

Within the *Khmuic* subbranch, in the jungles between Thailand and Laos, there is a tiny hunter-gatherer group known as *Mlabri*; 125 in Thailand and 24 in Laos, probably underenumerated; the language is now severely endangered as the group settles down, being replaced by *Hmong, Thai* or *Lao*.

Iduh[2] is a recently located moribund *Khmuic* language of the border between central Laos and north central Vietnam; of 200 in the group, fewer than 30 can speak the language.

Mang is a highly important group-level isolate within *MK* with about 2,200 people near the southern border of Yunnan and another 2,300 on the Vietnamese side of the border; in each country about 500 *Mang* still speak their language, which is severely endangered and poorly known. They are recognised as an ethnic group in Vietnam, but not in China.

Lai or *Paliu* is the northeasternmost *MK* language, spoken by under 500 of an ethnic group of 1,771 in northwestern Guangxi and southeastern Yunnan in China. It is very important for *MK* reconstruction. Some members of the group speak *Yi* rather than *Lai*, and all are multilingual, speaking *Zhuang, Miao* and *Chinese* as well. A third small endangered language of this subgroup, Pakan, was recently found in southwestern Guizhou.

In the *Viet-Mu'o'ng* branch of *MK*, all of the small groups speaking *Mu'o'ng* languages in Vietnam are lumped into the single *Mu'o'ng* ethnic group or in the smaller *Nguon* group. All other *Mu'o'ng* languages are spoken by tiny groups along the border between south central Laos and north central Vietnam, some in areas which are being inundated by dams, and nearly all are endangered. This includes *Sac* (about 1,000 in Vietnam), *May* (about 1,500 in Laos and Vietnam) and *Ruc* (about 500 in Laos and Vietnam), which are close to each other; another group comprising *Phong* (20,000: 18,165 in Laos and the rest in Vietnam), *Hung* (1,000 in Vietnam) and *Tum* (the last is an ethnic group of 2,042 in Laos); and a third cluster of *Arem* (1,000 in Laos and Vietnam), *Pakatan* (500 in Laos), *Bo* (2,500 in Laos), *Phonsung* (500 in Laos) and *Thavung*[3] (500 in Laos, 1,000 in Thailand). *Thavung* is spoken by about 200 adults in one village in Thailand, where it is known as *So*, a name usually used for a *Katuic* language also widespread in central Laos and across the river in northeastern Thailand. Apart from *Mu'o'ng* and *Nguon*, all these languages are very severely endangered.

Among the *Katuic-Bahnaric*[4] group languages, even groups with substantial populations are becoming endangered; but those with fewer speakers are particularly so. A severely endangered *Katuic* language recently located in Xekong Province of Laos by Theraphan Luangthongkum is *Chatong*, with 580 people in four villages, some of them fluent. She also located the *Dakkang* and *Triw* languages in the same area, with 1,198 and 1,328 people respectively, also with some fluent speakers; all three are undescribed apart from her work and endangered.

South Bahnaric Chrau is endangered because its traditional territory is near Saigon. The most endangered languages in this subbranch are *Kaco'*, about 1,000 people in northeastern Cambodia, located by Diffloth some years ago; also *Juk* (autonym) or *Suai* (exonym), 1,500 and *Swoeng* (autonym) or *Lavi* (exonym), 492 (or 584 according to the Lao census), both recently located and briefly described by Theraphan Luangthongkum in Xekong Province of Laos.

Pearic[5] group languages are widely distributed in tiny populations across western Cambodia and in very limited numbers across the border in Thailand. They are closely related to but distinct from *Khmer*. Some extremely small communities have maintained their languages, though the speaker populations were further reduced during the Khmer Rouge period. All are now endangered to moribund.

The largest population is speakers of *Chong* in Thailand along the western border of Cambodia; about 2,000 people and 500 speakers with the youngest now 22. *Song* or *Kasong*, usually also known to outsiders as

Chong, has a population of about 200 in eastern Thailand, with 40 speakers, the youngest of whom is now 30.

Samre has a population of about 100 displaced in Pursat Province of Cambodia and another 100 in eastern Thailand, of whom fewer than 20 speak it, the youngest now 45.

A *Pear* group – autonym unknown – in 3 or 4 villages near Kompong Thom has about 250 people, language status unknown but group size reduced from about 1,000 since 1975. The last two speakers of *Samrai* were in a refugee camp in Thailand in the 1980s; their present whereabouts is unknown. All the rest of their village was killed by the Khmer Rouge. At least one other *Pearic* language became extinct during the Khmer Rouge period.

Finally, the group usually called *Saoch* (which is the *Khmer* word for a kind of skin disease) and who call themselves *Su-ung* have an interesting history. Nearly the entire group was transported to western Thailand in 1833, leaving behind a small remnant. Of the remnant in Cambodia, 3 families comprising 17 speakers including children remained in 1993. Of the transported population, now called *Chu'ung*, *Sa-ong* or *Khamen Padong* 'Padong Khmer', 150 remain in the village, with 20 speakers of whom about ten are fluent, with the youngest semispeakers now 35.

The *Orang Asli* languages of Peninsular Malaysia in the *Aslian* group of *MK* are all endangered, mostly severely; some others are already extinct, and some dialects of the surviving languages are also extinct. *Northern Aslian* includes *Tonga'* or *Mos* in southern Thailand, closely related to *Kensiu* on the Thai/Malaysian border; also *Jehai, Batek*, and *Che Wong*. *Central Aslian* includes *Lanoh, Temiar, Semai* and *Jah Het. Temiar* and *Semai* are the least endangered of these. *Southern Aslian* includes *Semaq Beri, Semelai* and *Besisi*. Majority community attitudes are very negative.

3. Austro-Thai languages

The mainland *Austronesian* languages which are endangered fall into two genetic subgroups: the *Chamic* languages, mainly in southern Vietnam and northeastern Cambodia and one endangered language on the south central coast of Hainan in China, and the *Malay* languages.

The most endangered *Chamic* language is *Huihui* or *Tsat*, spoken by about 4,000 members of a group of 5,000 with Hui (Moslem) nationality in southern Hainan. This is also typologically interesting because it has become fully tonal, unlike other *Chamic* languages, due presumably to contact with tonal languages like *Chinese* which is replacing it.

There are four *Malay* group languages which are endangered in this area. *Moken* (2,000) further north and *Moklen* (4,000) further south are spoken by dwindling groups of seafarers along the coasts of southern Burma and the west coast of southern Thailand as far south as Phuket. *Urak Lawoi* is spoken by similar groups of about 3,000 ranging southwards from Phuket to beyond the Malaysian border. There are also about 2,000 *Duano, Desin Dola,* or *Orang Kuala* along the Malaysian coast just northwest of Singapore. All are endangered as these groups settle down; the *Duano* are gradually assimilating their speech back into local *Malay.*

Of the *Thai-Kadai* languages, the only *Thai* subgroup language which is very severely endangered is *Saek*, spoken in China by a few members of the Zhuang nationality, in Laos (2,459 by ethnicity, not all speak), and in Thailand. The total group population is about 20,000, but it is now divided into three communities out of contact with each other and the language is disappearing, at least in Thailand and in Laos, by being absorbed into local Lao.

Also in Laos is the *Phu Tai* group. This is an amalgamation which includes various southwestern *Thai* languages very close to *Lao*, some widely spoken such as *Thai Dam 'black Thai'* but also more or less endangered *Tai Daeng 'red Tai'*, *Tai Neua 'northern Tai'* (from Samneua Province of Laos) among others. Each of these has an original territory in northeastern Laos, and they are also found in the south where they were moved as war captives some time ago and are losing their original languages. The languages of several groups within the *Phu Tai* category are undescribed and potentially endangered.

The *Kam-Sui* or *Dong* subgroup of *Thai-Kadai* includes the *Dong, Li, Shui, Maonan* and *Mulao* nationalities in China. Endangered languages spoken by groups included within other nationalities include *Rau, Ten* or *Yanghuang*, about 20,000 speakers who are of *Buyi* nationality in southeastern Guizhou, somewhat endangered but not severely so; *Lajia*, also known as *Lakkia* in the western literature, about 9,000 speakers who are members of the *Yao* nationality in eastern Guizhou; moderately endangered; *Mak* (autonym) or *Mo* (Mandarin pronunciation of the same), about 5,000 speakers who are members of the *Buyi* nationality in southeastern Guizhou; quite endangered.

Unlike the *Thai* and *Kam-Sui* subgroups, all languages of the *Kadai* subgroup[6] are endangered, some very severely so. The only recognised Kadai nationality in China is the *Gelao* (438,192), two of whose four very distinct languages are moribund and two endangered; the total speaker population in the traditional area in western Guizhou is about 3,000 and rapidly decreasing, and descriptive work is urgent. There are also some communities to the south in Guangxi, Yunnan and Vietnam where some of the languages are also still spoken by another 2,400 people. The languages are:

1) *Hakhi* [ha^{33} k^{h}i?^{55}], Green Gelao, about 2,000 speakers around Guanling in west central Guizhou; other members of this ethnic subgroup are as far south as Vietnam, but do not speak the language.

2) *Tolo* [to^{33} luo?^{55}], White Gelao, under 1,000 speakers around Liupanshui in west central Guizhou; also over 2,000 further south in China (but of Yi, Yao or Zhuang nationality, not Gelao) and Vietnam.

3) *A-uo* [?a^{33} ?uo^{55}], Red Gelao; very few speakers but nearly 275,000 ethnic group members west of Zunyi in north central Guizhou; research is urgent! About 30 semispeakers calling themselves [va nto] including some children are in a Gelao community of over 400 people in northern Vietnam.

4) *Aqao* [?a^{33} qaw^{13}], spoken only by a few aged individuals near Puding, west central Guizhou. *Aqao* is the best described variety of *Gelao*, but more work is still needed.

There are also 1,500 group members enumerated in Vietnam, where they are also a separate nationality, the *Co'lao*. Between the 1982 and 1990 censuses in China, nearly 380,000 people formerly identified as Han Chinese reclaimed their former *Gelao* identity; but none of them speaks the language.

Gelao living further south include one village of *White Gelao* in Longlin, northwestern Guangxi who call themselves [tə^{33} ?lu^{53}]; the language is spoken there even by children; and another village with two elderly speakers of *Green Gelao* in the same area. In Malipo, southeastern Yunnan there are another 1,500 *White Gelao* speakers who call themselves [tə^{21} ?lɯ^{33}], and in Vietnam nearly 400 more. A village of over 400 *Red Gelao* in Vietnam has about 30 semispeakers, but most *Red* and *Green Gelao* in Vietnam and other *White Gelao* in southeastern Yunnan do not speak their traditional languages.

The northernmost *Kadai* language is *Qaw*, known locally as *Yi*; this should not be confused with the *Aqao* subvariety of *Gelao*, nor with the *TB Yi* nationality. Of about 3,000 *Qaw* in Gulin, Sichuan and in Bijie, Guizhou, it is believed that few if any speakers remain. All are members of the Gelao nationality.

There are six additional southern *Kadai* languages in China and Vietnam: 1) *Yerong*, over 300 people of *Yao* nationality in Napo County in Guangxi; 2) *Buyang* [puo^{11} ?jaŋ^{42}], about 3,000 people of *Zhuang* nationality in southeastern Yunnan; 3) *Pubiao* (Chinese name), *Pupeo* (Vietnamese name), *Laqua* in Benedict (1942) or [qa biaw³³] (own name), about 50 speakers in a group of 307 in Malipo County in Yunnan, and most of a group of 382 nearby in Vietnam. In China they are classified as Yi nationality, but in Vietnam they are a separate nationality. 4) *Lachi* (Vietnamese), *Laji* (Chinese) or *Lati* in Benedict (1942) is spoken by about 200 of the group of over 1,600 who call themselves [li¹³ pu³³ lio³³] in Maguan County in China where they are included in the *Yi* nationality, and by about 5,000 of 8,000 Lachi in Vietnam. 5) *Nung Ven* or *Ainh* with a viable speech community of 200 in far northern Vietnam, recently located by Edmondson; 6) *Laha* or *Khlaphlao* of Vietnam, 2,100, moribund in one village in Son La Province but spoken by all including children at villages in Lao Cai Province.

Within *Miao-Yao*, of some 18 languages in the *Miao, Yao, Bunu* and *She* clusters, three *Bunu* languages, *Ngnai* [hm nai], *Jiongnai* [kjɔŋ nai] and *Younuo* [ju nɔ] with as few as 1,000 speakers, are potentially endangered. The She nationality of eastern Guangxi and Guangdong in China has 634,700 members, of whom only about 1,000 still use the [huo nte] language near Huizhou in eastern Guangdong; the rest mainly speak *Hakka Chinese*.

4. Sino-Tibetan languages

As a result of the spread of standard northern *Mandarin* and major regional varieties of provincial capitals since 1950, many of the smaller local *Sinitic* (*Chinese*) varieties are disappearing by being absorbed into a larger regional *Sinitic* language, whether *Mandarin* or something else.

Within *TB* there are well over fifty endangered languages in this area, with many more still to be located, especially in southwestern China.

Of languages in the *Qiangic* branch of *TB* in western Sichuan, there are various small localised groups, all included within the Tibetan nationality, whose languages are endangered to various degrees. From south to north, they are the *Namuyi, Shixing, Ersu* (*Tosu* or *Lüzi*), *Muya, Ergong, Choyo, Zaba* and *Guichong*; also the *Baima* in southern Gansu.

In the Central *TB* branch there are five endangered languages. These include two small groups in southeastern Tibet, 800 [ta³¹ ʒuaŋ⁵⁵], known in the *Chinese* literature as *Darang Deng*, and 200 [kɯ³¹ mɑn³⁵], known in the *Chinese* literature as *Geman Deng*. There is one Taruang village in Burma where they are called Taraung, and a larger group of Taraon, Tayin or Tain, or formerly Digaru Mishmi in India. While endangered in China, it is less so in India. The Geman are also known as Kaman or Miju Mishmi in India; likewise endangered in China. There used to be more speakers in China, but many have gone to India.

Among the *Nu* and *Dulong* nationalities in China and the *Rawang* group in northern Burma, there are nine languages, eight of them *Nungish* with three endangered. The most affected of these is *Anung* (*Anong* or sometimes, *Along* in the *Chinese* literature), 6,000 people but only about 600 speakers, mostly over 40, in China; there are also several thousand speakers in Burma. Among the Rawang the *Lungmi* and *Dvngsar* languages are also becoming endangered.

The *Tujia* languages form a separate branch of *TB*, spoken by fewer than 60,000 of the 5,725,049 Tujia nationality of northwestern Hunan, southwestern Hubei and eastern Sichuan in south central China. They were concealed within the Han Chinese nationality until being identified and recognised in the 1950s. All speakers are bilingual in *Chinese*, and the language is increasingly endangered. It is also very interesting historically because it has so much *Chinese* contact material superposed on its *TB* core.

Within the large and complex *Burmic* branch of *TB*, *Burmese* itself contains a number of distinct regional sublanguages which are being submerged by influence from standard *Burmese*. These include *Tavoyan* and *Beik* or *Myeik* in the south; *Danu*, *Intha* and *Taungyo* in the northeast; and *Yaw* in the west.

Hpun is a nearly extinct language along the upper Irrawaddy. Survey work in the early 1960s found that the only fluent speakers of the two dialects of *Hpun* were in their 60s, with some younger semispeakers. Recent attempts to find fluent speakers have failed; only some very old semispeakers remain.

Within the Kachin culture complex, there are two severely endangered *Burmish* languages spoken in China: 400 *Bola* and 100 *Chintao* (*Xiandao* in *Chinese*) who are members of the Achang nationality. Due to language exogamy there are no monolingual speakers.

The *Gong* language was formerly spoken over a wide area of western central Thailand, along the branches of the River Kwai. It has disappeared from the original area, with the last speakers only recently deceased; but two communities which migrated to Suphanburi and Uthai Thani provinces to the northeast still maintain distinct dialects of the language; they are classified in the composite Lua 'hill tribe' of Thailand. Of 500 people in these two villages, about 80 still speak *Gong*: about 20 fluent speakers over 50 and additional semispeakers of varying ability as young as 30. Thai colleagues and I are working on this language, which is crucial for the understanding of *Burmic*.

Results of our recent surveys in some areas of Yunnan suggest that there may be fifty or more additional unreported endangered languages within the *Loloish* or *Yi* subbranch in Yunnan and Sichuan provinces of China, especially *Northern Loloish* languages. Further survey and descriptive work is extremely urgent!

Northern Loloish includes the 25,000 *Samei* of Guandu, east of Kunming, and the nearly 30,000 *Sanyie* of Xishan and surrounding areas just west of Kunming. Their languages, which have major internal dialect differences, are extinct or moribund in some villages, severely endangered in others, and endangered elsewhere. Another related language is *Samataw*, about 100 speakers and a larger number of semispeakers in a single large village of 2,500 on the southeastern outskirts of Kunming, where all fluent speakers are over 60 and even semispeakers are over 40; nevertheless the village primary school is trying to teach the language. Another similar language is *Ayizi*, a bit further east of Kunming; this language is moribund in nearly all locations; salvage work may still be possible, but as many villages now identify as Han Chinese, it is impossible to know the original size of the group. About ten villages have been identified, but in most no speech remains. For more details on these languages which we located around Kunming in the last few years, see Bradley and Bradley (2000).

The 5,391 *Gazhuo* of Xingmeng township in central Tonghai County are classified as *Mongol* nationality, but speak a *Northern Loloish* language. They are descendants of a *Mongol* army which settled about 700 years ago and married local women. There are no identfiable vestiges of *Mongol* in their speech. This language is also at risk as many young people do not speak it.

Eight known endangered *Central Loloish* languages are listed below; there are certainly others. One group is the *Micha*, with at least 50,000 very widely scattered across western Yunnan, intermingling with the Lalo and Lahu to the southwest, with the Lisu in the northwest, with the Lipo in the northeast, and overlapping with the Lolo over most of their range. While *Micha* is moribund or severely endangered in many villages, it is better-preserved in some; there are very substantial internal linguistic differences.

Overlapping with the Lisu in northwestern Yunnan are about 15,000 Laemae [$l\varepsilon^{21}$ $m\varepsilon^{21}$], in *Chinese Leimai* or *Leimo*, who traditionally spoke a distinctive variety of *Bai*, but now mainly speak only *Lisu*. *Laemae* is becoming endangered in the last small areas where it is spoken; there are no monolinguals.

A bit further east with seven villages in Lanping County and two in Lushui County are about 2,500 [zɑw⁵⁵ zo³³], in *Chinese Raorou*, who are members of the *Nu* nationality; about 1,000 of them still speak another endangered *Central Loloish* language.

The *Tanglang* language is spoken in one township in southwestern Lijiang County of Yunnan by all adults and some children; they are classified as *Yi* nationality.

The *Lamo* language is spoken by about 100 people, all also first language speakers of *Lipo*, in a cluster of villages further east still, in the northeastern part of Binchuan County. They are classified as members of the Lahu nationality, but their language is more similar to *Lisu* and *Lipo* than to *Lahu*. Few children are learning this language; we located it in 1999.

About 600,000 *Lalo* live in western central Yunnan, especially in Wenshan and Nanjian counties, but also in surrounding areas; however only about half speak the language, which is moribund in many peripheral areas and well-preserved only in some areas of concentration.

In addition to the *Lahu* nationality whose language is not now at risk, there is a distinct group of about 35,000 in south central Yunnan and 5,400 in northwestern Yunnan known as *Kucong* (*Chinese*) or *Lahu* (autonym). What they speak is closer to *Lahu* than to anything else, so when their application for status as a separate Kucong nationality in China was rejected in 1989, they were merged into the *Lahu* nationality. In Vietnam, which does not have the majority kind of *Lahu*, they used to be known as Cosung, but are now usually called *Lahu*.

In northeastern Jinghong County are the *Jinuo*, who were recognised as a separate nationality in China in 1978. Fewer than half speak the language; I have never met a young *Jinuo* who can speak the language, despite years of trying. It has at least two dialects and is very interesting, both for its complex tone sandhi and for its conservatism with initial consonants.

The following seventeen endangered languages are in the *Southern Loloish* group; there are almost certainly others in China. *Mpi* is spoken in one large village near Phrae in northern Thailand; they were transported there from China as war captives about 200 years ago. *Mpi* is still spoken by most of the 1,200 people in the village, but all are now trilingual, speaking *Northern Thai* as a Low and standard *Thai* as a High; use of *Mpi* is declining.

There are some smaller languages which fall within the Akha cultural orbit and are being absorbed into it. One example is *Akeu* [a⁵⁵ kə⁵⁵], spoken by over 10,000 people classified as Akha in Thailand, Burma and northwestern Laos, and as Hani in the southwestern tip of Yunnan in China. Their language is not intelligible to other *Akha* though it is quite closely related, and is being replaced by *Akha*. Another such is *Chepya* [tɕe¹¹ pjas¹¹] of northeastern Laos, a small group of unknown size. A third is *Muda* [mu³¹ ta̠³¹], a group of about 2,000 in Jinghong county, Yunnan, China.

All languages within the *Bisoid* branch are endangered: in China, Lao-mian of central Lancang County has about 5,000 group members and 4,000 speakers; *Laopin* of Menglian County has about 1,300 group members and fewer than 1,000 speakers; the knowledge of younger speakers is more restricted. The *Laomian* were amalgamated into the *Lahu* na-tionality in 1990; many others had doubtless already quietly integrated into the *Lahu* nationality, which calls them *Lawmeh* and includes them in their origin myth, suggesting longstanding contact. *Hpyin* in Burma was already reported as moribund in 1900, and has been replaced by *Lahu* in many domains. *Bisu* in Thailand (about 500 acknowledged group members, but far fewer speakers; two dialects have died in the last 20 years, but two villages speaking slightly different dialects remain), where the language is being replaced by *Northern Thai*, and a cluster of five languages within the *Sinsali* (formerly Phunoi) group in Laos. *Bisu, Hpyin, Laomian, Laopin* and the [law³³ pan¹¹] dialect of Phunoi are quite closely related, but the other four *Sinsali* languages, the main vari-ety and the other three known as [pʰɔŋ³³ ku⁵⁵], [law²¹ sɛŋ²¹] and [pi³³ su⁴⁴], differ from them and from each other. *Sangkong* is a further *Bisoid* language with about 2,000 speakers of *Hani* nationality nearby in Jing-hong County. A further *Bisoid* language is *Cong* of northwestern Viet-nam, with only 500 speakers in four villages, but said to be fairly well preserved and used by many children.

There are two severely endangered languages of another branch of the *Southern Loloish* group which are almost completely undescribed: *Bana* in northern Laos and *Sila* in northeastern Laos and northwestern Viet-nam. The few hundred *Bana* or *Bala* in Laos are included within the Kaw (Akha) ethnic group; in one village of northeastern Laos their lan-guage is being replaced by *Akha*, and in one village in northwestern Laos it is being replaced by *Lahu*. The 2,100 *Sila* or *Sida* are recognised as an ethnic group in Laos and in Vietnam, but their language is weakening.

All the Southeastern or '*Tonkin*' *Loloish* groups speak endangered lan-guages; four are listed here, but others may also be found in China. The [pʰu ɬa] or *Pula* of China are part of the Yi nationality; the *Phula* in Viet-nam are a separate nationality. This language is in decline in both areas.

Widely scattered in far south central Yunnan are the *Muji* people of *Yi* nationality, who speak a potentially endangered and virtually undescribed language which they call [ɬa³¹ ɣə⁵⁵] or [mu³¹ di³³]; the rest of the township speaks *Pula*. Fairly similar is *Laghuu*, spoken by 300 people in one village in far northern Vietnam. It is known in *Vietnamese* as *Xapho* but also classified as part of the Phula nationality.

In Funing County of southeastern Yunnan, about 5,000 people of *Yi* nationality speak [muɯaŋ^{51}], or in *Chinese Mo'ang*, another endangered language. In Guangnan County nearby, about 5,000 *Yi* people speak [k$\underline{A}^{33}$ θu$\underline{}^{31}$], reported in Chinese as *Gasu*, also endangered.

Most languages in the *Baric* branch of *TB* are in northeastern India; those found in Burma are some of the so-called *Luish* (from Manipuri *lui* 'slave') languages of western Burma. The only such language not on its last legs is *Sak*, autonym [atsaʔ], *Burmese* name *Thet*, with nearly 3,000 speakers in Bangladesh and about a thousand speakers of an ethnic population of 1,602 in Arakan State of Burma; but even *Sak* is declining and endangered. *Kadu* was the language of a pre-Burman kingdom in the north of Burma, and is still spoken there by a couple of thousand from an ethnic group of about 20,000. Closely related and in the same area is *Ganan*, with about 500 speakers of an ethnic population of 7,000. Both languages are moribund but fieldwork is at present impossible. Other *Luish* languages of Burma such as *Taman* and *Malin*, may already be extinct, as are some in Manipur.

5. 'Altaic' languages

In China as in Russia, every *Manchu-Tungus* language is at least endangered, and most are moribund. The *Jurchen* language of the rulers of the Jin Dynasty (1115–1234) is thought to be the precursor of the *Manchu* language of the rulers of the Qing Dynasty (1644–1911), but despite official support up to 1911, massive literature and a 1990 population of 9,846,776, the language in its homeland of Manchuria is extinct apart from three locations in northwestern Heilongjiang Province with a few remaining speakers, all over 50.

Manchu survives much better in Xinjiang, where the Xibo nationality is the remainder of Manchu armies left there during the Qing Dynasty. Of the 1990 population of 72,392, approximately 26,760 were estimated to speak the language, including some children, in the late 1980s (Wurm et al. 1987: C-5).

The *Nanai* language, formerly known as *Goldi*, is known as *Hezhe* in China. Of 4,254 Hezhe south of the Amur River in northeast Heilongjiang Province in 1990, about 40, all over 50, still spoke the language.

The *Ewenki* and *Oroqen* nationalities also form part of the cluster of *Tungus* languages that includes *Evenki* in Russia and Mongolia. Janhunen (1997) equates *Ewenki* with *Solon* in Russia and indicates that *Ewenki* and *Oroqen* are part of the same language cluster, but Whaley et al. (1999) suggest that they are distinct languages, and say that there are about 10,000 speakers, mainly over 50, in China and Russia. Of the 7,004 *Oroqen* in China in 1990, about 2,240 concentrated in Alihe *Oroqen* Banner were said to speak it then, but Whaley et al. (1999) report fewer now, also mainly over 50. Janhunen (1997) reports on the dialects of *Oroqen*: *Kumarchen* still spoken by a few children, *Orochen* and *Selpechen* with speakers mainly over 40, and *Birarchen* only a few old speakers.

The most endangered *Mongolic* language in China is *Kangjia*, with about 2,000 speakers who are members of the Hui (Moslem) nationality in Qinghai Province. *Eastern Yugur* and *Bao'an* are also beginning to be endangered.

In China, Turkic nationalities are primarily in the Xinjiang Uighur Autonomous Region. *Western Yugur* or *Yellow Uighur* with about 4,600 speakers is the most endangered of these languages.

6. Indo-European[7]

In this area there are two severely endangered *Portuguese* creoles, *Papia Kristang* of Melaka in Malaysia and *Patua* of Macao. *Kristang* is spoken among a group of former fishermen concentrated in one neighbourhood; the group population is about 10,000 people of whom about 2,150 speak it – most people now over 40, a third of those under 40, and some children; the language is being replaced by *Malaysian English*. *Patua* is spoken by fewer than fifty speakers over 70 years old among a group of about 10,000 to 15,000, of whom only about 5,000 are still in Macao; it has undergone extensive decreolization and will soon be extinct.

7. Ainu[8]

Ainu was formerly spoken in southern Sakhalin and the Kurile Islands, now part of Russia, and on the northern part of Honshu Island in Japan, but is now confined to Hokkaido Island in northern Japan and is moribund even there.

Ainu leaders claim up to 100,000 *Ainu* in Hokkaido; but official census statistics suggest only 23,830. Many people with *Ainu* background conceal it because of strongly negative attitudes among the Japanese majority community. Sawai (1998) discusses the current situation and attitudes among the *Ainu* from an insider's perspective. Of the four original dialects of *Ainu*, the *Sakhalin* and *Kurile* dialects are extinct, the *Northeastern Hokkaido* dialect is probably extinct and the *Southwestern Hokkaido* dialects are moribund despite recent revival efforts. In the Hidaka region which officially has 9,299 *Ainu* or 39 per cent of the total, the least moribund local variety is the *Saru* dialect of Hiratori town, with four relatively fluent female speakers in their 70s or older, and probably some slightly younger semispeakers who will acknowledge their *Ainu* ability after these speakers die. The *Shizunai* dialect is also in this area. The *Chitose* and *Horobetsu* dialects come from the area about 30km north of Hiratori, officially having another 7,330 Ainu or nearly 31 per cent of the total. The youngest speakers of any dialect of *Ainu* who learned it as children are at least 60, but revival efforts are underway.

8. Conclusion

In summary, in China, Japan and mainland Southeast Asia there are 145 identified endangered languages including 51 *Mon-Khmer*, 26 *Austro-Thai* including 5 mainland *Austronesian*, 17 *Thai-Kadai* and 4 *Miao-Yao*, 56 *Tibeto-Burman*, 9 *'Altaic'* including 5 *Manchu-Tungus*, 3 *Mongol* and 1 *Turkic*; 2 *Indo-European* creoles and *Ainu*. Long-extinct languages such as *Manchu-Tungus Jurchen* and *TB 'Nam'*, *Pyu* and *Xixia* are not included in these totals. In addition, a large number of *Sinitic* and *Burmese* local speech varieties are endangered and need further work.

The following table summarises the degree of endangerment of these 145 languages and the urgency and feasibility of research using the categories defined by Krauss (chapter 1, this volume). It should be noted that if field research becomes possible in Burma, there are at least eight further languages there which urgently need research. Furthermore, there is certainly a large number of unknown endangered *TB* languages in southwestern China, especially *Loloish* languages, so further work there is extremely urgent. However, as these languages have not yet been found, they are not included in tables.

Table 2. Languages of China and Mainland Southeast Asia:
Degree of endangerment and urgency of research

Level of endangerment	Total	Done	Not doing	Urgent feasible
a–	23	8	–	15
b	63	18	1	44
c	39	11	4	24
d	9	4	–	5
d–	11	5	3	3

Table 3 below shows endangered languages classified as as discussed above, with their endangerment status (a to d–), Set A factors (proportion of group population, child learners, domains and attitude), Set B factors (descriptions of related languages and of this language and feasibility of fieldwork), all on 1 to 4 scales. The Set B figures are followed by an asterisk where a language is currently under study and the status of documentation can be expected to improve. Numbering corresponds to the locations given on the map.

Table 3. Endangered languages of the region

	Language	Set A factors	Set B factors	Status
Mon-Khmer				
1	Mon	3,2,2,2	1,1,2*	a–
2	Nyahkur	2,2,2,2	1,1,4	c
3/4	Hu, Buxia	3,2,2,2	1,4,3	b
5/6	Buguo, Paijiao	3,2,2,2	1,4,3	b
7	Tai Loi	3,2,2,2	2,4,1	b
8	Danau	1,1,1,2	2,3,1	c
9	Phalok	1,1,1,2	2,1,4	d–
10	Lavua	3,3,2,2	1,2,4	b
11	Pasing/Bit	3,2,2,2	2,4,2	b
12	Mlabri	3,2,1,2	1,1,4*	b
13	Iduh	1,2,1,3	2,3,2	c
14	Mang	2,2,1,2	3,4,3	c
15	Lai	2,2,1,3	3,3,4	c

Table 3. cont.

	Language	Set A factors	Set B factors	Status
Mon-Khmer (cont.)				
16	Pakan	2,2,1,3	3,2,4	c
17/18	Sach, May	3,2,1,3	1,3,2	b
19	Ruc	3,2,1,3	1,1,3	b
20	Phong	3,2,2,3	1,3,3	a–
21/22	Hung, Tum	3,2,1,3	1,3,2	b
23/24	Arem, Pakatan	3,2,1,3	1,3,2	b
25	Phonsung	3,2,1,3	1,3,2	b
26	Thavung	2,2,1,3	1,3,4*	c
27	Chatong	3,3,2,3	1,3,2	c
28/29	Dakkang, Triw	3,3,2,3	1,3,2	b
30	Chrau	2,2,2,2	1,1,3	c
31	Kaco'	3,3,2,3	1,3,2	b
32/33	Juk, Swoeng	3,3,2,3	1,3,2	b
34	Chong	2,1,1,2	2,3,3*	c
35/36	Kasong, Pear	2,2,1,3	2,4,2	c
37	Samre	2,1,1,2	2,4,2	c
38	Samrai	1,1,1,2	2,4,2	d–
39A	Su-ung (C)	4,4,1,1	2,4,2*	a–
39B	Sa-ong (T)	1,1,1,2	2,4,4*	d
40	Tonga'	1,1,1,1	1,3,4	d
41/42	Kensiu, Jehai	2,2,1,1	1,2,3	c
43	Batek	2,2,1,1	1,3,4	c
44	Che Wong	2,2,1,1	1,3,4	c
45	Lanoh	2,2,1,1	1,3,4	c
46	Temiar	3,3,2,2	1,2,4*	b
47	Semai	3,3,1,1	1,3,4	b
48	Jah Het	2,2,1,1	1,3,4	c
49	Semaq Beri	2,2,1,1	1,3,4	c
50/51	Semelai, Besisi	2,2,1,1	1,3,4	c
Austronesian				
52	Huihui	3,3,1,2	2,3,3	b
53	Moken	3,3,2,3	2,3,1*	b

Table 3. cont.

	Language	Set A factors	Set B factors	Status
Austronesian (cont.)				
54	Moklen	3,3,2,3	2,3,4*	b
55	Urak Lawoi	3,3,2,3	1,3,4*	b
56	Duano	2,2,1,2	1,3,4	c
Thai-Kadai				
57	Saek	2,2,1,2	1,2,4	b
58	Tai Daeng	3,3,2,2	1,4,2	a–
59	Tai Neua	3,3,2,2	1,4,2	a–
60	Rau/Ten	3,3,2,2	1,4,4	b
61	Lajia	3,3,1,2	1,2,4	b
62	Mak	3,3,1,2	1,3,4	b
63	Hakhi Gelao	1,1,2,2	2,3,4	c
64	Toluo Gelao	1,1,2,2	2,3,4	c
65	A'uo Gelao	1,1,1,2	2,3,4	d
66	Aqao Gelao	1,1,1,2	2,2,4	d–
67	Qaw	1,1,1,2	2,3,4	d–
68	Yerong	3,2,2,2	2,4,4	c
69	Buyang	3,3,2,2	2,4,4	b
70	Pubiaw	3,2,2,2	2,4,4	c
71	Lachi	3,3,2,2	2,3,4	c
72	Nung Ven	3,3,2,2	2,4,2*	a–
73	Laha	3,3,2,2	1,1,2	b
Miao-Yao				
74	Ngnai	3,3,2,2	1,3,4	a–
75	Jiongnai	3,3,2,2	1,3,4*	a–
76	Younuo	3,3,2,2	1,3,4	a–
77	She	1,1,2,2	1,2,4*	d–
Tibeto-Burman				
78	Namuyi	3,3,2,2	2,3,4*	a–
79	Shixing	3,3,2,2	2,3,4	b
80	Ersu	3,3,2,2	2,2,4	b
81/82	Muya, Ergong	3,3,2,2	2,3,4	a–
83	Choyo	3,3,2,2	2,3,4	b

Table 3. cont.

	Language	Set A factors	Set B factors	Status
Tibeto-Burman (cont.)				
84	Zaba	3,3,2,2	2,3,4	a–
85	Guichong	3,3,2,2	2,3,4	b
86	Baima	2,2,2,2	2,2,4	c
87	Taruang	3,3,2,2	3,3,2	a–
88	Kaman	3,3,2,2	3,3,2	a–
89	Anung	2,2,3,2	1,3,2*	c
90	Tujia	1,2,2,2	3,2,3	d
91	Hpun	1,1,1,1	2,3,1	d-
92/93	Chintaw, Bola	3,2,2,2	1,3,3	b
94	Gong	1,1,2,2	3,3,4*	d
95	Samei	2,2,2,2	2,1,4	c
96	Sanyi	2,2,2,2	2,4,4	c
97	Samataw	1,1,2,2	2,4,4	d
98	Ayizi	1,1,1,2	2,4,4	d
99	Gazhuo	3,2,2,2	3,3,4	b
100	Micha	3,2,2,2	2,4,4	c
101	Laemae	2,2,2,2	2,4,4	b
102	Raorou	2,2,2,2	2,3,4	b
103	Tanglang	3,3,2,2	2,4,4	a–
104	Lamo	2,2,1,2	2,4,4	c
105	Lalo	3,222	2,2,4*	b
106	Cosung	3,2,2,2	1,3,3	b
107	Jinuo	3,2,1,2	2,2,4*	b
108	Mpi	3,3,1,2	2,2,4	b
109	Akeu	3,3,2,1	1,4,4	b
110	Chepya	3,3,2,2	1,4,4	b
111	Muda	3,3,2,2	1,4,4	b
112	Laomian	3,3,2,2	1,2,4*	b
113	Laopin	3,2,2,2	1,3,4	b
114	Hpyin	2,2,2,2	1,4,1	c
115	Bisu	2,2,2,3	1,2,4*	c
116	Sinsali	4,4,3,2	1,2,2*	a–

Table 3. cont.

	Language	Set A factors	Set B factors	Status
Tibeto-Burman (cont.)				
117	Lawpan	3,3,3,2	1,3,2	b
118	Phongku	3,3,3,2	1,3,2	b
119	Lawseng	3,3,3,2	1,3,2	b
120	Pisu	3,3,3,2	1,3,2	b
121	Cong	2,2,2,2	1,3,2	a–
122	Sangkong	3,3,3,2	1,4,3	b
123	Bana	1,1,2,2	2,4,3	c
124	Sila	2,2,2,2	2,4,3	b
125	Pula	3,2,3,2	2,4,3	b
126	Laghuu	3,3,3,2	2,3,4*	b
127	Mo'ang	3,3,3,2	2,4,4	a–
128	Gasu	3,3,3,2	2,3,4	a–
129	Sak	3,2,2,2	3,3,2	b
130/131	Kadu, Ganan	1,1,1,2	3,4,1	c
132/133	Taman, Malin	1,1,1,1	3,4,1	d–
Manchu-Tungus (in China)				
134	Manchu	1,1,1,2	1,1,3*	d–
135	Xibo	2,2,2,2	1,2,3	b
136	Ewenki	1,2,2,2	1,1,3*	c
137	Oroqen	2,2,2,2	1,1,3*	c
138	Hezhe (Nanai)	1,1,1,2	1,1,3*	d
Mongol (in China)				
139	Bao'an	3,2,2,2	1,2,4	a–
140	E. Yugur	3,2,2,2	1,2,4	a–
141	Kangjia	3,2,2,2	2,4,4	b
Turkic (in China)				
142	W. Yugur	3,2,2,2	2,2,2	a–
Indo-European (creole)				
143	Kristang	2,2,2,3	1,1,3*	b
144	Patua	1,1,2,2	1,3,4*	d–
Isolate				
145	Ainu	1,1,1,1	4,1,3*	d–

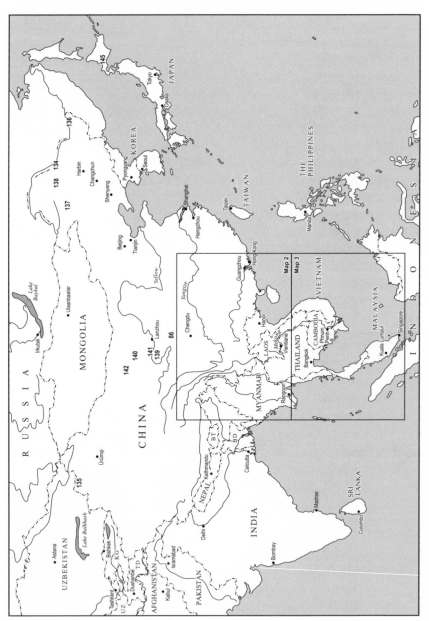

Map 19. China and Mainland Southeast Asia

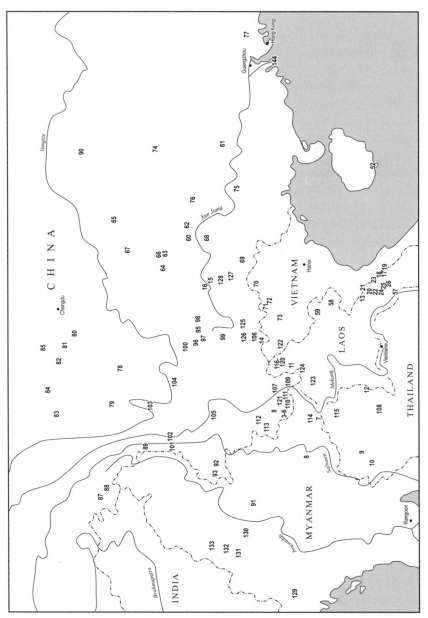

Map 20. Southern China and Northern Southeast Asia

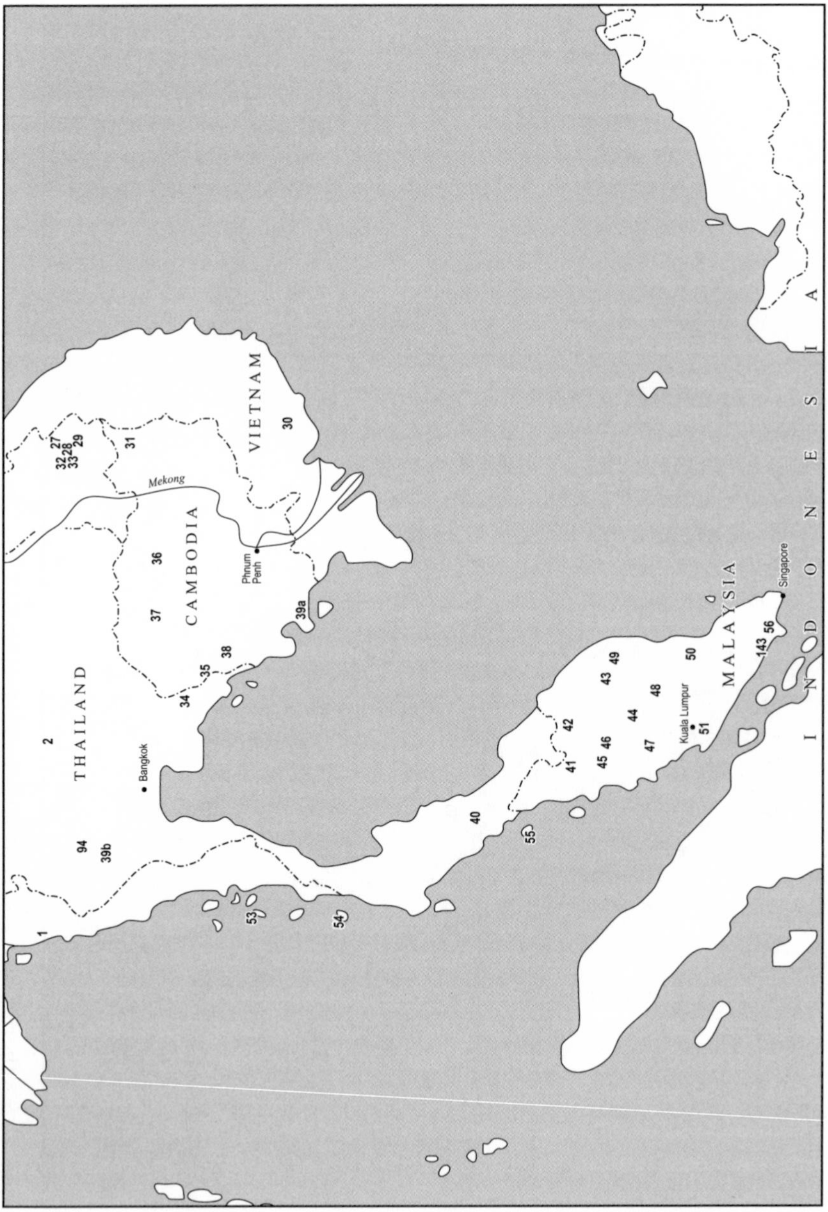

Map 21. Southern Mainland Southeast Asia

Notes

1. It is a pleasure to acknowledge the support of the UNESCO Endangered Languages programme and of the Australian Research Council (A59803475, Language maintenance for endangered languages, an active approach) and assistance from various institutions in China and Thailand. Data from a number of colleagues is included here, with specific acknowledgment in notes; I thank them all for their help! Of course all remaining shortcomings and errors are solely my responsibility.
2. I am grateful to Suwilai Premsrirat for this information.
3. The facts about *Thavung* are also from Suwilai Premsrirat.
4. Many thanks to Theraphan Luangthongkum for information on the 13 *Katuic* and *Bahnaric* languages of Xekong Province in southern Laos.
5. Suwilai Premsrirat and Gerard Diffloth have provided information on *Pearic* languages which I gladly acknowledge.
6. My sincere thanks to Jerry Edmondson for some of the information on the *Kadai* languages.
7. My grateful thanks to Alan Baxter for information on these two *Portuguese* creoles.
8. I am very pleased to thank Theresa Savage for much of the information on *Ainu* presented here.

References

Benedict, Paul K.
  1942   Thai, Kadai and Indonesian: a new alignment in Southeastern Asia.
           American anthropologist 44: 576–601.
Bradley, David and Maya Bradley
  2000   Language policy and language maintenance: Yi in China. In Bradley
           and Bradley (eds.) 74–96.
Bradley, David and Maya Bradley (eds.)
  2000   *Language maintenance for endangered languages: an active approach.*
           London: RoutledgeCurzon.
Janhunen, Juha
  1997   The languages of Manchuria in today's China. In Shoji and Janhunen
           (eds.) 123–146
Matsumura, Kazuto (ed.)
  1998   *Studies in endangered languages.* Tokyo: Hituzi Syobo.
Moseley, Christopher and Ronald E. Asher (eds.)
  1994   *Atlas of the world's languages.* London: Routledge.
Moseley, Christopher (ed.)
  2006   *Encyclopedia of endangered languages.* London: Curzon Press.

Sawai, Harumi
    1998   The present situation of the Ainu language. In Matsumura (ed.) 177–
                189.
Shoji, Hiroshi and Juha Janhunen (eds.)
    1997   *Northern minority languages, problems of survival. (Senri Ethnologi-*
                cal Studies, 44). Osaka: National Museum of Ethnology.
Whaley, Lindsay J.; Lenore A. Grenoble and Fengxiang Li
    1999   Revisiting Tungusic classification from the bottom up: a comparison
                of Ewenki and Oroqen. *Language* 75,2: 286–321.
Wurm, Stephen A. and Shiro Hattori (eds.)
    1981   *Language atlas of the Pacific area.* (Pacific linguistics C-66). Canber-
                ra: Australian Academy of Humanities.
Wurm, Stephen A.; K. T'sou, Benjamin; Bradley, David; Li Rong, Xiong Zheng-
hui, Zhang Zhenxing, Fu Maoji, Wang Jun and Dob (eds.)
    1987   Language Atlas of China. Hong Kong: Longman.

Chapter 14
Endangered Languages of South Asia

George van Driem

1. Introduction

Not only can ideas and memes go extinct, entire conceptualizations of reality are wiped off the map when languages go extinct. South Asia is an area with the greatest linguistic diversity in the Old World, with the possible exception of Papua New Guinea. Many languages in the area have gone extinct in documented history. For example, *Pyu* is an extinct *Tibeto-Burman* language of the Irrawaddy basin in what today is Burma. The language had an epigraphic tradition which endured well into the 12th century. Numerous languages have gone the way of *Pyu*. *Rangkas* was recorded in the Western Himalayas as recently as the beginning of the 20th century, but is now extinct. August Schleicher wrongly believed that the survival and extinction of languages was characterised by 'die Erhaltung der höher entwickelten Organismen im Kampfe ums Dasein' (1863: 28). However, the survival of individual languages is primarily determined by factors which have nothing to do with their intrinsic worth as a system for the articulation of human thought, but by economic, ecological and demographic factors affecting the individual language communities. The success of one language in outcompeting another has little or, in some cases, nothing to do with its grammatical propensities or lexical richness and refinement. Instead, the extinction of a language is a function of the histories of peoples, regions and language communities.

In addition to the socio-economic and demographic changes which cause language communities to assimilate to larger, often more exploitative groups, there are also trends and fashions within the linguistic establishment that impede the documentation of endangered languages. The most obvious has been the detrimental influence of Chomskyite formalism on the field of linguistics as a whole since the 1960s, leading to vast amounts of public and private funding and human resources being channeled away from research on languages. More recently, some funding bodies have undertaken to prescribe codes of conduct or research regimens. Linguists have been working on endagered languages for many decades, but now that 'endangered languages' has become a buzz phrase, there is also suddenly no shortage of people who would tell these linguists how precisely to go about conducting their work.

Where linguists have previously been working effectively, ethically and constructively with native language communities, now they will have to conduct their work with the meddlesome prompting of people sitting on the sideline. The codes of conduct currently being drafted have generally been inspired by the extreme situation which exists in North America and Australia, where colonial European populations have on a grand scale wiped out native peoples along with the languages they once spoke, and in their place set up modern Western societies with litigious Anglo-Saxon legal customs. The situation on the ground is already utterly different from one Asian country to the next. Therefore, codes of conduct inspired by the situation in North America and Australia are singularly inappropriate in other parts of the world. In practice, codes of conduct are more than superfluous, for they can actually hamper sound and ethical field research.

In a similar vein, in addition to conventional grammatical analysis and lexical documentation, it is helpful to document a language in the form of an audio recording. In fact, I have never met a field linguist who did not do this as a matter of course. Yet it serves no purpose to prescribe a format of audiovisual documentation to which the fieldworker must adhere in order to be eligible for funding. Recruiting a capable field linguist willing to document endangered languages is already a big challenge. Most people trained in linguistics are either not up to the task or unwilling to suffer the discomfort or brave the dangers involved. Putting extra hurdles in place, however well-intentioned, merely obstructs the documentation of what remains of mankind's endangered linguistic heritage.

2. Endangered language isolates of the Indian subcontinent

Each of the languages endangered with extinction discussed in this section represent so-called language isolates, i.e. languages which have not been demonstrated to belong to any other major language family or linguistic phylum. There is a theory connecting the *Nahali* language to *Austroasiatic*, although even this theory recognises that *Nahali*, if *Austroasiatic*, would constitute the only representative of its own distinct major branch of this large linguistic phylum. The Karasuk theory, advanced by myself on the basis of specific morphological evidence, holds that Burushaski forms a language family together with the Yenisseian languages.

Andamanese languages: All native languages spoken by the indigenous negrito peoples of the Andaman Islands are either extinct or threatened with imminent extinction. As a result of British colonial policies, just three of over a dozen native languages of the Andamans were driven extinct, along with the people who spoke them. The three surviving *Andamanese* languages are *Ōnge*, spoken on Little Andaman, *Sentinelese*, spoken on North Sentinel Island, and *Jarawa*, spoken in the interior of South Andaman. The 1981 census enumerated 31 speakers of *Jarawa*, 97 speakers of *Ōnge*, and a comparably small *Sentinelese* language community holding out on Sentinel Island. No reliable recent data are available. Historically the Andamanese used to give outsiders visiting the islands a hostile reception, but in view of their tragic history the prompt slaying of outsiders was in retrospect the best policy that the Andamanese could have had. Since the beginning of the 20th century, *Urdu* or *Hindi* had established itself as the dominant language because it was the lingua franca between the inmates of the penal colony established on the Andamans by the government of British India. Today *Bengali, Tamil, Malayalam* and *Telugu* are also significant minority languages spoken by the colonists who have settled the islands.

Vedda: The earliest Western account of the aboriginal *Veddas* of Ceylon and their language was written by Ryklof van Goens of the Dutch East India Company in 1675. Subsequently most Veddas were assimilated by the *Tamil* and *Sinhalese* speaking populations of the island, both linguistically and through acculturation and intermarriage. Policies implemented by the Ceylonese government in the 1950s and 1960s led to the displacement, fracturing and impoverishment of the last remaining *Vedda* language communities. The individuals who survived the devastation of their communities have been absorbed into modern Sinhalese society in terms of both lifestyle and language. It is not known whether there are still any surviving speakers of the original, albeit heavily *Indo-Aryanised Vedda* language, but the places to look would be at the Mahaweli Vedda Settlement Area at Hennanigala on the Kudu Oya, or in isolated households around either Dambana or Polonnaruwa. The *Rodiya* language, another language of Ceylon, is almost certainly extinct.

Nahali: The Nahali are mainly settled in and around the Gawilgarh Hills south of the Tapti river in Nimar and Ellichpur Districts of Madhya Pradesh, especially around the village of Tembi 40 km east of Burhanpur. The Gawilgarh Hills form part of the Vindhya and Satpuḍā chain, which separates the Deccan Plateau from the Gangetic plain. There are less than 2,000 speakers of *Nahali*. The *Nahali* language – also written as *Nihali* or

Nehali – has been heavily influenced by the *Austroasiatic* language *Korku*. It should be possible to do fieldwork using *Hindi* as the contact language.

Kusunda: *Kusunda* is the language of an ancient aboriginal relict group of Nepal. The four remaining Kusunda clans, which designated themselves by the Indo-Aryan names of Siṃha, Śān, Śāhī and Khān, split up in the middle of the 20th century. *Kusunda* speakers could still be found in the 1960s and 1970s, but the remaining Kusunda are generally individuals which have married into a sedentary agriculturalist community. Several individuals are known to remember the language of their parents, though none speak *Kusunda* as the language of daily communication. Individual Kusunda are known to be found around Damaul and near Gorkhā in central Nepal as well as further west in Dāfg and Surkhet. For those interested in finding the last speakers, more detailed clues and reports on their possible whereabouts are given in my handbook (van Driem 2001).

Burushaski: *Burushaski* is spoken in the high alpine valleys of Hunza-Nager and Yasin in northern Pakistan by about 80,000 people who call themselves Burúšo and their language *Burúšaski*. Some 50,000 Burúsho live in Hunza and Nager and some 30,000 live in Yasin. A considerable Burúsho population has also settled in Gilgit itself. The Burúsho area is surrounded on all sides by tracts of land where *Iranian, Indo-Aryan, Turkic* and *Tibetan* languages are spoken. The Burúsho for centuries enjoyed a high degree of local autonomy. In 1891, Hunza was conquered by the British after a bloody three-day struggle, and in 1947 the region became part of Pakistan. In 1972 President Bhutto abolished the autonomous Nager kingdom, and in 1974 the kingdom of Hunza was abolished. Between 1964 and 1968 the Karakoram highway was built, which has rendered the area easily accessible to outsiders. In addition to many older *Ṣiṇā* loans, Burushaski has become swamped with *Urdu* and *English* loan words. Bilingualism has led to the attrition of native morphosyntactic complexity in the speech of the younger generation. In 1992, Hermann Berger predicated that at the present rate of assimilation the language would be fully extinct within several decades.

3. Endangered Austroasiatic languages of the Indian subcontinent

The *Austroasiatic* language family is the most ancient linguistic phylum of mainland South and Southeast Asia. With the exception of the four languages *Khmer, Vietnamese, Khasi* and *Santhali*, each of the over two hundred *Austroasiatic* languages is threatened with extinction. Even the *Mon* language, which has an epigraphic and literary tradition dating back to the 7ᵗʰ century, is threatened with imminent extinction. The *Austroasiatic* languages of South Asia are the *Nicobarese* languages of the Nicobar Island and the *Munda* languages of the Indian Subcontinent.

Nicobarese languages: Over 20,000 people presently inhabit the Nicobar Islands, but not all of these speak a native language of the Nicobar Islands. The precise linguistic situation on the Nicobars is currently kept hidden from the scrutiny of foreign scholars by the Indian government. The names and locations of the language communities are known, however. *Pû* is spoken on Car Nicobar Island, *Tatet* on Chowra Island, *Taihlong* on Teressa Island, *Powahat* on Bompoka Island, *Nancowry* on the islands of Nancowry and Camorta, *Lâfûl* on Trinkut Island, *Téhñu* on Katchall Island, *Lo'ong* along the coast of Great Nicobar Island, *Ong* on Little Nicobar Island, *Lâmongshé* at Condul, and *Miloh* at Milo. The language *Shompen*, the most aberrant and idiosyncratic of the *Nicobarese* languages, constitutes a group unto itself. *Shompen* is spoken in the hinterland of Great Nicobar Island by the Shompen tribe. The 1981 census enumerated 223 members of the Shompen tribe.

South Munda languages: The *Munda* languages are divided into a southern and a northern branch. Despite the large number of speakers of a few of the *Munda* languages, bilingualism is widespread. At the present break-neck speed of assimilation, most *Munda* languages will not survive to the end of this century. All *Munda* language communities are under heavy demographic and socio-economic pressure to assimilate linguistically to the local *Indo-Aryan* majority language. We shall turn to the *South Munda* languages first. Juang has approximately 17,000 speakers in the Kyonjhar and Dhekānāl districts of Orissa. The *Kharia* dialects have over 190,000 speakers, concentrated mainly in the Choṭā Nāgpur, especially in Rāñcī district of Bihar, and in scattered communities in Orissa, West Bengal, Bihar, Assam and Madhya Pradesh. The language known variously as *Sora, Saora* or *Savara* has over 300,000 speakers in the Korāpuṭ and Gañjām districts of southern Orissa and in neighbouring parts of Andhra Pradesh. *Pareng* or *Gorum* is spoken by approximately 10,000 people in Nandpur and Poṭṭangī tālukā in Korāpuṭ. *Remo* or *Bonda* has approximately 2,500 speakers in the Jayapur hills of Korāpuṭ. *Gutob* or *Sodia* (also known as *Gadaba*, but not to be confused with the *Dravidian* language also named *Gadaba*) has just over 40,000 speakers in Kalāhāṇḍī, Korāpuṭ, Viśākhāpaṭnam and Bastar districts. The language known as *Geta ʔ, Gta ʔ, Dideyi* or *Didam* has about

3,000 speakers in the hills and plains on either side of the Sileru river in East Godāvarī district of Andhra Pradesh.

North Munda languages: *Santhali* or *Santali* is the only *Munda* language community with millions of speakers that may be large and resilient enough to resist the forces of linguistic assimilation in the course of the present century. *Korku*, the westernmost *Munda* language, has approximately 200,000 speakers in southwestern Madhya Pradesh and neighbouring parts of Maharashtra, especially in the Satpuḍā range and Mahādev hills. The diverse *Muṇḍārī* or *Horo* dialects, including *Hasada?*, *Naguri, Latar* and *Kera?*, together have approximately 750,000 speakers in the districts Rāñcī, Siṃhabhūm, Manbhūm, Hazārībāg and Palāmū of Bihar and in northern Madhya Pradesh and Orissa. *Ho* or *Kol* has just over 400,000 speakers in Siṃhabhūm district in Bihar. *Bhumij* may have as many as 150,000 speakers in scattered communities in Bihar, Orissa and Madhya Pradesh. The language of the semi-nomadic *Birhoṛ* is moribund, with less than 2,000 speakers in Siṃhabhūm, southern Palāmū, southern Hazārībāg, and northern and northeastern Rāñcī. The *Koḍa* dialects, which have been utterly neglected by scholars and evangelists alike, are spoken by about 25,000 people in scattered enclaves throughout the Choṭā Nāgpur. *Turi* is spoken by several thousand people living as small artisanal groups in West Bengal, Palāmū, Rāñcī, Siṃhabhūm, Rāygaḍh and Chattīsgaḍh. The *Asur* dialects count some 7,000 speakers on the Netarhaṭ plateau in southern Palāmū and northern Rāñcī as well as further south around Gumlā. The dialects collectively referred to as *Korwa, Koroa* or *Ernga* together have over 35,000 speakers in the Jaśpurnagar Tahsil of Rāygaḍh district and in Sargujā district of Madhya Pradesh and in Palāmū and Hazārībāg districts of Bihar.

4. Endangered Dravidian languages of the Indian subcontinent

Other than the four major *Dravidian* languages *Kanarese, Tamil, Malayalam* and *Telugu*, most minor *Dravidian* languages are spoken by small tribes and have not been systematically committed to writing. *Kanarese, Tamil* and *Malayalam* are *South Dravidian* languages. *Telugu* is the only *Central Dravidian* language not threatened with extinction.

South Dravidian languages: *Iruḷa, Toda, Kota* and *Badaga* are minor *South Dravidian* languages spoken in the Nilgiri Hills in the west of Tamil Nadu. Of these *Iruḷa, Toda* and *Kota* are most closely related to

Tamil and *Malayalam*, whereas *Badaga* can be said to be a major variant of *Kannada*. *Iruḷa* has only about 5,000 speakers. *Kota* and *Toda* are each spoken by about 1,000 people, *Kota* in the Kōttagiri portion of the Nilgiris, and *Toda* in the vicinity of Udagamaṇḍalam or 'Ootacamund', affectionately known as 'Ooty'. Although a close relative of *Kota*, *Toda* is aberrant and is said to have non-*Dravidian* features. *Badaga* has over 100,000 speakers. Another relative of *Tamil* and *Malayalam* is the *Kodagu* language, spoken by about 100,000 speakers in the 'Coorg' or Kodagu district of Karnataka in the vicinity of 'Mercara' city or Maḍkeri. *Tuḷu* is a totally distinct *South Dravidian* language with over a million speakers around the coastal city of Mangalore or Mafgalūru and along the coast from Kāsargoḍu in Kerala up as far as North Kanarā district in Karnataka. *Tuḷu* is written in an adapted form of the *Grantha* script, like *Malayalam*, and schoolbooks and Bible translations have been printed in *Tuḷu* since 1842. The *Kuruba* language is spoken by the thousand or so members of the Betta-Kuruba tribe in the hilly parts of Coorg. The Betta-Kuruba tribe constitute merely one tenth of all ethnic Kuruba, for other Kuruba tribes have adopted *Kannada*. The *Koraga* and *Bellari* languages each have roughly 1,000 speakers in the area around Kuṇḍāpura or 'Coondapoor' and Uḍupi or 'Udipi' in South Kanarā district of Karnataka. The recently discovered *Koraga* language is spoken by untouchables who are bilingual in *Kannada*. *Kurru* (including *Korava, Yerukula, Yerukala* and *Kaikudi*) is spoken by an estimated 100,000 nomadic tribesmen in Andhra Pradesh and neighbouring portions of Karnataka and Tamil Nadu.

Central Dravidian languages: *Central Dravidian* comprises the minor languages of the *Telugu-Kūi* group (*Gōṇḍi, Koṇḍa, Manḍa, Pengo, Kūvi* and *Kūi*) and the *Kolami-Parji* group (*Kolami, Naikri, Naiki, Gadaba* and *Parji*). Over two million speakers of *Gōṇḍi*, who call themselves either *Kōi* or *Kōya*, live in scattered communities in Madhya Pradesh, Maharashtra, Orissa and the north of Andhra Pradesh. *Koṇḍa* or *Kūbi* is spoken by the more than 15,000 members of the Konda Dora tribe in the districts of Viśākhāpaṭnam and Śrīkākulam in Andhra Pradesh and the neighbouring district of Korāpuṭ in Orissa. *Manḍa* and *Pengo* are spoken in Korāpuṭ and Kalāhāṇḍī districts in Orissa by an estimated 1,500 speakers. The languages *Kūi* or *Kū ʔi* and *Kūvi* are spoken by more than half a million members of the Kondho (also Kondh, Kandh or Khond) tribes in Gañjām, Kalāhāṇḍī, Baudh-Kondhamāḷ and Korāpuṭ districts in Orissa and in Viśākhāpaṭnam district in Andhra Pradesh. Christian missionaries have printed religious tracts in *Kūi* and

Kūvi using the *Roman* and *Oriya* scripts. *Kolami* is spoken by about 70,000 people in the hills of Yavatmāḷ and Vardhā districts in Maharashtra and in Adilābād district in Andhra Pradesh. An estimated 1,500 Yerku tribesmen in the hills of Canda district in Maharashtra speak the related language *Naiki*. There are roughly 50,000 speakers of *Parji* in Bastar district in Madhya Pradesh in the vicinity of Jagdalpur. In neighbouring Korāpuṭ district in Orissa, there are roughly 40,000 speakers of the various dialects of *Gadaba*, not to be confused with the *Muṇḍā* language of the same name, currently more usually called *Gutob*.

Northern Dravidian languages: The *Northern Dravidian* languages are all minor languages, i. e. *Brahui, Malto* and *Kurukh*. *Brahui* [*brā?ūī*] is spoken in Pakistan, mainly in Kalat and the adjacent districts of Hyderabad, Karachi and Khairpur, and in small communities in adjacent portions of Afghanistan and Iran. The language is spoken by about half a million members of the so-called indigenous Brahui tribes of the Kalat, the Sarawan tribes north of the Kalat and the Jhalawan tribes south of the Kalat. *Brahui* has been a written language for over three centuries, but a truly flourishing literary tradition has never developed. *Brahui*, like the *Indo-Aryan* language *Urdu*, is written in an adapted form of the *Persian* script. Traditionally, *Brahui* is considered to be either a separate branch of *Dravidian* or a member of *North Dravidian* alongside *Malto* and *Kurukh*. More than 100,000 people speak the *Dravidian* language of Malto, mainly in the Rājmahal Hills of central Bihar.

Kurukh, also written *Kuṟux*, and also known as *Oraon* or *Uraon* is spoken by roughly 1.5 million speakers, mainly in the hill tracts of the Choṭā Nāgpur in the states of Bihar, Madhya Pradesh, Orissa and West Bengal but also in scattered communities elsewhere in these states and even as far east as Assam and as far north as the foot of the Himalayas in the eastern Nepalese Terai, where about 15,000 people speak the *Dhangar* and *Jhangar* dialect. There are also a few scattered Uraon settlements on the Indian side of the Indo-Bhutanese border at intervals from the area south of Samtsi in the west to the area south of Samdrup Jongkhar in the east. Moreover, scattered Uraon communities are found throughout Assam, where they are referred to as 'Adibasis', and so lumped together with the various linguistically unrelated *Austroasiatic Muṇḍā* groups with whom they share their geographical provenance and their dark, at times nearly negroid appearance. The term "Ādivāsī" used in northeastern India literally means 'aboriginal', but, ironically and confusingly, the groups thus designated are, in fact, not aboriginal to northeastern Indian, but aboriginal to the Choṭā Nāgpur.

5. Endangered languages of Bhutan and Sikkim

The contrast between Bhutan and Sikkim in terms of the language endangerment situation could not be greater. With the possible exception of Singapore, Bhutan is the most *anglophone* country in all of Asia. The position of *English* in education, government and daily life is such that even *Dzongkha* itself, the national language which is actively propagated by the Royal Government of Bhutan, occupies a precarious position alongside *English*. On the other hand, the Royal Government of Bhutan fosters a policy of studying, documenting and preserving the native languages of the country as part of the national cultural heritage. Sikkim, on the other hand, has been swamped by colonists from Nepal and lost sovereignty in 1975 when it was annexed by India. The indigenous population groups of Sikkim, the Lepcha and the Drānjop, have been reduced to a minority of less than 10 % in their own native homeland. *Nepali*, an allochthonous language, has expanded in Sikkim to the detriment of all native languages, and *Nepali* has also made inroads into Bhutan. In comparison with Sikkim and Nepal, the sociolinguistic situation in Bhutan is characterised by far greater stability. In Bhutan, languages under threat are faced with encroaching endangerment and gradual extinction, but not with the cataclysmic upheaval and immediate endangerment which threatens almost all of the native language communities of Nepal. The only exception is *Lhokpu*, the most endangered language in Bhutan, which is threatened by linguistic assimilation to the surrounding communities of Nepali colonists in southwestern Bhutan. Here too *Nepali* is spreading at the expense of a native language. The least endangered language in Bhutan is the *Tshangla* or *Shâchop* language. *Tshangla* is a *Tibeto-Burman* tongue which constitutes a subgroup in its own right, spoken by a highly robust language community native to the eastern part of the kingdom. A *Tshangla* dialect is also spoken in an enclave around Pemakō, further east on the Indo-Tibetan border.

South Bodish languages: The four *South Bodish* languages are *Dzongkha*, *Drānjoke*, *J'umowa* and *Cho-ca-nga-ca-kha*. *Dzongkha* is the national language of the kingdom of Bhutan, but is actually native to just 8 out of 20 districts, all located in western Bhutan. Propagation of a standard form of the language highly influenced by the *Classical Tibetan* liturgical language or '*Chōke*'. The preeminent role of *English* in Bhutan threatens *Dzongkha* even though there are an estimated 160,000 native speakers of the language. The normative influence of *Chōke* threatens authentic grass roots forms of *Dzongkha*.

The sister language of *Dzongkha, Drānjoke,* used to be the national language of the Kingdom of Sikkim. However, since Sikkim was annexed by India in 1975, the land has been overwhelmed by a *Nepali*-speaking immigrant population which now constitutes over 90 % of the populace. As a result, young Drānjop are almost all raised in *Nepali,* and *Drānjoke* is now moribund.

J'umowa is spoken in the southernmost portion of the Chumbi valley, a sliver of former Sikkimese territory which was ceded to Tibet and is now wedged in between Sikkim and Bhutan. The Chumbi valley is known in *Tibetan* as *Gro-mo* or '*Dr'omo*' and in Dzongkha as *Gyu-mo* or '*J'umo*'. The *English* name for the Chumbi Valley is derived from the genitive adjectival form J'umbi 'of or pertaining to the Chumbi valley'. Based on the *Tibetan* pronunciation of the valley, the language is also known as '*Tromowa*' or '*Dr'omowa*'. This language, only spoken in the lower portion of the valley, is now moribund. *Cho-ca-nga-ca-kha* is spoken by approximately 20,000 speakers in Monggar and Lhntsi districts on both banks of the Kurichu. This language is under threat from *Tshangla* and *Dzongkha.* The closeness of *Cho-ca-nga-ca-kha* to *Dzongkha* means that assimilation to the *Bhutanese* national language is an easy process which involves the language being shorn of all its most interesting features, some of which are *Kurichu* linguistic substrate traits.

East Bodish languages: The *East Bodish* languages are the most archaic branch of *Bodish,* more conservative in some respects than *Old Tibetan.* *East Bodish* comprises *Dakpa, Black Mountain, Bumthang, Kurtöp, Kheng, Nupbikha, 'Nyenkha, Dzala* and *Chali.* Of these languages, four can be seen as dialects of a single *Greater Bumthang* language, i. e. *Bumthang, Nupbikha, Kheng* and *Kurtöp.* Yet all the other *East Bodish* languages are quite distinct, and their diversity reflects a great time depth. The particular language endangerment situation of Bhutan has already been discussed above in light of the country's relative sociolinguistic stability.

Bumthang is the native language of Bumthang district in central Bhutan, where four dialects of the language are spoken by an estimated 30,000 people. The dialect spoken in Trongsa is called *Nupbikha* 'language of the west', i. e. west of Bumthang. *Kheng* is the language of an estimated 40,000 people in Kheng district, now also known as Zh'āmgang, south of Bumthang in central Bhutan. *Kurtöp* is spoken by approximately 10,000 people in Lhntsi district, to the west of the Kurichu all the way north to the Tibetan border. The *Kurtöp* area is therefore east of the Bumthang area, whilst the *Kurichu* separates the *Kurtöp* area from the *Dzala* language area of northeastern Bhutan.

The other *East Bodish* languages are all quite distinct languages. '*Ny-enkha* is also known as *Henkha*, but the most popular name is probably *Mangdebi-kha* because this highly divergent *East Bodish* language is spoken by an estimated 10,000 people in the Mangde river valley. *Chali* is spoken by about a thousand people in a small enclave north of Monggar on the east bank of the Kurichu, consisting mainly of *Chali* itself and neighbouring *Wangmakhar*. *Dzala* is the spoken by about 15,000 people in northeastern Bhutan in Trashi'yangtse district and in Lhūntsi district east of the Kurichu. Chinese sources have reported over 40,000 speakers of the same language in the portion of Tibet just north of northeastern Bhutan and the adjacent part of Arunachal Pradesh. *Dakpa* is spoken by a few thousand people in Tawang, which now makes up the northwestern corner of Arunachal Pradesh, and in a few villages in eastern Bhutan abutting Tawang. The *Black Mountain* language is spoken by about 500 people in 6 different villages scattered throughout the southern jungle heartland of the Black Mountains in central Bhutan. This language is decidedly the most divergent and aberrant of all *East Bodish* languages. The language may, in fact, not be *East Bodish* at all, but represent another *Tibeto-Burman* language on its own which has been extensively relexified by *East Bodish*.

Lhokpu: *Lhokpu* constitutes a group unto itself within the *Tibeto-Burman* language family. The *Lhokpu* language is spoken in the hills of Samtsi District in southwestern Bhutan in two distinct language communities. The robust western community in the hills one day's march to the northwest of Samtsi bazaar comprises approximately 1,340 speakers in the villages of Sanglung, Sataka and Loto Kucu and Lotok. The eastern community comprises approximately 1,270 speakers in Tâba, Dramte and several associated hamlets near Jenchu, upstream from the town of Phntsho'ling on the Indo-Bhutan border. Language retention is better in the western community because there are fewer Nepali settlements nearby. The entire Lhokpu population is effectively bilingual in *Nepali*, and most of the hill tracts of southwestern Bhutan as well as a portion of the western Bhutanese duars used to be Lhokpu territory. The Royal Government of Bhutan has recognised the urgent language endangerment situation of the Lhokpu due to the influx of Nepali settlers into their traditional homeland, and *Lhokpu* is currently being grammatically and lexicographically documented under the auspices of the Royal Government of Bhutan.

Lepcha: The Lepcha have their own indigenous script and a literary tradition which dates back to the early 18th century. *Lepcha* is the language of the original populace of Sikkim. The kingdom of Sikkim, once comprised present-day Sikkim as well as most of present-day Darjeeling district. Outside of this area, *Lepcha* is also still spoken decreasingly within roughly 100 Lepcha households in Ilm district in eastern Nepal. The language is also spoken in Kalimpong or 'British Bhutan', i. e. the territory wrested from Bhutan which now forms the easternmost part of Darjeeling district. *Lepcha* is furthermore spoken in a few Lepcha villages in Samtsi District of southwestern Bhutan. Zongu district in Sikkim is the only remaining area where the Lepcha have not been outnumbered by Nepali colonists. The entire Lepcha area is bilingual. Despite spirited attempts to preserve the language, Lepcha has already effectively been lost everywhere in favour of *Nepali*. There are very few remaining households where the younger generation actively speaks the language, and these households are few and far between. The total number of fluent *Lepcha* speakers does not exceed a few thousand.

Gongduk: *Gongduk* is a previously unknown *Tibeto-Burman* language which was first discovered for scholarship in May 1991. The language, which has turned out to constitute a distinct and unique branch unto itself within the great *Tibeto-Burman* language family, is spoken by a dwindling population of just over a thousand people in a remote enclave along the Kurichu in Monggar district in east-central Bhutan. *Gongduk* is one of the two languages in Bhutan which has retained complex conjugations which reflect the ancient *Tibeto-Burman* verbal agreement system. The language community has survived intact for so long because of its remoteness and the relative general stability of language communities in Bhutan over time. Whereas some language communities are remote in the sense that they are many days on foot from a motorable road, the *Gongduk* speaking enclave has until recent historical times also been several days on foot from the nearest neighbouring language communities. This means that travellers had to carry their own provisions and sleep outdoors to reach the Gongduk area. This still holds true for two of the three approaches to the language community. Yet Bhutan has been transformed in recent decades by a network of narrow but motorable roads and a growing infrastructure of educational and health care facilities set up by a caring central government The *Gongduk* language community is opening up to the outside world, and a growing staff of civil servants who do not speak the language are now stationed there on a semi-permanent basis. Although there is still a fair number of genuine monolinguals, the situation is rapidly changing, and the future prospects for the survival of *Gongduk* are not good. The Royal Government of Bhutan has recognised the urgent language endangerment situation of the *Gongduk*, and the lan-

guage is currently being grammatically and lexicographically documented under the auspices of the Royal Government of Bhutan.

6. Endangered languages of Arunachal Pradesh

The Kho-Bwa languages: The four languages of the enigmatic *Kho-Bwa*
cluster in western Arunachal Pradesh, just east of Bhutan, are all endangered with imminent extinction. These are *Khowa* or *Bugun, Sulung* or
Puroit, Lishpa and *Sherdukpen. Khowa* is spoken by an estimated 800
people, more than half of whom reside in the two villages of Wanghoo
and Singchung near the district headquarters at Bomdila in West Kameng
district. *Sulung* is spoken by about 4,000 people, half of whom inhabit a
small area which straddles the northeastern hills of East Kameng and the
northwestern hills of Lower Subansiri district. In this area, they occupy
the northern and more inaccessible parts of the upper reaches of the Par
river. The Sulung have been compelled to lead a semi-nomadic existence
because they were lowest in the pecking order established by the peren-
nial internecine tribal warfare traditionally waged in the region. The Sulung were often enslaved by rival groups. Therefore, their actual area of
dispersal extends from the Bhareli river to the Subansiri, and small settlements of Sulung are interspersed with the villages of more numerous
groups such as the Tani and Hruso. *Lishpa* is spoken by about 1,000 people in Kameng district who pass themselves off as 'Monpa'. *Sherdukpen*
is spoken by less than 2,000 people who live mainly in the villages of Ru-
pa, Shergaon and Jigaon in the southwestern corner of Kameng district,
but are also settled in the area in and around the Tenga valley south of
Bomdila. Culturally the Sherdukpen are distinct from the other *Kho-Bwa*
language communities because they have adopted a Tibetan Mahāyāna
Buddhist "Hochkultur".

Hrusish languages: All three *Hrusish* languages are endangered with
imminent extinction. The Hruso or 'Aka' population is estimated at less
than 3,000 speakers. The Hruso live in the southeast of Kameng, where
they are concentrated in the Bichom river valley. Like the Bhutanese to
the west and the neighbouring Nishi tribes to the east, the Hruso or Aka
have historically observed the practice of raiding the plains to take back
slaves to the hills. *Dhímmai* or '*Miji*' is still spoken by about 4,000 people.
The Dhímmai inhabit about twenty-five villages and hamlets in the northeastern and north-central region of Kameng, i. e. in the Bichom river valley to the north of Hruso territory and also in the Pakesa river valley.

There are only about 1,000 speakers of *Levai* or '*Bongro*', who live in Kameng and also part of Subansiri.

Tani languages: *Tani* languages, formerly known as '*Abor-Miri-Dafla*' languages, are spoken by the many Adi and Nishi tribes and a few other groups such as the Milang which are not thus classified. An estimated 5,000 speakers of *Milang* live on the eastern fringe of the *Tani* area, abutting the territory of the Idu Mishmis. The Milang inhabit the three villages of Milang, Dalbing and Pekimodi in the upper Yamne valley in Mariyang subdivision of East Siang district.

Bangni, Nishi, Tagin and *Apatani* form a cluster. *Bangni*, traditionally known as *Western Dafla*, is spoken by roughly 23,000 people. In the north, the Bangni area straddles the Indo-Tibetan border. *Nishi*, formerly known as *Eastern Dafla*, is spoken by roughly 30,000 people. *Nah* is spoken in just seven villages of Taksing administrative circle in in Upper Subansiri district. *Sarak* or '*Hill Miri*' is spoken just east of the Apatani area by an estimated 9,000 people. An estimated 25,000 Tagin inhabit the northeastern quadrant of Subansiri district and Subansiri and adjoining parts of West Siang, including the towns of Denekoli and Taliha. The Tagin were driven to their present abode by the bellicose Pailibo and Ramo tribes. *Apatani* is the most divergent member of the *Nishi* group and has been exposed to the most *Tibetan* influence. An estimated 14,000 Apatani inhabit an enclave in the fertile valley of the Apatani Plateau in lower central Subansiri district, between the Nishi and Hill Miri, midway between the Panior and Kamla rivers.

Gallong, Bokar, Pailibo and *Ramo* form a cluster. *Gallong*, one of the two *Tani* languages which is endangered but not threatened with immediate extinction, is spoken by approximately 40,000 people in the southern half of West Siang district as far down as where the plains of Lakhimpur District begin in Assam. The largest Gallong village is Bagra with a population exceeding 3,000 near the West Siang district headquarters at Along. Approximately 3,500 speakers of *Bokar* live in 40 villages in the Monigong Circle of Machukha subdivision in West Siang district just below the peaks of the Indo-Tibetan border, as well as in several villages on the Tibetan side of the ridge. Just over 1,000 speakers of *Pailibo*, live along the banks of the Siyom or Yomgo river, in 9 villages in the Tato Circle and two villages in the Payum circle of West Siang district. Less than 800 speak *Ramo* in the upper Siyom valley in Mechukha subdivision of West Siang district to the northwest of the Pailibo area. Exclusively Ramo villages are located between Machukha and Tato, whereas elsewhere Ramo are mixed with Bokar and Memba settlers.

The remaining languages belong to the *Minyong-Padam* cluster, although nothing is in fact known about the *Ashing* language except its name. Its inclusion, therefore, is just a matter of geographical convenience. Whereas *Padam* is one of the two *Tani* languages which is endangered but not threatened with immediate extinction, *Tangam* is nearly extinct because most of the people who spoke the language became the victims of genocide. The endangerment situation therefore varies widely from language community to language community. Approximately 20,000 speakers of *Minyong* occupy the swathe of territory along the west bank of the lower Siang river, downstream of the *Bori* and *Karko* language communities and to the east of the Gallongs. Not much more than 2,000 speakers of *Bori* are settled along the Siyom and Sike rivers in an area enclosed by the Luyor hills on the east, the Piri hills on the west and on the north by the closing together of these two ranges. The totally undocumented *Ashing* language is spoken by less than 1,000 people who inhabit the northernmost headwaters of the Siang river near the Tibetan border, beginning from the village of Ramsing in the south and extending up as far as Tuting village in the north. Pango and Bomdo are the most numerous Ashing settlements. An estimated 2,000 speakers of *Shimong* remain on the left bank of the Siang in the northernmost portion of what used to be known administratively as the Siang Frontier Division. Yingkiong is the administrative centre in the Shimong area. Less than 200 speakers of *Tangam* remain in the northernmost portion of Siang district inhabiting the three villages of Kuging, Ngering, Mayum and a few neighbouring hamlets in the northeastern corner of the Adi tribal region of Arunachal Pradesh, along the upper reaches of the rivers Siang and Nigong. The Tangam were once numerous but were killed *en masse* by neighbouring tribes. *Karko* is spoken by a small tribe of just over 2,000 people found mainly in Karko village and surrounding hamlets, such as Ramsing and Gosang. About 600 speakers of *Panggi* live in the lower Yamne valley above the confluence of the Yamne and the Siang, in the villages of Geku, Sumsing, Sibum, Jeru and Pongging. *Padam*, formerly known as the '*Bor Abor*' or '*Great Abor*', is spoken by probably over 40,000 people in the tract of land between the Dibang, Siang and Yamne valleys in East Siang, from the Assam border in the south to the Sidip river in the north. *Mishing* or '*Plains Miri*' is spoken by less than 4,000 Hinduised people living in scattered settlements on the plains closely skirting the hills of Arunachal Pradesh. All the language communities of Arunachal Pradesh are threatened by *Hindi* which has been propagated in the area by the Government of India since the 1970s.

Midźuish languages: The *Midźuish* languages are referred to in older writings by the antique term *'Northern Mishmi'*. The two *Midźuish* languages, *Kaman* and *Zaiwa*, are both endangered. Approximately 9,000 people speak *Kaman* or *'Miju Mishmi'* along the upper reaches of the Lohit on both banks of the river around Parsuram Kund in Lohit district, and across the border in Tibet. Less than 200 people of the Zakhring and Meyor clans speak the *Zaiwa* language in the vicinity of Walong. This *'Zaiwa Mishmi'* is not to be confused with the utterly different *Burmic* language also named *Zaiwa*, which is spoken in parts of Yúnnán and Burma.

Digarish languages: The two *Digarish* languages, *Idu* and *Taraon*, are both endangered with imminent extinction. There are only an estimated 9,000 speakers of *Idu*, once known as *Chulikata* 'cropped hair' *Mishmi*. An estimated 6,000 speakers of *Taraon* are concentrated in the area between the Delei and Lati rivers in the east, the Kharem in the south and the Digaru in the west.

7. Endangered languages of the Brahmaputran plain and associated hill tracts

Brahmaputran is a major trunk of the *Tibeto-Burman* language family, comprising the three branches *Konyak*, *Bodo-Koch* and *Dhimalish* and may include a fourth branch *Kachinic* or *Jinghpaw*. The *Kachinic* languages are all endangered, not only by *Mandarin*, *Burmese* and *Assamese*, but also by the *Jinghpaw creole* which is used as a lingua franca between diverse *Kachinic* language communities. This form of *Jinghpaw* has been grammatically simplified and is shorn of the native morphosyntactic complexity which characterises the various local grass roots *Jinghpaw* languages. More information on the *Jinghpaw* languages can be found in the section on Southeast Asia. The *Bodo-Koch* branch of the *Tibeto-Burman* family consists of *Chutiya*, *Bodo-Garo* and the *Koch* languages. A number of *Bodo-Koch* languages mentioned and even scantily documented in British sources in the 19th and 20th century have since then gone extinct, e. g. *Hâjong*.

Deori Chutiya: There was once a large number of ethnic Chutiya, but the only group that had retained the original language at the dawn of the 20th century was the priestly Deori clan, who formerly officiated at sacrificial ceremonies for the Ahom kings. The 1971 census only counted 2,683 ethnic Deori in Arunachal Pradesh and 9,103 Chutiya in Assam. Today there are reportedly only few households in Lakhimpur and Sibsagar districts of upper Assam who still speak the language and one would have to make an effort to localise them.

Bodo-Garo languages: The *Bodo-Garo* cluster consists of *Kokborok, Tiwa, Dimasa* or '*Hills Kachari*', *Hojai*, '*Plains Kachari*', *Bodo, Mech* and *Garo*. The most divergent languages within this cluster are believed to be *Dimasa, Tiwa* and *Kokborok*. *Dimasa* is hardly documented and today very much under threat of extinction. The *Dimasa* live in the northern Cachar hills and portions of the adjacent plains, where they have largely been linguistically assimilated to their Bengali and Assamese neighbours. *Dimasa* is only spoken in isolated households, and local sleuthing would be required to find them. There is no description of *Hojai*, but old sources suggest some affiliation with the *Dimasa*. *Dimasa* and *Hojai* are distinct from *Plains Kachari*, but the speakers of all three dialects refer to themselves as '*Bodo*'. *Plains Kachari* or simply *Kachari* is the dialect spoken in Darrang district, upriver from Bodo proper and downriver from the Chutiya territory. The surviving *Kachari* language communities are rapidly being assimilated. The dialect spoken further downriver in areas such as Goalpara is generally referred to simply as *Bodo*. There is still a considerable number of *Bodo* speakers, but their communities are presently assimilating linguistically to *Bengali* and *Assamese* under heavy demographic and socio-economic pressure. *Meche* is a *Bodo-Koch* language often mentioned in British sources, but now perhaps extinct. If there are still households speaking *Meche*, they must be sought by a locally savvy linguist in Jalpaiguri district and neighbouring parts of Goalpara. The original Meche territory stretched from what today is Jhāpā district in the eastern Nepalese Terai all the way across the Bhutanese duars as far as modern Goalpara district.

Kokborok, formerly known as '*Hill Tippera*' is spoken in the low rolling hills of Tripurā. At the time that India gained its independence from Great Britain, at least 70% of the people in Tripurā were Kokborok and merely 30% were Bengali colonists. Today the Kokborok constitute just a 30% minority in their own tribal homeland, having been swamped by Bengali immigrants, especially from the area which now constitutes the country of Bangladesh. Bengali colonists now make up over 85% of the population. There are an estimated 800,000 ethnic Kokborok, but the vast majority has abandoned their ancestral language or is in the process of doing so. *Tiwa*, also known as '*Lalung*', is spoken by about 35,000 people settled in Kamrup and Marigaon districts and in the Karbi Anglong, formerly known as the Mikir Hills. *Garo* is the only *Bodo-Koch* language not threatened with imminent extinction. About 200,000 of the 250,000 people living in the western half of the Meghālaya, known as the Garo Hills, speak *Garo*. An additional 50,000 *Garo* speakers live in the Assamese districts of Goalpara and Kamrup and in Mymensing District of Bangladesh, which all skirt the Garo Hills. Some *Garo* even live further south in the Bangladeshi hinterland, e. g. about 15,000 in Modhupur.

The Koch languages: The *Koch* languages are *Pānī Koch, A'tong, Ruga* and *Rabha*. *Koch* proper is still spoken by only approximately 300 people along the western fringe of the Garo Hills near Dalu in the vicinity Garobadha. The speakers are known as Wanang or Pānī Koch 'Water Koch'. Several thousand speakers of *A'tong* live in the southeast of the Garo Hills reside in and around Somasvarī and Bāghmārā. The A'tong speak a *Koch* language, but identify themselves as 'Garo' and are already bilingual in their native *A'tong* and in *Garo*. The Ruga or Rugha are a small group in the south of the Garo Hills. No data are available on the number of *Rugha* speakers. The Rabhas inhabit the territory where the Brahmaputra meanders around the highlands of the Meghālaya and bends south towards the Bay of Bengal after flowing westward across the plains of Assam. The prehistoric Rabha ethnic area may originally have extended as far east as Guwahati. There are at least 150,000 ethnic Rabha in Assam, and in 1993 the Rabha Hasong Demand Committee even put the number of ethnic Rabha as high as 375,000. Yet there are no more than several thousand speakers of the *Rabha* language. Most Rabhas speak *Bengali* or *Assamese*. *Rabha* is only still actually spoken in a number of villages in Goalpara District between Goālpārā proper and Phulbārī, inc. Bardāmal, Mātiā, Majerburi and Mākuri. However, even here the younger generation is already fully bilingual in *Assamese*, and most young Rabhas have a better command of *Assamese* than they have of *Rabha*.

Dhimalish languages: *Dhimalish* includes the *Toto* and *Dhimal* languages. *Toto* is spoken by a small tribal group at the town of Êoṭopārā in Baksā or Mādārīhāṭ subdivision of Jalpgu district in the Indian state of West Bengal nearby the Bhutanese border town of Phntsho'ling. In November 1994, there were 176 Toto families with a total number of 992 *Toto* speakers. Although this language of the Bhutanese duars is officially spoken on the Indian side of the border today, the Royal Government of Bhutan has recognised the precarious situation of this community and commissioned grammatical investigation of the language, which is currently being prepared for publication. On the basis of British sources, it is known that the range of *Toto* speaking settlements was once far larger than it is today.

The Dhimal live in Jhāpā and Moraf districts in the eastern Nepalese Terai. There are two distinct *Dhimal* language communities, an eastern conglomeration of 16 villages in Jhāpā district to the east of the Kafkāī-māī or Māī river, with an estimated 3,000 speakers, and a western tribe of over 25,000 speakers to the west of the river inhabiting about 24 villages in western Jhāpā and 51 villages in Moraf district. The current Dhimal population has recently been estimated as high as 35,000 people, though the 1991 census somehow only counted 16,781 Dhimal. The language is rapidly being lost in favour of *Nepali*, however, because the Dhimal are a 10% minority in their own native areas. The groups in the same region which are sometimes identified as Jhāṅgaḍ Dhimāl are speakers of the *Dravidian* language *Jhangar*.

Konyak languages: The *'Northern Naga'* or *Konyak* languages are spoken in Arunachal Pradesh, Nagaland and adjacent areas of Burma. Two clusters can be distinguished, the first comprising the languages *Konyak, Wancho, Phom, Khiamngan* and *Chang*, and the second comprising *Tangsa* and *Nocte*. *Tangsa, Nocte* and *Wancho* are spoken in Arunachal Pradesh, whereas *Konyak, Phom* and *Chang* are spoken to the southwest in Nagaland. There are approximately 30,000 Wanchos in approximately 41 villages grouped into eleven confederacies, known as Jan, in the southwestern tip of Tirap district between the foothills and the Patkoi range. To the south of the Wancho, in Nagaland, live approximately 70,000 speakers of *Konyak*. South of the Konyak live about 19,000 speakers of *Phom*. To the southeast of the Phom, approximately 16,000 *Chang* occupy the hinterland of Nagaland, stretching back into the high range which divides India from Burma. An unknown number of speakers speak *Khiamngan*, and the precise wherabouts of this language community is unknown. There were about 20,000 Tangsa in Changlang and Miao subdivisions of Tirap district. The *Jogli, Moklum* and *Lunchang* languages are dialects of *Tangsa*, divergent enough to warrant separate documentation and each spoken by well over a thousand people. The Noctes live in central Tirap to the northeast of the Wanchos and to the west of the Tangsas. There are approximately 28,000 Nocte.

Karbí: *Karbí* or *Mikir* is spoken in the Karbi Anglong or 'Mikir Hills' of Assam as well as in the neighbouring districts of Kamrup, Nowgong and Sibsagar. The language is not a *Brahmaputran* language, but a taxon unto itself within the *Tibeto-Burman* language family. There are over 150,000 Mikir, the vast majority of which reside in the Karbi Anglong. Half of the *Karbí* are bilingual in *Assamese*, and amongst the younger generation the ancestral language is being abandoned at an alarming rate in favour of *Assamese*.

8. Endangered Tibeto-Burman and Daic languages of the Indo-Burmese borderlands

Ao languages: The *Ao* languages are spoken in central Nagaland. These are *Chungli Ao, Mongsen Ao, Sangtam, Yimchungrū, Lotha, Yacham* and *Tengsa*. *Lotha* is the most robust with about 35,000 speakers. All the other *Ao* languages together have about 65,275 speakers. Over one third of the population of Nagaland are not indigenous Tibeto-Burmans, but Indo-Aryan settlers. Due to the many languages spoken in Nagaland, the increased mobility of all population groups and the use of *Assamese* and *Nagamese*, a low-status *Assamese-based creole*, as lingua franca, all the *Ao* languages are threatened with extinction.

Angami-Pochuri languages: There are two language clusters, one of consisting of *Angami, Chokri, Kheza* and *Mao*, and the other of *Pochuri, Ntenyi, Maluri, Sema* and *Rengma*. There are roughly 30,000 speakers of *Angami* and an estimated 65,000 speakers of *Sema*. The other languages are all spoken by far smaller populations. For example, ther are about 9,000 speakers of *Rengma*.

Zeme languages: The linguistic territory of the *Zeme* languages lies in the southwestern corner of Nagaland and the northwestern portion of Manipur, where the languages *Zeme, Liangmai, Nruanghmei, Mzieme, Puiron, Khoirao* and *Maram* are spoken. There are no good population counts for these language communities. There were 26 *Zeme* speaking villages in 1901, whereas the 1971 census returned 406 *Khoirao*, 19,968 *Maram* and 17,360 *Rongmai*. All *Zeme* languages are threatened with extinction. The direction of linguistic assimilation is generally towards *Meithei*, a robust *Tibeto-Burman* language which is the official language of Manipur, spoken by over one million people.

Tangkhul languages: Tangkhul territory covers the northeastern quadrant of Manipur. The two languages are *Tangkhul* in the north and *Maring* in the south. The 1971 census returned 58,167 ethnic Tangkhul in Manipur, and no separate data were available on Maring. *Tangkhul* is being lost in favour of *Meithei* and is nearly extinct. It is not known whether *Maring* is already extinct or still survives in certain households.

Mizo-Kuki-Chin languages: Some languages of this branch are not yet endangered, e. g. *Mizo*, also known as *Lushai*, spoken by 300,000 people. Precise numbers for other language communities are not available, but it is certain that all these languages are vanishing fast. *Thadou, Kom, Chiru, Gangte, Lamgang, Anal* and *Paite* are spoken by dwindling numbers of speakers in Manipur, where these communities are being linguistically assimilated to the *Meithei* speaking majority. The small *Lakher* language community in southern Mizoram is assimilating to the *Mizo* speaking minority. The *Simte, Zo, Vaiphei, Tiddim Chin, Falam Chin, Haka Chin* and various *Southern Chin* language communities in Burma are being linguistically assimilated by the *Burmese* speaking majority. The small *Hrangkol, Chorei, Bawm, Kom* and *Hmar* language communities in Tripura, southern Assam and the northern tip of Mizoram are all assimilating to the *Assamese* or *Bengali* speaking majority.

Mru: *Mru* is a *Tibeto-Burman* language in a class by itself. The estimated 40,000 speakers of *Mru* in the central hills of the Chittagong in southeastern Bangladesh are losing their language in favour of *Bengali.*

Sak languages: The *Kachinic* branch consists of the *Sak* languages and the *Jinghpaw* dialects. The *Sak* languages, formerly also known as '*Luish*' languages, are *Sak, Kadu, Andro* and *Sengmai. Andro* and *Sengmai* went extinct in the course of the 20th century. The descendants in Manipur now speak *Meithei.* In 1911, *Kadu* was still spoken by at least 11,000 people in the portion of the Burmese district of Katha adjacent to Manipur. It is unknown whether there are any hamlets or households in which the language is still spoken. The Chakmas of the northern Chittagong Hill tracts have adopted *Bengali,* but the *Chak, Cak* or *Sak* in the southern Chittagong hill tracts still speak their ancestral *Tibeto-Burman* tongue. The Sak are separated from the Chakma by bands of territory inhabited by speakers of the *Mru* language and of the *Arakanese* dialect of *Burmese.* A mere 1,500 speakers of *Sak* were counted in 1981 in the area of Alaykhyong, Baichiri, Nakhali et Nakhyongchari near the Burmese border east of Cox's Bazar.

Daic languages: *Ahom* is an ancient *Daic* language introduced into the lower Brahmaputra valley in what today is northeastern India with the incursion of a Daic tribe in 1228. A Daic élite led by prince Sukāphā imposed its language and culture upon a Bodo-Koch populace, but their language ultimately went extinct and all that survives are chronicles known as *Buranjis.* Subsequently other Daic groups migrated into northeastern India, such as the Khampti and Tai Phake or 'Phākial', who arrived in the mid 18th century. Today the Khampti predominantly inhabit the southeastern corner of Lakhimpur district in Assam and neighbouring portions of Lohit district in Arunachal Pradesh, and an unknown but dwindling number of ethnic Khampti still speak their ancestral *Daic* language. The roughly 2,000 Buddhist speakers of *Tai Phake* inhabit the six villages of Nam Phakial, Tipam Phakial, Bar Phakial, Namman, Namchai and Lang in Tinsukia and Dibrugarh districts. The Tai Phake are already all bilingual and speak *Assamese* in addition to their native language.

The Tai Nora are a Northern Shan group who fled to the Patkoi Hills to escape persecution by the Jinghpaw at the beginning of the 19th century, later moving to Jorhat subdivision of Sibsagar district. Most of the Tai Nora have lost their native *Daic* tongue, whereas the few Tai Nora who continue to speak the language usually identify themselves and their language as *Khamyang*. The Tai Rong or Tai Long 'Great Tai' are a Shan group who settled in northeastern India in 1825, likewise settling in Jorhat. The approximately 2,000 speakers of *Aiton* or *'Shām Doāniyās'* are also a Northern Shan group who fled to avoid persecution in the 19th century and settled in small numbers in Lakhimpur and Sibsagar districts and the Naga Hills.

9. Endangered languages of Nepal

The 1971 census returned 220,000 speakers of all the *Rai* languages taken together. After the Nepalese Revolution did away with repressive language policies in 1990, it became popular to identify oneself as a speaker of one's ancestral language even when one no longer spoke it. In the 1991 census, 80 % of the 525,551 Rai people reportedly still spoke their native language, but this outcome is the product of collective wishful thinking. All *Rai* languages are moribund and will go extinct within one or two generations at the present rate, being lost in favour of *Nepali*. A comparable situation exists amongst the Limbu. The *Kiranti* languages consist of the *Limbu group, Eastern Kiranti, Central Kiranti* and *Western Kiranti*. Sometimes the *Limbu* and *Eastern Kiranti* languages are grouped together under the heading of *Greater Eastern Kiranti* languages.

The Limbu group: There are an estimated 300,000 ethnic Limbu in eastern Nepal and a portion of western Sikkim. It is sometimes claimed that language retention is as high as 80 %, but these figures belie the dire situation of these languages. The most conservative *Limbu* language, *Phedāppe*, will probably go extinct when today's generation of young adults takes the language to the grave with them because virtually nobody in the *Phedāppe* language community is currently raising their children in *Limbu*. The linguistic situation is comparable in the even smaller *Chathare* language community. The situation is slightly better in the larger *Pāñcthare* language community to the west of the Tamor. Yet even the prospects for *Pāñcthare* as well as *Tamarkhole*, the *Limbu* dialect spoken in northeastern Limbuvān, look bleak. Under the currently prevailing sociolinguistic conditions *Limbu* is likely to be completely extinct by the end of this century unless measures are taken to revitalise the language through the primary school system.

Eastern Kiranti languages: *Eastern Kiranti* consists of the *Upper Aruṇ* and *Greater Yakkha* languages. The languages of the *Greater Yakkha* cluster are *Yakkha, Chiling* and the *Athpahariya* dialects. *Yakkha* is on the verge of extinction. There are reportedly only a few isolated households where the language is still spoken on a daily basis, though there is a slightly larger number of elderly Yakkha throughout the former Yakkha territory who can remember the language, but have no fellow speakers with whom to speak it. *Chiling* is a *Rai* language spoken by about 3,000 people in the hamlets and villages of Āfkhisallā in Dhankuṭā district. The language has managed to survive surprisingly well amongst the approximately 600 households where it is spoken. Language retention amongst the Chiling younger generation is still relatively good, but under the present sociolinguistic conditions it is highly unlikely that the next generation of speakers will be raised in the language. The *Athpahariya* dialects are spoken by the indigenous people of Dhanku district, who are now vastly outnumbered by settlers from outside. There is significant dialectal diversity within the *Athpahariya* dialects area. For example, the *Belhare* variety is somewhat distinct. Comprehensive grammatical and lexical documentation of the *Athpahariya* dialects is a matter of great urgency. There are probably only several hundred elderly speakers, and these languages are all now on the verge of extinction.

The *Upper Aruṇ* or *Yakkhaba* languages are *Yamphu, Lohorung* and *Mewahang*. The *Yamphu* is spoken by less than 3,000 people in the upper Aru valley in the north of Safkhuvā Sabhā district. *Lohorung* is spoken by an estimated 4,000 people in a language community in the central portion of Safkhuvā Sabhā district on the left bank of the Aruṇ. *Mewahang* is spoken by a comparable number of speakers north of the Safkhuvā river and to the east of the Aruṇ. The southern portion of the Mewahang area is flooded with Indo-Aryan colonists as well as Newar, Ghale and other Tibeto-Burman migrants from more westerly parts of Nepal. These language communities are all bilingual in *Nepali*. In terms of language they have fared surprisingly well until today. Yet these communities are now being subjected to unprecedented upheaval due to the economically motivated emigration of their members to urban centres elsewhere and the likewise economically motivated influx of monied outsiders into these areas. Not only are indigenous languages of the Himalayas endangered by the construction of roads into their areas, the socio-economic detrimental effects of roads on indigenous populations are often observed, studied and reported. In Nepal roads have generally benefitted outsiders moving in and had deleterious economic effects on local people, but this is a message which development banks, aid organizations and governments do not want to hear.

Central Kiranti: The *Central Kiranti* languages comprise the *Khambu* group and the *Southern Kiranti* languages. The *Khambu* group encompasses *Kulung, Sampang, Nachiring* and probably *Sām*. *Kulung* is spoken by an estimated 15,000 people, mainly in Solukhumbu district but also in neighbouring portions of Safkhuvā Sabhā district. *Nachiring* is spoken downstream from the Kulung area, just above the confluence of the Hofgu and the Dūdhkosī and in the swathe of territory which lies between Hulu and the Rāva river in Khoṭāfg district. There are only an estimated several hundred speakers of the language, all quite elderly and often isolated from other speakers. *Sampang* is spoken in the Khārtamchā, Phedī and Pāthekā areas of Khoṭāf district and in adjacent parts of Bhojpur district to the east. Although there may be over 1,000 speakers, increasingly fewer members of the younger generation are learning the language. The Sām inhabit the territory which straddles both Safkhuvā Sabhā and Bhojpur districts along the Irkhuvā River, a western tributary of the Aruṇ. It is uncertain whether there are any remaining speakers of the language, but patient sleuthing in the area could uncover a remaining *Sām* speaking household.

The *Southern Kiranti* languages are *Bantawa, Chintang, Dungmali, Chamling* and *Puma*. They are spoken in the lower hills region between the Dūdhkosī and the Aruṇ. The Sunkosī which runs through this area cuts through Chamling territory, but in the east, where the river has already descended onto the plains, it more or less coincides with the southern border of Bantawa territory. Two of the *Southern Kiranti* languages, *Bantawa* and *Chamling*, are respectively the largest and second largest *Rai* language in terms of numbers of speakers. Yet hardly any young people speak these languages. *Bantawa* is the language native to Bhojpur district. *Dungmali* is spoken in the northeastern quarter of Bhojpur district, north of the Pikhuvā river, covering the territory on the right bank of the Aru across the river from Yakkha territory. *Chintang* is spoken in just the two villages of Chintāf and Ḍāḍāgaù in Dhankuṭā district, just west of the *Chiḷiṅg* language area further along the same ridge. *Chamling* is spoken in Khoṭāf and Udaypur districts, south of the Rāva Kholā and east of the Dūdhkosī, and on both banks of the Sunkosī, especially to the northeast of the river. The number of ethnic Chamling have been estimated to be as high as 30,000, but language retention is poor in most areas. Language retention amongst the younger generation is reported to be highest in communities on the southwest bank of the Sunkosī, such as Balamtā. Puma is spoken in Dipluf and Cisopānī in the southeastern corner of Khoṭāf district, about 10 km north of the Sunkosī to the west of the Bufvā river.

Western Kiranti: *Western Kiranti* consists of the *Thulung, Tilung,* the *Chaurasiya* group, the *Upper Dūdhkosī* languages and the *Northwestern Kiranti* languages. *Thulung* is spoken mainly in the southern part of Solukhumbu district and in the territory surrounding the confluence of the Solu river and the Dūdhkosī. *Thulung* is so distinct within *Kiranti* that it is viewed as a group on its own, termed *Midwestern Kiranti.* The number of Thulung has been estimated at 8,000, but the language is being lost. *Tilung* is a *Kiranti* language about which very little is known except the name and the approximate location. The language is spoken only by an indigenous minority in the triangle of land between the lower course of the Dūdhkosī and the part of the Sunkosī below the confluence in the southwestern portion of Khoṭāf district. There are few remaining speakers.

The *Chaurasiya* group comprises the languages *Ombule* or *'Wambule'* and *Jero. Ombule* is spoken around the confluence of the Dūdhkosī and Sunkosī. The *Jero* speaking area is contiguous with Ombule territory and lies to the northwest of the Ombule area on both sides of the Sunkosī. There are approximately 15,000 Chaursaiya people, speaking either *Jero* or *Wambule,* and language retention is rapidly waning in the younger generation.

The *Upper Dūdhkosī* languages are *Dumi, Kohi* and *Khaling.* There are less than eight speakers of *Dumi* east of the Lidim river, all of whom are very elderly. There are unsubstantiated reports of middle-aged speakers around Aiselukharka on the west bank of the Lidim. The Dumi homeland is the area between the Rāva and the Tāp rivers. *Kohi* is an undescribed *Rai* language related to *Dumi.* The language is still spoken in and around the village of Sufdel along the upper headwaters of the Rāva in Khoṭāf district. Language retention amongst the young is still good, but the language community is very small. *Khaling* is spoken by about 15,000 people in Solukhumbu district in the mountains on either side of the Dūdhkosī from Bupsā above Jumbhif as far downstream as Kilimpī, just above the confluence of the Hofgu river and the Dūdhkosī.

The *Northwestern Kiranti* languages are *Hayu, Bahing, Sunwar* and perhaps *Surel.* If there are any elderly speakers of *Hayu* remaining, they would most likely be found in the villages of Muḍhājor, Barḍāḍā, Mānedihī, Adhamarā or in some neighbouring hamlet. *Hayu* was once spoken in a corridor of land, along the Mahābhārat Lek range alongside the Sunkosī above its confluence with the Likhu river, primarily in Rāmechāp and in neighbouring portions of Sindhulī and Kābhrepālañcok districts. *Bahing* is also on the verge of extinction. The language has been lost or language retention is poor in most Bahing villages. There are a few exceptional villages with exceptional households, however, within the Bahing homeland area in Okhaldhufgā district and neighbouring parts of Solukhumbū. *Sunwar* is the most northwesterly of the *Kiranti* languages, and it is now spoken only by a small and dwindling minority out of the approximately 30,000 ethnic Sunwar. The Sunwar homeland is the river valleys of the Likhu and Khimtī, tributaries of the Sunkosī and Tāmākos respectively. The Surel live in the village of Surī near Hāleśvara in Dolakhā district. Their language is spoken by at least several hundred people, and some claim that it represents a more archaic stage of the *Sunwar* language.

Newaric: The *Newaric* languages are *Newar,* Barām and *Thangmi.* *Newar* is the *Tibeto-Burman* language of the urbanised civilization of the Kathmandu Valley. The language has an epigraphic tradition dating back to 1171 AD. Land deeds survive in Newar from as early as 1114, and the Newar literary tradition dates back to 1374. There are over a million Newar. None the less *Newar* is a language endangered with imminent extinction. All Newars are bilingual in *Newar* and *Nepali. Nepali* is a language originally not native to the Nepali capital. Today the native Newar are vastly outnumbered in their native homeland of the Kathmandu Valley.

At a *Tibeto-Burman* workshop held at the University of California at Santa Barbara on 28. July 2001, the Newar scholar Dayā Ratna Śākya went as far as to proclaim that 'the more educated the Newar, the less likely he is able to speak Newar'. This is a damning observation to have to make about the language that has been the daily means of communication for a society that yielded one of the most advanced pre-modern societies and has produced sublime art and a refined culture and acted as the midwife for the birth of numeous schools of philosophy. The drastic sociolinguistic changes which have overwhelmed the culturally and technologically advanced *Newar* language community since the conquest of the Kathmandu Valley by Pçthvī Nārāyaṇ Śāh in 1768 may serve as a metaphor for the convulsive changes which are now overwhelming language communities all over the world as they increasingly come under siege by expansive languages such as *English.*

There is a large *Newar* language community, but few families are raising their children in *Newar.* It has even been claimed that none do so. Though the language community is still large in absolute terms, the language may already have reached the point of no return. The prospects may be slightly better for other *Newar* dialects, which are at any rate not mutually intelligible with the *Newar* language of Kathmandu and Pāṭan. The situation is in fact not much better for the *Newar* dialect spoken in Bhaktapur, but the highly divergent *Paharī* and *Citlfāg* dialects and the Dolakhā *Newar* language could conceivably hold out for another generation. The *Paharī* and *Citlfāg* dialects are spoken by rural groups at localities within the Kathmandu Valley and surrounding hill tracts, whereas the *Dolakhā Newar* language is spoken far away in Dolakhā district.

Barām is still spoken in just one village in Gorkhā district in central Nepal, i. e. Ḍáḍāgaù near Pīpal Ḍáḍā in the Tākukoṭ area. Ethnic Barām can be found throughout Gorkhā district as well as in Dāhdif and Nuvākoṭ districts. However, in these areas only a few very elderly and isolated individuals can be found with some fragmentary recollection of the language. There are only a few hundred speakers of Barām, but the fluent speakers are all middle-aged to elderly and together number far less than a hundred. *Thangmi* is spoken by approximately 30,000 people, mainly in the northern portion of Dolakhā district, but also in eastern Sindhupālcok. Language retention is poor amongst the younger generation.

Shingsaba: *Shingsaba* or *Lhomi* are a cis-Himalayan *Bodish* group with a distinct language. Not much is known about the language, but *Shingsaba* may not even be a *Bodish* language, but one heavily influenced by *Tibetan*. The language may have some affinity with the *Kiranti* or *Tamangic* languages. Just over 4,000 speakers were reported in the 1970s. The Shingsaba live in villages on the steep slopes of the upper Aru upstream from the Hedāfnā area in Safkhuvā Sabhā district as far as the Tibetan border, e. g. in the villages of Cyāmṭāf and Kimāthafkā. The Shingsaba area is surrounded by the towering Lumbā-Sumbā Himāl, Umbhak Himāl and Kumbhakarṇa Himāl.

Magaric: *Magaric* includes the *Magar* dialects spoken by the *Southern Magar* septs and *Kham* or *Northern Magar*. According to the 1991 census data on language retention, only 430,264 out of 1,339,308 ethnic Magar or one third of the Magar population in Nepal still speak the *Magar* language, but this return is higher than the real number. Actual language retention is sadly just a fraction of this number. The Magar have been a highly mobile group since the dawn of the Gorkha conquest in the 18th century, and most Magar communities have abandoned their language in favour of *Nepali*. The language is primarily still spoken in small communities found between the Bherī and Marsyāfdī, especially in the districts Pālpā, Syāṅjā, Tanahù and Gorkhā. The original home of the Magar was known as Bāhra Magarát 'the twelve Magar regions', which comprised all the mid hill regions of Lumbinī, Rāptī and Bherī zones. The Magar still live in these areas as well as in adjacent parts of Gaṇḍakī and Dhavalāgiri zones. There is great dialectal variation within *Magar*, and because of major differences in grammar and lexicon the various dialects merit separate studies. *Kham* is also a distinct language spoken by at least 30,000 people in the upper valleys of Rukum and Rolpā districts in west-central Nepal and in adjacent portions of Bāgluf district, separated from the Magar area proper by several days' walk. Most *Magar* dialects are on the verge of extinction, with few children being raised in *Magar* anywhere. The prospects for *Kham* are slightly better in the short term.

Chepangic: Chepangic consists of *Chepang* and *Bhujeli*. *Chepang* is spoken by only 25,097 out of 36,656 ethnic Chepang or two thirds of the Chepang, who live in Makvānpur, Citvan and Dhādif districts, south of the Triśulī river, north of the Rāptī river and west of the highway connecting Heṭaùḍā to Kathmandu. *Chepang* proper is spoken to the east of the Nārāyaṇī river, whilst Bhujelī is spoken by at least 2,000 people in Tanahù district to the west of the Nārāyaṇī. The Chepang have until recently lived as semi-nomadic hunter-foragers, but their habitat has been largely deforested and rendered accessible by roads and settlers from elsewhere in Nepal. The work of Christian missionaries has pitted the converted against the traditionalist Chepang. Therefore, the Chepang are now entering modern Nepalese society as a fragmented and socio-economically depressed group, compelled to assimilate both linguistically and culturally in order to survive at all.

Raji and Raute: The Raji and Raute are two groups who have until recently lived as semi-nomadic hunter-gatherers in the western Nepalese Terai and the adjoining portion of Pithaurāgaḍh district in Uttarkhaṇḍa. The Raji and Raute groups have been compelled to abandon their traditional lifestyle and adopt a sedentary existence by Nepalese and Indian government resettlement programmes. This has left most Raji and Raute destitute and prey to alcoholism and other social ills. Just 472 Raji were counted in 1988 in the Indian district of Pithaurāgaḍh, where they had been resettled in four villages in Dhārcūlā tehsil, four villages in Ḍiḍihāṭ tehsil and one village in Campāvat tehsil. The 1991 census of Nepal returned 3,274 Raji and 2,878 Raute by ethnicity, and 2,959 *Raji* by mother tongue. The Raji are primarily settled in Dāf-Deukhurī district. Since 1979 the Raute have been settled at two places in Ḍāḍeldhurā district. In addition, several hundred Raute still lead a nomadic lifestyle, led by the septuagenarian headman Man Bahādur Raskoṭī. This traditional group has resorted to modest forms of trading in jungle commodities and crafts, since much of their original forest habitat has been destroyed. Unverified reports would indicate that the resettled groups have largely lost the ancestral language, whereas the itinerant band of Raute is still known to speak *Raute*. Traditionally the Raute used to migrate from Pyūṭhān in the east to Ḍoṭī district in the west. Most recently, the itinerant group has been operating in Surkhet.

Dura: The *Dura* language is a *Tibeto-Burman* language which was spoken until the 1970s in the heartland of Lamjuf between the Pāùdī and Midim rivers. The last speakers passed away in the 1980s. The surviving *Dura* data have been collated in Leiden. The precise position which *Dura* occupied within the *Tibeto-Burman* language family has yet to be determined.

Gurung: *Gurung* is a *Tamangic* language. The *Tamangic* group includes *Gurung, Tamang, Thakali, 'Narpa, 'Nyishangba, Gyasumdo, Chantyal, Kaike* and perhaps *Ghale*. According to the 1991 census data on language retention, 227,918 out of 449,189 ethnic Gurung or about one half of the Gurung population still speaks the *Gurung* language. Gurungs live in the districts Gorkhā, Kāskī, Lamjuf, Parbat, Syāñjā, Tanahù and Dhādif. *Gurung* comprises three dialects with a low degree of mutual intelligibility between them: (1) a relatively homogeneous western *Gurung* dialect in Kāskī and Parbat, (2) a heterogeneous eastern dialect group in Lamjuf, Gorkhā and Tanahù, and (3) a southern dialect in Syāñjā. All *Gurung* language communities are abandoning the language in favour of *Nepali*. Probably no young children are being raised in the language, so that all dialects of the language are likely to go extinct after the present generation of speakers expires.

Tamang: According to the 1991 census data on language retention, 904,456 or nearly 90 % of the 1,018,252 ethnic Tamang reported *Tamang* as their first language. Though already in a precarious position, *Tamang* is not yet as endangered as the other *Tamangic* languages. *Tamang* language communities are found dispersed throughout central and eastern hill regions of Nepal, especially in the districts Kābhrepālañcok, Makvānpur, Sindhupālcok, Nuvākoṭ, Dhādif, Sindhulī, Rāmechāp, Bāgmatī, Dolakhā and Rasuvā. A majority of 83 % of the population in the sparsely populated district of Rasuvā in Bāgmatī zone is Tamang speaking. There is a clear distinction between the western and eastern dialects of *Tamang*, whereby the Triśulī river demarcates the linguistic boundary between the two varieties, with transitional dialects found in western Makvnpur. *'Murmi'* is an obsolete term for *Tamang*. The Humlī Tāmāṅ 'Tamangs of Huml' and Mugulī Tāmāṅ 'the Tamangs of Mugu' are not linguistically Tamangs, but *Limirong Tibetans* and *Mugu Tibetans* respectively.

Thakali: The Thakali are a *Tamangic* language community in the Kālī Gaṇḍakī river valley, an affluent area because of the trade in salt and other commodities between Tibet and India in olden days and today because of tourism. The majority of the ethnic Thakali are economically successful, no longer speak *Thakali* and have moved out of their native homeland to Kathmandu and abroad. Many of the remaining *Thakali* speakers are originally outsiders of other ethnic groups who have settled in the Thakali portion of the Kālī Gaṇḍakī river valley in order to make a livelihood and have assimilated as best they can to the Thakali both linguistically and culturally. Particularly, the Towa, who were originally speakers of the '*Loke* dialect of *Tibetan*, have moved from the neighbouring Bāhra Gāù area and mastered the *Thakali* language, though they are looked down upon by the Thakali, who refer to them by the derogatory name Arangsi Karangsi. *Thakali* was spoken by 7,113 people according to the 1991 census. A comparable number of people speak *Seke*, a related and mutually intelligible dialect spoken in an enclave further upstream, surrounded on all sides by *Tibetan* speaking settlements. The speakers of *Seke* are known as Shopa.

Manangba: The *Manangba* dialects include '*Nyishangba*, *Gyasumdo* and '*Narpa*, spoken respectively in the upper Manang valley, the lower Manang valley, and in the 'Nar and Phu valleys, east of the Annapūrṇā Himāl massif. The 1971 population estimate for the '*Nar-Phu* dialect area was approximately 500, whilst the 1971 census put the number of Mananba in Manang proper at approximately 2,600. The latter figure revealed that at the time the Manangbas already effectively constituted merely one third of the population of their native homeland in the Manang valley. A sociolinguistic detail relevant to any field linguist is that the speakers of *Manangba* dialects generally resent the qualifications Manangba or Manāṅe, both of which have acquired a derogatory connotation. Instead, these people prefer to be known as 'Gurungs'.

Kaike and Chantyal: *Kaike* is another *Tamangic* language spoken by approximately 2,000 people in several villages in Dolpo district. The language is also known as '*Tārālī Khām*' or '*Tārālī Magar*'. This name is taken from the toponym Trākāoṭ 'star fort', the main town in Tichurong, where these people live. *Chantyal* is spoken in the hills south of the Thakali area between the Myāgdī and Bherī rivers on the steep western and southern slopes of the Dhaulāgiri massif. The Chantyal until recently worked the copper mines of the area. Approximately only 2,000 of the 10,000 ethnic Chantyal still speak the language. The ethnic Chantyal are divided into two groups, one in the northeast, in Myāgdī district, and the other in the southwest, in Bāgluf district, the two areas being separated by a ridge. The Bāgluf Chantyal had ceased to speak *Chantyal* by the 19th century. The Myāgdī Chantyal still speak the language in certain villages,

e. g. Mafgale Khānī, Dvārī, Ghyás Kharka, Caurā Khānī, Gurjā Khānī, Kuhine Khānī, Thārā Khānī, Pātle Kharka, Mālāmphār and Malkābāf, as far as the Rāhughāṭ Kholā.

Ghale: *Ghale* is a *Tibeto-Burman* language which may, in fact, not be *Tamangic*, but may phylogenetically constitute a group on its own within the *Tibeto-Burman* language family. The number of *Ghale* speakers was estimated at 12,000 in 1975. The language is spoken in the northern portion of Gorkh district, where there are 33 Ghale villages and hamlets, and in an adjacent portion of Dhdif district. The main *Ghale* speech community lies in the area surrounding and north of the town of Bārpāk, which has about 650 houses. Traditionally, the Ghale have been ethnically classed with the Gurung, with whom they may intermarry. The designation 'Ghale Gurung' is even heard, though others repudiate that they are Gurung. The inaccessibility of the area has protected the language thus far. Yet even in this remote northern part of Gorkhā district, language death is inevitable, given the present pace of linguistic assimilation to *Nepali* in Nepal.

10. Endangered languages of Tibeto-Burman languages of the Western Indian and Pakistan Himalayas of Nepal

West Himalayish: The 10 *West Himalayish* languages are spoken in scattered enclaves in the western Indian Himalayas, between Jammu and Kashmir in the west-northwest and the modern state of Nepal in the east-southeast. *Rangkas* was recorded at the beginning of the 20th century, but is now extinct. *Zhangzhung* went extinct even earlier, and used to be spoken to the north of the Himalayas across a large portion of western Tibet until it was wiped out by *Tibetan* towards the end of the first millennium AD. All surviving *West Himalayish* languages are severely endangered.

The three languages *Manchad, Tinan* and *Bunan* are spoken in Lahul district in what today is the Indian state or Himachal Pradesh. *Manchad* is spoken along the Candra or Upper Chenab river by approximately 15,000 people who have adopted the Hindu religion, and whose language has adopted many *Indic* loanwords. The term 'Manchad' means 'lower valley' in the local *Tibetan* dialect. The language has also been called '*Paṭanī*' or '*Paṭṭanī*' after the Paṭan or Paṭṭan valley, where it is spoken from Tandi as far upstream as Thirot. *Tinan* is spoken on the Chenab immediately downstream from the Manchad area, from Tandi as far downstream as Sissu Nullah, particularly in the area known as Gondhla. The 1981 census counted 1,833 speakers of *Tinan*. *Bunan* is spoken in the Gahar or Gahr valley which covers both banks of the Bhāgā river from Tandi northeast to Kyelong. The Bhāgā is a tributary emptying into the Chenab from the north. The 1981 census enumerated 3,581 speakers of *Bunan*.

Kanashi is a special language within this branch of the family, spoken in just the one village of Malāṇa near Kulu in Kulu district of Himachal Pradesh. *Kinnauri* is spoken in Kinnaur district of Himachal Pradesh. It is unknown what percentage of the 59,154 people enumerated in the 1981 census for Kinnaur district actually still spoke the language. *Rangpo* or *Rangpo* is spoken along the northeastern fringe of Garhwal, confined to the area of the Nītī and Māṇā valleys in Jośīmaṭh subdivision of Cāmolī district, north of Badrināth along the upper course of the Alaknandā river and around the lower course of the Dhaulī-Gafgā river above its confluence with the Alaknandā at Jośīmaṭh. There are an estimated 12,000 remaining speakers of *Rangpo*. *Darma* and *Byangsi* are spoken further west in the Indian-Nepalese borderlands, straddling the Indian districts of Almoḍā and Pithaurāgaḍh in the area that used to be known as Kumaon as well as in the Nepali district of Dārculā. *Darma* is spoken in spoken in the uppermost portion of the Darmā valley, drained by the river Dhaulī and bounded on the north by Tibet. At the beginning of the 20th century, 1,761 speakers of the language were counted. No more recent statistic is available. Immediately to the east of the Darmā valley lies the Mahākālī river valley, which is the home to the Byangsi. The 1991 census counted 1,314 Byangsi in Nepal. A form of *Byangsi* was recorded by Sten Konow under the name '*Chaudāngsī*'.

Central Bodish languages: Europeans call *German* and *English* 'languages', rather than treating them respectively as a hinterland dialect and an insular dialect of *Dutch*. However, Westerners tend to treat languages in other parts of the world as 'dialects' which are just as distinct from each other phonetically, phonologically, morphologically and lexically as *German* and *English* are from *Dutch*. The same applies to what are generally referred to in the West as '*Tibetan* dialects'. The Standard or Central dialect of *Tibetan*, spoken in Lhasa, is not an endangered language, even though the language is undergoing heavy lexical and even grammatical influence from *Mandarin*, the language of the occupying forces. *Kham* and '*Amdo Tibetan* also still represent lively language communities. However, many other '*Tibetan* dialects' are endangered. Linguistically, it is more correct to refer to these languages as *Central Bodish* languages, and not as '*Tibetan* dialects'. These include the many diverse languages spoken in the western extremity of Tibet, parts of which now lie in the modern states of Pakistan and India, as well as the languages spoke in the sBas-yul 'hidden lands', as the high alpine valleys on the southern flank of the Himalayas have been referred to from the Tibetan perspective.

The *Central Bodish* languages of western Tibet are in many respects the most conservative of the *Tibetan* languages and also amongst the most endangered. They are spoken in the parts of Tibet which ar now located in the modern states of Pakistan and India, in the areas of sBal-ti 'Bālti', Burig 'B'urik' or 'Purik', La-dwags 'Lada' of 'Ladakh', sBi-ti 'Biti' or 'Spiti', and Zangs-dkar 'Z'angkar'. In the western Indian Himalayas, the languages of the 'hidden lands' include *Jāḍ*, spoken mainly in Bagorā village, just 17 km south of Uttarkāśī on the banks of the Bhāgīrathī, where the Jāḍ were resettled after the Indo-Chinese conflict of 1962. Some settlements are also found in Purolā, Rājgaḍhī, and Bhaṭvārī sub-divisions. Their original homes lay on the Indo-Tibetan border.

In Nepal, several *Central Bodish* languages are spoken in enclaves on the southern slopes of the Himalayas which show characteristics divergent from *Central Tibetan* proper. These include the dialects spoken by the Limirong Tibetans in the extreme northwest of Karṇālī zone in the district of Humlā, the Tibetans of Mugu and the Karmarong Tibetans in northwestern Nepal, the dialect of *Dol-po 'D'ōlpo'*, the dialect of Mustang known as *'Loke*, the dialect of the Nupri or Lārkyā Bhoṭe below Manāslu Himāl in Gorkhā district, the dialect of the *Tsum* in a few villages along a tributary of the Buḍhī Gaṇḍakī known as the Shar, the community of *Khaccaḍ Bhoṭe* 'mule Tibetans' north of Dhāibuf and northeast of Nuvākoṭ, the 'Langthang Tibetans south of the 'Langthang Himāl and north of Jugal Himāl and Gosāīkuṇḍ, the well-known Sherpa in the mountains surrounding Mt. Everest and in Solu Khumbu, and a small population living at Ha-lung, known in Nepali as Olāfcuf Golā, and at Tāpke Golā and Thudam in the northeastern extremity of Nepal around the headwaters of the Tamor.

In Bhutan, three endangered *Central Bodish* language communities account for nearly 15,000 people. The Brokpas of Sāphu Geo in 'Wangdi Phodr'a district in the north of the Black Mountains speak a dialect called *Lakha* 'language of the mountain passes' or *Tshangkha*. There are an estimated 8,000 speakers. *Brokkat* is a *Central Bodish* language spoken by the Brokpa community of 300 speakers at Dur in Bumthang district in central Bhutan. A *Central Bodish* language is spoken by approximately 5,000 people at Mera and Sakteng in eastern Bhutan. A number of Tibetan enclaves are also spoken in Arunachal Pradesh, south of the McMahon line on the Indian side of the Indo-Tibetan border.

Other Bodish languages: *Jirel* is a poorly documented *Bodish* language spoken by about 3,000 people in the Jirī and Sikrī valleys of Dolakhā district in northern central Nepal The name Jirel is the Nepali adjectival form of the place name Jir. *Kāgate* is spoken in the mountains between the Likhu and Khimtī rivers in the northeastern part of Rāmechāp district by the Kāgate Bhoṭe 'paper Bhutiya' because their ancestors used to manufacture paper. The Kāgate call themselves 'Yuba', which likewise signifies 'paper maker', and pass themselves off as 'Tamang' to outsiders. The number of speakers was estimated at about 1,000 in 1974. There is another group of 'Sherpas', who are not recognised as Sherpas by the Sherpa proper, mentioned above. Whilst the Sherpas around Mt. Everest and in Solu Khumbu speak a *Central Bodish* language, the Sherpa of Yol-mo or 'Ōlmo', an area known in *Nepali* as Helambū north of Sindhupālcok, speak a distinct *Bodish* language.

11. Endangered Indo-European languages of South Asia

Indo-European languages are spoken throughout the north of the Indian subcontinent and on Ceylon. All of these are *Indo-Iranian* languages belonging to *Iranian, Nuristani* and *Indo-Aryan* branches. *Nuristani* sometimes still goes by the name *'Kafiri'*, and *Indo-Aryan* is sometimes still called *'Indic'*.

   Iranian languages: Older stages of *Iranian*, such as *Avestan, Old* and *Middle Persian, Pehlevi, Parthian, Sogdian, Chorasmian, Bactrian, Sarmatian* and *Khotanese*, have gone extinct or have effectively been superseded by later stages of *Iranian*. The modern languages *Persian* or *Fārsī, Darī, Tājikī, Kurdish, Baluchi* or *Balōčī*, and *Pashto* or *Pakhto* are flourishing. Yet a number of *Iranian* languages are spoken only by small and dwindling language communities. *Ossetian* is spoken in the north-central Caucasus. *Tātī* is spoken in parts of Azerbaijan, and *Āzarī, Tāleshī, Semnānī, Gīlakī* and *Māzanderānī* are spoken in the southwestern Caspian littoral. *Gurānī* is spoken in several areas in the Zagros east of the Tigris, *Zāzā* or *Dimli* is spoken in eastern Turkey and western Iran. There is considerable dialectal heterogeneity in southwestern, southeastern and central Iran. Other endangered Iranian languages of eastern Afghanistan and neighbouring parts of Pakistan include *Parācī*, spoken in three valleys along the southern flank of the Hindu Kush, and *Ōrmuṛī*, spoken in the area around Barakī-Barak in Afghanistan and at Kāṇīgrām in Pakistan. The archaic and highly endangered *Pāmir* languages spoken by communities along the Āb-i Panja river in southern Tajikistan, in Badakhshan province of northeastern Afghanistan and neighbouring portions of Chi-

nese Turkestan, include Śughnī, Rośanī, Bartangī, Rośorvī, Sariqōlī, Yāz-
ghulāmī, Wakhī, Zēbākī, Sanglīcī and Iśkāmī. Closely related to *Paśtô* are
Yidgha, spoken in the Lutkuh valley of Pakistan, and *Munji*, spoken in
the Munjān valley of northeastern Afghanistan. *Yaghnōbī* is still spoken
by a small community in an alpine valley around the headwaters of the
Yaghnōb in Tajikistan. There are no reliable up-to-date statistics for the
precise numbers of speakers of these endangered language communities.

Nuristani languages: All *Nuristani* languages were already faced with
imminent extinction before Afghanistan was turned into a war zone by
the Soviet Union under Brezhnev and later by the Taliban and warring Islamists from countries like Saudi Arabia and Pakistan. The *Nuristani* languages are spoken by tribesmen whose ancient *Indo-Aryan* ancestors
took refuge in the inaccessible mountain valleys of the Hindu Kush in
Nuristan. These tribes have no literary tradition of their own and were
collectively called Kāṅirī 'infidels' until they were converted to Islam after Nuristan was conquered by the Afghans in 1896. The *Nuristani* languages from north to south are *Kati, Prasun, Waigali, Ashkun, Gambiri*
and *Zemiaki*. *Kati*, formerly also known as *Bashgali*, is perhaps still spoken by about 20,000 speakers. All the other *Nuristani* language communities are much smaller than *Kati*. *Prasun*, the most aberrant of the
Nuristani languages, is spoken in 6 villages in the high alpine valley along
the headwaters of the Peč, wedged in between the Kati speaking areas in
the Ktiwī valley and the upper Bashgal valley. *Waigali* is spoken in the
Waigal valley, a northern tributary of the Pe. *Gambiri* or *Tregāmī* 'three
villages dialect' is spoken not only at Gambr, Kaṭār and in the Tregām valley southeast of lower Waigal in the direction of the Kunar river. The *Ashkun* speaking area lies between the Peč and the Alingar and in valleys
along the upper drainage of these two rivers and their minor tributaries.
Zemiaki, first identified as a 6th quite distinct *Nuristani* language by Edelman and Grünberg-Cvetinovič in 1999, is spoken in a small enclave south
of the Peč river, south of the Waigali area but immediately surrounded on
all sides by *Dardic* language communities. The *Nuristani* languages are
not only highly important from the point of view of understanding the
population perhistory of South and Central Asia, they exhibit numerous
peculiar typological features of great interest to cognitive linguistics.

Dardic languages: The most endangered *Indo-Aryan* languages are
the heterogeneous and archaic *Dardic* languages, spoken in small alpine
communities. The 5 clusters of *Dardic* languages are the *Ṣi ṇā* cluster, the
Kōhistānī cluster, the *Kunar* group, the *Citrāl* group and *Paśaī*. *Ṣi ṇā* and
Kashmiri are not themselves endangered, but other languages of the *Ṣi ṇā*

group are threatened with extinction. These are the archaic *Phalūṛa* and *Sāwī* dialects, related to *Ṣi ṇā*, and the endangered *Ḍumākī* language is of great historical importancve because it is believed to be related to the language of the gypsies. *Ḍumākī* is spoken by a less than 600 elderly Ḍoma in Hunza, who traditionally belong to the lowly minstrel and blacksmith castes in what is now northern Pakistan. The *Khōistānī* languages are *Baśkarīk, Torwālī, Maiyá, Tirāhī,* and the language of *Woṭapūr* and *Kaṭārqalā*. *Baśkarīk* or *Gāwrī* is spoken around the headwaters of the Swāt and in the Panjkora valley. *Torwālī* is spoken in the upper Swāt valley. *Maiyá* is spoken between Ṣiṇī and Pashto speaking territory. *Tirāhī* is spoken in a few villages southeast of Jalalabad in eastern Afghanistan. The language of *Woṭapūr* and *Kaṭārqalā* is spoken in a few villages on the Peč in eastern Afghanistan. The *Citrāl* languages are *Khowār* and *Kalaṣa*. *Khowār*, the language of the Khō tribe, is the main language of the great Citrāl valley. *Kalaṣa* is spoken by members of the Kalaṣ tribe in the western side valleys of southern Citrāl. The nearly extinct languages of the *Kunar* group are spoken by small communities found around the confluence of Citrāl and the Bashgal, i. e. Damēlī, Gawar-Bātī, Ningalāmī and Śumāśtī. *Gawar-Bātī* or *Narisātī* is spoken in a few villages on the Kunar river. A divergent language is or used to be spoken by a dwindling number of speakers at Ningalām on the Peč. Another divergent but related language is or used to be spoken at Śumāśt. *Damēlī* is likewise spoken in just one village. The *Paśaī* language is spoken in lower Kunar and in Laghmān and was once spoken over a larger area than it is today.

Western Pahāḍī and Central Pahāḍī: The three branches of *Indo-Aryan* known as *Western Pahāḍī*, literally 'montane', *Central Pahāḍī* and *Eastern Pahāḍī* do not together form a linguistic taxon, as the nomenclature misleadingly suggests, but merely share the feature of designating groups of alpine language communities. *Western Pahāḍī* languages are spoken from the western portion of Dehr Dn district in Uttar Pradesh, through Himachal Pradesh all the way west into Jammu and Kashmir. The 1961 census of India distinguished over 60 highly divergent and poorly documented *Western Pahāḍī* languages known by a welter of local dialect names, including *Bafgāṇī, Jaunsarī, Sirmaudī, Baghāṭī, Mahāsuī* (formerly known as *Kihūṇṭalī*), *Haṇḍūrī, Kuluī, Maṇḍeālī* in the area formerly known as Maṇḍe Rājya, *Cameālī* in the area once known as in Cambā-Rājya, *Kāfgḍī*, Bharmaurī (or *Gāḍī*), Curāhī, Pafgvālī, Bhadravāhī, Bhalesī, Khaśālī and Pāḍrī. The *Central Pahāḍī* languages are the *Garhwali* and *Kumaoni* dialects (*Gaḍhvālī* and *Kumāunī*), spoken in Garhwal and Kumaon, together forming an area known today as Uttarākhaṇḍ. All the *Western* and *Central*

Pahāḍī languages are endangered because these areas are increasingly being linguistically being assimilated by larger language communities, e. g. *Urdu, Panjabi, Hindi*. *Eastern Pahāḍī* is represented by the successful and growing *Nepali* language. The success and spread of *Nepali* not only has conferred upon the language the dubious honour of being a 'killer language' throughout the Nepal, Sikkim and parts of Bhutan, but ironically also of threatening the archaic and divergent western dialects of *Nepali* itself.

Indo-Aryan languages with possible allophylian substrate: The Tharu in the Terai speak *Indo-Aryan* dialects collectively known as *Thāruvānī*, which is not a language as such but a cover term for various *Terai* dialects of Bhojpuri, Maithili and especially *Awadhi* as spoken by ethnic Tharu. The original *pre-Indo-Aryan* languages spoken by the Tharu are extinct, but survive in the form of substrate words used within households, so that doublets exist for certain words. For example, in *Citvan Thāru* alongside *Indo-Aryan* yāṇkhī 'eye' there exists a form tèḍ 'eye', reminiscent of the *Manchad* form tira 'eye'. These original *Tharu* substrate words are being lost because not every household preserves them. The differences between the *Tharuwani* dialects and the local *Indo-Aryan* languages spoken by the high castes have never been properly or systematically studied and documented. Varieties of *Tharuwani* have been investigated by Christian missionaries, but they have kept their linguistic findings to themselves and used their knowledge mainly for the production of hymnals and Christian literature. As the Tharu are being continuously assimilated into mainstream culture, the vestiges of their ancestral language and the peculiar features of *Tharuwani* are being lost through increasing linguistic assimilation to the mainstream *Awadhi, Maithili, Bhojpuri* and *Nepali* language communities.

Three other *Indo-Aryan* languages of Nepal are in the thores of death. Most speakers of the *Danuwar, Darai* and *Majhi* or *Bote* language communities have already assimilated linguistically and culturally to modern Nepali mainstream culture. The main Darai settlements are in Citvan, Tanahù, Gorkhā, Navalparāsī and Pālpā districts. According to the 1991 census data on language retention, only 6,520 out of 10,759 ethnic Darai or less than two thirds of the Darai still speak the *Darai* language, which exhibits biactantial verbal morphology. The Danuwar or Danuvār are native to Sindhulī and Udaypur districts in the Inner Terai, but Danuwar are also settled in the hills of Kābhrepālañcok and Sindhupālcok districts and in the Terai districts of Sarlāhī, Mahottarī, Dhanuṣā and Sirāhā. According to the 1991 census data on language retention, only 23,721 out of 50,574 ethnic Danuwar or roughly just half of the Danuwar still speak the *Danuwar* language. The group known as Majhi or Bote live along the Nārāyaṇī or Saptagaṇḍakī river and its tributaries in the districts of Bāgluf, Parvat, Syāñjā, Gulmī, Pālpā, Kāskī, Gorkhā, Tanahù, Parsā, Citvan and Navalparāsī as well as in the Terai and hills of the districts of Rāmechāp, Sindhulī, Sindhupālcok, Kābhrepālañcok and Dhanuṣā. The 1991 census data on language retention show that only 11,322 out of 55,050 ethnic Majhi or just one fifth of the Majhi still speak the *Majhi* language.

A number of other inadequately documented *Indo-Aryan* languages spoken in the hills of Nepal, the *Nepalese Terai* and *Manipur* have now nearly vanished. The *Kumāle* or *Kumāhle* language is spoken by a potter's caste in the central Terai and adjacent central hills. The total number of speakers was estimated at 3,500 in the early 1950s, but only 1,413 speakers of the language were counted in the 1991 census. The original language of the *Bátar* in the eastern Terai, especially Moraf district, may have already vanished. A dwindling number of Ganagāí in eastern Bihar, the eastern Nepalese Terai and West Bengal still speak *Afgikā*. In Manipur, the *Indo-Aryan* language known as *Bishnupriya Manipuri* or *Viṣṇuprīya Maṇipurī*, served as an *Indo-Aryan* contact language and lingua franca between the 13th and 19th centuries, which had undergone influence of the *Meithei* language native to the region. In 1964, there were still reportedly 114 speakers of *Bishnupriya Manipuri*.

References

Berger, Hermann
  1992   Das Burushaski – Schicksale einer zentralasiatischen Restsprache (vorgetragen am 12. Januar 1991), *Sitzungsberichte der Heidelberger Akademie der Wissenschaften* (Philosophisch-historische Klasse, Jahrgang 1992, Bericht 1). Heidelberg: Carl Winter Universitätsverlag.
van Driem, George
  2001   *Languages of the Himalayas: An ethnolinguistic handbook of the Greater Himalayan region, containing an introduction to the symbiotic theory of language.* Leiden: Brill.
van Goens, Ryklof
  1675   Extract uyt de Beschryving van den Staat en Gelegenheid van het Eyland Ceylon, de Landen van Madure, Zuyder-Choromandel, Malabar, en Canara. Reproduced on pp. 204–246 in François Valentyn. 1726. *Agtste Boek: Beschryvinge van het Eyland Ceylon.* Dordrecht: Joannes van Braam, and Amsterdam: Gerard onder de Linden.
Government of India
  1969   *Census of India, 1961.* New Delhi: Ministry of Home Affairs, Office of the Registrar General.

Government of India
  1983   *Census of India, 1981*. New Delhi: Ministry of Home Affairs, Office
          of the Registrar General.
His Majesty's Government of Nepal
  1995   *Statistical pocket book*. Kathmandu: Central Bureau of Statistics.
Nigam, R. C.
  1971   *Survey of Kanauri in Himachal Pradesh* (Census of India 1971, Mono-
          graph No. 3). Delhi: Language Division, Office of the Registrar.
Schleicher, August
  1863   *Die Darwinsche Theorie und die Sprachwissenschaft: Offenes Send-
          schreiben an Herrn Dr. Ernst Häckel, a. o. Professor der Zoologie und
          Direktor des zoologischen Museums an der Universität Jena*. Weimar:
          Bühlau.
Shakya, Daya Ratna (i. e. Day Ratna kya)
  2001   'The sociolinguistic position of Newar', paper presented at the Work-
          shop on Tibeto-Burman Languages and Linguistics, held during the
          Linguistic Society of America 2001 Summer School for Linguistics.
          University of California at Santa Barbara.
Singh, Balwant
  1988   *Census of India*, 1981, Series 24: Andaman and Nicobar Islands, Part
          IX: Special Tables for Scheduled Tribes. Delhi: Controller of Publica-
          tions.

Chapter 15
Warramurrungunji Undone:
Australian Languages in the 51st Millennium

Nicholas Evans

1. Initial orientation to Australian languages

Australia has been occupied by humans for around 5,000 years, and its initial colonization represents the first known major ocean crossing. Thereafter, though there were minor contacts with Indonesia, there is no clear archaeological evidence of subsequent major waves of immigrants until the British established the first European colony in Sydney in 1788. While agriculture and then state-based societies developed on all other continents the original inhabitants of Australia were able to continue living as hunters, fishers and gatherers throughout 50 millennia.

Virtually all scholars agree that *Australian* languages are all related at a deep level. This makes Australia unique in being the only continent entirely occupied by related languages, though the degree of time depth is such that the term 'phylic family' is more appropriate than 'family' to describe the relationship.[1] It also makes the *Australian* language family specially significant because of its likely great time depth. This phylic family comprises around 250 languages, or about 700 distinct linguistic varieties if one follows Aboriginal practice in how to measure language diversity; they are relatively uniform phonologically but exhibit enormous variation in grammatical organization.

Because Australia was the only continent entirely occupied by hunter-gatherers in historical times, its sociolinguistic situation holds great significance for our understanding of the processes of language change in a social universe entirely made up of small groups. Nettle (1999: 93) argues that 'there would have been more language diversity in the world, certainly in relative terms and perhaps absolutely, before the origin of agriculture', so *Australian* languages are vital to understanding the forces that have shaped linguistic diversification for the 99 % of our evolutionary history during which all humans were hunter-gatherers (Livi-Bacci 1992). Certainly the pattern described by Nettle, according to which languages spoken by hunter-gatherers rarely have over 5,000 speakers, is played out in Australia where the average number of speakers per language would have been somewhere between 1,000 and 3,000, with some languages counting hardly more than 50 speakers and the maximum size for any one language unlikely to have exceeded 5,000.

In the oral traditions of north-western Arnhem Land, the first human to enter the continent was a woman, Warramurrungundji, who came out of the sea on the Cobourg Peninsula. As she heads inland, she puts groups of people into particular areas and decrees which languages should be spoken where. Unlike the Judaeo-Christian tradition which sees the aftermath of Babel as a negative outcome punishing humans for their presumption, the Warramurrungunji myth reflects a point of view much more common in small speech communities: that language diversity is a good thing because it shows where every comes from and belongs.[2] Widespread multilingualism meant that even languages differing radically in their grammatical organization posed little obstacle to inter-group communication.

Genetic diversity is not evenly distributed over the continent. Of the 25 or so language families found on the continent, all but one are confined to the north-western one-eighth of the continent (*Map 23*). The remaining seven-eighths is covered by a single family, Pama-Nyungan.

The extraordinarily rich intellectual production of this 50,000 year flourishing, some of which I will touch on briefly in this chapter, is now collapsing over most of the continent, under the impact of the colonial language *English* and its associated culture of monolingualism. Indeed Australia is probably the continent currently experiencing the most rapid and drastic effects of language loss. It seems likely that by 2088 (three hundred years after the first European colonization), at most a dozen indigenous languages of the continent will have viable speech communities – i. e. a 95 % extinction rate, over the three centuries of European rule that will then comprise one two-hundredth of the continent's history of occupation, of the accumulated linguistic legacy of the preceding fifty millennia.

Map 22 gives a preliminary impression of the fragility of the current situation. Of the 605 language varieties mapped (territories based on estimates of traditional locations), only 25 have over 1,000 speakers, and only 36 have over 500 speakers. The vast majority (526/605) have fewer than 100 speakers. The distribution of 'healthy' languages exhibits a clear geographical pattern – they are confined to those parts of the continent furthest from urban settlements, such as the Western Desert, Arnhem Land and the Torres Strait. Even having a 'remote' location, however, is no guarantee that a language is healthy – examples of extinct languages from quite remote locations are *Wurrugu* from the Cobourg Peninsula and *Linngithigh* from Cape York.

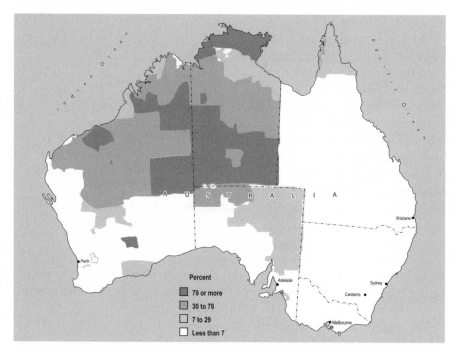

Map 22. Indigenous language speakers as proportion of indigenous population
(map S1.5 from the ABS website; reproduced from McConvell and Thieberger 2000)

2. Special characteristics of Australian languages

In this section I give a taste of some of the ways *Australian* languages are
important for our general understanding of linguistics, exhibiting characteristics that are totally or largely absent elsewhere in the world.

  As an undergraduate student of psychology at the Australian National
University in the 1970s, excited by reading Whorf's *Language, Thought
and Reality* for the first time, I asked my lecturer why all the 'exotic' language examples were *Amerindian* and none *Australian*. He replied that
'we don't know much about *Aboriginal* languages, but they don't seem to
be as different or interesting as *American Indian* ones'. Perhaps he
wouldn't have said this if he had been more aware of the research going
on at the time in the Linguistics department a few hundred metres away,
but it was a characteristic response to the somnolent history of indifference to *Australian* languages that had characterised most of the two centuries since white occupation of the continent.

Although there were some honourable exceptions, the overwhelming impression until the 1960s is one of neglectful, amateurish and uninspired efforts that rarely succeed in documenting the languages in a way remotely comparable to the work being carried out by Boas, Sapir and their students in North America, or by Dutch scholars in Indonesia. It was not until the 1970s – 200 years after the British claimed New South Wales, and at a time when a huge number of languages had already disappeared completely – that the first reasonable grammars and dictionaries of *Australian* languages began to appear (see Austin 1991 for a good survey).

We now have around thirty high-quality grammars and workmanlike grammars of as many again (see below for the situation with dictionaries and text collections). However, the concentration of typological and genetic diversity in the north-west (and the fact that most languages of the south-east became dead or moribund before modern research could be undertaken) means that our coverage is far from even.

In many cases, earlier descriptions simply failed to notice central and interesting facts about the language – if we had ticked these languages off as 'already described' on the basis of the short descriptions available, we would have missed the really crucial lessons they have to offer the science of linguistics. I will describe three examples of this in §2.1., concentrating on grammar and phonology, the heartland of the last three decades of research. In §2.2.–2.4. I look at some broader problems where our understanding is much further behind: lexicon and texts (§2.2.), special registers (§2.3.), and the area of multilingualism and the use of linguistic variation more generally to index differences in social group membership (§2.4.).

2.1. Grammar, phonology, and the unimaginable human language

One of the most exciting things about fieldwork is its potential to continuously broaden our preconceptions of what is possible for the human mind, by stumbling upon 'unimaginable' languages – those that would never have been thought possible.[3]

Work on *Australian* languages has had its fair share of such revelations since the 1960s, whether it be *Dyirbal* [1], the first langGuage in which ergative syntax was comprehensively described (Dixon 1972), *Warlpiri* [2], for which the work of Ken Hale and others has uncovered the workings of non-configurational syntax in greater detail than any comparable language (e. g. Hale 1983) or, more recently, the way in which many north-western languages break their representation of event structure into two parts – a small set of generic verbs that carves up the semantic space of event representations into one or two dozen main types, and a larger set of coverbs that combines with these to portray the event in detail (see e. g. Schultze-Berndt 2000, McGregor 2002).

In most cases it was far from obvious, at the stage of initial survey work that led to descriptions at the level of a short grammar, where the most interesting issues would arise. In each of above cases the interest of the language only became evident when 4 conditions came together – the opportunity for detailed and sustained research, an open-minded linguist with a flair for noticing new issues, outstanding native speakers with an interest in the work, and a favourable intellectual climate.

It is certainly not the case that either the prior existence of a grammatical sketch or of detailed knowledge of a closely related language would lead a researcher to suspect what treasures lay beneath the surface. I now consider two examples of how easy it is to overlook these even when relatively good survey-level documentation is available.

(a) *Kayardild* [3] is spoken in the South Wellesley Islands in north-west Queensland. It is closely related to *Yukulta* [4], with which it shares around 80 % of its vocabulary, and a little less closely related to *Lardil* [5], on Mornington Island. Sandra Keen, who undertook research on *Yukulta* in 1969-70, described the situation as follows: 'the small amount of comparative work done indicates that *Yukulta, Gayardilt* [= *Kayardild*] and *Yanggal* [6] [= *Yangkaal*] belong as dialects of one language while *Lardil* is a different but closely related language. *Yukulta, Gayardilt* and *Yanggal* have considerable grammatical similarity as well as a high percentage of shared vocabulary and speakers of these dialects can hold quite detailed conversations with each other' (Keen 1983). Hale (1983), on the basis of fieldwork on Mornington Island that concentrated on *Lardil* but included brief recordings of *Yangkaal*, made similar observations. Any setting of research priorities that de-prioritized work if good descriptions of closely-related languages already existed would certainly not have identified *Kayardild* as needing special attention in the 1980s.

Luckily other developments led, quite fortuitously, to more detailed research. In 1981 Ken Hale visited Mornington Island to present the *Lardil* with draft copies of a *Lardil-English* dictionary. The Kaiadilt community, by then concerned about the fact their language was not being passed on, asked Hale whether a similar project could be undertaken for their language and a chain of events led to the community approaching Bob Dixon, who, to my great good fortune, asked me if I would be interested in doing my Ph.D. on the language.

As it turns out, *Kayardild* is a superb example of an 'unimaginable language', and although it shares most of its vocabulary with *Yukulta* and the phonological differences are only slight, its grammar is organized in a quite different way. Perhaps its most outstanding feature is the way it keeps passing down all information from higher syntactic levels, so that each word projects up a host of information about all structural levels above it, rather than just its local environment. This can be illustrated by the phenomenon of multiple case marking. To say 'with a/the boomerang', the word for 'boomerang' is inflected with the instrumental case (1) – nothing unusual about this, from the perspective of *Russian* or *Latin*. If you go on to say 'with brother's boomerang', as in (2), you notice that the instrumental spreads over the whole phrase, being placed outside the genitive case on 'brother' as well as on 'boomerang'.

1. *wangal-nguni*
    boomerang-INSTR
    'with the boomerang'

2. *thabuju-karra-nguni*   *wangal-nguni*
    brother-GEN-INSTR   boomerang-INSTR
    'with brother's boomerang'

Although somewhat unusual typologically, double case-marking is far from unique – as well as being found in many other *Australian* languages, it is a trait found in *Central Cushitic* in Ethiopia, the ancient near East, and the Caucasus – see Plank (1995) for a collection of descriptions and a historical survey. But in *Kayardild* this is only the beginning. If you then embed (2) in a clause in the past tense, each noun phrase other than the subject takes an additional ablative suffix, as illustrated in (3).

3. *dangka-a*   *burldi-jarra*   *yarbuth-ina*
    man-NOM   hit-PAST   bird-ABL

    thabuju-karra-nguni-na   *wangal- nguni-na*
    brother-GEN-INSTR-ABL   boomerang-INSTR-ABL
    'the man hit the bird with brother's boomerang'

This is an example of the 'modal case' system, which gives *Kayardild* a second way of giving information about tense/mood, linked with but partly independent of its verb inflections; it originated through the use of case to mark inter-clausal relations ('from/after spearing the fish, the man cooked it') and then became an independent marker of tense/mood when the main clause got ellipsed. In fact, it is precisely because *Kayardild* is so close to *Yukulta* (which has the interclausal use) that we have been able to figure out the historical origins of modal case. Among all the world's languages, only *Kayardild* and *Lardil* have modal case systems, and various changes that have taken place in *Lardil* (such as the specialization of one of the modal cases to the point where its basic use has been lost) makes it much harder to work out what is going in *Lardil* than in *Kayardild*.

To top things off, there is a fourth layer of case marking in *Kayardild*. When one clause is embedded in another and certain other conditions are met (e. g. the two clauses not having the same subject), every word in the subordinate clause takes a further case suffix (most commonly the 'oblique', historically a dative). An example is (4); note that while the nominative on 'man' in (3) is simply replaced (basically because the nominative only goes on words that have missed out on getting in any other case), all other words (including the past-inflected verb 'hit') just tack on the 'complementizing' oblique suffix after all other inflections; in the case of *thabuju* 'brother' this means it ends up with 4 case suffixes. No other language in the world takes case stacking to this extreme – comparative morphological evidence shows that *Lardil* once had it, but various radical phonological changes that have chopped off the ends of *Lardil* words have produced a somewhat different system in the modern language.

4. *ngada*   *kurri-jarr,*   *dangka-ntha*   *burldi-jarra-ntha*
    1sgNOM   see-PAST   man-OBL   hit-PAST-OBL

    yarbuth-inaa-ntha   *thabuju-karra-nguni-naa-ntha*
    bird-ABL-OBL   brother-GEN-INSTR-ABL-OBL

    wangal-nguni-naa-nth
    boomerang-INSTR-ABL-OBL
    'I saw that the man had hit the bird with brother's boomerang'

This does not exhaust the unique features of *Kayardild* grammar (see Evans (1995) for a detailed description). For example, in addition to 'normal' case inflections like those just given, which leave nouns as nouns, there is another whole set that turns nouns into morphological verbs capable of taking the full range of verbal inflections (but which still function as nouns syntactically) – a counter-example to the often-made claim that inflections do not change word-class. The point is that here is a prime 'unimaginable' language whose importance was still masked when we had quite full information on two closely related languages – and also one where it would have been very difficult to work out the system had we not already had outstanding descriptions of *Yukulta* and *Lardil*. It would also have been impossible to figure out its structure if research had begun twenty years later – the number of fluent speakers has dwindled from around 40 in 1982 to under 10 in 2000. Most crucially, the fact that the generation who would now be in their 60s has been disproportionately affected by premature deaths mean that there is effectively only one bilingual speaker left, yet it was the bilingual generation (all born between 1935 and 1945) who were the key to understanding how the language functioned. The premature loss of this generation would certainly not have been predicted, though retrospectively it reflects where the major health stresses of the transition from traditional to mission to 'modern' living conditions have fallen most heavily.

(b) *Dalabon* [7] is spoken in central Arnhem Land. The pioneering Australianist Capell published a grammar of it in 1962 as one of 4 exemplified in his book *Some Linguistic Types in Australia*. Capell's grammar typifies the way a sketch grammar can overlook centrally interesting and unusual facts about a language – in this case, I believe, because most of the data was based on a questionnaire which only allowed the investigator to find what had already been foreseen as a possibility. Consider the following pair of sentences (adapted from Alpher 1982):

5. *darruh-ko*   *barra-h-bo-n*
    brother-DYAD   3dual(harmonic)-REALIS-go-PRES
    'They two, brothers, go.'

6. *be-ko*   *ke-h-bo-n*
    man's.son-DYAD   3dual(disharmonic)-REALIS-go-PRES
    'They two, father and son, go.'

As this pair illustrates, the pronominal prefixes on the verb, in addition to person and number, are sensitive to a social factor usually called 'harmonicity': the harmonic forms are used if members of the referent set are in the same generation (or even-numbered generations, such as grandparents and grandchildren), while the disharmonic forms are used if they are in odd-numbered generations (e. g. parent and child).

The existence of kinship-sensitive pronominal prefixes was completely overlooked by Capell's grammar. The most likely explanation for this is that it was largely based on a survey-type questionnaire, used widely by himself and others from the 1940s to the 1960s. Although this included a thorough examination of paradigmatic combinations like 'we two saw the dog', 'we three saw the dog', etc., it did not ever try to vary the kin relationship between the members of a set like 'we two' – presumably because no-one had reported this as being relevant at the time, the first published discovery of the phenomenon in any language being Hale (1966) for *Lardil*. It was only when Barry Alpher began work on *Dalabon* in 1974 that this material came to light, partly because of the involvement in this research of a native *Dalabon* speaker, David Jentian Nangan-golod, who was training in linguistics at the then School of Australian Linguistics.

Now it is perfectly understandable that Capell, as the first investigator to report on the language, should overlook many significant features, and his sketches have been put to good use by subsequent investigators (though we still lack a comprehensive description of *Dalabon*). My point is that survey work is inherently prone to overlooking the most interesting features of languages, and hence provides a poor guide to locating unusual grammatical and phonological characteristics.

2.2. Lexicography and texts

The trajectory of scientific interest since the 1960s has favoured work on grammars at the expense of dictionaries, which have remained 'the poor cousin of grammatical description' (Austin 1991). A recent survey of Australian lexicography by Goddard and Thieberger (1997) listed only 17 'reasonably large' dictionaries of *Australian* languages, even though their definition of 'reasonably large' is an unambitious '2,000+ entries'. Only 5 out of the 25 *non-Pama-Nyungan* families are represented in this list. Yet for most non-linguists dictionaries are the most important type of documentation – certainly the speech communities themselves are more interested in dictionaries than in grammars; encyclopaedic dictionaries are an excellent source of cultural documentation relevant to community-based enterprises as diverse as eco-tourism, gathering of wild plant seeds for native nurseries, or documentation of bark paintings. For historical linguistics the lack of good lexical documentation remains the single greatest handicap to detailed work.

A successful initiative in the early 1990s, resulting from a one-off grant by the Federal Government to the Australian Institute of Aboriginal and Torres Strait Islander Studies, encouraged linguists to bring out provisional versions of dictionaries based on materials they had already gathered, leading to the publication of dozens of dictionaries and word-lists. However, the interaction of the much slower gestation time of dictionaries than grammars with the short funding cycle of most supporting institutions has made it hard to establish the sort of twenty-year project needed to produce proper dictionaries. Although there are isolated cases of comprehensive dictionaries produced by individual researchers (e. g. Alpher 1991), it has more often been the case that good dictionaries reflect long-term projects, based in the community or a local language centre, that have gathered lexical material and written definitions as part of a more wide-ranging program of language work. In some cases this has involved missionary organizations who over the years have built up a team comprising native speakers engaged in Bible translation (e. g. the *Wik-Mungkan* [8] dictionary by Kilham et al 1986).

The most successful dictionary-making program has been based in Alice Springs at the Institute for Aboriginal Development, which so far has produced three excellent dictionaries (Goddard's 1992 *Pitjantjatjara/ Yankunytjatjara* [9] to *English* dictionary, Henderson and Dobson's 1994 *Eastern* and *Central Arrernte* [10] to *English* dictionary, and Green's 1992 *Alyawarr* [11] to *English* dictionary). Crucial to the quality of their dictionary-making programs has been (a) cooperation of trained linguists with native speakers who combine practical training in lexicography with an on-going range of language-related jobs such as interpreting, language teaching, cultural documentation, and producing vernacular literacy materials (b) parallel production of several dictionaries with sharing of ideas and techniques between them (c) success in bringing together sufficient funding, over a relatively long term, to build stable lexicography teams (d) the capability of publishing their own materials.

Text material has lagged even further behind grammars than dictionaries have; the seriousness of this gap is becoming more apparent as linguistics makes more and more use of extensive corpora. Publishing of bilingual texts has neither been commercially feasible nor a high academic priority, and many text collections, submitted to publishers as bilingual, have had to excise much of the vernacular text as the price of publishability. Exceptions (see Laughren 2000 for a fuller listing) include Strehlow's (1971) 'Songs of Central Australia', the collection of *Warlpiri* [2] 'dreamings and histories' in Napaljarri and Cataldi (1994), of *Kunwinjku* [12] texts in Nganjmira (1997), and, more academically oriented in terms of glossing and linguistic commentary, Heath (1981) on *Nunggubuyu* [13] and Schebeck (1974) on *Adnyamathanha* [14]. In recent years it has been local *Aboriginal* language centres that have led the way in the publication of bilingual text materials, which tend to be directly written in the vernacular rather than transcribed from speakers. As with dictionaries, text collections are valued by the speech communities themselves because of the high content of cultural information; they are also useful 'insurance' against an overly-narrow focus by linguists on the questions of the day.

2.3. Multilingualism in speech communities

There is growing interest in the question of how linguistic diversity is engendered and maintained (e. g. Nettle 1999), and in the social mechanisms that favour its development. Australia provides a clear example of how small, culturally similar groups that are in regular contact and whose members normally know a number of neighbouring languages, consistently develop and maintain language diversity. The reigning social model over much of Australia posits a direct relationship between land and language (e. g. Merlan 1981), as well as between language and particular social groupings, such as clans. Individuals then derive the right to be recognized as speakers of particular languages indirectly, through their membership in clan or other groups:

Figure 1. The indirect relationship between individuals and 'their' languages

This ideology leads to a widely-maintained distinction between speaking and owning a language: a statement that 'X speaks Y' may simply mean that 'X belongs to the group associated with the country where Y is spoken', and some other person who actually speaks Y fluently because of their life history, but does not belong to the requisite grouping, may not be volunteered as a speaker. I discuss elsewhere (Evans 2001) some of the difficulties this can create in discoveringlast speakers.

The mapping of language onto country creates an interesting range of sociolinguistic practices (see e. g. Brandl and Walsh 1982, Trigger 1987). It is a regular practice to change the language one is speaking when entering a new territory, to address particular locales (e. g. wells, or dangerous places) in the local language, for characters in myths to switch languages as they move about the country (sometimes this metonymic device may be the only indication that a character has moved from one place to another), and for large-scale song and myth cycles to incorporate a number of 'legs', each in a different language and typically told by different speakers in relay – as if the Odyssey, say, passed through half-a-dozen *Mediterranean* languages and story-tellers as the action shifted.

Typically there is no etiquette that all participants in a conversation should speak the same language, and it is quite normal to witness multilingual conversations in which each participant speaks their own language. This is one factor that may help speakers of critically endangered languages remain fluent the fact that their conversational partners don't speak their languages doesn't mean that they have to give it up. It is striking how often, compared to cases reported in some other parts of the world, the 'last speakers' of *Australian* languages have had an excellent command of their morphosyntactic intricacies (see e. g. Harvey's (1992) grammar of *Gaagudju* [15] and Dench's (1995) grammar of *Martuthunira* [16], both based on work with last speakers).

It is also a widespread practice for a number of languages in a region to be organized into an overarching system, such that speakers' metalinguistic awareness extends well beyond their 'own' speech community or territory. The clearest example is in North-Eastern Arnhem Land (Morphy 1977, Wilkinson 1991), where each language variety is associated with one of two patrimoieties; features distinguishing 'moiety lects' (e. g. dropping of final vowels) cross-cut features distinguishing dialect groupings set up on geographical grounds (e. g. loss of initial syllables of some pronouns). The social processes by which differentiation of new social groups (e. g. clan splits) lead to the formation of new 'patrilects' in very small-scale speech communities have been described for Western Cape York by Smith and Johnson (1986).

So far little theorization in sociolinguistics has appreciated the importance of carrying out detailed work on super-speech-communities made of many interlocked and intermarrying small languages – and obvious this is hard to achieve until basic grammatical and lexicographic work has been carried out (though see Sutton 1978 for an example of what is possible). Psycholinguistics, with its belief in a 'critical period' based on observations of language-learning in large, literate speech communities, may also discover surprises if it were to tackle the problem of second- lan-

354   *Nicholas Evans*

guage learning in speech communities where it is normal for adults to keep learning new languages throughout their lives. This is also relevant to the question of whether languages can still be passed on even when they are not learned as children. In short, full documentation of language use in such communities is one of the highest priorities if we are to understand the forces that have shaped linguistic diversity for the majority of our human past, in which speech communities throughout the world are likely to have been small.

2.4. Special language functions

A commonly used index of language endangerment is to look at the encroachment of a replacing language on the 'language functions' of the threatened language. Frequently cited functions include 'religious practice', 'education', 'inter-ethnic communication' and so forth. However, if we take seriously the emic premise of examining functions from within the perspective of each speech community, we need to allow for the possibility that there exist culture-specific functions that we would never have imagined before undertaking detailed field research. These are of particular scientific interest for the way they encode interpersonal relationships in language, and because in many cases they embody an indigenous tradition of analysis that gives great insight into semantic structure.[4]

2.4.1. Respect registers

Many *Australian* languages have special 'respect registers', sometimes known as 'brother-in-law languages' or 'mother-in-law languages', which are used as a polite way of talking between certain types of relative. They normally involve substitution of a proportion of the vocabulary, which may range from a few words to virtually every word in the language, by different lexical items, while leaving the grammar intact. For example in *Uw-Oykangand* [17], a language of Cape York, a man talking to a potential mother-in-law must use a special register known as *Olkel-Ilmbanhthi*; to speak this one leaves affixes and function words like 'I' intact but replaces the remaining vocabulary items (Alpher 1993: 98):

7a. *Alka-nhdh*   *idu-rr*   *ay*
    spear-INSTR   spear-PAST   I
    'I speared it with a spear.' (ordinary register)

7b. *Udnga-nhdh*   *yanganyunyja-rr*   *ay*
   spear-INSTR   spear-PAST   I
   'I speared it with a spear.' (respect register)

Because respect registers typically have fewer words than the everyday register, their meanings are correspondingly more general, and several linguists have used this as a way of investigating semantic structure by studying the many-to-one meaning relationships between everyday register words and their respect-register equivalents (Dixon 1971, Evans 1992).

There have been few comprehensive studies of respect registers, and most have been based on what a few old people remember rather than observations of actual use. This is partly because it takes time for fieldworkers to discover their existence, but also because respect registers are far more fragile than the everyday form of a language, not being mastered until well after adolescence. For example, at Oenpelli all children still learn *Kunwinjku* [12] as their mother tongue, but the youngest two generations are not mastering the respect register, known as *Kunbalak* or *Kunkurrng*, to the great concern of the speech community. This has prompted Andrew Manakgu, a *Kunwinjku* linguist working at the *Kunwinjku* Language Centre, to specially produce a book of stories with parallel *Kunwinjku* and *Kunbalak* versions as an attempt to restore knowledge of this register in the younger generations (Manakgu 1998).

2.4.2. Trirelational kin terms

Another way in which many *Australian* languages reflect a sensitivity to kinship relations between speaker and hearer is through systems of 'trirelational' kin terms, which offer a number of ways of referring to kin based on simultaneously figuring out the relationship of the referent to speaker and hearer. Consider the following terms from the *Gun-dembui* or trirelational register of *Gun-djeihmi* [18]; all are ways of referring to the mother of speaker and/or hearer in a range of circumstances:

8. *al-garrng*   'the one who is *your mother* and *my daughter*, given that I am your mother's mother'

   al-doingu   'the one who is *your daughter* and *my mother* (given that you are my mother's mother)'

   al-gakkak   'the one who is *your maternal grandmother* and *my mother*, given that I am your mother'

> *arduk gakkak* 'the one who is *my maternal grandmother* and *your mother*, given that I am your mother'
>
> *al-bolo* 'the one who is *mother of one of us* and *mother-in-law of the other*, given that we are husband and wife'

These systems are important for cognitive psychology because of the way they require the speaker to take two perspectives at once – their own and that of their interlocutor. See Merlan (1989) and Laughren (1982) for discussions of two such systems.

Not surprisingly, given the fact that the ability to outgrow an egocentric perspective only comes with maturity, they are not mastered until mid-adulthood (though we have no proper developmental studies), and their correct use is regarded as polished and courteous. Like respect registers, with which they may coexist in the same language,[5] the fact that they are not mastered until adulthood renders them particularly fragile.

2.4.3. Initiation register

A further type of special register is that taught to ceremonial initiates in certain *Australian* communities as part of the process of formal religious education. I shall briefly discuss two of these here – *Jiliwirri* and *Damin* – to give some idea of how important they are as part of humankind's intellectual heritage; this point has been elaborated elsewhere by Hale (1999), who is responsible for most of the research on which this section is based.

Warlpiri [2] initiates learned, as part of the process of initiation, a special register known as *Jiliwirri* (Hale 1971), based on the principle of replacing all lexical items (though not grammatical affixes other than pronouns) with their opposites. As the following example shows, to convey the proposition 'I am sitting on the ground', one must use a *Jiliwirri* utterance which would translate literally into everyday *Warlpiri* as 'someone else is standing in the sky':

9. *ngaju*   *ka-rna*   *walya-ngka*   *nyina-mi*
    I   PRES-1sg   ground-LOCATIVE   sit-NONPAST
    'I am sitting on the ground.' (ordinary *Warlpiri*)

10. *kari*   *ka-ø*   *nguru-ngka*   *karri-mi*
    other   PRES-3sg   sky-LOCATIVE   stand-NONPAST
    'I am sitting on the ground.' (*Jiliwirri*)

Jiliwirri has been used to investigate antonymy in *Warlpiri* lexical semantics, including such non-obvious issues as whether the perception verbs 'see', 'hear' etc. have antonyms, and on how one determines antonyms for natural species names like 'red kangaroo'. See Hale (1971) for full discussion.

Even more spectacular is a special initiation register known as *Damin*, which was taught to *Lardil* [5] men on Mornington Island as part of their initiation as Warama (second degree initiates) – see Hale and Nash (1997) and McKnight (1999). It is said to have been created by an ancestor known as Kaltharr (Yellow Trevally fish), and has a rich inventory of sounds, some echoing what 'fish talk' would sound like. In fact, its phoneme inventory is unique among the world's languages in employing 5 distinct airstream initiation types: pulmonic egressive (the normal type in all other *Australian* languages), pulmonic ingressive (the ingressive lateral fricative *l**, velaric ingressive (nasal clicks like *n!*), labiovelar lingual egressive (*p'*) and glottalic egressive (*k'*).[6] Of these, the pulmonic ingressive and labiovelar lingual egressives are found nowhere else in the world's languages, at least as phonemic elements.

Because grammatical affixes are simply taken over from everyday *Lardil*, it is only the lexical roots that display these special phonemes, as can be illustrated by the following sentence equivalents from everyday *Lardil* (11a) and *Damin* (11b): *Damin* substitutes *n!aa* for *ngada*, *didi* for *ji-* and *l*ii* for *yak-*, but leaves the grammatical suffixes intact (other than allomorphic differences between postconsonantal *-ur* and postvocalic *-ngkur*).[7]

11a. *Ngada*   *ji-thur*   *yak-ur*
    I   eat-FUT   fish-OBJ
    'I will eat fish.'

11b. *N!aa*   *didi-thur*   *l*i-ngkur*

Equally unique is the semantic structure of *Damin*, which maps the many thousand lexical items of everyday *Lardil* into around 200 words by a combination of highly abstract semantics, extended polysemic chains, paraphrase, and supplementation by hand signs. In the above example, *n!aa* does not simply correspond to *ngada* 'I' but can denote any group including ego, which in *Lardil* includes 9 possible pronouns, representing the three-dimension matrix formed by *ngada* 'I' plus $2 \times 2 \times 2$ combinations of the oppositions dual vs plural, inclusive vs exclusive, and harmonic vs disharmonic. Likewise *didi* does not simply correspond to *jitha* 'eat' but also includes all actions of harmful affect, such as *barrki* 'chop', *betha* 'bite', *bunbe* 'shoot', and *kele* 'cut'. The net effect is to produce a totally indigenous analysis of the semantics of the entire vocabulary into a small number of elements, and Hale (1982: 32) justifiably refers to *Damin* as a 'monument to the human intellect'. Elsewhere he has drawn attention to the fact that its association with rituals outlawed by the missionaries in power on Mornington Island meant that its transmission was interrupted well before the transmission of everyday *Lardil*, as well as to the invisibility of this astounding achievement to the outside world:

The destruction of this intellectual treasure was carried out, for the most part, by people who were not aware of its existence, coming as they did from a culture in which wealth is physical and visible. Damin was not visible for them, and as far as they were concerned, the Lardil people had no wealth, apart from their land. (Hale 1998: 211–212)

Each of the special registers described in this section has been developed to fulfil particular 'language functions' that lie outside the usual typology of written vs. spoken, high vs. low that we are familiar with from the languages of literate societies. In addition to their sociolinguistic interest, all bring unusual and sometimes unparalleled semantic insights into the study of the 'everyday' forms of the corresponding languages. At the same time they are among the most fragile and easily-overlooked phenomena in need of documentation – in other words, they are normally much more sensitive to loss than the 'normal' language. Indeed, as we saw in the case of the *Kun-balak* and *Kun-debi* registers of *Kunwinjku*, it may happen that an apparently-healthy language is regarded by its speakers as under threat precisely because one or more of these special functions is no longer being carried out. It is essential that prioritizations of needs for language documentation not overlook these exceptionally interesting language varieties, whose existence often does not emerge until detailed work has been carried out on the everyday variety.

3. Assessing endangerment across the continent

I lack the space here to give full figures on the status of every language on the continent. Rather, I shall summarize the overall picture, give some examples illustrating some of the difficulties of assessment, and point the reader to more comprehensive sources.

Only since 1986 questions about language been asked in the Australian census, and only in the last census (1996) have indigenous languages been identified individually by name. The exact current form of the question – 'do you speak a language other than *English* at home?' – has various difficulties, such as disallowing the possibility that the individual speaks more than one language other than *English*, and allowing for self-reporting errors. The existence of multiple language names and spellings causes confusion in interpreting the results, although in some areas assistance given to the census-takers helped standardize this. Finally, confidentiality requirements mean that for languages with very low numbers of speakers the figures are not made available, obviously a grave shortcoming when dealing with endangered languages.

Before census figures began being compiled, a number of surveys had been published, beginning with Oates and Oates (1970), which attempted a complete listing of languages, giving estimates of speaker numbers, language viability (including the proportion of the population who still use the language), documentation of grammar/phonology, vocabulary, text/ tape, and names of investigators involved with the language. At the stage when they compiled this the status of many varieties as distinct languages or dialects was still unclear (see *Notes* to *Figure 2* for two examples).

More recently, comprehensive 'handbooks' have appeared for several regions: Central Australia (Menning and Nash 1981), the Kimberleys (McGregor 1988), the Pilbara (Sharp and Thieberger 1992), and Western Australia south of the Kimberleys (Thieberger 1993); the latter two overlap in coverage. Each of these gives estimates of speaker numbers and language situation, detailed information on available sources, school programs and language learning materials, and basic word lists.

Significantly, the first three handbooks were commissioned by local Aboriginal organizations:[8] an important development since the mid 1980s has been the setting up of Aboriginal-run regional 'Language Centres' acting as a local focus for language maintenance, documentation and archiving (Laughren 2000 has a full listing), and these have played an important role in involving community members in a wide range of language activities, as well as in matching researchers with speech communities and negotiating acceptable conditions of involvement by academic researchers.

A further set of figures, for the whole of Australia, was compiled by Schmidt (1990) as part of a nation-wide survey commissioned by the Australian Institute of Aboriginal and Torres Strait Island Studies (AIATSIS) in Canberra. Schmidt's figures on speaker numbers draw on a number of the above sources plus additional surveys in some areas. However, they only extend to 90 languages: the 20 languages she identifies as 'healthy/strong', defined as 'one which is transmitted to children and actively spoken by all generations in a wide range of social contexts' (p. 2), and ranging from 200 to 3,000+ speakers, plus a further 70 'severely threatened' languages estimated to have at least 10 speakers (p. 5), and ranging upwards from 10 to 1,000 speakers. The author notes that this list is not exhaustive, and than languages with fewer than 10 speakers are not listed at all. Additional comprehensive figures are the constantly-updated source Ethnologue, and Wurm's 1999 listing of endangered languages, both compiled from a number of sources.

The difficulties in coming up with accurate figures are illustrated in *Table 1*, which compares sources for a number of languages that I have worked on sufficiently to come up with my own estimate, and to make a sober assessment of claimed knowledge. The discrepancies are representative of the mistakes that arise when figures are quoted without intensive investigation on the language having been undertaken, but also of the way in which speaker numbers can collapse very quickly in communities with life expectancies decades below those for non-indigenous Australians. For *Kayardild* [3], for example, Wurm's estimate of 50 speakers in 1981 would not have been far out; the decline to the current figure of 8 simply reflects the death of most *Kayardild* speakers in the last 20 years.

They also show how speakers of languages believed extinct can still come out of the woodwork, as happened with *Ilgar* [19]; another recent example is the Kimberley language *Andajin* [20] (Saunders 1999).[9]

Finally, it illustrates the fact that a small number of *Australian* languages are actually increasing in number, usually through a combination of demographic growth and language shift by speakers of neighbouring languages. *Kunwinjku* (*Bininj Gun-wok*) is an example of this (Evans 2003): the more than doubling since the 1980s estimates reflects both factors. Families at Korlobidahdah outstation in Central Arnhem Land, for example, have shifted in the last three generations from being bilingual in *Dalabon* and the *Kune* dialect of *Bininj Gun-wok*, to being monolingual *Kune* speakers (with some *English*); the youngest residents of this community who know *Dalabon* are in their late 40s. In this case, as in many other expanding indigenous languages, a major factor favouring *Bininj Gun-wok* growth is its role as a lingua franca in the staging of traditional religious ceremonies. In other cases one indigenous language has spread at the expense of others through its use as a lingua franca on missions – see Smith (1986) on the displacement of Kugu *Muminh* [24] by *Wik-Mungkan* at Aurukun.

Table 1. Examples of speaker estimates of selected languages from various sources

	Oates and Oates 1970	Ethnologue 1988	Black 1983 (NT only)	Schmidt 1990	Wurm 1999	Australian Census 1966	My assessment
Tangkic family							
Kayardild [3]	[no figures]	no mention	no mention	70	50 in 1981, lower today	no mention	6
Lardil [5]	'Entire population of Mornington Island'	50 possibly	no mention	50	possibly 50 in 1981	no mention	1
Gunwinyguan family							
Dalabon [7] (Ngalkbon)	33*	100–200 (< Black 1983)	100–200	100–200	100–200 in 1983	no mention	20
Kunwinjku (Bininj Gunwok) [12]	180	900 inc. L2 speakers	400–900	900	no mention	1403	1500–2000
Iwaidjan family							
Iwaidja [21]	120	180 (< SIL)	180	180	180 in 1983	no mention	c. 100
Garig [22]	**	no mention	no mention	no mention	no mention	no mention	0
Ilgar [19]	**	no mention	no mention	no mention	no mention	no mention	2 'hearers'
Marrgu [23]	12	4 possibly (< Wurm and Hattori 1981)	no mention	no mention	'recently extinct'	no mention	1 semi-fluent

* Oates and Oates (1970) discuss the language I am calling *Dalabon* here under three headings: *Gun-dangbon* (which they mistakenly list as a dialect of *Kunwinjku* ("*Gunwinggu*"), *Dalabon* and *Boun*. The figure given here adds the figures for these three together.

** Oates and Oates do not mention *Ilgar*; they mistakenly subsume *Garig* as a variant of *Iwaidja*.

In the last two years an important initiative has led to a comprehensive compilation of data on *Australian* languages, the State of *Indigenous* Languages audit. This was commissioned by Environment Australia and treats indigenous languages as part of the nation's natural and cultural heritage. An important feature is that, since it has been introduced as part of a 5-yearly round of reporting, it will be possible to make time-based comparisons from subsequent surveys. The current report (McConvell and Thieberger 2000) includes a full data-base, remarks on factors affecting language maintenance, as well as recommendations for data-gathering methods that will produce a more accurate picture for future audits.

Although this section has focussed on the problems of accurate assessment, it is worthwhile concluding this with some overall approximate statistics revealing the extent of endangerment and extinction.

Of the 250 or so *'linguist's languages'* (i. e. grouping together dialects as one language on structural grounds, in a way that speech community members may not acknowledge as valid) spoken in Australia prior to European colonization, fewer than 20 are being passed on to children today, and fewer than one hundred have more than ten fluent speakers. The number that are extinct is harder to quantify exactly, though Wurm 1999 lists 131 extinct languages.

Another way of taking stock is by language family. Of the 25 language families shown on *Map 2*, only 6 contain 'healthy' languages: *Pama-Nyungan* contains more than half the 'healthy' languages, including *Warlpiri* [2] (3,000+), *Arrernte* [10] (3,000+), *Western Desert* [25] (4,000+), *Yolngu-Matha* [26] (2,500+), *Kala Kawaw Ya* [27] (3,000+), *Wik Mungkan* [8] (1,000), *Nyangumarta* [28] (700–800), and *Thaayorre* [29] (500). Five other language families contain the remaining 'healthy' languages: *Tiwi* [30] (1,400) and *Anindilyakwa* [31] (1,000+) are family-level isolates, *Southern Daly* contains *Murrinhpatha* [32] (900+), *Gunwinyguan* contains *Bininj Gun-wok* [12, 18] (1,500), and the *Maningrida* family contains *Burarra* [67] (400–600) and *Ndjébbana* [33] (200–). Of the remaining 21 families, 6 or extinct or virtually so – these are *Gaagudju* [15] (family-level isolate), *Umbugarlan, Geimbiyo, Larrakiyan, Limulngan* and *Kungarakany* (isolate). For a further 7, their 'largest' language numbers fewer than 20 speakers – these are *Tangkic* (largest language *Kayardild* [3], 8–10), *Anson Bay* (largest language *Batjamalh* [34], 20), *Eastern Daly* (largest language *Matngele* [35], perhaps 10), *Western Daly* (*Marrithiyel* [36] and *Marri-Ngarr* [37] have around 20 each), *North Daly* (*Malak-Malak* [38], perhaps 10), and *Wagiman* [39] (10?). In the 8 further families, the healthiest languages are severely threatened, with speaker numbers between 20 and 200: these are *Maran* (*Alawa* [40], perhaps 50), *Iwaidjan* (*Iwaidja* [21] and *Maung* [41], perhaps 150 each), the *Wardaman* group (*Wardaman* [42], 30), *Mindi* (*Jaminjung/Ngaliwurru* [43], 50–150), *Garrwan* (*Garrwa* [44], 200) *Jerragan* (*Kija* [45], perhaps 100), *Worrorran* (*Ungarinyin* [46], 100–), *Bunaban* (*Bunaba* [47], 100), *Nyulnyulan* (*Bardi* [48], 75). *Meryam Mir* [49], the only *Papuan* language spoken in Australia, has around 200 speakers, none fluent under 40.

There have been many positive turn-arounds in public policy and attitudes towards indigenous languages in the last decades – including public recognition, provision of (some) interpreting services, support for regional language centres, appearance of indigenous languages on the airwaves, return of some Aboriginal lands to their traditional owners, some introduction of *Aboriginal* languages into schools (though bilingual education has actually been scaled down in the last few years), and language revival programs such as the *Kaurna* [50] revival program in Adelaide (see Laughren 2000 for a survey of these developments). However, it is not clear that this has significantly retarded the rate of language loss, and other factors, such as the penetration of *English*-language television and videos into remote areas, appear to be at least as powerful in accelerating language loss. It is unlikely that Australia will lose the dubious distinction of being the continent in which language loss is proceeding most rapidly.

4. Priorities for documentation: a survey of the Australian situation

A situation such as that described in §3 obviously places a large number of languages on the high-priority list for documentation, and prioritising them is an invidious task. In this section I give a brief personal view of the 4 main factors I believe should be taken into account in formulating research in the decades to come.

Firstly, there are languages about which virtually nothing is known, and very low numbers of speakers remain. Examples are *Pakanha* [51] and *Ayupathu* [52] in Cape York, virtually undescribed, and with a couple of fluent old speakers each (Barry Alpher p. c.), or *Andajin* [20] in the Kimberleys, for which a speaker has recently been discovered. Probably fewer than ten languages are in this category. Clearly research with languages like this is high-risk, since the speakers could die at any time, and it depends very much on the personality and state of health of the last individuals, but there have been some very successful documentation projects in similar situations (*Martuthunira* [16] and *Gaagudju* [15] being two, as mentioned above).

Secondly, there is a large number of languages with a number of speakers ranging from half-a-dozen to 200, and some sort of limited documentation. Effective research is less risky in such situations than when there is only one or two speakers, and particularly important when the language belongs to a family that has yet to be well-described. But, as also pointed out in §2.1., a 'family-level sampling' approach risks overlooking languages that may turn out to have something equivalent in interest to *Kayardild* [3] multiple-case or *Dalabon* [7] disharmonic pronouns, and there are scores of other languages where it is still feasible to carry out detailed research and the descriptions are relatively rudimentary: among the many examples are *Thaayorre* [29], *Koko-Bera* [53], *Karajarri* [54], *Ngardi* [55], *Ngarinyman* [56], *Ngarla* [57], *Ngarluma* [58], *Kurrama* [59], and *Yanhangu* [60] (all *Pama-Nyungan*), *Kunbarlang* [61] (*Gunwinyguan*), *Marri-Ngarr* [37], *Marri-Sjabin* [62], *Marri-Amu* [63] and *Magatige* [64] (*Western Daly*), and *Gwini* [65] (Worrorran). (Though in the time since this article was originally written, major new projects on Karajarri, Yanhangu and Kunbarlang have commenced).

Thirdly, as indicated in §2.2., special registers such as mother-in-law varieties, initiation languages, and systems of trirelational kin terms have great sociolinguistic and semantic interest and are of major cultural importance to the communities that use them, but are far more fragile than the basic register of the language. The fragility and importance of such subsystems is often overlooked in assessing priorities for documentation, and does not usually appear on lists of speaker numbers. For example, *Tiwi* [30] is known to have had a special 'spirit language', which appears to be a pool of formerly tabooed terms from which names can be drawn (Hart 1930). Yet I know of no recent source setting out the extent to which it is still known. Typically, too, the existence of such special registers only becomes apparent when research on the ordinary variety is well-advanced.

Fourthly, there are many speech communities where it would be more useful and interesting to take the multilingual speech community, rather than individual languages, as the unit of investigation, because of the many unusual ways in which multiple codes are organized for purposes of social identification and cultural elaboration, as outlined in §2.3. In many cases where critically endangered languages are encapsulated within slightly less endangered ones (e. g. *Amurdak* [66] in Iwaidja, or some of the *Wik* languages within *Wik-Mungkan*), taking the multilingual speech community as the domain for research reduces the dependence of a project on the survival of one or two speakers, and is more efficient in terms of gathering cultural information since in situations like gathering plant vocabulary speakers normally volunteer material on several languages at once. Taking the multilingual community as the focus of research also helps gives insights into language contact effects (e. g. between *Ngarinman* [56] and *Jaminjung* [43] across the *Pama-Nyungan / non-Pama-Nyungan* border).

1	Dyirbal	35	Matngele
2	Warlpiri	36	Marrithiyel
3	Kayardild	37	Marri-Ngarr
4	Yukulta	38	Malak-Malak
5	Lardil	39	Wagiman
6	Yanggal	40	Alawa
7	Dalabon	41	Maung
8	Wik-Mungkan	42	Wardaman
9	Pitjantjatjara/Yankunytjatjara	43	Jaminjung/Ngaliwurru
10	Eastern and Central Arrernte	44	Garrwa
11	Alyawarr	45	Kija
12	Kunwinjku	46	Ungarinyin
13	Nunggubuyu	47	Bunaba
14	Adnyamathanha	48	Bardi
15	Gaagudju	49	Meryam Mir
16	Martuthunira	50	Kaurna
17	Oykangand	51	Pakanha
18	Gun-djeihmi	52	Ayupathu
19	Ilgar	53	Koko-Bera
20	Andajin	54	Karajarri
21	Iwaidja	55	Ngardi
22	Garig	56	Ngarinyman
23	Marrgu	57	Ngarla
24	Muminh	58	Ngarluma
25	Western Desert	59	Kurrama
26	Yolngu-Matha	60	Yanhangu
27	Kala Kawaw Ya	61	Kunbarlang
28	Nyangumarta	62	Marri-Sjabin
29	Thaayorre	63	Marri-Amu
30	Tiwi	64	Magatige
31	Anindilyakwa	65	Gwini
32	Murrinhpatha	66	Amurdak
33	Ndjébbana	67	Burarra
34	Batjamalh		

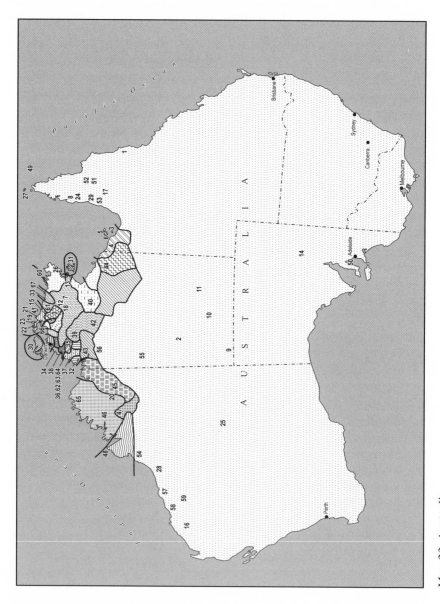

Map 23. Australia

5. Final remarks

In closing it is worth remarking on the rapidly evolving changes to the relationship between researcher, research institution, speaker, and local community. As indigenous groups become less disenfranchised, the relationships between all parties have become more complex. One form this has taken has been the drawing up of a code of ethics for linguists working in indigenous communities in Australia by the Australian Linguistic Society in the 1980s, more or less simultaneously with the drafting of a statement of linguistic rights by the *Aboriginal* Languages Association, an indigenous national association. There has been considerable debate about issues of intellectual property, responsibilities of the linguist to the language community, appropriate training of members of the language community as part of the research process, and a trade-off between outside researchers' goals and those of the community (e. g. an agreement to produce pedagogical or dictionary materials in return for community support for research on a more 'academic' topic, such as syntax or phonology) – see e. g. Wilkins (1992). It is now normal for regional language centres to expect full consultation on such matters as part of the process of planning, execution and 'bringing back' of research projects.

Although some academics have seen this as an unwelcome limitation on their intellectual freedom, and there have been rare cases where it has created difficulties in publishing their research, the net effect has been to make for a richer and more interesting understanding of *Australian* languages, better able to incorporate the cultural insights of native speaker researchers. Some examples of the fecundity of such 'two-way research' were given in §2.2. under the discussion of lexicography and text material. As we strive to document what we can of the extraordinary linguistic legacy that will fade away over the next century, a research process that combines the questions and insights of insiders with those of outsiders stands the best chance of describing languages, on their own terms and in ways that capture possibilities beyond our current imaginations.

Notes

1. There is a single exception to this within Australia's political borders, though not on the continent proper: *Meryam Mir*, spoken in the eastern Torres Strait between Australian and Papua New Guinea, belong to the *Trans-Fly* family whose other members are located in Papua New Guinea.

2. On similar attitudes in Melanesia see Laycock (1982: 33), who quotes a Sepik man saying 'it wouldn't be any good if we all talked the same; we like to know where people come from'.

3. It is a peculiar fact about linguistics that practically none of the most astonishing typological features eventually discovered empirically have been anticipated through prior speculation, whether by philosophers or armchair linguists. This is in marked contrast to the natural sciences where, for example, mathematicians had anticipated the possible existence of the Einsteinian universe by playing speculatively with non-Euclidean geometry, or chemistry, where the likely existence of a large number of elements was deduced by Mendeleev before they were discovered.

4. This is by no means exhaustive – e.g. I omit the special systems of sign language, of interest to our understanding of grammatical and semantic structure – see Kendon (1988), Wilkins (1997).

5. In fact it is possible to see both as special registers: mother-in-law registers index a simple two-value opposition in terms of kin relationships (respectful vs unmarked) but do so by distinct words over the whole vocabulary, whereas tr-irelational kin terms index a much larger set of relationships between speaker and hearer (as indicated by the translations for (8)), but only register this on that part of the vocabulary dealing with kinship.

6. These forms are cited in a practical orthography. See Hale and Nash 1997.

7. This is slighly oversimplified, since the allomorph *-ngkur* is restricted to Damin and may represent an archaic post-vocalic form – see Hale (1973).

8. The Institute for Aboriginal Development in Alice Springs commissioned the Central Australian handbook; this institution has a broader brief than just language but includes a very active language department (see discussion of lexicography in §2.2.). The Kimberley survey was commissioned by the Kimberley Language Resource Centre, and the Pilbara survey by the Pilbara Aboriginal Language Centre.

9. As far back as Tindale (1974: 225), the group inhabiting Ilgar country (though labeleled Gaari by him) was described by him as 'a now extinct people'. Charlie Wardaga, a knowledgeable *Ilgar* speaker, came forward as an *Ilgar* speaker during research for a Native Title hearing by anthropologist Jeannie Devitt in 1994.

References

Alpher, Barry
    1982   Dalabon dual-subject prefixes, kinship categories, and generation skewing. In Heath, Merlan and Rumsey (eds.) 1–18.
    1991   *Yir-Yoront lexicon. Sketch and dictionary of an Australian language.* Berlin: Mouton de Gruyter.
    1993   Out-of-the-ordinary ways of using a language. In M. Walsh and Colin Yallop (eds.) *Language and culture in Aboriginal Australia.* 97–106.

Austin, Peter
   1991   Australian Aboriginal languages. In Michael G. Clyne (ed.) *Linguis-
           tics in Australia: trends in research*. Canberra: Academy of the Social
           Sociences in Australia. 55–74.
Black, Paul
   1983   *Aboriginal languages of the Northern Territory*. Darwin: School of
           Australian linguistics.
Brandl, Maria and Michael Walsh
   1982   Speakers of many tongues: toward understanding multilingualism
           among Aboriginal Australians. In G. R. McKay (ed.) *Australian Ab-
           origines: sociolinguistic studies*. (*International journal of the sociology
           of language* 36). Berlin: Mouton. 71–81.
Capell, Arthur C.
   1962   *Some linguistic types in Australia*. Sydney: Oceania Linguistic Mono-
           graph 7.
Dench, Alan
   1995   *Martuthunira, a language of the Pilbara region of Western Australia*.
           Canberra: Pacific Linguistics.
Dixon, R. M. W.
   1971   A method of semantic description. In D. D. Steinberg and L. A. Ja-
           kobovits (eds.) 436–471.
   1972   *The Dyirbal language of north Queensland*. London: Cambridge Uni-
           versity Press.
Evans, Nicholas
   1992   Multiple semiotic systems, hyperpolysemy and the reconstruction of
           semantic change in Australian languages. In Michael Morrissey and
           Günter Kellermann (eds.), *Diachrony within synchrony: language,
           history and cognition*. Bern: Peter Lang. 475–508.
   1995   *A grammar of Kayardild, with historical-comparative notes on Tangkic*.
           Berlin: Mouton de Gruyter.
   2000   Iwaidjan, a very un-Australian language family. *Linguistic typology*
           4,1: 91–112.
   2001   The last speaker is dead – long live the last speaker! In Paul Newman
           and Martha Ratcliff (eds.) *Linguistic fieldwork*. Cambridge: Cam-
           bridge University Press. 250–281.
   2003   *Bininj Gun-wok: a pan-dialectal grammar of Mayali, Kunwinjku and
           Kune*. Canberra: Pacific Linguistics.
Goddard, Cliff
   1992   *Pitjantjatjara / Yankunytjatjara to English dictionary*. (2nd edition).
           Alice Springs: Institute for Aboriginal Development.
Goddard, Cliff and Nicholas Thieberger
   1997   Lexicographic research on Australian Aboriginal languages 1968-
           1993. In Tryon and Walsh (eds.) 175–208.

Green, Jenny
    1992   *Alyawarr to English dictionary.* Alice Springs: Institute for Aborigi-
            nal Development.
Grimes, Barbara F.
    1988   *Ethnologue. Languages of the World* (11th edition). Dallas: Summer
            Institute of Linguistics.
Hale, Kenneth L.
    1966   Kinship reflections in syntax: some Australian examples. *Word* 22:
            318–324.
    1971   Notes on a Walpiri tradition of antonymy. In Steinberg and Jakobo-
            vits (eds.) 472–482.
    1973   Deep-surface canonical disparities in relation to analysis and
            change: an Australian example. In T. A. Sebeok (ed.) *Current trends
            in linguistics 8: Linguistics in Oceania.* The Hague: Mouton. 401–
            458.
    1982   The logic of Damin kinship terminology. In Heath, Merlan and Rum-
            sey (eds.) 31–37.
    1983   Warlpiri and the grammar of non-configurational languages. *Natural
            language and linguistic theory* 1,1: 5–47.
    1998   On endangered languages and the importance of linguistic diversity. In
            Lenore A. Grenoble and Lindsay J. Whaley (eds.) *Endangered lan-
            guages: Language loss and community response.* Cambridge: Cam-
            bridge University Press. 192–216.
Hale, Kenneth L. and David Nash
    1997   Damin and Lardil phonotactics. In Darrell Tryon and Michael Walsh
            (eds.) *Boundary rider: essays in honours of Geoffrey O'Grady.* Can-
            berra: Pacific Linguistics. 247–259.
Hart, Charles W. M.
    1930   Personal names among the Tiwi. *Oceania* 1,3: 28–290.
Harvey, Mark
    1992   *The Gaagudju people and their language.* Unpublished Ph.D. Thesis,
            University of Sydney.
Heath, Jeffrey
    1981   *Nunggubuyu myths and ethnographic texts.* Canberra: Australian In-
            stitute of Aboriginal Studies.
Heath, Jeffrey, Alan Rumsey and Francesca Merlan (eds.)
    1982   *Languages of kinship in Aboriginal Australia.* Sydney: Oceania Lin-
            guistic Monographs No. 24.
Henderson, John and Veronica Dobson
    1994   *Eastern and Central Arrernte to English dictionary.* Alice Springs: In-
            stitute for Aboriginal Development.
Keen, Sandra
    1983   Yukulta. In R. M. W. Dixon and Barry J. Blake (eds.) *Handbook of
            Australian languages, Vol. 3.* Canberra: Australian National Univer-
            sity Press. 190–304.

Kendon, Adam
1988   *Sign languages of Aboriginal Australia.* Cambridge: Cambridge University Press.

Kilham, Christine, Mabel Pamulkan, Jennifer Pootchemunka and Topsy Wolmby.
1986   *Dictionary and source book of the Wik-Mungkan language.* Darwin: Summer Institute of Linguistics.

Laughren, Mary
1982   Warlpiri kinship structure. In Heath, Merlan and Rumsey (eds.). 72–85.
2000   Australian Aboriginal languages: their contemporary status and functions. In R. M. W. Dixon and Barry J. Blake (eds.) *Handbook of Australian languages, Vol. V.* Melbourne: Oxford University Press. 1–32.

Laycock, Don
1982   Linguistic diversity in Melanesia: a tentative explanation. In Rainer Carle, Martina Henschke, Peter W. Pink, Christel Rost and Karen Stadtlender (eds.) *GAVA': studies in Austronesian languages and cultures, dedicated to Hans Kähler.* Berlin: Dietrich Reimer. 31–37.

Livi-Bacci, Massimo
1992   *A concise history of world population* (transl. Carl Ipsen). Cambridge, Massachusetts: Blackwells.

McConvell, Patrick and Nicholas Thieberger
2000   *The state of indigenous languages in Australia.* Canberra: Australian Institute of Aboriginal Studies.

McGregor, William B.
1988   *Handbook of Kimberley languages. Volume 1. General information.* Canberra: Pacific Linguistics.
2002   Verb classification in Australian languages. MS.

McKnight, David
1999   *People, countries and the Rainbow Serpent.* Oxford: Oxford University Press.

Manakgu, Andrew
1998   *Kunbalak. Stories for Kunwinjku young people in mother-in-law language, ordinary Kunwinjku and English* (2nd edition). Kunbarllanjnja (Oenpelli): Kunwinjku Language Centre.

Merlan, Francesca
1981   Land, language and social identity in Aboriginal Australia. *Mankind* 13,2: 133–148.
1989   Jawoyn relationship terms: interactional dimensions of Australian kin classification. *Anthropological linguistics* 31,3/4: 227–263.

Morphy, Frances
1977   Language and moiety: sociolectal variation in a Yu:lngu language of north-east Arnhem Land. *Canberra anthropology* 1,1: 51–60.

Napaljarri, Peggy and Lee Cataldi
1994   *Yimikirli – Warlpiri dreamings and histories.* San Francisco: Harper Collins.

Nash, David (ed.) and Kathy Menning (comp.)
1981   *Source book for Central Australian languages.* Alice Springs: Institute for Aboriginal Development.
Nettle, Daniel
1999   *Linguistic diversity.* Cambridge: Cambridge University Press.
Nganjmira, Nawakadj
1997   *Kunwinjku spirit.* Melbourne: Miegunyah Press.
Oates, William J. and Lynette F. Oates
1970   *A revised linguistic survey of Australia.* Canberra: Australian Institute of Aboriginal Studies.
Plank, Frans (ed.)
1995   *Double case: agreement by Suffixaufnahme.* Oxford: Oxford University Press.
Pym, Noreen (with Bonnie Larrimore)
1979   *Papers on Iwaidja phonology and grammar.* Darwin: Summer Insitute of Linguistics, Australian Aborigines Branch.
Saunders, Thomas
1999   A first look at Andajin. Paper presented at Australian Linguistics Conference, University of Western Australia, Perth, September 30, 1999.
Schebeck, Bernhard
1974   *Texts on the social system of the Atynyamaṯaṉa people, with grammatical notes.* Canberra: Pacific Linguistics.
Schmidt, Annette
1990   *The loss of Australia's Aboriginal language heritage.* Canberra: Aboriginal Studies Press.
Schultze-Berndt, Eva
2000   *Simple and complex verbs in Jaminjung.* A study of event categorization in an Australian language. Proefschrift, Katholieke Universiteit Nijmegen.
Sharp, Janet and Nicholas Thieberger
1992   *Bilybara. The Aboriginal languages of the Pilbara region of Western Australia.* Port Hedland: Wangka Maya, The Pilbara Aboriginal Language Centre.
Smith, Ian
1986   Language contact and the life or death of Kugu Muminh. In Joshua A. Fishman, Andrée Tabouret-Keller, Michael Clyne, Bh. Krishnamurti and Mohamed Abdulaziz (eds.) *The Fergusonian impact: in honor of Charles A. Ferguson on the occasion of his 65th birthday, volume 2: Sociolinguistics and the sociology of language.* Berlin: Mouton de Gruyter. 513–532.
Smith, Ian and Steve Johnson
1986   Sociolinguistic patterns in an unstratified society: the patrilects of Kugu Nganhcara. *Journal of the atlantic provinces linguistic association* 8: 29–43.

Steinberg, D. D. and L. A. Jakobovits (eds.)
1971   *Semantics.* Cambridge: Cambridge University Press.
Strehlow, Theodor G. H.
1971   Songs of Central Australia. Sydney: Angus and Robertson.
Sutton, Peter
1978   Wik: Aboriginal society, territory and language at Cape Keerweer, Cape York Peninsula, Australia. University of Queensland: unpublished Ph.D. Dissertation.
Thieberger, Nicholas
1993   *Handbook of WA Aboriginal languages south of the Kimberley Region.* Canberra: Pacific Linguistics.
Thieberger, Nicholas and William B. McGregor (eds.)
1994   *Macquarie Aboriginal words.* Macquarie University: Macquarie Dictionary.
Tindale, Norman B.
1974   *Tribal boundaries in Aboriginal Australia.* (2nd edition). Berkeley: University of California Press.
Trigger, David
1987   Languages, linguistic groups and status relations at Doomadgee, an Aboriginal settlement in north-west Queensland, Australia. *Oceania* 57: 217–238.
Tryon, Darrell and Michael Walsh (eds.)
1997   *Boundary rider: essays in honour of Geoffrey O'Grady.* Canberra: Pacific Linguistics.
Wilkins, David
1992   Linguistic research under Aboriginal control: a personal account of fieldwork in Central Australia. *Australian journal of linguistics* 12,1: 171–200.
1997   Handsigns and hyperpolysemy: exploring the cultural foundations of semantic association. In Tryon and Walsh (eds.) 413–444.
Wilkinson, Melanie
1991   Djamparrpuyngu: a Yolngu variety of Northern Australia. Ph.D. Dissertation, University of Sydney.
Wurm, Stephen
1996   *Atlas of the world's languages in danger of disappearing.* Paris/Canberra: Unesco Publishing/Pacific Linguistics.
forthcoming a. Alphabetical list of entries for threatened and extinct languages.
forthcoming b. Australian Aboriginal languages which are endangered in some form, and additional extinct ones.

Chapter 16
Threatened Languages in the Western Pacific Area from Taiwan to, and Including, Papua New Guinea

Stephen A. Wurm

1. General introduction

The question of language endangerment is a very complicated issue. There are two different aspects to it, one sociolinguistic, the other purely linguistic. The sociolinguistic one refers to the declining use of a threatened language by shrinking numbers of its speakers, and deals with the reasons, and circumstances of such events. The linguistic one concerns changes in the manner in which a language is used, the reduction of the number of its different registers, as well as changes and simplifications in its structure, and lexical composition, and semantic changes in its lexicon with all this resulting from a linguistically-oriented endangerment of the traditional form of that language. There may be no or only little decline in the use by its speakers, of a language thus affected, and it may be little affected in its sociolinguistic role and functions, except for the reduction in the number of the sociolinguistically determined application of its registers. It is not necessarily threatened as far as its survival is concerned, but it is not identical with, or sometimes rather different from, the language that it was before these changes took place.

There is disagreeement among linguists as to whether or not such a language should be regarded as being in danger because of its deviating from its traditional form, and whether its endangerment could, or should, be graded according to the severity of it being affected, though in ways which differ from the sociolinguistic gradings of endangerment. Some linguists, and many of the speakers of such languages, regard languages thus affected as new forms of the traditional languages, which may function quite well sociolinguistically, and remain different from a dominant language which may have caused them to be thus affected through its pressure. A frequent phenomenon found in a language thus affected is a change in its semantic setup which moves it from its traditional one in the direction of that of the influencing dominant language. In the Pacific and Australia, there are a comparatively small number of known cases of languages which have been affected in one or several of the ways mentioned above (Wurm 1986, 1992).

The sociolinguistic form of language endangerment manifests itself in a continuing reduction of the number of its speakers, usually from the bottom up, with the children speakers becoming fewer and fewer first, and the age of most of the youngest speakers steadily increasing. As a rule of thumb and a hallmark, the following categories are usually distinguished — *Potentially endangered language* (P): children are more and more inclined not to use and even not to learn the language; *Endangered language* (E): the youngest speakers are young adults; *Seriously endangered language* (S): the youngest speakers are middle-aged or beyond middle age; *Moribund language* (M): there are only a few aged speakers left. The symbols P, E, S, M will be added at the end of each of the language entries given here later to indicate where a given language is believed to be placed on the scale of sociolinguistic endangerment. This scale can mainly be applied when a language is becoming more and more threatened by pressure from a dominant language and culture, and by attitudes and actions of its speakers and carriers. However, there are situations in which the justifications for this scale do not apply, and the grades of endangerment have quite different underlying causes. For instance, an indigenous language which has a very small number of speakers and traditionally never had more (e. g. the members of a semi-nomadic tribe in a remote part of the Amazon forest, or in western non-peninsular Irian Jaya), and has a healthy number of children speakers, may have to be regarded as endangered or even seriously endangered, and the existence of its speakers as threatened or seriously threatened, if there are plans by members of the dominant population to imminently start extensive logging, mining, or oil-drilling etc. in the tribal area. This would result in the transplanting of the members of the tribe into an unfamiliar hostile environment or worse still, their random scattering or even extermination, with serious or even fatal results for their language. Similar situations can result from natural catastrophes such as volcanic eruptions, tsunamis such as the very powerful one which in November 1998 almost wiped out the speakers of four languages on the northwest coast of Papua New Guinea, though one of these languages had over 4,000 speakers of whom perhaps now only 100-200 are left who happened to be absent from the disaster area when the tsunami hit. Major floods, landslides, rampant epidemics, and local warfare, are other factors leading to the demise of quite healthy, but very small languages.

It may have to be pointed out that not infrequently, though by no means always, the linguistic endangerment tends to accompany the sociolinguistic endangerment, though the opposite is not so common. With seriously endangered and moribund languages, a number of the last speakers, or most of them, often tend to speak a simplified and structurally and lexically reduced form of the language, which frequently shows the influences from a dominant language which have been mentioned above. It is interesting to note that with sociolinguistically seriously endangered and moribund languages which had large numbers of speakers before, the simplification and reduction characteristics mentioned above seem to appear earlier and more generally, and with more of the speakers, than with languages which had few or very few speakers (50–200) before, when the language was still healthy. In many such cases, the last surviving fluent speakers still have a perfect or near-perfect command of the full form of their language, whereas with languages which originally had many speakers (1,000 or thousands) and which are only endangered or even only potentially endangered, many speakers begin to speak a form of the language which shows some of the linguistic shortcomings mentioned above.

In the following section on language endangerment in the Pacific area today, and in the listing of languages following it, 'language endangerment' and its grades as indicated refer only to their *sociolinguistic* endangerment. Observed cases of linguistic endangerment in the Pacific area are relatively few to date, and this paper has as its focus the problem of the disappearance of threatened languages for which the establishment of sociolinguistic endangerment is more relevant.

Turning to the social factors threatening languages sociolinguistically, the following may be mentioned in addition to the pressure from large and dominant languages and attitudes and actions by their speakers already mentioned above: economic and social sidelining, isolation and oppression, poverty, and other adverse circumstances resulting in a reduction and loss of ethnic pride and the feeling of ethnic identity of the speakers.

2. Language endangerment in the Pacific area today

Until quite recently, the Pacific area was, with few exceptions, a part of the world least affected by language endangerment, in spite of the prevalence and multiplicity of small to very small languages in a number of its regions. Apart from Australia which had one of the very worst records of language endangerment and extinction in the world until a few decades ago, the only areas with a bad record were those with a significant and dominant metropolitan population from outside the Pacific area, i. e. New Caledonia and to a much lesser extent French Polynesia (French), Hawaii (American), and Taiwan (Chinese). Since the establishment of the State of Indonesia, its record has been getting progressively worse to the present day, though the results of this are still a long way from being as catastrophic as in Australia (or the USA, Canada and elsewhere), because of the shallowness of the time elapsed since Indonesia has come into being, and the absence of policies aimed directly at the destruction of local languages (which were formerly typical of other countries such as Australia, the USA, Canada, the former USSR, Taiwan, etc.), though indirect policies favouring the *Indonesian* language alone did contribute much to endangering local languages, as did the frequent dislocation of whole communities through transmigration and forced removal (such as that of a considerable part of the population of Timor where several languages were affected).

The reasons for the relatively low incidence of language endangerment in the Pacific area are essentially threefold: the first is the low to very low presence of a dominant outside population in most areas, with the exception of those mentioned above, with Indonesia a special case. So is New Zealand in a positive sense: its local language, *Maori*, was near extinction at the beginning of the 20th century, but was rescued by positive official attitudes long before such positive approaches became the norm in countries like Australia, Canada, and Taiwan, and in present-day Russia. The second reason is the widespread presence of stable bi- and multilingualism in many parts of the Pacific area. This allows speakers of a local language to acquire a good knowledge of a major large language which may correspond to a dominant language elsewhere (e. g. *Tagalog* in the Philippines, *Tok Pisin* in Papua New Guinea, etc.), without abandoning, or being obliged to abandon, their own language as is so common in other parts of the world. In many areas of the Pacific, speakers of local languages simply add their knowledge of a major large language to their already existing repertoire of two or often several languages. The third reason is that in Pacific areas in which there are very many different local languages such as Papua New Guinea, Irian Jaya, parts of Island Melanesia, the Philippines etc., the speakers of the local languages took great pride in them and regarded them as important symbols of their ethnic identity, which was a powerful reason for them to maintain them and not to abandon them in favour of another, larger, and more important and useful, language. Unfortunately, this favourable attitude of the speakers towards their own languages has been gradually waning in recent years in Papua New Guinea and elsewhere because of the increasing mobility of the population. This caused many speakers to lose touch with their own speech community, and resulted in very frequent intermarriages between speakers of different languages with *Tok Pisin* becoming more and more frequently the family language where the parents are from different linguistic backgrounds. The interest of children in their own small local languages has been reduced by elementary education being in only a small number of the 800 or so languages of Papua New Guinea, the same being the case with broadcasting. Many children now tend to prefer the major lingua franca and national language *Tok Pisin* to their own. Similar situations are observable in other parts of the Pacific area in which there is a multiplicity of small to very small languages.

The number of different languages is very large in the Pacific area under discussion here. In the entire insular Pacific area there are about 960 *Austronesian* languages (some of them in a few mainland Southeast Asian Pacific rim areas), about 750 *Papuan* languages, and a very small number of other languages such as *Japanese* and *Ainu* in Japan, and two varieties of *Chinese* on Taiwan — a total of over 1,700 languages. Of these, 193 languages are in some way in danger in the Pacific regions covered in this paper, with about 40 more in areas further east in the Pacific, a total of about 233 threatened languages. (In addition, there are 20 threatened pidgin and creole languages in the area covered in this paper, and 4 more in areas further east, a total of 24.) The breakdown of the figure of 233 for various regions is as follows:

Taiwan 7; Philippines 14; Malaysia: Sarawak 3, Sabah 1; Indonesia: Sumatra 2, (Java 2 creoles), Kalimantan 1, Sulawesi 36, Maluku 22 (+ 1 creole), Nusa Tenggara (Timor-Flores) 8 (+ 1 creole); Irian Jaya 64 (+ 1 pidgin); Papua New Guinea 65 (+ 15 pidgins and creoles). Of the 41 languages further east about 30 are in the Solomon Islands (including the Santa Cruz Archipelago) and Vanuatu; the remaining 11 are in New Caledonia, Micronesia and Polynesia (+ 1 pidgin and 1 creole in Micronesia, and 1 of each in Polynesia).

3. List of threatened languages

3.1. Western Pacific area, from Taiwan to, and including, Papua New
   Guinea

In this list, a bird's-eye view is given of significant factors relating to the
endangerment status of every language with broad approximations. After
the language name, the approximate number of extant speakers is given.
This is followed by A, under which four factors are listed. Points a)–d) are
indicated in numbers 1–4 as follows:

Set A

a) What percentage of the ethnic group does the number of extant speakers approximately represent:
   1. under 10%
   2. around 20–30%
   3. around 40–60%
   4. 70–100%

b) To how many children is the language still being passed on:
   1. none
   2. a few
   3. 30–50%
   4. 60%–close to all

c) How many of the roles and functions of the language have been passed
on to another language:
   1. all, except perhaps the family circle
   2. most of the important ones
   3. some important ones have been kept
   4. few or none

d) What is the attitude of the speakers towards their own language:
   1. negative
   2. neutral
   3. mildly supportive
   4. strongly supportive

Two hyphenated numbers indicate: a difference in the language areas
(e. g. distinct villages); or a situation falls between two neighbouring numbers (e. g. b) 2–3 about 15%); or inadequate or unreliable information
available.

The A set is followed by a B set. Under B, the following information is given. Points a) to c) are indicated by number 1 – 4.

Set B

a) Is the language closely or distantly related to an already known, studied, or large not threatened language:
   1. closely related
   2. distantly related
   3. very distantly related if at all, or a special case, i. e. a linguistically, sociolinguistically or otherwise important language for study, even if it is closely or distantly related to a known language
   4. language isolate

b) How much information is available on the language:
   1. well documented
   2. good sketch
   3. a little known
   4. (almost) unknown

c) What are the circumstances under which fieldwork in the language area itself could be carried out:
   1. bad to very bad and impossible
   2. some risks
   3. reasonably safe
   4. good

The B set is followed by a single letter code indicating the degree of endangerment of the language referring to the categories explained above, i. e.

Status – Degree of endangerment

P   potentially endangered
E   endangered
S   seriously endangered
M   moribund

Table 1. List of threatened languages

Language	Speakers	Set A				Set B			Status
		a	b	c	d	a	b	c	
Taiwan									
Babuza	3–4	1	1	1	2	1	2	4	M
Kanakanabu	6–8	1	1	1	2	1	2	4	M
Kavalan	5–6	1	1	1	2	1	2	4	M
Nataoran	5	1	1	1	2	1	3	4	M
Saaroa	5–6	1	1	1	2	1	2	4	M
Saisiyat	3,200	3	2–3	2	3	1	1–2	4	E
Thao	5–6	1	1	1	1	1	4	4	M
Philippines									
Adasen	4,000	4	3–4	2	2–3	1	2	4	P
Agta, Alabat Island	30	2–3	2	1	2	1	2	4	S
Agta, Camarines Norte	150	3	2	1	3	1	2	4	E
Agta, Central Cagayan	500	3	2	1	3	1	1	4	E
Agta, Isarog	5–6	1	1	1	1	1	3	4	M
Agta, Mt. Iraya	150	2–3	2	1	1	1	3	4	E
Alta, Northern	200	3	2	1	2	2	3	4	E
Arta	15	1	1–2	1	1–2	2	3	4	M
Ata	2–5?	1	1	1	1	1	3	4	M(D?)
Atta Faire	300	3	2	1	2	1	2	4	E
Ayta Sorsogon	15–20	1	1	1	1	2	3	4	M
Ayta, Bataan	500	3	3	2	3	1	3	4	E
Batak	200	3	3	2	3	2	1	4	E
Ratagnon	2–3	1	1	1	1	2	3	4	M
Borneo (Sarawak, Sabah, Kalimantan)									
Abai Sungai	400	3	3	1	2	1	3–2	4	E
Kanowit	100	2–3	1–2	1	1–2	1	3	4	E
Lengilu	3–4	1	1	1	2	1	2	3–3	M
Punan Batu	30	3	2–3	2	2	1	3	4	S
Sian	50	3	2–3	2	2	1	3	4	E
Indonesia: Sumatra									
Enggano	700	3	2–3	1	2	2	1	4	E
Lom	2–10?	1	1	1	2	2	4?	4	S, M?

Table 1. cont.

Language	Speakers	Set A				Set B			Status
		a	b	c	d	a	b	c	
Indonesia: Sulawesi									
Ampibabo Lauje	6,000	3–4	2–3	3	2	1	3	3	E
Andio	1,700	3	3	2	3	1	2	3	P
Bahonsuai	180	3	2	1	2	1	3	3	E
Baleasang	3,000	4	3	3	3	2	2	3	E
Baras	200	3	2	1	1–2	1	3	3	E
Besoa	3,000	3	3	2	3	1	2	3	P
Boano	2,000	4	3	3–4	3	1	2	3	P
Budong-Budong	50	2	2	1	2	1	3	3	S
Busoa	500	4	3	2	3	1	3	3	P, E
Dakka	1,200	3	2–3	2	2	1	3	3	P
Dampal	1–2	1	1	1	1	1	2	3	M
Dampelas	2,000	2	2	1	1–2	1	2	3	E
Dondo	13,000	4	3	3–4	3	1	2	3	P
Kalao	400	3	3–4	1–2	2	1	3	3	P
Kodeoha	1,000?	3	3	2	3	1	3	3	P
Koroni	400	3	3	2	3	1	3	3	P
Laiyolo	600	3	2	2	2	2	2	3	E
Lauje	32,000	4	3	3–4	3	1	3–2	3	P
Lemolang	1,800	3	3	2	2	2	2	3	P
Lolak	50	1	1	1	2	1	2	3	S
Napu	4,000	3	3	2	2	1	2	3	P
Padoe	5,000	3	3	3	2	1	3–2	3	P
Panasuan	800	3	3	3	2	2	3–2	3	P
Pendau	3,200	3	3	3	2	2	1	3	P
Rahambuu	4,000	3	3	3	2	1	3	3	P
Saluan, Kahumamahon	1,500	3	2–3	2	2	1	3	3	P
Taje	1–2	1	1	1	2	1	2	3	M
Tajio	12,000	3–4	3	3	2	1	3–2	3	P
Taloki	500	3	3	2	2	1	3	3	P
Talondo'	400	3	2–3	1	2	1	3	3	P
Tialo	30,000	3	2–3	2–3	2	1	1	3	P
Tomadino	500	3	2	2	2	1	3	3	P

Table 1. cont.

Language	Speakers	Set A				Set B			Status
		a	b	c	d	a	b	c	
Indonesia: Sulawesi (cont.)									
Tombelala	1,000	3	2	1	2	1	2	3	P
Totoli	15,000	3	2–3	2–3	2–3	1	2–3	3	P, E
Waru	300	3	2	1	2	1	3	3	P
Wotu	4,500	3	3	2	2	1	3	3	P
Indonesia: Maluku									
Alune	12,000	3–4	2–3	2	1–2	2	2	3	E
Amahai	30	1	1	1	2	1	3	3	M
Aputai	120	3	2	1	2	1	3	3	E
Benggoi	320	3	3	1	2	1	3	3	P
East Makian (Taba)	10,000?	2–3	1–2	2	2	1–2	2	2–3	E, S
Emplawas	220	3	3	1	2	1	3	3	P
Gebe	2,000?	3	3	1	2	1?	3	3	P
Kadai	200	2–3	2–3	1	1–2	1	3	3	E
Kaibobo	250	2–3	2–3	1	1–2	1–2	2	3	E
Kao	200?	3	2–3	1	1–2	1	3	3	E
Lisela	9,000	3–4	2–3	2	2	2	3	3	E
Lola	800	3–4	2–3	1	2	1	3–2	3	E
Loun	2–3	1	1	1	2	1	3	3	E
Nila	1,500	3–4	2–3	1	2	1	3–2	3	E
Oirata	600	3	2	1	1–2	2	2	3	E
Paulohi	5–6	1	1	1	1–2	1	3	3	M
Salas	30	2–3	1	1	1–2	2	3	3	S
Saparua	8,000	3–4	2–3	1	1–2	2	3–2	3	E
Serili	300	3–4	2–3	1	2	1	3	3	P
Te'un	900	3	2–3	1	1–2	2	3	3	E
Ujir	900	3–4	2–3	1	2	1	3–2	3	E
Indonesia: Timor-Flores area, Nusa Tenggara									
Adabe	800	4	2–3	2	2	2	3	2–3	P
Habu	800	3–4	2–3	1	2	1	3–2	2–3	P
Helong	8,500	3–4	2–3	2	2	1	3–2	2–3	P
Kairui-Midiki	1,500	3–4	2–3	1	3–2	1	2–3	2–3	P
Maku'a	20?	1	1	1	1–2	2	3–2	2–3	M

Table 1. cont.

Language	Speakers	Set A				Set B			Status
		a	b	c	d	a	b	c	
Indonesia: Timor-Flores area, Nusa Tenggara (cont.)									
Naueti	700	3	2–3	2	2	2	3	2–3	P
Palu'e	2,000	3	2–3	1	1–2	1	3	2–3	E
Waima'a	2,000	3	2–3	1	2	1	3–2	2–3	P
Indonesia: Irian Jaya									
Anus	70	3	2	1	2	1	3	2–3	E
Arguni	150	3	2	1	2	1	3	2–3	P
As	230	3–4	2–3	1	2	1–2	3	2–3	P
Auye	300	3	2	1	2	1	3	2–3	P
Awera	70	3	1–2	1	2	2	3	2–3	E
Awyi	350	3–4	2–3	1	2	2	3	2–3	P
Bedoanas	180	3	1–2	1	1–2	1	3	2–3	P, E
Biak	30,000	3–4	2–3	2	1–2	1	1	2	P
Bonerif	20?	2	2	1	1–2	1	3	2–3	S, M
Burate	100?	3–4	2–3	1	2	2	3	2–3	E
Dabra	90?	3–4	2–3	1	2	2	3	2–3	E
Damal	4,000	3–4	2–3	1	2	1	3–2	2–3	P
Demisa	400–500	3–4	2–3	1–2	2	2	3	2–3	P
Doutai	70–100	3	2	1	1–2	1–2	3	2–3	E
Dubu	110	3–4	2–3	1	2	2	3	2–3	P
Duriankere	30?	3	1	1	1–2	2	2	2–3	S
Erokwanas	200	3–4	2–3	1	2	1–2	3	2–3	S
Fayu	350	3–4	2–3	2	2	1–2	3	2–3	P
Foya	20?	1–2	1	1	1–2	1	3	2–3	P
Iresim	70?	3–4	2	1	1–2	1	3–2	2–3	E
Isirawa	1,800	3–4	2–3	1–2	2	1	3–4	2–3	P
Itik	80	3–4	2–3	1	2	1	3	2–3	P
Kaiy	220	3–4	2–3	1	2	1–2	3	2–3	P
Kapori	30–40?	3	2	1	1–2	2–3	3–4	2–3	E, S
Karas	100	3	2	1	1–2	1	3	2–3	E
Kayupulau	50	1	1	1	1–2	1	3	2–3	S
Keder	180	2–3	2	1	1–2	2	3	2–3	E
Kembra	20?	2–3	2	1	2	4	4	2–3	M

Table 1. cont.

Language	Speakers	Set A				Set B			Status
		a	b	c	d	a	b	c	
Indonesia: Irian Jaya (cont.)									
Kofei	100?	3–4	2?	1	1–2	1	3	2–3	E
Koneraw	200	3–4	2–3	1	2	1	3	2–3	P
Kowiai	500	3–4	2–3	1–2	2	1	3–2	2–3	P
Kwansu	300	3–4	2–3	1	2	1	3	2–3	P
Kwerisa	15–50?	2	1	1	1–2	1	3	2–3	M
Legenyem	250	3–4	2–3	1	2	1	3	2–3	P
Liki	5–6	1	1	1	1–2	1	3	2–3	M
Mander	20	1–2	1	1	1	1	3	2–3	S
Mansim	5	1	1	1	1	2	1	2–3	M
Maremgi	40	2–3	2	1	2	1	3	2–3	E
Massep	25	1–2	1–2	1	1–2	1	3	2–3	S
Momuna	2,000	3–4	2	1–2	2	1	1–2	2–3	P
Mor2	20–30	1–2	1–2	1	1–2	2	3	2–3	S
Moraori	50	3–4	2	1	2	1–2	2	2–3	E
Narau	80–90	3–4	2	1	2	1	3	3	E
Obokuitai	120	3–4	2–3	1	2	2	1–2	2–3	P
Onin	500	3–4	2–3	1	2	1	2–3	2–3	P
Ormu	500	3–4	2–3	1	2	1	3	2–3	P
Pauwi	80?	3–4	2–3	1	2	4	1	2–3	P?
Saponi	4–5	1	1	1	1–2	1	3	2–3	M
Sauri	280	3–4	2–3	1	2	2	3	2–3	P
Sause	250	3–4	2	1	2	2	3	2–3	E
Senggi	100	3–4	2–3	1	2	2	3	2–3	E
Sobei	1,000	3–4	2	1	2	1	3	2–3	E
Taikat	500	3–4	2–3	1	2	1	3	2–3	P
Tarpia	300	3	2	1	2	1	3	2–3	E
Tause	300	3–4	2–3	1	2	1–2	3	2–3	P
Taworta	140	3–4	2–3	1	2	1–2	3	2–3	P
Tobati	100	1	1	1	1–2	1	3–2	2–3	S
Tofamna	90	3–4	2–3	1	2	2–3	3–4	2–3	P
Uhunduni	14,000	3–4	2–3	1–2	2	2	2	2–3	P
Usku	20?	1–2	1–2	1	1–2	2–3	3–4	2–3	S

Table 1. cont.

Language	Speakers	Set A				Set B			Status
		a	b	c	d	a	b	c	
Indonesia: Irian Jaya (cont.)									
Wano	3000	3–4	2–3	1–2	2	2	3–4	2–3	P
Wari	150?	3–4	2	1	2	2	3	2–3	E
Woria	5–6?	1	1	1	1–2	1–2	3	2–3	M
Yoki	20?	2–3	1–2	1	1–2	4	4–3	2–3	S
Papua New Guinea									
Abaga	4–5	1	1	1	1–2	2	3	1	M
Ak	75	3–4	3	1	2	1–2	2	1	E
Amto	200	3–4	2–3	1	1–2	3	3	4	E
Anuki	500	3–4	2	1	2	2	3	4	E
Arapesh, Bumbita	2,200	3	2	1	1–2	2	2	4	P
Arawum	60	3	2	1	1–2	2	3	4	E
Ari	50	3	2–3	1	1–2	1	3	4	E
Atemble	60	3–4	2	1	1–2	1	3	4	E
Bagupi	50	3–4	2	1	1–2	2	3	4	E
Bepour	50	3–4	2	1	1–2	2	3	4	E
Bilakura	30	3	2	1	1–2	2	3	4	S
Bothar	50	3–4	2	1	1–2	1	3	4	E
Bulgebi	50	3–4	2	1	1–2	2	3	4	E
Dengalu	110	3	2	1	1–2	1	3	4	S
Doga	200	4	2	1	2	2	3	4	E
Dorro	80	3–4	2	1	1–2	1	3	4	E
Dumun	35	3	1–2	1	1–2	2	3	4	S
Faita	50	3–4	2	1	1–2	2	3	4	E
Gapun	80	3	1	1	1–2	3–4	2–1	3–4	(E), S
Garuwahi	200	3–4	2–3	1	2	1	2	4	P
Gorovu	15	2	1	1	1–2	1	2	4	M
Kaki Ae	260	3–4	2–3	1	2	3	1	4	P
Kamasa	6–8	1–2	1	1	1–2	1	2	4	M
Kaningara	300	3–4	2–3	1	2	1	3	4	P
Kawacha	12	1–2	1	1	1–2	1	2	4	M
Koiari, Grass	1,700	3–4	2	2	2	1–2	1	4	P
Koitabu	2,700	3–4	2	2	2	1–2	1	4	P

Table 1. cont.

Language	Speakers	Set A				Set B			Status
		a	b	c	d	a	b	c	
Papua New Guinea (cont.)									
Kowaki	25	3	2	1	2	2	3	4	S
Kuot	900	3–4	2	1	2	2–3	1	4	P
Likum	80	3	2	1	1–2	1	3	4	E
Magori	100	3	2–3	1	1–2	2	1	4	P, E
Mari	80	3–4	2	1	2	1	3–2	4	E
Mawak	25	3	1–2	1	1–2	2	3	4	S
Mindiri	80	3–4	2	1	1–2	1	3	4	E
Moere	50	3–4	2	1	1–2	1	3	4	E
Mosimo	50	3–4	2	1	1–2	2	3	4	E
Murik	1,000	3–4	2	2	2	1–2	2	4	P
Musan	70	3–4	2	1	1–2	3	3	4	E
Musom	200	3–4	1–2	1	1–2	1	1	4	E
Mussau-Emira	3,500	3	2	2	1–2	3	3	4	E
Mwatebu	120	3	2–3	1	2	1	3	4	P, E
Nauna	100	3	2	1	1–2	1	3	4	P, E
Onjab	150	3–4	2	1	1–2	2	3	4	E
Papapana	120	3–4	2	1	2	1	3	4	P, E
Papi	70	3–4	2	1	2	2–3	3	4	E
Piu	100	3–4	2	1	1–2	1	3	4	E
Puari	30–40?	1	1	1	1–2	1	3	4	S
Samosa	90	3–4	2	1	1–2	2	3	4	E
Sera	40?	1	2	1	1	1	3	4	S
Sissano	300?	1	2	1	1	1	2	4	S
Som	80	3–4	2	1	1–2	1	3	4	E
Suarmin	140	3–4	2	1	1–2	2–3	3	4	E
Sumariup	80	3–4	2	1	1–2	1	3	4	E
Susuami	10	1	1	1	1	2	3–2	4	M
Taap	6–8	1	1	1	1–2	1	3	4	M
Taulil	800	3–4	2	1	2	2	2	4	P
Tenis	30	3	1–2	1	1–2	1	3	4	S
Turaka	25	2–3	1–2	1	2	2	3	4	S
Uya	90	3–4	2	1	2	1	3	4	E

Table 1. cont.

Language	Speakers	Set A				Set B			Status
		a	b	c	d	a	b	c	
Papua New Guinea (cont.)									
Vehes	70	3	2	1	1–2	1	3	4	E
Wab	120	3–4	2–3	1	2	1	3	4	P, E
Warapu	300?	2	2	1	1–2	2	3	4	E, S
Yapunda	60	3–4	2	1	2	1	3	4	E
Yarawi	1	1	1	1	1	1	3	4	M
Yimas	300	3–4	2	2	2	1–2	1	4	P

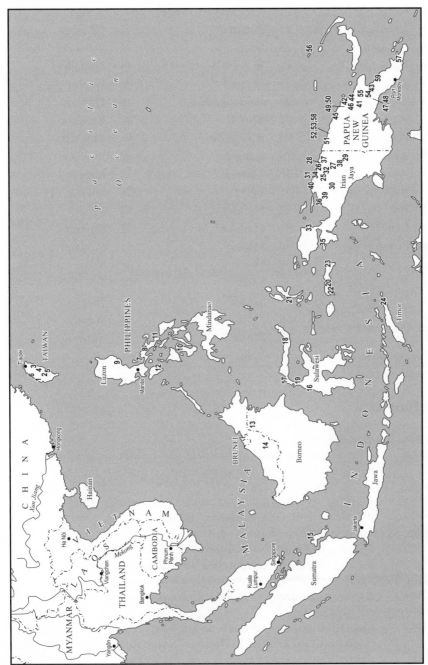

Map 24. Western Pacific Area from Taiwan to, and Including, Papua New Guinea

1	Babuza	21	East Makian (Taba)	41	Abaga
2	Kanakanabu	22	Paulohi	42	Bilakura
3	Kavalan	23	Salas	43	Dengalu
4	Nataoran	24	Maku'a	44	Dumun
5	Saaroa	25	Bonerif	45	Gapun
6	Thao	26	Duriankere	46	Gorovu
7	Agta, Alabat Is	27	Kapori	47	Kamasa
8	Agta, Isarog	28	Kayupulau	48	Kawacha
9	Arta	29	Kembra	49	Kowaki
10	Ata	30	Kwerisa	50	Mawak
11	Ayta Sorsogon	31	Liki	51	Puari
12	Ratagnon	32	Mander	52	Sera
13	Lengilu	33	Mansim	53	Sissano
14	Punan Batu	34	Massep	54	Susuami
15	Lom	35	Mor2	55	Taap
16	Budong-Budong	36	Saponi	56	Tenis
17	Dampal	37	Tobati	57	Turaka
18	Lolak	38	Usku	58	Warapu
19	Taje	39	Woria	59	Yarawi
20	Amahai	40	Yoki		

References

Grimes, Barbara E. (ed.)
  1996   *Ethnologue, languages of the world.* 13th edition. Dallas, Texas: Summer Institute of Linguistics, Inc.
Nekitel, Otto
  1998   *Voices of yesterday, today and tomorrow.* Language, culture and identity. New Delhi: UBS Publishers' Distributors Ltd.
Wurm, Stephen A. and Shirô Hattori (eds.)
  1981–83 *Language atlas of the Pacific area.* Canberra: Australian Academy of the Humanities, in collaboration with the Japan Academy.
Wurm, Stephen A.
  1986   Grammatical decay in Papuan languages. *Pacific linguistics* (Series A) 70: 207–211.
  1992   Change of language structure and typology in a Pacific language as a result of culture change. In Dutton, T. (ed.), *Culture change, language change, case studies from Melanesia. Pacific linguistics* (Series C) 120: 141–157.

Chapter 17
The Languages of the Pacific Region:
the Austronesian Languages of Oceania

Darrell Tryon

1. Introduction

The linguistic focus of this chapter is the vast *Oceanic* subgroup of the *Austronesian* language family, see *Map 25*.

In geographical terms, the area covered extends from just west of the Irian Jaya border in Indonesia to the far reaches of the eastern Pacific, Easter Island and Hawaii.

In terms, of languages, then, the chapter focuses on the six Austronesian languages spoken in Irian Jaya which are members of the *Oceanic* subgroup[1] together with all of the *Austronesian* languages of Papua New Guinea, the Solomon Islands, Vanuatu, New Caledonia, Fiji, Polynesia and Micronesia, a total of around 500 languages.

1.1. Methodology

This paper addresses a number of factors which make the South Pacific a unique area. These include:

- Why such a multiplicity of languages?
- Why such linguistic diversity?
- Factors contributing to language endangerment.
- Current measures being taken to protect/preserve language and materials

The final section of the chapter contains a listing of all of the languages which are members of the *Oceanic* subgroup of *Austronesian* with fewer than 500 speakers, together with locations, approximate numbers of speakers, and an evaluation of degree of endangerment.

1.2. Why such a multiplicity of languages?

In the Pacific there is a distinction to be drawn between Melanesia (Papua New Guinea, Solomon Islands, Vanuatu, New Caledonia and Fiji) and the island states which make up Polynesia and Micronesia.

In terms of language classification, there are two distinct language families represented in the South Pacific region, the widespread *Austronesian* or *Malayo-Polynesian* family, (Tryon 1995 ed.) and the group of languages known as the *Papuan* family (located right across the New Guinea cordillera and in parts of New Britain, New Ireland and Bougainville in eastern Papua New Guinea and on parts of the Indonesian islands of Alor, Pantar and Timor). The *Papuan* languages have not all been proven to be genetically related, although it appears likely that they will in due course. What has been demonstrated is that 500 of the 750 *Papuan* languages are members of what has been called the *Trans-New Guinea* Phylum (Pawley 1998, Ross 2000).

In this chapter, discussion is limited to those languages which are members of the *Oceanic* subgroup of the *Austronesian* family, some 500 languages, see the tree diagram below. The *Papuan* languages are treated by Wurm (this volume).

In Melanesia, characterised by its egalitarian social structures, there is a great multiplicity of languages, approximately $1,000^2$, spoken by small communities, usually without hereditary chiefly structures. These communities or clusters of communities (usually corresponding to a single language or dialect) are headed by a big-man or entrepreneur who through prestations (usually the sacrifice of pigs and the distribution of food crops) has risen to the top of his micro-society through the indebtedness of a good number of his fellow community members to him. For the guiding principle of Melanesian societies is that each gift received by a beneficiary incurs a corresponding obligation or debt towards the donor. Those obligated fall under the power of the donor or big-man, for until a debt is repaid, the beneficiary remains obligated to his benefactor, who may request goods or services in the interim. Indeed reciprocal gift-giving is the sole means of cementing relationships in most Melanesian societies. These Melanesian micro-societies average only a few hundred (and occasionally a few thousand) souls, normally only a few villages. Each society is fiercely proud of its own language/dialect, paraded like a badge or emblem.

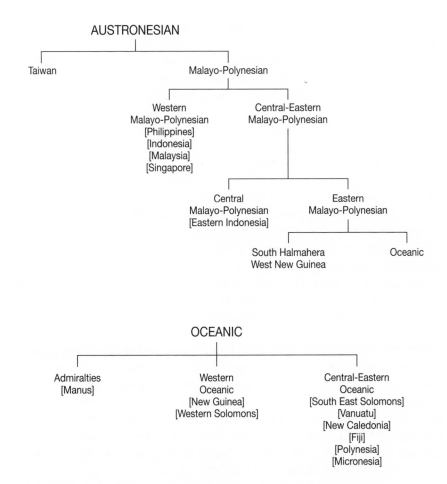

Figure 1. Tree diagram Oceanic subgroup of the Austronesian family

Apart from these factors, the topography of Island Melanesia makes regular communication between distant communities difficult, for there are literally hundreds of islands involved, the larger ones being mountainous and difficult of access. Until colonial times, relations between communities were often hostile. Cumulatively, all of these factors have created an ideal environment for language separation and diversification in the Melanesian region.

In Polynesia and Micronesia, in striking contrast to Melanesia, there are large political units, pyramoidal societies headed by hereditary chiefs or even kings/queens. Tonga, for example, is ruled by King Taufa'ahau IV, while Samoa is divided into three chiefly groups led by paramount chiefs. The social organization of Polynesia and Micronesia has meant in fact that in this region there is normally a single language per state or island group, in stark contrast with Melanesia. As a consequence there are very few languages under threat there compared to the alarming situation in Melanesia.

1.3. Why such linguistic diversity?

Not only are there an astonishing number of languages spoken in the south-west Pacific, but these languages show a high degree of diversity among themselves. This factor adds to the urgency and importance of recording and adequately documenting representative languages in the Melanesian region.

The causes of the formidable linguistic diversity which characterises Melanesia have been discussed elsewhere (Lynch 1981, Pawley 1981). Essentially language diversity in Melanesia is attributable to two factors: first is the isolation factor, referred to above, and inter-tribal hostility and rivalry stemming from traditional Melanesian social organization. Another important factor is language contact between Austronesian and Papuan-speaking populations. For Papuan settlement in Melanesia is of great antiquity, up to 50,000 years in Papua New Guinea, while the Austronesian-speaking populations in Oceania are no more than 4,000 years old. (Spriggs 1997). In Papua New Guinea and the Solomon Islands this contact has been a major contributing factor to language diversity, both on the Austronesian and Papuan side of the equation.

The relevance of linguistic diversity here is simply that of obtaining a satisfactory record of the markedly different linguistic systems which have resulted from the interface between languages of these two unrelated and systemically different language families.

1.4. What are the causes of language endangerment in the Pacific?

In areas which are remote from urban centres there is little threat to the continuance of existing social and linguistic arrangements. The nearer these communities are located to urban centres, the greater the threat to language survival. Indeed, those languages in the area which is the focus of this survey which are classed as endangered, seriously endangered, moribund or already extinct are almost invariably located in or near urban areas. Since rapidly increasing urbanization is one of the major demographic transformations which currently marks the Asia-Pacific region, even languages with relatively large numbers of speakers are quite rapidly becoming endangered and impoverished under pressure from either local trade languages, pidgins and creoles, and metropolitan languages introduced by colonising powers in the nineteenth century. Even a language with over 100,000 speakers, such as *Tahitian*, spoken in French Polynesia, is seriously under threat as its younger speakers mix *French* and *English* elements in with it, as the modern technological and electronic age pervades all strata of Tahitian society.

Another factor, intimately connected to the urbanization phenomenon, is the movement of young students away from their home areas for purposes of education. Almost all students who undertake secondary schooling do so away from their home villages and/or islands, and those who advance further inevitably end up in capital or provincial cities. Since paid employment is found mainly in these areas, students rarely return to their home communities, but rather contribute to the urban sprawl which increasingly characterises the Asia-Pacific region.

Another factor which plays an important role in terms of language endangerment is government attitude to and use of language as a nation-building instrument, especially in Melanesia. In Vanuatu, for example, at independence in 1980, there was no single language used or understood by the whole population, some students in the former Anglo-French Condominium having been 'educated' in *French* and others in *English*. The nearest thing to a national language was *Bislama*, an *English-based pidgin*, commonly used among ni-Vanuatu of different language backgrounds (there are 113 distinct vernaculars spoken in Vanuatu for a population of under 200,000). Since independence *Bislama* has become the national language, and very much the dominant language in urban agglomerations.

In Melanesia nowadays there are many marriages between partners of different vernacular language backgrounds, predominantly but not exclusively in urban areas. Young people from different islands come together in these areas, basically for education, but increasingly in search of a paid job, as the Pacific is quite rapidly moving from subsistence to cash economy, even in rural areas. The children born of these unions almost invariably grow up with either an *English-based pidgin* or a variety of *English* or *French* as their mother tongue. The consequences for the transmission of the parental mother tongues are not difficult to foresee.

While this phenomenon is most acute in Melanesia, it is not uncommon in Polynesia and Micronesia, where one would imagine that larger political units and a single local vernacular would constitute a bastion against invading metropolitan languages. It came as a surprise to me that mixed race Tahitians in their thirties and forties, for example, confessed with embarrassment that they could not express themselves in *Tahitian*, but only in *French*, in spite of having Tahitian mothers.

The major point to be made here is that a small number of speakers of a language does not per se constitute a major threat to the survival of many of the *Austronesian* (or indeed *non-Austronesian* or *Papuan*) languages of Oceania. Much more significant are the ravages wrought by galloping urbanization, the displacement of young students during the education process, and the exigencies of nation-building in states composed of micro-societies, each speaking a distinct, if related, language. Of course there are other factors which impinge on language endangerment, quite apart from the threats posed by increasing globalization and monoculturalism. In Melanesia, especially, evangelization is increasingly carried out in an *English-based pidgin*, rather than a local vernacular, especially since the beginning of the 1970s. This simply exacerbates the pressure on local vernaculars, particularly as their relevance is becoming limited to the village level, while population mobility is on the increase.

At the same time, while languages covered by this survey are potentially, although not necessarily, endangered by having only a small number of speakers, there is a corollary, namely that numbers of languages with relatively large numbers of speakers should also be classed as endangered. In this survey, for example, *Takia*, an Austronesian language of Papua New Guinea, with 16,000 speakers is a good case in point.

While *Takia* has a substantial number of speakers, Ross (personal communication) informs me that there are no longer any monolingual *Takia* speakers, but that all *Takia* speakers are bilingual in *Tok Pisin*, the major *English-based lingua franca* of Papua New Guinea, while many also speak *English* with varying degrees of competence. He reports that over the past two or three generations many Takia have moved from their island home (Karkar I.) to the mainland of Papua New Guinea seeking paid employment in provincial centres and towns. Even in cases where both parents speak *Takia*, it is common for the children to grow up speaking *Tok Pisin* and *English*. Typically, young Takia students have moved away from their home area for purposes of education, the great majority not returning home to live. When they marry, they often take partners from other areas, their children growing up speaking either *Tok Pisin* or *English*.

Even for the stay-at-homes, *Takia* language use is under pressure as its domains of use are gradually reduced. Many Takia are literate, but when they write they usually write in *Gedaged* (the earlier lingua franca of the Lutheran Church), *Tok Pisin* or *English*. Interaction in other domains, for example at the hospital, at the wharf or on the plantation, takes place almost exclusively in *Tok Pisin*. This scenario is just a single example of what is the daily experience of many speakers of languages with nominally thousands of speakers in Melanesia today.

2. The language record: Fragility of materials and their preservation

It is widely believed that a considerable proportion of the languages of the Oceanic region will disappear over the next thirty to fifty years as the effects of globalization are felt, even in the Pacific islands. In most areas little is being done to arrest the progress of this threat, either by the governments or the people of the Pacific states, whose attention is focussed more on issues of governance and economic stability.

In some areas Pacific Islanders are, however, making considerable efforts to record and preserve their own languages for future generations. In Vanuatu, for example, some sixty community representatives, nearly all speaking different mother tongues, all *Austronesian*, have been undergoing linguistic and ethnographic training at the Vanuatu National Museum (formerly the Vanuatu Cultural Centre). This has taken the form of annual workshops, beginning in 1980, funded until recently by the Australian Government's South Pacific Cultures Fund.[3]

The motivation for this activity was simply that many high-ranking big-men and chiefs had expressed great concern at the Malfautmauri or Vanuatu National Council of Chiefs. The major concern was that much traditional knowledge was being lost with the death of a number of Vanuatu elder senior statesmen and that languages were becoming seriously endangered due to the inroads being made by *Bislama*, the *Melanesian Pidgin* used as a lingua franca throughout Vanuatu, as well as the languages of education, *English* and *French*. So it was that the Vanuatu Cultural Centre initiated a series of workshops in order to address the problem.

During the initial workshops, in the early 1980s, emphasis was placed on the recording of oral tradition, mainly folk-tales, for later transcription and publication for use in schools. The transcription phase involved orthography design for those languages which had no existing mission orthography. Once the 'fieldworkers' (as they are known in Vanuatu) felt comfortable writing and reading transcriptions of field recordings, they quickly suggested that the compilation of dictionaries was indispensable for the preservation of their individual languages.

In order to create dictionary files, (in a pre-computer era) a semantic domains system was adopted, beginning, for example, with visual domains such as 'the house', 'the ocean', 'the trees'. Each year a different domain was chosen and researched for the following workshop. Before many years we moved on to conceptual domains such as 'the family', 'death', 'birth', and 'land' among many others. This led to the idea of making each of these domains a chapter heading for an ethnography of the particular fieldworker's society and culture, written by the fieldworker himself in his own language, the lexicon from which was to be extracted and added to existing dictionary files. In this way there is now a double output from each fieldworker's research in his home community: a dictionary (or rather an annually updated dictionary file in the first instance), and a draft ethnography of that community.

As mentioned above, a well-known adage in the Pacific is that 'knowledge is power'. What this in fact means is that only some knowledge is public and that much of it is secret. Many of the 'fieldworkers' expressed concern that often cyclones and tropical storms damaged or even destroyed the language materials that they had produced, which meant that their work had to begin again *ab initio*. This destruction applied not only to materials produced during the annual workshops, but also to notebooks and tape-recordings of traditional knowledge, genealogies, music and the like, much of which is secret knowledge not to be transmitted beyond the immediate family or clan. For in Vanuatu it is not uncommon for elderly people to write down or record such information to be passed on to their heirs after their death. However, there was always a fear that this practice was unsafe as the information might fall into the wrong hands. Even more common is for an elderly and infirm person to summon a younger relative when they feel that their hold on life is insecure, and attempt to pass on as much traditional, and usually secret, knowledge as possible in the time remaining to them. Often the elderly leave their run too late, with the result that much traditional information is lost with the passing of each generation.

In order to respond to this situation, a novel proposal was developed at the Vanuatu Cultural Centre, namely the construction of what has become known as a 'Taboo Room', which is a cyclone-proof air-conditioned room, rather like a bank vault, in the middle of the Vanuatu Cultural Centre. The Vanuatu fieldworkers and numerous other ni-Vanuatu who have learned about the Taboo Room (whose existence is now well-known nation-wide) come and deposit copies of their dictionary files and ethnographic field note-books and tape-recordings there, much as one makes a bank deposit. Only the depositor or his/her nominee may withdraw or consult the materials, managed by the Vanuatu Cultural Centre staff. The originals are usually kept at home in the village of the individual fieldworker. If they should be destroyed by cyclones, fire, rats or predatory children, they can easily be replaced and new copies made.

During the first ten years of the Vanuatu Cultural Centre Fieldworkers' Program, 1980–1990, replacement of damaged ethnographic materials and dictionary files was still an onerous undertaking, as cyclones strike at least one or two islands during the cyclone season (December–April) every year. Post-1990 Vanuatu entered the computer age, so that now dictionary files are kept on hard disk or backed up on diskette, and a hard copy lodged in the Taboo Room archive along with the note-books and tape recordings.

In the various islands the fieldworkers have become unofficial cultural officers, overseeing the work of overseas researchers on behalf of the Vanuatu Cultural Centre, through whom all social science research is co-ordinated and authorised. In addition to lexicography and ethnography, many of the fieldworkers also receive training in archaeology and ethno-musicology, working in tandem with visiting overseas professionals. At the conclusion of the annual Vanuatu Cultural Centre workshops, the fieldworkers return to their villages and become teachers themselves, passing on the skills and knowledge which they have gained that particular year.

Since 1980, the fieldworkers' network has grown from 10 to 66 men fieldworkers. In 1994, a women's fieldworker network was established, which at the time of writing has grown to 33. The Vanuatu Cultural Centre Fieldworkers Network is unique in the Pacific. There are only two simple rules applied, no politics and no religion. The only topic tolerated is culture, the traditional culture or cultures of Vanuatu. The fieldworkers receive no salary. They are nearly all important traditional leaders or members of their families who are proud of their individual languages and cultures, their badge of identity, so much so that they are prepared to devote considerable time each month to fostering language and cultural enhancement and preservation in their home areas.

As noted above, there are over 100 different languages still spoken in Vanuatu today, with an average of roughly 1,500 speakers per language, often less. Because of the traditional social organization of Vanuatu society, there is considerable importance laid upon one's identity and culture, not just through language, but also through traditional dress, music, dance and music, to say nothing of architecture. It is this pride in community identity which has motivated the Vanuatu language recording and preservation program. It is this attitude, too, which ensures that languages with only a hundred or so speakers, very much endangered by world standards, remain safe for the time being, and will probably remain so just so long as they remain sheltered from the forces of globalization.

3. The establishment of priorities for recording endangered languages

A final point, in the context of language endangerment concerns the establishment of priorities for the recording of such languages in the face of limited financial resources. If it is not possible to fund the systematic recording of endangered languages, it would perhaps be wisest to facilitate the recording of languages with no known close relatives, for the maintenance and recording of linguistic diversity is a prime linguistic concern.

For languages which satisfy this criterion, namely if one had to choose between two previously unrecorded language isolates, for example, would it be more advisable to record a language on the point of disappearance, very seriously endangered, spoken by very few speakers, and perhaps imperfectly recalled, or a language which is still fully functional, but potentially endangered, such as *Takia* (referred to above) for example? Such a choice would be invidious. However, it is a very real question. If the aim is to facilitate as complete a recording of an endangered language and culture as possible while there is still time, then in my opinion it would be more beneficial to science to support the language described in the second scenario. For experience in Oceania has shown that what is known as 'salvage linguistics' often recovers only incomplete systems, which, while invaluable in themselves, lack the roundedness which would be achieved by as complete a recording as possible of a fully functioning system.

What follows is a listing of the *Austronesian* languages of Oceania with fewer than 500 speakers, the languages which in principle appear the most endangered, with an assessment of their degree of endangerment. However, the caveats introduced in the discussion above must also be taken into account.[4] The actual number of speakers may not be a reliable guide to language endangerment. For this reason, a number of the languages with fewer than 500 speakers, in a Pacific context, have been ranked here as either only potentially endangered or "unendangered".

In terms of criteria used, I have adopted those used by Stephen Wurm in his complementary presentation (*Chapter 16, this volume*), as follows:

In the tables, *Set A* provides the following information:

a) Percentage of the ethnic group represented by remaining speakers:
1. under 10%
2. approx. 20–30%
3. approx. 40–60%
4. 70–100%

b) Percentage of children to whom the language is passed on:
1. none
2. a few
3. approx. 30–50%
4. 60–100%

c) Roles and functions of the language passed on to another language:
1. all, except perhaps the family circle
2. most of the key roles
3. some key roles retained
4. most key roles retained

d) Attitude of speakers towards their own language:
1. negative
2. neutral
3. mildly supportive
4. strongly supportive

Set B provides the following information:

a) Relationship to a language for which good data are available:
1. closely related
2. distantly related
3. very distantly related
4. language isolate

b) Information available on the language:
1. well documented
2. good sketch available
3. poorly known
4. (practically) unknown

c) Fieldwork conditions:
1. very poor, hazardous
2. some risks
3. reasonably safe
4. good

These data are followed by a single-letter evaluative code, as follows:

Wurm notation (*chapter 16, this volume*)		Krauss notation (*chapter 1, this volume*)	
P	potentially endangered	A	unstable, eroded
E	endangered	B	definitely endangered
S	seriously endangered	C	severely endangered
M	moribund or extinct	D	critically endangered
D	extinct	E	extinct

Assessments are based on data from the following sources:

CB	Beaumont 1972
TD	Dutton 1971
E	Ethnologue 1992
SH	Holzknecht 1989
McE	McElhanon 1984
PL	Lincoln 1977
MR	Ross 1988
SIL	Grimes (ed.) 1992
DT	Tryon 1995
T&H	Tryon and Hackman 1983
W&H	Wurm and Hattori 1981

Table 1. Table of Endangered Austronesian languages (Oceanic)

Language	Speakers	Set A	Set B	Status
Irian Jaya				
Bonggo , SIL 1975	435	3,3,2,2	2,4,2	E (B)
PNG				
Apalik (W. New Britain) E 1992	300	4,3-4,3,4	2,3,3	E (B)
Aribwatsa (Morobe) SH 1989	1	1,1,4,3	2,3,2	M (D)
Bina (Central) W&H 1981	2	1,4,2,1	1,3,2	M (D)
Bosilewa (Milne Bay) Census 1972	350	3-4,3-4,3,3	1,3,3	P (A–)
Budibud (Milne Bay) Census 1972	170	3-4,4,3,3	1,3,3	P (A–)
Doga (Milne Bay) SIL 1975	200	4,2,2,2	2,3,4	E (B)
Duwet (Morob) SH 1989	398	4,3,3-4,3	2,3,2	P (A–)

Table 1. cont.

Language	Speakers	Set A	Set B	Status
PNG (cont.)				
Garuwahi (Milne Bay) Census 1972	40			M(D)
Gitua (Morobe) McE 1978	483	4,3-4,3-4,4	1,1,2	OK
Gumawana (Milne Bay) Census 1972	250	4,3,3,4	1,1,2	OK
Hermit (Manus) PL 1977	20	4,3,3,4	1,2,1	M (D)
Kaiep (E.Sepik) W&H 1981	150	,3,3,3	2,3,2	P (A–)
Kandas (N Ire) CB 1972	480	4,3-4,3-4,3	2,2,2	P (A–)
Kilenge (New Britain). MR 1988	440	4,4,3,3	1,2,2	P (A–)
Kis (E Sepik) PL 1977	216	3,2-3,1,1-2	2,1,4	E (B)
Koro(Manus) SIL 1983	400	4,4,3-4,3	1,2,2	P (A–)
Lenkau (Manus) SIL 1982	250	4,4,3-4,3	1,2,2	P (A–)
Likum (Manus) PL 1977	100	3,3,3,1-2	1,3,4	P (A–)
Loniu (Manus) PL 1977	460	4,4,3-4,1-2	1,3,4	P (A–)
Magori (Central) TD 1971	200	3,2-3,1,1-2	2,1,4	E (B)
Malalamai (Madang) PL 1977	340	3,2-3,1,1-2	2,1,3	E (B)
Malasanga (Morobe) SIL 1991	435	4,4,3,3	2,2,2	P (A–)
Matukar (Madang) 1981 W&H 1981	219	4,4,3,3	1,3,2	OK
Mindiri (Madang) W&H 1981	95	3-4,2,1,1-2	1,3,4	E (B)
Minigir (E New Britain) E 1992	300	3-4,4,4,3	2,3,3	OK
Miu (W New Britain) SIL 1982	395	3-4,4,4,3	2,3,2	OK
Mokoreng (Manus) W&H 1981	200	3-4,4,4,3	1,2,2	OK
Mondropolon (Manus) W&H 1981	300	3-4,4,4,4	1,2,2	OK
Musom (Morobe) SH 1989	140	3-4,1,1,1-2	1,1,4	E (B)
Mwatebu (Milne Bay) Census 1972	170	3,2-3,1,2	1,3,4	P (A–)
Nafi (Morobe) SH 1989	160	3,3,3,2	2,3,2	E (B)
Nauna (Manus) PL 1977	130	3,2,1,1-2	1,3,4	P (A–)
Nenaya (Morobe) McE 1978	315	3,3, 3-4, 3-4	2,3,3	OK
Nuguria (North Solomons) W&H 1981	200	4,4,4,4	1,2,3	OK
Nukumanu (N Solomons) DT 1981	200	4,4,4,4	1,2,3	OK
Numbami (Morobe) McE 1978	270	3-4,4,3-4,3,3	1,1,3	P (A–)
Okro (Manus) W&H 1981	200	3-4,4,4,4	1,2,4	OK

Table 1. cont.

Language	Speakers	Set A	Set B	Status
PNG (cont.)				
Ouma (Central) W&H 1981	4			M (D)
Papapana (N Solomons) PL 1977	150	3-4,2,1,2	1,3,4	P (A–)
Piu (Morobe) SIL 1970	130	3-4,2,1,1-2	1,3,4	E (B)
Sengseng (W New Britain) SIL 1992	455	4,3-4,3-4,3	2,2,2	OK
Sepa (Madang) W&H 1981	270	3-4,3-4,3,3	2,3,2	P (A–)
Sera (Sandaun) W&H 1981	435	1,2,1,1,	1,3,4	S (C)
Takuu (North Solomons) DT 1981	250	4,4,4,4	1,1,3	OK
Tench (New Ireland) CB 1972	50	3,1-2,1,1-2	1,3,4	S (C)
Uruava (North Solomons) PL 1977	5			M (D)
Vehes (Morobe) McE 1978	100	3-4,3,3,3	1,2,2	OK
Wab (Madang) PL 1977	145	3-4,2-3,1,2	1,3,4	S (C)
Wampur (Morobe) SIL 1990	360	4,4,3-4,4	1,2,3	OK
Wataluma (Milne Bay) Census 1972	190	4,4,3-4,4	1,2,3	OK
Watut North (Morobe) SH 1989	465	4,4,4,3	2,2,2	OK
Solomon Islands				
Asumboa (EOI) SIL 1990	60	3,2,3,3	3,2-3,2	E (B)
Buma (EOI) T&H 1983	60	3-4,2-3,3,3	3,2-3,2	E (B)
Faghani (Makira) T&H 1983	300	4,3-4,4,4	1,2-3,3	P (A–)
Kokota (Isabel) SIL 1990	200	3,3-4,3,3	2,2,2-3	E (B)
Laghu (Isabel) T&H 1983	5	3,2,4,3	2,3,2-3	S ©
Nembao (EOI) T&H 1983	280	3,3,3,3	3,2-3,2	E (C)
Sikaiana (Malaita) T&H 1983	485	4,4,4,4	1,2,2-3	OK
Tanema (EOI) T&H 1983	5	3-4,3,3,3	3,2-3,2	D ©
Tanimbili (EOI) T&H 1983	100	3-4,3,3,3	3,2-3,2	E (B)
Vano (EOI) T&H 1983	5	3,2,4,3	3,2-3,2	M (D)
Zazao (Isabel) T&H 1983	166	3,3,3,3	2,2-3,2-3	S (C)
Vanuatu				
Aore (Santo) DT 1995	1			M (D)
Araki (Santo) DT 1995	105	3,2,3,3	2,3,3	S (C)
Aulua (Malakula) DT 1995	300	4,4,4,4	2,3,3	OK
Baki (Epi) DT 1995	200	3-4,3,3-4,4	3,2,3	P (A–)
Bierebo (Epi) DT 1995	450	3-4,3,3-4,4	3,2,3	P (A–)

Table 1. cont.

Language	Speakers	Set A	Set B	Status
Vanuatu (cont.)				
Bieria (Epi) DT 1995	170	3-4,3,3-4,4	3,2,3	S (C)
Fortsenal (Santo) DT 1995	150	4,4,4,4	3,3,2	S (C)
Hiw (Torres) DT 1995	120	4,4,4,4	2,3,3	E (B)
Katbol (Malakula) DT 1995	450	4,4,4,4	2,3,3	OK
Koro (Banks) DT 1995	105	4,4,4,4	2,4,2	E (B)
Labo (Mal) DT 1995	350	4,3-4,4,4	4,3,2	E (B)
Lakona (Banks) DT 1995	300	4,4,4,4	2,3,2	E (B)
Lametin (Santo) DT 1995	150	4,4,4,4	1,3,2	P (A–)
Larevat (Mal) DT 1995	150	4,4,4,4	2,3,2	P (A–)
Lehali (Banks) DT 1995	150	4,4,4,4	2,4,3	E (B)
Lehalurup (Banks) DT 1995	90	4,4,4,4	2,4,3	S (C)
Letemboi (Mal) DT 1995	305	4,4,3-4,3-4	2,2,2	S (C)
Lingarak (Mal) DT 1995	210	4,4,4,4	2,3,3	P (A–)
Litzlitz(Mal) DT 1995	330	4,4,4,4	2,3,3	P (A–)
Lorediakarkar (Santo) DT 1995	50	3-4,2,3,3	3,4,3	S (C)
Maewo Cent (Maewo) DT 1995	350	4,4,4,4	1,3,3	P (A–)
Mafea (Santo) DT 1995	50	3-4,3,3-4,3	1,2,3	E (B)
Maii (Epi) DT 1995	100	4,4,4,4	1,3,2	P (A–)
Malmariv (Santo) DT 1995	150	4,4,4,4	1,3,2	P (A–)
Malua Bay (Malakula) DT 1995	300	4,4,4,4	2,3,2	P (A–)
Maragus (Mal) DT 1995	10	3-4,2-3,3,3	3,4,3	M (D)
Morouas (Santo) DT 1995	150	4,4,4,4	2,3,2	P (A–)
Mosina (Banks) DT 1995	400	4,4,4,4	2,3,3	P (A–)
Mpotovoro (Mal) DT 1995	180	4,4,4,4	2,3,3	P (A–)
Narango (Santo) DT 1995	160	4,4,4,4	2,4,3	P (A–)
Nasarian (Mal) DT 1995	20	2-3,2,3,3-4	2,3,2	S (C
Nati (Mal) DT 1995	10	2-3,2,2,3	2,3,3	S ©
Ninde (Mal) DT 1995	250	4,4,4,4	1,2,3	P (A–)
Nokuku (Santo) DT 1995	160	3-4,4,4,4	1,2,3	P (A–)
Piamatsina (Santo) DT 1995	150	4,4,4,4	3,3,3	P (A–)
Polonombauk (Santo) DT 1995	225	2-3,2-3,4,4	3,3,3	P (A–)
Repanbitip (Mal) DT 1995	90	4,4,4,4	3,3,3	E (B)
Rerep (Mal) DT 1995	375	4,4,4,4	2,3,2	P (A–)

Table 1. cont.

Language	Speakers	Set A	Set B	Status
Vanuatu (cont.)				
Roria (Santo) DT 1995	150	4,4,4,4	2,3,2	P (A–)
Seke (Pentecost) DT 1995	300	4,3-4,4,4	2,3,3	E (B)
Shark Bay (Santo) DT 1995	225	3-4,3,3,3-4	2,3,3	E (B)
Sowa (Pentecost) DT 1995	20	4,3-4,3-4,4	3,3,3	S ©
Tambotalo (Santo) DT 1995	50	4,3-4,3-4,4	3,3,3	S ©
Tangoa (Santo) DT 1995	375	4,4,4,4	1,2,4	P (A–)
Tasmate (Santo) DT 1995	150	4,4,4,4	2,3,3	P (A–)
Toga (Torres) DT 1995	315	4,4,4,4	2,3,3	P (A–)
Tutuba (Santo) DT 1995	150	3-4,3-4,4,4	1,3,3	E (B)
Ura (Erromango) DT 1995	10			M (D)
Valpei (Santo) DT 1995	300	4,4,4,4	1,3,3	E (B)
Vinmavis (Mal) DT 1995	210	4,4,4,4	2,3,3	P (A–)
Vunapu (Santo) DT 1995	375	4,4,4,4	1,3,3	P (A–)
Wailapa (Santo) DT 1995	100	4,4,4,4	2,3,3	P (A–)
Wusi (Santo) DT 1995	170	4,4,4,4	1,2,3	E (B)
New Caledonia				
Arha (Rivierre pc)	250			S (C)
Arho (Rivierre pc)	10			M (D)
Bwatoo (Rivierre pc)	300			P (A–)
Haeake (Rivierre pc)	100			P (A–)
Haveke (Rivierre pc)	300			P (A–)
Hmwaveke (Rivierre pc)	300			P (A–)
Mea (Rivierre pc)	300			P (A–)
Neku (Rivierre pc)	200			S (C)
Nemi (Rivierre pc)	325			OK
Pije (Rivierre pc)	100			S (C)
Pwaamei (Rivierre pc)	325			P (A–)
Pwapwâ (Rivierre pc)	130			P (A–)
Vamale (Rivierre pc)	150			E (B)
Sîchë (Rivierre pc)	30			M (D)

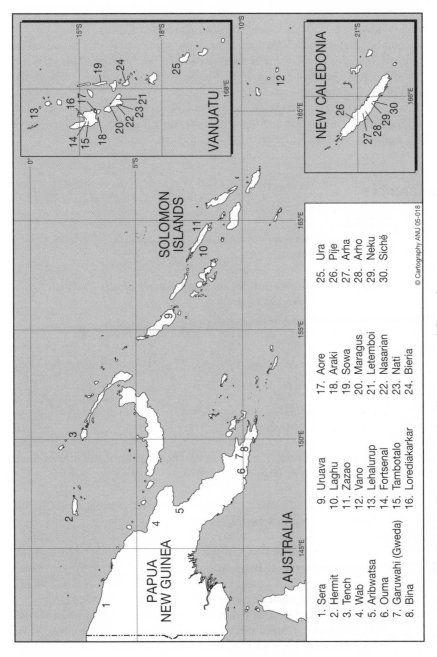

1. Sera
2. Hermit
3. Tench
4. Wab
5. Aribwatsa
6. Ouma
7. Garuwahi (Gweda)
8. Bina

9. Uruava
10. Laghu
11. Zazao
12. Vano
13. Lehalurup
14. Fortsenal
15. Tambotalo
16. Lorediakarkar

17. Aore
18. Araki
19. Sowa
20. Maragus
21. Letemboi
22. Nasarian
23. Nati
24. Bieria

25. Ura
26. Pije
27. Arha
28. Arho
29. Neku
30. Sichë

© Cartography ANU 05-018

Map 25. Pacific Region: the Austronesian Languages of Oceania

Notes

1. *Bonggo, Kayupulau, Ormu, Sobei, Tarpia* and *Yotafa* (*Tobati*).
2. This number includes the 500 Papuan languages spoken in Papua New Guinea, excluded from this chapter, but treated in the chapter by Wurm (this volume).
3. The SPCF was discontinued in 1997. Funding currently comes through the AusAID small grants scheme.
4. For detailed comments on the *Austronesian* languages of Papua New Guinea, I am indebted to my colleague Malcolm Ross (Australian National University). Comments on the remainder are based on my own field research.

References

Beaumont, Clive L.
    1972   *History of research in Austronesian languages*: New Ireland. Pacific Linguistics, Series A, No. 35: 1–41.
Dutton, Tom E.
    1971   *Languages of southeast Papua*: a preliminary report. Pacific Linguistics, Series A, No. 28: 1–46.
Grimes, Barbara F. (ed.)
    1992   *Ethnologue*: Languages of the World. Dallas, Texas: SIL.
Holzknecht, Susanne
    1989   *The Markham languages of Papua New Guinea*. Pacific Linguistics, Series C, No. 115.
Lincoln, Peter C.
    1977   *Listing Austronesian languages: Part 1 – Oceanic languages*. University of Hawaii. Mimeo.
Lynch, J. D.
    1981   Melanesian diversity and Polynesian homogeneity: the other side of the coin. *Oceanic linguistics* 20: 95–129.
McElhanon, Kenneth. A.
    1984   *A linguistic field guide to the Morobe province, Papua New Guinea*. Pacific Linguistics, Series D, No. 57.
Pawley, Andrew
    1995   Melanesian diversity and Polynesian homogeneity: a unified explanation for language. In Hollyman, Jim and Andrew Pawley (eds.) *Studies in pacific languages and cultures in honour of Bruce Biggs*. Auckland: Linguistic Society of New Zealand. 269–309.
    1998   The trans New Guinea Phylum hypothesis: a reassessment, In Miedema, Jelle; Odé, Cecilia and Rien A. C. Dam (eds.) *Perspectives on the Bird's Head of Irian Jaya, Indonesia*. Amsterdam & Atlanta: Rodopi. 655–690.

Ross, Malcolm
   1988   *Proto Oceanic and the Austronesian languages of Western Melanesia.*
           Pacific Linguistics, Series C, No. 98.
   2000   Grouping Papuan Languages: one more attempt. Paper presented at
           the Australian Linguistics Society Conference, University of Mel-
           bourne, 7.–9. July 2000.
Spriggs, Matthew
   1997   *The Island Melanesians.* Oxford: Blackwell
Tryon, Darrell T. and Brian D. Hackman
   1983   *The languages of the Solomon Islands:* an internal classification. Pa-
           cific Linguistics, Series C, No. 72.
Tryon, Darrell T.
   1981   *Towards a classification of Solomon Islands languages.* Papers from
           the Third International Conference on Austronesian Linguistics. Pa-
           cific Linguistics, Series C, No. 74: 97–108.
Tryon, Darrell T. (ed.)
   1995   *Comparative Austronesian dictionary.* Berlin: Mouton de Gruyter.
           (4 vols).
Wurm, Stephen A. and Shiro Hattori
   1981   *Language atlas of the Pacific area.* Canberra: The Australian Acade-
           my of the Humanities in collaboration with the Japan Academy.

Names Index

General Index

Language Names Index

424   *Language Names Index*